D1547450

I. A. RICHARDS

I. A. RICHARDS

ESSAYS IN HIS HONOR

Edited by
REUBEN BROWER
HELEN VENDLER
JOHN HOLLANDER

New York
OXFORD UNIVERSITY PRESS
1973

Copyright © 1973 by Oxford University Press

Library of Congress Catalogue Card No: 73-82661

Permission to use copyright material is hereby gratefully acknowledged:

To The Viking Press, Inc., and Laurence Pollinger, Ltd., for "Piano" from *The Complete Poems of D. H. Lawrence,* edited by Vivian de Sola Pinto and F. Warren Roberts. Copyright © 1964, 1971 by Angelo Ravagli and C. M. Weekley, Executors of the estate of Frieda Lawrence Ravagli.

To Holt, Rinehart and Winston, Inc., and Jonathan Cape, Ltd., for "Range-Finding" from *The Poetry of Robert Frost,* edited by Edward Connery Lathem. Copyright 1916, © 1969 by Holt, Rinehart and Winston, Inc.; copyright 1944 by Robert Frost.

To Alfred A. Knopf, Inc., and Faber and Faber, Ltd., for lines from "The Idea of Order at Key West" from *The Collected Poems of Wallace Stevens.* Copyright 1923, 1931, 1954 by Wallace Stevens.

To Norma Millay Ellis for "First Fig" from *Collected Poems,* Harper and Row. Copyright 1922, 1950 by Edna St. Vincent Millay.

To Harcourt Brace Jovanovich, Inc., and Routledge and Kegan Paul, Ltd., for excerpts from *Practical Criticism* and *Principles of Literary Criticism* by I. A. Richards; and for poetry and prose from *Internal Colloquies* by I. A. Richards, © 1957, 1958, 1959, 1960, 1971 by I. A. Richards.

To Harcourt Brace Jovanovich, Inc., and Faber and Faber, Ltd., for lines from "The Waste Land" by T. S. Eliot.

Printed in the United States of America

Editorial Note

In the application of these principles to purposes of practical criticism, as employed in the appraisement of works more or less imperfect, I have endeavoured to discover what the qualities in a poem are, which may be deemed promises and specific symptoms of poetic power, as distinguished from general talent determined to poetic composition by accidental motives, by an act of the will, rather than by the inspiration of a genial and productive nature. In this investigation, I could not, I thought, do better, than keep before me the earliest work of the greatest genius, that perhaps human nature has yet produced, our *myriad-minded* * Shakespeare.

* Ἀνὴρ μυριόνους, a phrase which I have borrowed from a Greek monk, who applies it to a Patriarch of Constantinople. I might have said, that I have reclaimed, rather than borrowed it; for it seems to belong to Shakespeare, *de jure singulari, et ex privilegio naturae.*

COLERIDGE, *Biographia Literaria,* Chapter XV

"Myriad-minded"—the term that Coleridge "reclaimed, rather than borrowed" for Shakespeare—might well be reclaimed a second time for the writer who has done most in the twentieth century to renew and extend Coleridgean study of literature and language. For present-day readers of the above sentences from the *Biographia,* the echoes—if that is the right word—are inimitably Ricardian: "principles . . . practical criticism . . . specific symptoms of poetic power." Many of us date our interest in the nature of imagination ("poetic power") and our introduction to the study of language from our first readings of *Principles of Literary Criticism.* One purpose of this volume is to recall and record the impact of Richards' writing on nearly two generations of critics, teachers, poets, philosophers, experts in linguistics—the list could easily be extended. A larger aim has been to suggest the many if not "myriad" facets of Richards' thought and life. Though the essays that follow represent a fair number of Richards' interests and fields of action, they are not all-inclusive in their range. We could wish that there were more adequate representation of Richards' work in aesthetics and the visual arts, in the philosophy of science, and linguistic theory, and that there were a fuller account of his educational ventures from China to the U.S.A. to Africa. A quick review of the critical bibliography (pp. 321–64) will reveal that there are further ranges to be explored in the intellectual and personal history of I. A. R.

June 1973   R.B.
                                                                       H.V.
                                                                       J.H.

Contents

Poems for I. A. R.

ROBERT PENN WARREN *Time as Hypnosis,* 3

RICHARD EBERHART *Salute,* 5

JOHN HOLLANDER *Examples,* 7

ROBERT LOWELL Goodbye Earth *by I. A. Richards,* 13 *Death,* 14

Beginnings and Transitions:
I. A. Richards Interviewed by REUBEN BROWER, 17

Essays

JOAN BENNETT *"How It Strikes a Contemporary": The Impact of I. A. Richards' Literary Criticism in Cambridge, England,* 45

M. C. BRADBROOK *I. A. Richards at Cambridge,* 61

WILLIAM EMPSON *The Hammer's Ring,* 73

ANGUS FLETCHER *I. A. Richards and the Art of Critical Balance,* 85

W. K. WIMSATT *I. A. R.: What To Say About a Poem,* 101

CHARLES L. STEVENSON *Richards on the Theory of Value,* 119

CLEANTH BROOKS *I. A. Richards and the Concept of Tension,* 135

GEOFFREY H. HARTMAN *The Dream of Communication,* 155

HELEN VENDLER *Jakobson, Richards, and Shakespeare's Sonnet CXXIX,* 179

B. F. SKINNER *Reflections on Meaning and Structure*, 199

ELSIE DUNCAN-JONES *A Reading of Marvell's* The Unfortunate Lover, 211

BASIL WILLEY *I. A. Richards and Coleridge*, 227

KATHLEEN COBURN *I. A. R. and S. T. C.*, 237

JOHN PAUL RUSSO *Richards and the Classical Tradition*, 245

ERIC A. HAVELOCK *The Sophistication of Homer*, 259

L. C. KNIGHTS *Literature and the Teaching of Literature*, 277

DENYS THOMPSON *Teacher's Debt*, 295

RICHMOND LATTIMORE *Prospero*, 303

JANET ADAM SMITH *Fare Forward, Voyagers!* 307

A Bibliography of the Books, Articles, and Reviews of I. A. Richards, by JOHN PAUL RUSSO, 321

CONTRIBUTORS, 367

His frame was firm, his powers were bright,
Tho' now his eightieth year was nigh.

I. A. RICHARDS

Poems for I. A. R.

ROBERT PENN WARREN

Time as Hypnosis

(To I. A. Richards, this poem about a country snowfall of
far away and long ago, which I hope he will explicate.)

White, white in that dawnlight, the world was exploding, white
Light bursting from whiteness. What
Is the name of the world?—for

Whiteness, all night from the black sky unfeathering,
Had changed the world's name, and maybe
My own, or maybe it all was only
A dream I was having, but did not
Know it, or maybe the truth was that I,
Huddling tight in the blankets and darkness and self,
Was nothing, was nothing but what
The snow dreamed all night. Then light:

Two years and no snow in our section, and two years
Is a long time when you are twelve. So,

All day in a landscape that had been
Brown fields and black woods but was now
White emptiness and arches,
I wandered. The white light
Filled all the vertiginous sky, and even
My head until it
Spread bright and wide like another sky under which I
Wandered. I came

To a place where the woods were, stood under
A crazed geometry of boughs black but
Snow-laden and criss-crossed with light, and between
Banks of humped snow and whiteness of ice-fret, saw
Black water slide slow, and glossy as sleep.

I stared at the water, and staring, wondered
What the white-bellied minnow, now deep in
Black leaf-muck and mud, thought.
I thought of the muskrat dim in his mud-gloom.

Have you ever seen how delicately
Etched the print of the field mouse's foot in fresh snow is?
I saw the tracks. But suddenly, none. Nothing
But wing-flurried snow. Then, small as a pin-head, the single
Bright-frozen, red bead of a blood-drop. Have you ever
Stared into the owl's eyes? They blink slow, then burn:
Burn gold in the dark inner core of the snow-shrouded cedar.

There was a great field that tilted
Its whiteness up to the line where the slant, blue knife-edge of sky
Cut it off. I stood
In the middle of that space. I looked back, saw
My own tracks march at me. Mercilessly,
They came at me and did not stop. Ahead,
Was the blankness of white. Up it rose. Then the sky.

Evening came, and I sat by the fire, and the flame danced.

All day, I had wandered in the glittering metaphor
For which I could find no referent.

All night, that night, asleep, I would wander, lost in a dream
That was only what the snow dreamed.

RICHARD EBERHART

Salute

To Ivor and Dorothea

After the action of action, what?
Thought. Gut!
Vessel down the ways,
Baby down the sluiceways.
Gut! Thought! What?

Pot, Shot, Got, Lot.
Pillar of salt, Gestalt.
Baghavadgita, here?
Buddha, better still Prince?

I threw myself into action
Acting like an actor a part.
Fool, clown, tragedian!
Riots riotous! Crotch!

After the action of action, what?
More action? More thought? More gut?
Violence! Yes, a pence.
A penny for the world's violence.

How to escape a poem?
The old glory men, Keats, Hopkins.
Negative capability,
Pied beauty.

We Americans love craze.
We will do anything.
Walt said he had children,
We are liars all.

Seventy bats fly out
From my study, every evening.
Nature is with us! Bats!
I do not want to be the Exterminator.

Bats in the attic,
A pain in the wing,
A poem in the evening,
Lust everywhere!

Bats, hornets, toads, ants,
I love you, creatures of life,
Gorge yourselves on earth,
Winter is coming.

Examples

Descartes' Wax

Ah yes, the wax: this piece just now unhived, now in my hand—
Honey-smelling yet, that honey yet flower-smelling, those flowers
(Say, they are purple clover, outgrowing the white)
Still remembering their houses of grass, whose green breathings
Themselves lead back into redolence, in eternal regress,
Stirred by the mind's winds; while in its house of silence,
This wax, tawnier than the honey, shines with a noble yellow,
Lion-color, golden as a beast from which strength is plucked,
A hardened blob: warmth will make it give, warmth of the near
      candle's glowing mind
Lump of cerebrum: my thumbnail lines it into two lobes which caresses
      will spread
Or curl
And then, and then anything
A waning of sameness: but from where—
Hoard of forms hidden in a high mountain cave? the sky's inexhaustible
      grayblue Morpheum?—
Will it take shape?

Russell's Monarch

"The present king of France is bald";
For some years he has gone without the fiction of false hair,
Fringed with a slipped, half-glory of white, while a corollary gleam
Shines from his pate in the bright light, above a land of green,
As he stands for a moment, ivory orb and cue in either hand,
In the grand billiard-room at Monterreur,
Still suggesting some of his earlier pictures: as on the east terrace back
        at Montraison
In the clear light that spoke silently of betrayals, he stood watching,
First the light itself and then, distantly, welcoming clouds.
And he sighed for the truth.
Or as in state of some kind, with much plum-colored velvet swagged
        behind him,
The heavy, dripping sleeve of an abstract arm whose hand may be
        pointing somewhere,
Or keeping something out of sight.
But if one is mistaken about him, finds out he has crowned nonentity
        with the pinchbeck of language,
Elevating him who could not even be considered a pretender,
Then say, rather "The present king of France" is bald, is too crude an
        instance;
For the blunders by which we climb, those mistakes our handholds
Are less stark than the rocks we seek to rise above,
And these: the fullness and the curl of wigs, moving above a sea of
        shoulders,
Or reposing broodily on their wooden eggs at night—
Are our additions to what is given, our patches for what is always
        being taken away.

Taking the Case of the Donkeys (Austin)

Spare philosophers in a bright field stand shooting at donkeys
Across the cold distance of rocky ground on which they are not
Toward pasture, and the gray, earnest ones grazing there,
One of whom finally drops, hit by accident,
Another, by mistake; but both by an unrelenting intent that they serve
      not as beasts of burden,
But, winged with the Exemplary, as creatures of the mind's flight.
The philosophers may not love them—their deaths are so ridiculous!—
But that would be because the philosophers are exemplary as well;
Dropping their rifles to the misty ground, and slowly merging with its
      colors,
They amble toward the melted beasts and ride them solemnly
Out of our sight.

Moore's Beasts

"Tame tigers growl"

Or not, as the case may be;

But some tame tigers who do not exist are ever silent of throat,

Just as they are never narrowed of eye.

Silence of paw is something else: I have been brushed by the passage of
        fiery fur

And heard soft padfall, like the slopping of something damp in the
        long hallway;

I have heard the rip and then the shredding of stretched canvas

As, patiently standing, one paw against the golden foliage of frame,

One of them came to know, after weeks of contemplation,

That a landscape of dim forests must, in fact, go.

An ounce of tears watered the carpet and his face.

I have heard them lying half asleep along the hard terraces, their
        guarded breathing.

But mostly these children of fear are seen and not heard,

Passing across open doors, slow huge heads turning dark corners,

Looking back down corridors as if—and what can one make of the
        silences of our beasts?—

Regretful: unhurried, but surely regretful.

$7 + 5 = 12$ (Kant)

I think I see why this one: two primes aimed at the all but inevitable
      composite
—The one which should, had we two subsidiary thumbs, have been our
      numberer,
A reasonable base for those airy towers untopped, paling into distances—
But, out of some gentleness, not stepped crudely upward,
Five and seven and then their sum—as if climbing were all that vertical
      scales were for—
Instead more warmly abstract: dipping in order to rise, but barely
      whispering of that,
Nor of mystery taken and pent up in hand.
Hand in hand, their *tableau vivant* never over,
They yet bow and smile, asserting a truth radiant even in daylight,
Like what lay somewhere between the given and the found,
Always golden and unspeakably glittering down in the cellars.

Dorothea Richards

I.A.R., Kandersteg, Switzerland, 1957.

Goodbye Earth by I. A. Richards

Sky-high on the cover of *Goodbye Earth*
you flash and zigzag like a large hummingbird—
heavy socks and climber's knickerbockers,
sleeves rolled, shirt open at the front;
an upended pick, your prisoner's ball and chain,
penitentially attached to your wrist.
Here while you take your breath enthused, I see
the imperishable Byronics of the Swiss Alps
change to a landscape for your portrait,
casual, unconventional, innocent, earned—
gratuitous rashness and serpentine hesitation.
It is not a picture but a problem;
you know you will move on; the absolute,
bald peaked glare-ice, malignly beckons . . . goodbye earth.

ROBERT LOWELL

Death

This, our one intimate metaphysical—
today tomorrow, death looks fair on all.
Ivor you know the matter with this subject,
"My vanity won't let me believe in my death.
In this generous world-throw, ought but vanity,
death never catches those life speeds." You thought
"A doubtful suicide should choose the ocean;
who knows he might reach the other side?
If my coin falls heads, I'll see the other side. . . .
We still go foothill shuffling every weekend;
climbing's dull past sixty unless you risk your life."
Hob-Alpine Spirit, you saved so much illusion
by changing its false coin to words—your shadow
on the blind bright heights . . . absconds to air.

Beginnings and Transitions:
I. A. Richards Interviewed by Reuben Brower

I.A.R. Good morning, Ben. Shall we sit as we did when you first came to Magdalene to see me? How many years ago is it?

R.B. It will be forty years in late September or early October when I had the nerve—I don't know whether you can remember that—to stop you on the street and ask you if you would like to supervise me, and then I went to your rooms.

I.A.R. There was that big window, looking out into the Master's garden. Suppose you sit on that side as I remember you did, and I'll sit this side. Here we are again. Isn't it extraordinary what a part accident plays in our life? There was another time we sat on opposite sides of a window. It was in a railway train going up by Amherst somewhere. There you were, and the contact was resumed. Pure accident.

R.B. Do you know at all how you first developed an interest in poetry? Was that accident too?

I.A.R. It seems so. You know, I think, I was laid up all my early teens with TB. A very near squeak. And as I had unlimited leisure, I read and read . . . Suddenly I got engulfed by Kipling. I was reading a story (in *Many Inventions*) where Muller, the Inspector General of Woods and Forests, meets Mowgli, the grown-up Mowgli, in the woods. He recites to himself in a kind of German English. I was so overwhelmed by this that I really set to work to find out what it was. And sooner or later someone said " 'Dolores.' Swinburne." I'd never heard of "Dolores." And I doubt if I had heard of Swinburne. But, hearing, I ran down immediately to the drawing room where there was a funny old collection called The International Library of Famous Literature. About twenty volumes with little bits and pieces of everybody in it.

R.B.   I've heard of it.

I.A.R. I turned up Swinburne in the index and of all things on earth, found *The Battle Chorus* from *Erechtheus*. About ten lines later I couldn't see the book. I just blubbered my way through the rest of the excerpt. I had to lie down on my back on the hearthrug with the book propped up on my chest to keep the tears out of the line of vision.

> From east to west of the south sea-line
> Glitters the lightning of spears that shine. . . .

I didn't know that was going to send me, after many days, to the *Iliad*. But that opening

> Ill thoughts breed fear, and fear ill words; but these
> The Gods turn from us that have kept their law.
>   Let us lift up the strength of our hearts in song
>   And our souls to the height of the darkling day.
>   If the wind in our eyes blow blood for spray,
>   Be the spirit that breathes in us life more strong.
>   Though the prow reel round and the helm point wrong
>   And sharp reefs whiten the shoreward way
> For the steersman time sits hidden astern
>   With dark hand plying the rudder of doom. . . .

And so on and so on. This stayed with me, after a very few readings.

For me, it was the divine vision. I've never, therefore, been able to think critically about it—though I do recall that when I found "Dolores," soon after, I decided that Muller had much improved what he quoted. But the *Erechtheus* stood by me. At fearsome moments it was a talisman to restore courage. And it took me to Cambridge. One day in class at Clifton a marvelous old schoolmaster—we called him Cabby Spence because he was the picture of an old-fashioned cabby—asked, "Does anyone here know which were the flowers, the sacred flowers of Athens?" I couldn't help myself.

> Violet and olive leaf purple and hoary,
> Song wreath and story the fairest of fame,
> Flowers that the winter can blast not or bend;
> A Light upon earth as the sun's own flame,
>   A name as his name,
>   Athens, a praise without end.

That suddenly made me a classroom figure. And by pure accident again someone said I ought to try for an exhibition. I did and won a twenty-pound exhibition—twenty pounds a year at Magdalene. Quite enough to dazzle me: an opportunity to get away to Cambridge a year earlier than usual.

R.B.   What was this master in? Was he a master in English?

I.A.R.   Fifth form. And he was a master of English . . . really. And of enormous influence on me. He read to his class what he himself wanted to read and let them come along. He'd suddenly come in one morning and read us the whole of William Morris' "Defence of Guinevere." I'll never forget that, you know. One year he suddenly thought, "I'll reread the *Purgatorio* . . ." and gave it us —skipping little right through. That's unusual.

R.B.   Very. Did you worry much about language that early? As such?

I.A.R.   No. Not till I got to Cambridge.

R.B.   Now how does the transition take place between this kind of young interest: it's still very present with you—I've just heard you recite Swinburne—to, somehow or other, the Moral Sciences? Did you do the Moral Sciences Tripos first? Of course there was no English Tripos.

I.A.R.   There was no English Tripos. I went up in 1911 and stayed there till '15. Taking a year out through TB trouble again. I was laid up on Dartmoor. A break of a year and a very good thing too . . . another fine accidental intervention that let me do some miscellaneous reading. But this is what happened about the Moral Sciences. I was supposed to be a History Exhibitioner, you see. I had a most understanding Supervisor, very young, a newcomer at Magdalene, Frank Salter, who remained a close friend until his death in 1970. I went to him one morning in a grim mood and said I didn't think History ought to have happened. I didn't see why we should study it. I was getting no benefit. I had nothing against him. Frank Salter simply said, "You know, what you'd better do is come to lunch on Tuesday." So I came to lunch and there was Frank Salter in tennis clothes. He apologized. Said he'd had a snack and he was going out to play tennis and left me alone with a little white-faced, large-glittering-spectacled undergraduate, four years older than me. A Senior, when I was a very raw Freshman. And we sat and had lunch together there in Frank Salter's rooms. And Ogden, it was C.K. Ogden, proceeded to tell me what I would have to read in every possible subject being taught at the University, who my chief instructors would be and why they would teach me the sort of doctrines they taught. He thoroughly believed in the economic and social determination of doctrine. I was given a view of Cambridge University teaching such as no other could have given me. And at the end, characteristically, he took me off to his rooms and sold me two books. I decided at that lunch table to read Moral Sciences. I didn't know before that there was any such thing.

R.B.   What stage was he at then?

I.A.R. He was a Classic, waiting. He was supposed to be in that anomalous situation, hanging about, hoping that some College would pick him up. Some teaching job or perhaps a by-fellowship: the beginnings of a career. Everybody had put him down as a future Professor in Classics . . . without any doubt whatever. He just was unbelievable as an intelligence. Perfect recall and all those sorts of things. And very lively spirit. Well, that settled me. I went into Moral Sciences and then I got enthralled by G.E. Moore.

R.B.   I was going to ask you if Moore wasn't a key point.

I.A.R. He was. I don't think I ever understood anything. But it was complete subjugation. I got really interested in language because I felt something must be done to stop the leakage of information that was going on there all the time. I knew I didn't understand Moore or what he was at. I always thought if I went back to him for a whole course of lectures once again an inkling would come. But . . . no.

R.B.   Was he already asking, "What do we mean?"

I.A.R. Incessantly.

R.B.   Lovely irony in that, isn't there?

I.A.R. Yes. Moore was vocally convinced that few indeed could possibly *mean* what they *said*. I was silently persuaded that they could not possibly *say* what they *meant*. These two balanced one another perfectly. Anyhow, I didn't do too badly in the Moral Sciences. Then I went away from Cambridge and cultivated other pursuits . . . which come into the picture again by accident. I got another attack of my lung trouble and went up to North Wales to cure it. It seems rather unlikely, but I became— for those days: nothing like the standards of today—a rather skilful cragsman. I was fairly good at floating up difficult rocks.

R.B. How did this interest in mountaineering come about? Who started you?

I.A.R. Whymper, I think, and Ruskin. I was a devotee of the fourth volume of *Modern Painters* while at Clifton. Whymper's *Matterhorn* sent me to Ruskin's. I was re-reading the other day Ruskin's "mica flake" paragraph and realizing again what a prodigious influence it must have had on me. May I read it to you?

R.B. Please do.

I.A.R. "Modern Painters," Volume 4, Chapter XVI, paragraph 17.

> Is not this a strange type, in the very heart and height of these mysterious Alps—these wrinkled hills in their snowy, cold, grey-haired old age, at first so silent, then, as we keep quiet at their feet, muttering and whispering to us garrulously, in broken and dreaming fits, as it were, about their childhood—is it not a strange type of the things which "out of weakness are made strong"? If one of those little flakes of mica-sand, hurried in tremulous spangling along the bottom of the ancient river, too light to sink, too faint to float, almost too small for sight, could have had a mind given to it as it was at last borne down with its kindred dust into the abysses of the stream, and laid, (would it not have thought?) for a hopeless eternity, in the dark ooze, the most despised, forgotten, and feeble of all earth's atoms; incapable of any use or change; not fit, down there in the diluvial darkness, so much as to help an earth-wasp to build its nest, or feed the first fibre of a lichen;—what would it have thought, had it been told that one day, knitted into a strength as of imperishable iron, rustless by the air, infusible by the flame, out of the substance of it, with its fellows, the axe of God should hew that Alpine tower; that against *it*—poor, helpless, mica flake!—the wild north winds should rage in vain; beneath *it*—low-fallen mica flake!—the snowy hills should lie bowed like flocks of sheep, and the kingdoms of the earth fade away in unregarded blue; and around it—weak, wave-drifted mica flake!—the great war of the firmament should burst in thunder, and yet stir it not; and the fiery arrows and angry meteors of the night fall blunted back from it into the air; and all the stars in the clear heaven should light, one by one as they rose, new cressets upon the points of snow that fringed its abiding place on the imperishable spire?

R.B. So mountains weren't just a gymnasium to you.

I.A.R. I had Ruskin's rebuke to the Alpine Club by heart while I was still a schoolboy, before I had any dream of ever owning an ice-axe. "The mountains themselves, which your own poets used to love so reverently, you look upon as soaped poles in a bear-garden, which you set yourselves to climb and then slide down again with shrieks of delight . . . red with cutaneous eruption of conceit and voluble with convulsive hiccup of self-congratulation."

R.B.   But still you took to climbing.

I.A.R.   Yes, and, for a while, was good enough at it to take those pleasures seriously.

When I got over my TB, I decided to go back to Cambridge and get a medical qualification in order to become a psycho-analyst.

R.B.   This is where physiology comes in.

I.A.R.   Physiology and much more; psychological reading and reflexion beyond any I'd tried to do as an undergraduate. And what was in those days theory of linguistics and communication. Since that lunch with Ogden, I'd not met him again. We had everything in common, but we didn't meet. And then, here's another accident.

Armistice Day. 11 o'clock on the 11th day of the 11th month, 1918. Pandemonium broke out in Cambridge. I spent some time climbing up the pinnacle in the middle of the market place . . . which has since been removed. I was sitting on top of that and enjoying the scene when I heard a name. I came down to King's Parade to see a crash of glass breaking. Ogden, by that time, was the owner of three shops in Cambridge; one was a picture gallery, the others were book stores. There he was, standing by the door of one of them, busy at a peculiar trick. He used to take his glasses up to the top of his head and press the corners of his eyes with his fingers. He could distort the lens slightly and get better vision . . . so he believed. Partly because his hands were over his eyes and mouth, nobody recognized him. I took my stand beside Ogden. Twenty or thirty drunken medical students were sacking the shop. Pictures were coming out through the plate glass in very dangerous fashion . . . Duncan Grant, Vanessa Bell, Roger Fry . . . right out into the street; it was very lucky no one spotted Ogden. He'd have been in the river. That night he came to call on me, to see if I could help him in recognizing any of the rioters. And later, in the small hours, we stood together on the little winding stair in 1, Free-School Lane and for the first time we talked together—for three hours, outlining the whole *Meaning of Meaning.*

R.B.   Already?!

I.A.R.   We agreed so easily on every point then. Twenty years later there came a time when we couldn't write a line to one another without grossly misunderstanding. It happens. But that was the moment when *The Meaning of Meaning* came into being.

R.B.   Had he already been pursuing things like that?

I.A.R.   Yes, for twenty years perhaps.

*   *   *

Now here's the next thing. Where my mountaineering comes in. I was suffering continuously from Hand to Mouth Disease, as Ogden called it. Very poor. I had to be careful. And I got tired of this life in Cambridge. It looked as though it would be twenty years before I got anywhere. So I went round to that Enchanter, Manny Forbes, of Clare College.

R.B.   Oh yes, I was hoping Manny would come in.

I.A.R.   Manny comes in very very much. He was the most saintly spirit I have ever had to do with . . . very bizarre.

R.B.   I heard him lecture.

I.A.R.   Well, you can see how he wouldn't strike everybody in the same way. But when you got to know him—spellbinding. I remember meeting him at the corner of King's Parade and Benet Street. He had a pile of books higher than his head in his arms. And a Newnhamite passing by took pity on him and said, "May I help you?" Manny, holding some of his books with his chin and so forth said, "Pray do not disturb me; I have the stability of a pregnant Kangaroo."

R.B.   Marvelous!

I.A.R.   Always like that. I went to Manny because he knew all the Lairds of the Mountain Hebrides. I got him to write me a set of letters which would smooth my way to becoming a professional guide for mountaineering in Skye. We wrote the letters together, and he fell in love with the scheme. After we'd done it, we sat down by the fire and started talking about Wordsworth. Two hours later Manny tore up the letters and found another bit of paper. He could get two signatures, he told me, from people in the English school, just forming then, which would enable me to lecture next year . . . and collect fifteen shillings a head from anyone who came six times to the course. And that worked out. I only had to see Chadwick and Q and Aubrey Attwater and one or two others. And next year I came back and lectured: one course for distinction on Principles of Literary Criticism and the other course for lucre—on the Contemporary Novel.

R.B.   Would this be about 1921? Or something like that?

I.A.R. More like 1919, when the English Tripos was just beginning.

R.B.   You've got to get in one more strand at this point. There is *The Foundations of Aesthetics*. Did that grow partly, I suppose, from Ogden, too?

I.A.R. That was a pure fluke, again, another fluke. It's the only time, I think, between the wars, that I didn't spend the entire summer in the Alps. I went out, I think it must have been in '20, to the Alps. I was rather unlucky . . . on an early expedition; and knocked myself out. And I gave up the season, a thing I never had to do any other year, and went back to Cambridge. In low spirits. And there I ran into a man I'd met once before, James Wood, who was staying in Cambridge. A good painter and a very close friend of Ogden's. He started talking art talk to me, and I said, "Why don't we spend some of our time as a triumvirate? Sorting out this art talk." I was doing bits and pieces of the *Meaning of Meaning* already.

R.B.   You must have been, to get that done by '23.

I.A.R. We did it all in a very queer way. Here is the picture of the three of us doing it. James Wood in the corner bicycling slowly upside down, doing his Muller's exercises, and supplying the ideas. It would be very late at night. Ogden lying on an immense high day-bed he had. We always called it Sardanapalus's Death Bed. Ogden would be on the Death Bed, pen in hand, writing it all down. And I would be walking up and down, doing a good deal of phrasing and rephrasing. The triumvirate would have sessions far into the night, being kept going by an ozone machine Ogden had picked up which produced sparks about a foot long and a tremendous smell of the Underground. But Ogden thought it was Brighton, and transported Brighton into Cambridge. He went to live in Brighton the later part of his life.

R.B.   Well, now, that interest . . . had you been reading Clive Bell and Vernon Lee and those people on your own?

I.A.R. Yes. And so had James Wood.

R.B.   And Roger Fry, did he come in quite soon?

I.A.R. Quite soon. But Roger Fry was a bit different from the others, I

I.A.R. at the American Academy of Arts and Letters, 1968.

felt. I saw a lot of him later. In his whimsical way he touched realities.

R.B.   What about other minds that played some part in your experience then. You have mentioned Moore, and of course Ogden. How soon did Wittgenstein come to Cambridge and mean anything to you? Or didn't he mean much to you?

I.A.R.   He didn't, you know—ever. But he was very daunting and impressive. He turned up, the first time I saw him, at Moore's classes. Moore would lecture twice a week and at a third meeting we were expected to ask him questions. And almost nobody ever dared . . . to do it twice. So it tended to be a bit like a Quakers' meeting. Silence all round. Moore was quite unwittingly very savage. He would have to put his hands over his head and scream if you didn't use exactly the language that he would have used. If you used your own, he was baffled. Ogden—it was partly the impishness of the man—found a very distinguished physicist, A.A. Robb, who thought he had antedated and altogether outclassed Einstein. Robb was a huge Irishman with a head like a melon. And he completed it by always wearing a bowler hat, a *chapeau melon:* really a very odd figure for a great philosopher-mathematician. Ogden persuaded him to come to Moore's lectures, and he asked Moore a very simple question. He said, "When you say you see the sun, what do you think you see?" "The sun." "But, you know, about sunset, you can't see the sun. The sun is below the horizon. It's the refraction of the earth's atmosphere which enables you to see an image of the sun. Quite in a different location from where the sun is." Moore went nearly helpless with rage. "I can't see the sun," he cried. "I can't see the sun!" Everything broke down; that was what we were used to. And then suddenly there was this incredibly beautiful young Austrian, Wittgenstein, Lucifer before his Fall, oh, the most noble thing you ever saw. Rumour then had it he was an aeronautical engineer who had come to consult Russell as to whether any of Russell's and Whitehead's performances would assist him in some problems in aerodynamics. If so, he got involved deeper than he knew. Russell sent him to Moore. Wittgenstein started asking Moore questions. For the first time in our many years' experience of Moore, Moore was submissive, gentle, doing his best to understand. It was a complete reversal. Mohammed was gone to the mountain. It was most extraordinary. And from that moment came Wittgenstein's dominance over Moore and over Cambridge. It went up preternaturally.

R.B. I was wondering whether your meeting with Wittengenstein had much to do with how you thought about language.

I.A.R. I shouldn't think it had. I was very negative. Wittgenstein was a personality who required utter devotion. And I've never been able to be even amused in any way with anyone who makes such enormous claims. People who saw much of Wittgenstein acquired what I irreverently christened "Saint Wittgenstein's Dance." They twitched and they pulled faces and they stopped to stare upwards . . . in the manner of the Master. And I shrank away from it all. I had one long session with Wittgenstein when I came back from one of our visits to China. First week. He came to breakfast and in the end we gave him supper. It was an all-day business, walking round Magdalene Garden and then coming in to talk. Various people joined us from time to time to relieve the strain. It was heavy. He pointed out to me early that there were two mistakes in *Tractatus*. I said, "Oh, that's no trouble, is it? It will be reprinted next year, I believe, and you can put an errata slip in." I realized as I said it that I had lost caste. He was staring at me like a Pillar of Society looking at a self-confessed rapist. "How could I," he said, "how could I touch it? It is my child." I just couldn't deal with that. And later he spent about an hour trying to convince a small group that if anyone were to drink one drop of perfectly pure water, he would die instantly. He had beliefs of that order . . . amongst the other things. He was a very odd character in many ways. I wrote a poem much later . . . about his lectures in Trinity. I used to go to them occasionally. They weren't lectures. You've heard descriptions, haven't you?

R.B. Yes, I have. When you say lectures: wasn't this still a very small group?

I.A.R. About twenty people, lying down in deck chairs. He thought that that was more propitious—they were supposed to be relaxed. And Moore was in an armchair, at his elbow, taking down every syllable. When Wittgenstein would start a sentence ten times, Moore would write it on his pad ten times up to the point where he broke it off. Absolute devotion. Most peculiar. It gave me the creeps.

R.B.   Well, now, we'll round another corner. How did you turn from
         that intense interest in meaning to the *Principles?*

I.A.R.   It grew out of my current lecturing, and I am a little tired of its
         being taken as my final word. I've certainly had enough of the
         first sentence: "A book is a machine to think with." That was
         just borrowed from Le Corbusier. "A house is a machine to live
         in. A chair is a machine to sit on. A book is a machine to think
         with." But it was a very early use of Le Corbusier, before he was
         much of a figure. It was James Wood who brought Le Corbusier
         to my attention. He read in the arts very very widely. But I like
         Principles still: parts of it; and I like what Hugh Gaitskell said of
         it. He came to Harvard to give the Godkin Lectures. Somebody
         introduced us. And I said, *"Principles of Literary Criticism,"* and
         he said, "No, Principles of Intellectual Rectitude. That's what I
         learned through that book."

         What mattered was that I was interested in psychology, a
         rather old-fashioned psychology: pre-behavioristic, although I did
         know a good deal about behaviorism and did something towards
         joining them up. But my psychology came out of G.F. Stout, out
         of the big James Ward article in the Encyclopedia Britannica,
         and William James's two volumes, *The Principles of Psychology.*
         Those were the real formative things. Those and Sherrington's
         Integrative Action of the Nervous System to put the physiology
         in it. I was someone really saturated in psychology and neurology
         making up a book about the literary approaches. That was a bit
         of luck really. Two quite different concerns crossing at a crucial
         point.

R.B.   Then *Practical Criticism* . . . which was perhaps even more up-
         setting.

I.A.R.   It was to me. It went home. That and *Interpretation in Teach-
         ing,* which in my own private judgment is a much better, bigger
         book.

R.B.   I agree also that it's a very much neglected book, most unjustly
         neglected.

I.A.R.   It was written too fast. Did I tell you what happened with that
         book? It is worth putting on record. The Rockefeller Foundation
         had just begun to take me up. They took me up for about ten
         years. John Marshall said, for them, "Will you write an equiva-
         lent to *Practical Criticism* about prose? Do the lectures. Write

the book, and we'll have a big conference in New York. And get everyone to come and we'll try and make this a subject: *Interpretation.*" So I did. I gave a course. I collected the protocols. Enormous quantities of them. I saw Marshall again, when I'd got my materials piled up. And he said, "Now you've got to put down a figure that represents the worth of what you're going to do for the Foundation. I gave it a lot of thought and with great daring came up with the sum of $600. Then I had six weeks given me to write the book. It so happened that Dorothea caught scarlet fever. And was wafted off to an isolation hospital in Tooting Graveney. I wasn't allowed to do anything but stay away, and I wrote night and day. I found the extracts from the protocols (which took some finding), and arranged them and wrote the whole book in six weeks. It doesn't, I know, seem possible.

R.B.   The last part of the book saw you going in at least two directions toward a new kind of analysis of uses of language. I suppose it was the beginnings of *The Philosophy of Rhetoric?*

I.A.R.   I wrote that in those same six weeks. It's a derivative built from bits and pieces that I didn't use in *Interpretation in Teaching.* There is a sort of proportion sum: *Philosophy of Rhetoric* is to *Interpretation in Teaching* as *Science and Poetry* is to *Principles of Literary Criticism.* Each was a replaying on a more popular level, as I thought.

    Interpretation in Teaching has been out of print. But now, after all these decades, I am glad to say Routledge are reissuing it.

R.B.   In writing it, were you still thinking of how you could directly help teachers of literature?

I.A.R.   Yes. I was . . . and more than just teachers of literature.

R.B.   This is where you made the big transition.

I.A.R.   This is where it is. Actually, those two books sickened me for life of trying to read examination papers fairly. It's too hard to judge how foolish a comment really is and there are too many, too big a proportion of foolish comments. Do you know when I decided to back out of literature, as a subject, completely, and go into elementary education, I learnt something. I learnt where the academic railway tracks are. I was crossing the railway tracks in a most sinister fashion. I was told so again and again. Russell had tried to do it, you know. He'd founded a school and written a book on education. And people had said, "No wonder. He hadn't anything more to say." There's a very severe penalty attaching to going the wrong way across the railway tracks.

R.B.   The guilt feeling, yes.

I.A.R.   And in a way you are betraying a cause, showing things up. All that sort of thing. I remember one extraordinary moment when I was talking with T. S. Eliot. He was staying with Pickthorn, then the Junior Burgess (Member of Parliament) for Cambridge. I went round, Pickthorn had to go out and Eliot seemed hungry for serious conversation. I knew Eliot pretty well. He'd come and stay with us. But I always had a difficulty in making him talk about truly serious matters. He preferred not to on the whole.

R.B.   This was characteristic always, wasn't it?

I.A.R.   I thought so. He may have had special cronies with whom he could be intimate, but with me he usually dodged it. But at this point I took courage and asked him very, very straight, to advise me. Would I be making a mess of things . . . if I did what I in fact did. And he was about the only man I asked that question of who was cordially ready to approve. He had authority and dignity, Eliot had, that made you weigh his opinion. I was much comforted that he thought it would be a good thing to do.

R.B.   One wouldn't have expected him to have seen why you were doing it.

I.A.R.   I expect I took a good deal of trouble trying to spell it out.

R.B.   That transition must have been really something. *Interpretation in Teaching* is sort of the grand hinge from one way to another.

I.A.R.   From things which had been strangely successful to things very much otherwise.

R.B.   There is another transition I'm curious about. Your transition to Plato.

I.A.R.   I suppose that was partly due to Coleridge, to finding out that he was even more a Platonist than he himself sometimes knew. But, more still, making a Basic English version of *The Republic*. I'd neglected Plato. Everybody I knew in Cambridge had. They were strangely unaware of Plato. He didn't seem to be alive in any of them. They didn't seem to think he was anything but a Spartan anticipator of Mussolini or something as silly. That kind of thing was the View. It's very significant to me that for some reason or other even that noble figure, G.E. Moore, after being a distinguished Classic, when he turned to philosophy, never—so far as I know—made any reference to anything he'd learnt from Plato.

R.B. And yet the kind of debate Moore said, at least, he wanted—it sounds as though he didn't want it when he got it—would be the essence of dialectic. After all, he was always asking Socratic questions.

I.A.R. He was. And answering them himself. Wouldn't allow other people to answer them. He shows extraordinarily little concern with any other thinker than Moore. A dangerous sign, maybe, in him. A great mind, but—so it seems to me now—strangely immature: in some ways intellectually childlike.

R.B. What's interesting is that you should have come out of the very heart of what one thinks of as the scientific, positive Cambridge, and made this transition where there was almost nobody around doing it. I suppose there was a little "Platonizing" in some corners of Cambridge . . . did Lowes Dickinson mean anything to you?

I.A.R. Yes.

R.B. He would have been one of the great exceptions.

I.A.R. He was. Of course, old Goldie was glorious really in lots of ways. But I don't think he had at the time any influence on me on that front. He *had* a tremendous influence on me politically. A *Modern Symposium* was a book I would be able then to recite. It was a sort of Bible. And we joined up through his passion for things Chinese. But it was James (Jas) Wood who first awakened my interest in the multiple potentialities of Chinese phrases. We compared different translations of them together in a kind of rapture. It was he who brought the Chung Yung into our *Foundations.* Typically, he made "The Lodge of Leisures" a catchword among us. H.A. Giles had translated the Chinese collection of yarns as *Stories from a Chinese Studio.* Jas Wood pointed out that in the English translation of Soulié de Morant's version it was *Tales from the Lodge of Leisures.* We delighted in having such a name for wherever we might be doing our hardest work. It must have been an inverse impulse that made us give a really clamant title to the little book we had so enjoyed writing.

R.B. This reminds me of another deviation or transition: *Mencius on*

Gyorgy Kepes

I.A.R., 1972.

the Mind. Is that picking up your early *Meaning of Meaning* interest? Or is it also looking into the very next step, which seems
to me to be broadly connected with translation?

I.A.R. Both perfectly true. It was a sort of natural growth for me in
Peking. Here was I doing my best to take part in academic activities which illustrated incomprehension—unknown, unrecognized
failure of understanding and on such a scale, always hitting you.
I felt I must do something. So I got together a very able team of
four and I sat in more or less as secretary. I didn't pretend to any
Chinese. I could just distinguish one character from another, but
I didn't know anything. I couldn't be sensitive to the terrific,
universe-wide, reverberations. And these four people were so
sensitive in their various ways, and they did their best to explain
to me some of the key things. I took . . . curiously enough . . .
the passages in Mencius which might be parallel to passages in
Coleridge.

R.B.   That's just the question I was about to ask. *Coleridge on Imagination, Mencius on the Mind.* Isn't there some deliberate coming together here?

I.A.R.   Yes, but with a difference. What got into *Coleridge on Imagination* was a sort of free reconstruction. I wasn't so much concerned to say what Coleridge had thought as to suggest what might be done with what he had said.

R.B.   This too was a transition.

I.A.R.   It was. In my then view it was being scientific.

R.B.   Which many people didn't understand. It baffled many "pure scholars." Because they didn't see that what you were trying to do—as I understood it—was to show us what could be rescued and continued.

I.A.R.   Yes, that is exactly right. And I tried to do something for Mencius of the same sort. Only I had to lay out the problems much more thoroughly in Mencius. My informants (and I had to rely on them), although they were devout Mengtzists, or whatever you call it, were very diverse in their understanding of the Master. I came to feel that this diversity was what mattered.

R.B.   Well, I gathered from that book that it was just this very variety of interpretation that you were talking about. The book gave you an enormous opportunity for it. This was where I came in, incidentally. You were getting the proofs of Mencius just at that time. And occasionally I used to sit by your side on the sofa in Magdalene when you were tearing your hair out over these choices of Mencius and saying to yourself sometimes: "Whatever did I mean?"

I.A.R.   One way and another Mencius taught me so much that I got the Rockefeller to stake me to go back and try to found a movement in China for teaching English in a way that would make it more useful to the Chinese, for understanding what they (and we) most need. And there I learnt a lot of politics again.

R.B.   You and Ogden had already worked out the vocabulary of Basic English.

I.A.R.   He did it. It's Ogden's, all the detail; the general plotting is a good deal me, but all the hard work was Ogden's . . . tremendous, too. The way he did it was as individual as it was original.

R.B.   Can you reconstruct how the two of you thought of doing this at all? If I may say so, this was a really new idea.

I.A.R. Ogden had been playing with artificial languages for perhaps ten years.

R.B. Had he gone back to . . .

I.A.R. He'd read Wilkins and Leibnitz; he knew Newton's proposals backwards. He was deep in it, and in all the artificial languages too. He had a gift for that kind of thing. And when he wrote a chapter, in *The Meaning of Meaning*, "On Definition," at the end of it we suddenly stared at one another and said, "Do you know this means that with under a thousand words you can say everything." If a word can be defined in a descriptive phrase of not more than ten words, you can substitute the descriptive ten words for the word and get rid of it. Over-simple, extremely—but, for most purposes, good enough. We found we'd worked out the principles for such rephrasings in writing that Chapter. And at the end of it, we very nearly switched to a new task. I remember I went home to Clifton and spent my time drafting what was to be Basic. And Ogden had been doing exactly the same thing in my absence. When we came together again we said, "Look here, shall we drop the *Meaning of Meaning* because this is a much bigger thing." It was only half written, the book, you see, and this *was* a much bigger thing. But Ogden had got himself deeply involved. He'd already set up the publication of *The Meaning of Meaning*. Did you ever hear how that was done? He created a project which finally grew to two hundred volumes called The International Library of Psychology, Philosophy and Scientific Method—just in order to print the *Meaning of Meaning* among suitable supporting works.

He had been publishing then, very successfully, a penny weekly magazine, which he turned into a digest of the world news as an aid to the war. When all *that* was put an end to by drunken medicos rioting on Armistice Day, he wrote a letter to the subscribers, some 15,000, including Charlie Chaplin, I remember, saying that the unexpired part of their subscription would be met by their receiving instead of the penny Weekly a Quarterly— very handsomely produced. He designed the Quarterly so that each page of it was four pages of *The Meaning of Meaning*. That cut down expense and trouble. So we wrote the *Meaning of Meaning* in a tremendous hurry for publication, in bits and pieces quarter by quarter. We cut up the *Cambridge Magazine* proofs as they came in and I pasted them on the walls of my room. In time we had the whole book pasted up there. So we could put a *not* in any sentence we thought would benefit from having a *not* put into it. Oh, it was fun! That's how we did it.

R.B. I suppose this interest—going over into Basic—is very much a part of your move to this Cambridge, isn't it.

I.A.R. Couldn't be more so. Though, actually, I came in '39 because of the war. When it broke, I went to the man I knew best in the field: Stephen Gaselee, Senior Ambassador, Librarian of the Foreign Office and a Fellow of Magdalene. I asked what I should do. I didn't care to get out of the war, and I had in my pocket an invitation to come to Harvard. The answer was: If you've got an invitation to Harvard, you've got to go. So I came. The invitation was mainly the work, I think, of David Stevens of the Rockefeller. They fixed up my appointment here because they wanted some Basic English texts turned out and some people trained and so on. They gave me an endowment for three years.

R.B. You would think now with all the new interest in the teaching of English as a second language all over the world, that there would be lessons to be learned from Basic.

I.A.R. Anyway, my gifted collaborator, Christine Gibson, and I turned out, through the years, a great amount of rather fundamental redesign of instruction—for Beginning Reading and Languages— in all the Media. I hope more people will be using it along with our other derivatives from Basic. Otherwise, I fear a big experimental resource for education will be missed. But I have put all that in my paperback: *Design for Escape.*

R.B. It seems natural to go on now to translation because these two interests are one, aren't they?

I.A.R. I never thanked you rightly for that dedication to me of your *On Translation.* That was enheartening.

R.B. That book really started from looking in Magdalene at those proofs of *Mencius on the Mind.* (I very nearly did Classics in college, but soon shifted to a combination of Greek and English.) It suddenly dawned on me then that here was a whole interest that I had been on top of, though unconscious of. But what I would like to ask about is the step from that kind of analytical interest to your actually trying your hand at translation?

I.A.R. Making Basic or Everyman's versions? Well, I needed to do that for China. But I also felt that there was a population here in the schools that would benefit from something really lucid. So, there we are. And I'm quite happy about the way *The Wrath of Achilles, Why So, Socrates?* and the *Republic* hold to their purpose . . . and are serving it. It's not every purpose. There must be a variety of interpretations aimed at different companies of addressees.

R.B. Right. The attempt to get *everything* into the scholarly translation finally defeats the reader.

I.A.R. It produces the Loeb versions—thank everyone for them.

R.B. Right in the middle of all this comes *How to Read a Page*. At least it was published in 1942. This seemed like a very good shot at Chicago and its Great Books Program and the way it was conducted.

I.A.R. You hit the nail on the head. I had admired Mortimer Adler immensely but I somehow got irritated by *How to Read a Book*. So I wrote a counter-blast: *How to Read a Page*. Instead of a hundred *books*, chosen regardless of what translation, version or anything, I wanted to take just a hundred *words* and then I revolted again and made it a hundred and three. And it so happens that the Great Books are now a hundred and three. It was partly a bit of fun. But it was a very serious book, unusable, I know now, for the populations I hoped I was addressing. I did have one surprise. It was made into a paperback. And about six months after that, I suddenly got a telegram from the editor of the paperback series, who simply said, "Hold on to your hat. They've ordered 15,000 of it." And I looked forward, as you imagine, to next year's returns. I think they sold forty-two copies the next year. It didn't go down where it was hoped it would go down. One has to be used to that.

R.B. It went down . . . perhaps where the ground was prepared . . . with the teachers who at that time were feeling, as I was—many of us were—feeling really swamped by the Chicago sort of thing. And all of our effort had been, you know, in the opposite direction. There were so many badly conceived courses that just grabbed Great Authors right and left, and threw them in. No consideration of what translation, or of how the teacher could intelligently teach a translation.

I.A.R. Or how much a mind can take in by the week.

R.B.   Let's not end on this because I'm interested in the experiments you are now active in. I suppose it was Basic that led you to thinking about visual media?

I.A.R.   Yes, because I had to draw, I had to turn *English through Pictures I* into comic strip technique. That's an awfully good little book that Dr. Wiese produced about the man who invented the comic strip, Rodolphe Töppfer: *Enter the Comics* (University of Nebraska Press, 1965).

R.B.   She was in my translation seminar when she was working on that.

I.A.R.   I learnt a lot from it. What happened was very simple. I'd long wanted to have a comic strip version for teaching Basic. I did the sequencing, the over-all design; I drew the pictures for the book myself and then, very mistakenly, got a draughtsman to redo them. And he gave them a kind of woodenness that I'm against. There's a great deal of thinking involved in drawing *really clear* diagrammatic representations of meanings. It's a way of studying meanings that's unexpectedly revealing. It started me on what may be a key idea: that the multiplicity of our channels is our best hope. The eye can check what the ear hears and vice versa. Our habits of writing may teach us a great deal about what we're saying. I found myself recently having twice written on a single page *competition*—very clearly, in my clearest handwriting—in place of *composition*. It hadn't occurred to me in oral or visual words so sharply ever before that any composition is a competition between the choices that are open to it. Here was my hand —unknown to me—speaking for a deeper awareness: writing *competition*. It was reminding me, drawing my attention to a primal fact.

*   *   *

R.B.   I hoped we might end on your poetry. Were you always writing verse?

I.A.R.   Almost never, until recently. It was a very queer set of impulsions, not accidental, that led me to write verse. I was finishing a play called *A Leak in the Universe*; it seemed definitely to require a lyrical component. So I just had to write the lyrical component. And that got me into it.

R.B.   And this would be about when?

I.A.R.   I must have been sixty, or over. The *Leak* is quite late (Playbook,

New Directions, 1956). It is listed in my *Internal Colloquies*: my
poems, up till 1970.

R.B.   And you've gone on.

I.A.R.   As Robert Lowell said to me recently: "Why not, if writing verse
is the most fascinating thing there is to do?" Perhaps I might
close this self-indulgent talk with my latest poem? It's not, I
hope, my last. The title is *Acquiescence*.

His young Mont Blanc could say,
  For Shelley, what he would.
    O serene Throne
    Unseen, Unknown!
Mine, threescore years away,
  For other searchings stood:

Spoke to me of Beyonds
  But too well gainable,
    Of means and aims
    Dwindling to games.
Now what in me responds
  To the Unattainable?

Lo! Ruskin's Matterhorn!
  Not Whymper's mortal prize.
    That craze dispelled,
    The Unbeheld
Returns, as if reborn,
  To disillusioned eyes.

Hence, to the Lodge of Leisures
  With easy steps and few,
    Being intent
    Less to repent
Than re-appraise those pleasures,
  Assess these aches anew.

Study the antic flight
  From shiver to sun to shade;
    The fervours past,
    The rigours last
Into the chills of night
  That shake strong hearts afraid.

Now the proud rage for doing,
  That passion for What's On,
    That feckless
    Restlessness,
That frenetic pursuing . . .
  Had best be seen as gone.

Hopes that would hint of treasures
  Repaying such to-do
    Have stept ahead
    As leaves are sped.
So redesign your measures,
  Align your ends anew.

Sorrows that might not tell
  Of Loss beyond your thought:
    Yearnings forbid,
    By chagrin hid.
Old strains and dreads as well:
  Old aches gone where they ought.

From what may this forefend?
  Such transformations steal
    So past recall
    Through all;
Foreshadowings so impend,
  How sense now how we feel?

Who less than ever guess
   What we may yet conceive
      So insecure
      Each "To be sure . . ."
In which we acquiesce;
   Nor know for what to grieve.

Failure comes first: first
   Forepang, gathering strength;
      To have so failed,
      Left unfulfilled
What most we tried: the worst
   Now realized, at length.

Each muscle that won't pull,
   Each sense and joint to stall,
      Enacting old
      Assaults gone cold,
Speaks to us, to the full,
   Of what might now appall.

The body wearing out
   Backs still each changed regime:
      What to refuse,
      What not accuse,
Learning to live with gout . . .
   Mind has its graver theme.

Parallel though: to keep
   Viable itself,
      Being not,
      Now, longer what
It was, but half-asleep,
   The old codes on the Shelf.

What we might do has sought
   To shape and set our scope.
     Which shutting in,
     We may begin
Refurbishing our thought,
   Untarnishing our Hope.

Of what? Ah, none can tell.
   But see what's risen there:
     That Towerer, sheer
     Transcending fear,
Whereby, composed, to dwell,
   Dare, share, forbear.
   And murmurings spare.

The Alps, July–October 1972

Essays

JOAN BENNETT

"How It Strikes a Contemporary":
The Impact of I. A. Richards' Literary Criticism
in Cambridge, England

In 1922, when I.A. Richards came back to Cambridge, the condition of English studies here was exceptionally propitious. Three years before, in 1919, I had sat for the first examination in English under new regulations. These recognized that English "Literature, Life and Thought" from Chaucer to the present day was an adequate field of study leading to an honours degree. Further developments were to take place, and soon it would be possible to study "English literature and its background" throughout the three undergraduate years. Under the fairly elastic headings "life and thought" and later "its background" much could be, and was, included. I myself, in 1919, was more keenly aware of what had been shed. I had come up to Cambridge in 1916 to read for the "Medieval and Modern Language" Tripos in French and English. In both languages this meant paying some attention to philology and learning to translate from early texts; for English one needed Anglo-Saxon and Middle English. Much excellent instruction was given to me both in College and in the lecture rooms in Cambridge, but I profited very little by it all, and I was delighted to find that I need display no knowledge of pre-Chaucerian English in my final examination. The linguistic options remained, as they still do; but from this time the emphasis for a student of English could be on the history of thought, the theory of criticism and the analysis of major literary works, rather than on the history of the language and the history of literature. Thus two years before Richards came back to give lectures for students of English, a revolution had occurred. There was an atmosphere of excitement and expectancy. Because of the changes in the regulations and the consequent opportunity for new directions in teaching, a newcomer

45

trained in another discipline, a man of vision and enthusiasm as well as sound judgment, could influence the development of English studies at least for a generation. This is what happened and, indeed, the influence of I.A.R. is still operative fifty years later.

I need not go into the question why or how the new English options came into being. The story is told in some detail, and with a vivid account of some of the personalities involved, in *The Muse Unchained* (1958), by E. M. W. Tillyard, and Basil Willey, in *Cambridge and Other Memories* (1968), enriches it with some brilliant character-portraits. Especially relevant to my theme is his evocation of the person-ality of Mansfield Forbes who was I.A.R.'s friend and the herald of his coming, and whose probing and eccentric style can be detected among the audience-contributions in the book *Practical Criticism*. Basil Willey writes:

> Manny was a most unusual being, hard to describe convincingly to anyone who never knew him. Someone called him the "little wizened old boy of forty," and indeed both his face, which was wrinkled yet childlike and ingenuous, and his manner, which was at once naive and sophisticated, justified that description. He answered to Coleridge's description of the man of genius, who is able to "carry on the feelings of childhood into the powers of manhood; to combine the child's sense of wonder and novelty with the appearances, which every day . . . had rendered famil-iar." Appropriately enough, he lectured on ideas of childhood and parenthood in Blake and Wordsworth, and for sheer brilliance, unexpectedness, insight and originality these lectures were un-rivalled. They were also extremely funny, Forbes possessing among his many gifts the power of inventing whole terminologies and classifications of his own, such as "Nor-Petal" for poets like Wordsworth who think that Skiddaw pours forth streams more sweet than Castaly, and "Sou-Petal" for those like Byron or Shelley who flee either imaginatively or actually (or both) to Italy or Greece. In more ways than one Forbes was a Coleridgean type; his lectures were a tissue of digressions; they eddied, but pro-gressed little and had little orientation. As likely as not, half-way through a course on the Romantics he would still be talking about the early Blake. And so it is not surprising that, if ever he planned a *magnum opus*, he never achieved one, indeed, he left nothing behind him at his early death but an eccentric History of Clare College and an eccentrically-decorated house in Queens' Road. But none of this mattered; Manny had a truly seminal mind, an imagination from which ours caught fire, and an ex-traordinary sureness of taste and rightness of judgment.

Every phrase of this brings back memories of Forbes and of his lectures in 1919 when H.S. Bennett and I were among the audience at that course on the Romantics. Two thirds of the way through the term Forbes was still exploring Blake's *Songs of Innocence* and *Songs of Experience* and giving us odd but evocative *viva voce* renderings of them. He was developing a theory that words in poems had not only an exact stress and time (indicated by the metre, the rhythm and the sense), but that one must also discover a right pitch of voice for certain key words. Once, after I.A.R.'s return to Cambridge, he and Forbes tried out this theory in a lecture. Each of them gave a *viva voce* rendering of D. H. Lawrence's poem *Piano*. Most of the audience already knew the poem, having attended I.A.R's "Practical Criticism" course. To demonstrate his theory about pitch Forbes read in a falsetto voice the word "poised" in the line "And pressing the small poised feet . . ."; his idea was, perhaps, that this would illustrate the weightlessness of feet merely touching the pedals. The effect, however, was irresistibly comic. I.A.R. followed in what he called the "neutral style" of reading. His reading followed with complete fidelity the poem's rhetorical structure and, in so doing, allowed the poet's thought and feeling to emerge. Most of us were, I think, convinced of the superiority of the "neutral style." Forbes probably was too, since no one could have been more receptive or less obstinate than he.

As a university lecturer Forbes was a brilliant amateur, as indeed was Richards; there was an unusual opportunity to recruit such amateurs in the 1920's. To be appointed as a lecturer required no defined qualifications, such as a Ph.D. or published works. For some time after the first World War the number of undergraduates was swollen by the addition of returned warriors to the normal inflow of school-leavers. The supply of teachers had to meet their needs. Then as now individual teaching was provided and in most Colleges every undergraduate would have an hour's weekly meeting with his teacher, alone or with one other student. Most of these teachers were also giving lectures in the University. They had, however, in those days no fixed salary; they were paid according to the number of students who attended the course. This had obvious disadvantages, but amateur-status was not, I think, among them; on the contrary it usually meant that each lecturer chose to talk on the subject that excited him—each was "in love with" his subject. In this sense they were amateurs; so were they also in the sense that many had taken no degree in English. Manny Forbes was an historian who was passionately interested in the arts, in architecture and sculpture, no less than in literature. In a lecture he might wander far afield from the announced subject, or the lecture might be postponed, or it might exceed the announced time. The only predictable certainty was that, if the lecture took place, it would be intellectually exciting. Of course, there were no other lecturers as brilliantly eccentric as Forbes, but there were others who were amateurs in the study of English literature and whose outstanding distinction was won in other fields. There was, for instance, the historian G.G. Coulton; he lectured on medieval life and thought in relation to medieval literature and so became a pioneer in that study of the social and intellectual background of literature which was to become characteristic of English studies in this University, and later in many others. The subject was also already widening to include some comparative literature. Dr. A.B. Cook, Professor of Classical Archaeology, lectured to us on Greek and Roman tragedy—his lectures on the former enthralling, on the latter, to me, tedious. Already, over-riding language barriers by using translations, the study of English included the major tragedies in European literature. I.A.R. was to make his contribution to a theory of the primacy of tragedy among literary forms.

I.A.R. himself had studied, not English literature, but philosophy. He obtained a First Class in the Moral Science Tripos in 1915 and returned to Cambridge as College lecturer in English and Moral Science at his own College, Magdalene, in 1921. In the second term of that year he gave a course of lectures on the novel; in the first and second terms of 1922 he gave courses on the Theory of Criticism, and again in the first term of 1924. At first he was not technically a good lecturer. He turned his back on the audience too frequently and for too long, while he scribbled on the board scarcely legible phrases, or scarcely intelligible diagrams. He broke many pieces of chalk. By the end of his hour he had seldom, or never, reached the promised goal. This could have been a device for retaining the audience or leading it to recognize the supreme importance of the withheld subject, for instance "metaphor" which was our will-o'-the-wisp throughout a term. But certainly I.A.R's postponements were not consciously a trick to retain the audience. There was no need for this: his lecture room was always well filled. In those early years he was a nervous lecturer and he was unaware how small a quantity of new ideas can be conveyed to an audience in fifty-five minutes. It is probable that the most effective lecturers retain both these characteristics, but gradually learn, as he did, to disguise them. Meanwhile I.A.R's lectures were spell-binding, partly because we could not fail to notice that he was breaking not only chalk but new ground. The ideas now extant in *Principles of Literary Criticism* (1925) were taking shape.

It would be absurd to attempt a summary of this seminal book; instead I will try to recall and explain the force of its impact. It was valuable at that time to be presented with a basis for literary criticism, rational, man-centred, rooted in utilitarianism. In the *Principles* I.A.R. always raises the basic question "what does this contribute to the good of man?" His own ideas had been nurtured by the study of moral philosophy from Plato and Aristotle to John Stuart Mill and G.E. Moore. I am not competent to guess what each contributed towards his own formulations, but it is clear that his thought was permeated by questions raised and answered in terms of ethical value. Fundamental to his thinking is his assumption that the purpose of art is the benefit of man and that the artist's tools are such as can effect this. In this sense his explorations are always psychological and moral:

> The Arts are our storehouse of recorded values. They spring from and perpetuate hours in the lives of exceptional people, when their control and command of experience is at its highest, hours when varying possibilities of existence are most clearly seen and the different activities which may arise are most exquisitely reconciled, hours when habitual narrowness of interests or confused bewilderment are replaced by an intricately wrought composure. (Ch. IV, p. 32)

There have been recent developments which seem to challenge this account of what the arts are—but it applies unquestionably to what they have been. I.A.R. in the nineteen-twenties was aware of the threat of change; in the following chapter he writes:

> It is perhaps premature to envisage a collapse of values, a transvaluation by which popular taste replaces trained discrimination. Yet commercialism has done stranger things: we have not yet fathomed the more sinister potentialities of the cinema and the loud-speaker. . . . (Ch. V, p. 36)

This and what followed acted as a clarion-call summoning many to the defence of the old values. Out of such inspiration, for example, *Scrutiny* arose, and the educational works of Denys Thomson. In *Principles of Literary Criticism* I.A.R. calls for defenders of literary values that were taken for granted by Spenser, by Milton and by Wordsworth. What is new is that he describes such values in psychological terms. He considers, for instance, how the work of art affects the recipient.

> When we say that anything is good we mean that it satisfies, and by a good experience we mean one in which the impulses which make it are fulfilled and successful, adding as the necessary qualification that their exercise and satisfaction shall not interfere in any way with more important impulses. (Ch. VIII, p. 58)

A similar picture of what happens within the mind is developed in his account of the effect of tragedy in Chapter XXXII, entitled "The Imagination." I.A.R. is here acknowledging his allegiance to Coleridge and he asks:

> What clearer instance of the "balance or reconciliation of opposite and discordant qualities" can be found than Tragedy. Pity, the impulse to approach, and Terror, the impulse to retreat, are brought in Tragedy to a reconciliation which they find nowhere else, and with them who knows what other allied groups of equally discordant impulses. Their union in an ordered single response is the catharsis by which Tragedy is recognised, whether Aristotle meant anything of this kind or not. This is the explanation of that sense of release, of repose in the midst of stress, of balance and composure, given by Tragedy, for there is no other way in which such impulses, once awakened, can be set at rest without suppression.
>
> It is essential to recognise that in the full tragic experience there is no suppression. The mind does not shy away from anything, it does not protect itself with any illusion, it stands uncomforted, unintimidated, alone and self-reliant.

In such passages I.A.R. gave us glimpses of the critical insights of Coleridge, the ethical emphases of Matthew Arnold and the then recent psychological discourses of Freud. In Chapter VIII he had invoked Matthew Arnold's conception of the critic's function:

> To set up as a critic is to set up as a judge of values. . . . For the arts are inevitably and quite apart from any intentions of the artist an appraisal of existence. Matthew Arnold when he said that poetry is a criticism of life was saying something so obvious that it is often overlooked. The artist is concerned with the record and perpetuation of the experiences which seem to him most worth having. (Ch. VIII, pp. 60–61)

There was a risk that I.A.R's directives, like Arnold's own, might lead disciples to look for quality only where the writer's intention was manifestly and consistently serious. As far as I know none of the first generation of I.A.R's intellectual progeny paid much attention to a light-hearted poet such as Herrick, nor to such witty or ironical novelists as Sterne or Peacock. But it was not, I think, I.A.R's intention to reject the comical or the gay in art. His concern was to destroy a then still active notion that art should be "for Art's sake." He devoted a whole, though brief, chapter to this shibboleth, Chapter X, ending:

> The reader must be required to wear no blinkers, to overlook nothing that is relevant, to shut off no part of himself from participation. If he attempts to assume the peculiar attitude of disregarding all but some hypothetically-named aesthetic elements, he joins Henry James' Osmond in his tower, he joins Blake's Kings and Priests in their Castles and Spires.

I think the Art for Art theory died of neglect soon after.

Among the many valuable achievements of *Principles of Literary Criticism*, as of the later *Practical Criticism*, was the provision of verbal tools to insure that we knew what we were talking about. For example I.A.R. alerted us to the danger of confusing two quite different activities by calling them both "criticism." That term, he suggested, should be confined to evaluative judgments; on the other hand comments upon diction, metre, structure, etc., should be called technical: "All remarks as to the ways and means by which experiences arise or are brought about are technical, but critical remarks are about the values of experiences and the reasons for regarding them as valuable, or not valuable." (Ch. III, p. 23) Once stated the distinction may seem obvious; it is however not always observed, even by professional critics. Similarly illuminating was his definition of rhythm in Chapter XVII, especially for those of us who had either studied manuals of prosody, or felt guilty for not doing so. After a brilliantly clear and amusing introduction to the subject of metrics in its relation to the sound of poetry, I.A.R. sums up his central point as follows:

> This texture of expectations, satisfactions, disappointments, surprisals, which the sequence of syllables brings about is rhythm. And the sound of words reaches its full power only through rhythm. Evidently there can be no surprise and no disappointment unless there is expectation and most rhythms are made up

as much of disappointments and postponements and surprises and betrayals as of simple, straightforward satisfactions. Hence the rapidity with which too simple rhythms, those which are too easily "seen through" grow cloying and insipid unless hypnoidal states intervene, as with much primitive music and dancing and often with metre.

Throughout a long life of teaching I have been guided by this account, without consciously even remembering it. More commonly than of old, students may come to a University to read English literature without ever having thought about the relation between, for instance, metre, rhythm and the total effect of a poem. Some will read verse aloud making no pause at the end of a line, exactly as if it were prose. I.A.R's account of rhythm can help partly because it is independent of technical terms. It points to the effect of metre, not to the techniques that govern it. By its directive towards expectation and surprise, it indicates how rhythm may depend upon metre. Consequently it can alert the ear of a reader who knows nothing about prosody to the achieved rhythms of any of the great English masters of verse, Milton or Pope, Donne or Tennyson, Hopkins or Yeats, each playing so differently and with such subtle mastery upon "a texture of expectations."

Principles of Literary Criticism was published in 1925; in the same year I.A.R. gave the first of his courses of lectures called "Practical Criticism," the fruits of which were published in the book of that name in 1929. The audience at these lectures was exceptionally miscellaneous; in the book Richards speaks of a total audience of about sixty. Probably two thirds of this number were undergraduates, most of them studying for the English Tripos. The remaining third included young graduates in their twenties, most of them doing some teaching for their Colleges. Among these were a few of outstanding brilliance and promise, for instance William Empson and F.R. Leavis. Mansfield Forbes also was sometimes present and frequently if not always contributed to what Richards called the "protocols" (comments on the poems). This diversity in the audience accounts for the extremely diverse quality of these comments, ranging from absurd callowness and egotism to amazing subtlety and awareness of the poet's intention and craftmanship. Richards' friend T.S. Eliot contributed at least once, though I have no knowledge that any contribution of his appears in the book. I.A.R. told some of us that he and Eliot differed in their evaluation of Long-fellow's *In the Church Yard at Cambridge*, a poem which divided the

audience in unusual ways, partly because almost all present were ignorant of its cultural background and therefore perplexed about the plain
sense of the opening stanza. A modern American audience similarly composed might find Lawrence's *Piano* baffling. I myself, eagerly attending
the Practical Criticism courses in 1925 and in 1927, was elated to learn
that Richards thought well of Longfellow's poem; I was more proud to
be on the same side as the lecturer than dismayed at differing from the
poet. Looking back, and sometimes recognizing my own contributions,
I find I was twice chargeable with lazy or careless reading, but was on
the whole sensible, if uninspired, a fair sample of the average youngish
graduate present. Such people to-day would be far better educated as
"practical critics" than we were.

In his Introduction to the book Richards gives an account of his
intentions and of his procedure in the lecture room. He defines his
three aims:

> First to introduce a new kind of documentation to those who
> are interested in the contemporary state of culture, whether as
> critics, as philosophers, as teachers, as psychologists, or merely as
> curious persons. Secondly to provide a new technique for those
> who wish to discover for themselves what they think and feel
> about poetry, and why they should like it or dislike it. Thirdly to
> prepare the way for educational methods more efficient than those
> we use now in developing discrimination and the power to un-
> derstand what we hear and read.

These aims were operative throughout both courses. "Documentation"
was supplied by notes on each poem contributed by almost all members
of the audience. Printed sheets were given out, each containing a group
of poems, without date, title or name of author; poems likely to be
widely known were avoided. The written notes were to be informal and,
of course, the writers would remain anonymous. I.A.R. collected these
notes after we had had one week to consider each of four poems (in
one case, in the second course, five poems). In his next lecture, a week
later, he discussed the results. Comments which illustrated types of
misreading and consequent misjudgment were read out, also some that
expressed valuable insights. As can be imagined there could be painful
moments for some members of the audience, caught out in careless
reading, even though no one but themselves could know of their failure.
On the whole however, those hours in the lecture room were hilarious,
salutary and revealing. Except where a comment was as arrogant as it

was absurd, Richards skilfully steered us towards mutual tolerance and
shared amusement, as well as towards greater humility, and above all
towards more alert attention to the words on the page.

The most startling and inescapable result of this experiment was the
discovery of widespread incomprehension of meaning at the most elementary level. Each of the thirteen poems was rejected by some members of the audience who had misunderstood the words, the grammar
or the logical sense. For example the notes on Christina Rossetti's *Spring
Quiet* showed that many misconstrued the fourth line in the third stanza:

Full of sweet scents
Are the budding boughs
Arching high over
A cool, green house.

Ignoring the comma in line four, they assumed that the poet referred to
a green-house or conservatory and wrote dismissively, for instance, that:

> Green houses are not usually cool, though I suppose they might be
> if anyone were foolish enough to erect them under arches of bud-
> ding boughs.

Donne's Holy Sonnet VII:

At the round earth's imagined corners blow
Your trumpets, angels . . .

was, predictably, unintelligible to many, because of their ignorance of
its scriptural and theological backgrounds; but it was surprising how
many readers failed to suspect their own ignorance as a cause of misunderstanding. Conversely, however, many praised Edna St. Vincent
Millay's *The Harp-Weaver* because they failed to understand it. As this
poem is unlikely to be well known, I will quote I.A.R.'s prose paraphrase in *Practical Criticism*, before giving examples of satisfied misapprehension; he notes:

> Since at best only some twenty readers construed it, and the
> remaining two-thirds wittingly or unwittingly failed, it seems im-
> perative to begin with a prose paraphrase. Here it is:
> "You should not think of death, for you will not die. It is
> inconceivable that God having made you so perfect will let you
> perish, since you are his masterpiece. Whatever may perish, your
> loveliness is too great to be lost, since when God dies your image
> will be permanently retained as a memorial of his skill as a creator."

Absurd though this is it unquestionably represents exactly what the poem says. The following is a comment typical of several that are reproduced in *Practical Criticism:*

> I am sure it is a good sonnet, but it takes a lot of getting at. I like the rhythms and the words please me immensely, but in spite of many readings I have not yet arrived at its precise meaning. Obviously the lady will die, physically, but whether her loveliness is to be preserved in the minds of others is more than I can fathom.

This writer has not faced the possibility that the poem is nonsensical. At the close of his discussion of the poem I.A.R. notes that, though many were puzzled by and some mistrusted the poem:

> Only two coupled these suspicions with detailed observation of the matter and manner of the poem and it is these observations that we seek in criticism.

He quotes them both, the first sober and lucid:

> This one offers cheap reassurance in what is to most men a matter of deep and intimate concern. It opens with Browning's brisk no-nonsense-about-me directness and goes on with a cock-sure movement and hearty alliteration. It contains echoes of all the best people. It is full of vacuous resonances [quoting an example of this] and the unctuously poetic.

The second is in the inimitable impressionistic style of Manny Forbes, ending with a summing up as follows:

> A sort of thermos vacuum, "the very thing" for a dignified picnic in this Two-Seater sonnet. The *"Heroic" Hectoring* of line 1, the hearty *quasi* stoical button-holing of the unimpeachably-equipped beloved, *the magisterial finger-wagging* of "I tell you this"!! Via such conduits magnanimity may soon be laid on as an indispensable, if not obligatory, modern convenience.

But a majority of the audience were impressed by the seeming complexity of idea and force of feeling.

Before moving on to what I.A.R. learnt and taught as a result of his experiment it may be useful to look at one whole poem and some typical reactions to it. I choose Lawrence's *Piano* because of its high quality and because responses to it were especially revealing:

Softly, in the dusk, a woman is singing to me;
Taking me back down the vista of years, till I see

A child sitting under the piano, in the boom of the tingling strings
And pressing the small, poised feet of a mother who smiles as she sings.

In spite of myself the insidious mastery of song
Betrays me back, till the heart of me weeps to belong
To the old Sunday evenings at home, with winter outside
And hymns in the cosy parlour, the tinkling piano our guide.

So now it is vain for the singer to burst into clamour
With the great black piano appassionato. The glamour
Of childish days is upon me, my manhood is cast
Down in the flood of remembrance, I weep like a child for the past.

The "protocols" show that there were three main obstacles between the
readers and this poem: (1) their inability to understand the two events
recorded in it and their relation to each other in time; (2) in consequence, their inability to follow the poet's thought and feeling; (3)—
perhaps a main cause of (1) and (2)—their deafness to the poem's
rhythm. For examples of all these incapacities the following selection
of protocols will serve (the numbers are those printed in the book; 8 is
the number of the poem):

> 8.1   If this, on further inspection, should prove not to be silly,
> maudlin, sentimental twaddle, I have missed the point. Such it
> certainly seems to me, and I loathe it. It is a revelling in emo-
> tion for its own sake, that is nothing short of nauseating. More-
> over, it's badly done. I object to "cosy", and "tinkling" used of
> a piano that elsewhere "booms" or is "appassionato. . . ." If this
> be poetry, give me prose.
> 8.22   The second verse, which should have been the most poig-
> nant, is especially uninspiring. And I don't think the lady singing
> at the piano would have been very pleased to hear her efforts de-
> scribed as "bursting into clamour."
> 8.4   A very vivid piece of prosy poetry—if one may call such a
> string of pictures poetry. I find some charm in the thoughts but
> none in the verse or very little. Contrast the last line of each
> verse with Swinburne's "Thou hast conquered, oh pale Galilean;
> the world grows grey at thy breath." The same metre, but what
> a difference of sentiment. I can't really like this.

I.A.R. remarks: "That he should misquote his Swinburne altering its
slow, weary rhythm ('the world has grown grey from') is just what we
should expect."

The poem did not, however, defeat all members of the audience;
there were four positive responses to it, all of them showing much greater

comprehension of the story-line than did the dismissive ones. Two of
these follow:

> 8.7 It is difficult to pass judgment on this poem. The communi-
> cation is excellent, and the experience one familiar to most peo-
> ple. I suppose this emotional reversion to an ordinary incident of
> one's childhood, and the indulgence in grief for it simply because
> it is past, is really sentimental. The striking thing is that the poet
> (D.H. Lawrence? or American?) knows quite well that it is so,
> and does not try to make capital out of the sentiment. The sim-
> plicity and accuracy with which he records his feelings—and the
> justness of the expression, not pitching the thing up at all—
> somehow alters the focus; what might have been merely senti-
> mental becomes valuable—the strength of the underlying feeling
> becoming apparent through the sincerity and truthfulness of the
> expression.

I.A.R. interpolates, "Another useful note of analysis is added in 8.71":

> Associations make it difficult to judge this poem impartially.
> The first verse is sentimental, but pleasing; it is curious that the
> poet feels sentimentality coming upon him—"in spite of myself"
> —and he gives way to it entirely. The last two lines of the second
> verse particularly show sentimentality—a shallow and languish-
> ing feeling—but yet they convey adequately the qualities of the
> evenings they describe, thus we can scarcely accuse the poet of
> sentimentality.
> The poem is extremely simple, and whether it is itself weak or
> no, it well describes a certain psychological state of mind. The
> poet can convey pictures. The poem, I think, succeeds in doing
> what it set out to do.

I.A.R. pertinently questions "Whether . . . on the evidence before
us" we can assume that the poem "is so simple."

Part II of *Practical Criticism*, containing the "protocols," has probably been the most frequently read and has undoubtedly provided the
most entertainment. But it is upon Part III, "Analysis," and Part IV,
"Summary and Recommendations," that the influence and value of the
work depend. Here is to be found what I.A.R. deduced from the strange,
comical, dreadful evidence of how poems can be mis-read, and the guide-
lines he laid down for the avoidance of the revealed pitfalls. He deduced
that the meaning of a poem may comprise (i) the sense (prose
meaning, argument, story-line or the like), (ii) the feeling (about any
or all of these within the poem), (iii) the tone (the way in which the
reader is invited to respond) and (iv) intention (sum-total of the poet's

guidance within the poem). All the bracketed elucidations are merely
my own interpretations of I.A.R's key words. For more than forty years
this fourfold definition of a poem's meaning has proved a valuable
guide for readers. However, the fourth has sometimes been misunderstood and I.A.R. seems to have foreseen a possibility of this since, in
Appendix A, he returns to it and recognizes that:

> *Intention* may be thought a more puzzling function than the
> others. We may admit the distinction between sense, feeling and
> tone, but consider that between them they cover the uses of lan-
> guage, and that to speak of intention as a fourth additional func-
> tion is to confuse matters. There is some justification for this.
> None the less there are plenty of cases, especially in drama, in
> dramatic lyrics, in fiction which has a dramatic structure, in some
> forms of irony . . . where this additional function may assist
> analysis. [He adds that] intention . . . controls the relation
> among themselves of the other functions [sense, feeling, tone].

Throughout I.A.R's explanation of "intention" it is obvious that he is
attending exclusively to what can be discovered within the work itself.
When Dr. W.K. Wimsatt published his influential essay "The Intentional Heresy" in *The Verbal Icon* he may not have meant to deny the
importance of "intention" discoverable by close reading. What concerned him was, I think, the temptation to substitute for such reading
outside information of a biographical kind. It is this that, he insists, is
irrelevant. It was totally absent from *Practical Criticism* because, for
experimental purposes, the poems were anonymous and dateless. In
normal reading, however, it is wise to extend our search for "intention"
a little beyond the confines of the poem. A date, a name, or familiarity
with a genre can prevent misreading, as is evident in I.A.R's instances
of the forms in which failure to identify intention are most likely to
arise. Instances abound of irrelevant criticism, poor stage production,
impercipience of ironic effects and so forth that can be remedied by
knowledge external to the work itself. This is always knowledge that was
fully in the writer's possession and that he expected the discerning
reader to supply. When I.A.R. gave his lectures and when he wrote the
book he paid little attention to this need for some knowledge external
to the work. The impact of his work perhaps gave rise to too exclusive
emphasis upon the words on the page.

However that may be, the influence of the two works I have tried to
describe has been of incalculable value. It would I believe be impossible

to set up a similar experiment for undergraduates reading English to-day and discover a comparable incapacity to read. Training in attention to the words on the page is given in school classrooms; there are books (too many perhaps) made solely to provide a variety of samples, in case the teacher cannot find his own. The school-leaving examinations that in England admit students to study English literature at a University all include some tests of "practical criticism", in which the candidates are presented with passages of prose or verse and invited to appraise, compare or give some account of them involving close reading. More importance is attached to this type of paper than to literary papers on books and authors studied in class. Because of I.A.R's influence it is widely recognised that the ability to respond fully to a writer's fourfold meaning is the most indispensable ability for a student of literature. It now seems almost ridiculously obvious, but it was not so before 1925. In fact it was many years later than that, at my own College, we abandoned all other types of tests for would-be students of literature than tests of their ability to understand and to appreciate passages of prose and of verse and to express ideas in good English. These two exercises have proved better guides to selection than general questions about authors studied at school.

But the impact of I.A.R. was wider and deeper than this suggests. He was concerned with the teaching of English literature because he believed that, as Shelley wrote in the *Defence of Poetry*, "poetry is the record of the best and happiest moments of the happiest and best minds." This should be obvious to all who read Richards' books, as it was obvious to us who listened to him. I lay stress on it, however, because in 1961 I read a short history of criticism by a young man who wrote as follows:

> Richards is, of all the major English critics, the one most difficult to visualize with a book of verse in his hands. His interest in poetry seems abstracted to the point where all English poetry is an illustration of an aesthetic principle or a mass of data to provide experiments towards a theory of communication.

This is the exact reverse of the truth. I.A. Richards, now himself a poet of distinction, was an exciting and trustworthy interpreter partly because his response to each poem was not only intellectually alert, but also intuitive and strongly felt. This was evident in the way he read a poem, or indeed a passage of good prose, as well as in his interpretations.

M. C. BRADBROOK

I. A. Richards at Cambridge

Joan Bennett has described the early days of the Cambridge English School; ten years later, in 1927, I came up to her College, so that my pupil years cover what, in his *Cambridge and Other Memories,* Basil Willey has termed the Heroic or Golden Age—the period between 1928, when the Tripos was reformed for the first time in a way that made it unique in English studies, and the period when Richards withdrew gradually to Peking and then to Harvard. In the Lent Term, 1939, his name appeared for the last time in the Lecture List, giving a course on Practical Criticism on Tuesdays at 12.

I suppose my pupillage might be said to have ended in 1936, when I was elected to a teaching Fellowship at Girton; from that critical era of graduate unemployment round 1933–36, I gratefully remember the kindness of Richards in helping me to obtain the Allen Scholarship from Cambridge University. A little lunch party at Magdalene with his friend Frank Salter represented the civilized substitute for an interview. Richards was always eager to meet and to talk with the young. Perhaps this explains why in his eightieth year he is still able to explore fresh paths and to experiment in new forms.

In his Clark Lectures for 1968, *English Literature in Our Time in the University,* F.R. Leavis treated "our time" in terms of "the past that is present"—in terms of Eliot and Lawrence, that is, of the late twenties and early thirties. Each generation carries about with it its own youthful Cambridge, its own Golden Age—that period in life when the power of education is strongest, the ability to respond and adapt at its greatest.

The Cambridge English School was created by Ivor Richards' generation. As Eustace Tillyard, Basil Willey, F.R. Leavis and Joan Bennett [1] all attest, it was Mansfield Forbes who shaped its earliest forma-

---

1. E.M.W. Tillyard, *The Muse Unchained,* Bowes and Bowes, 1958, p. 15; Basil Willey, *op. cit.,* pp. 20–21; F.R. Leavis, *op. cit.,* pp. 14–17; Joan Bennett, in this vol., p. 45.

tion; it was Mansfield Forbes who brought Richards into the English School. But Forbes died in 1936, and is now almost a forgotten figure, for he left behind only a History of Clare College and his beautiful house on the Backs. True, there had been a Chair of Anglo-Saxon at Cambridge since 1878 (first occupied by W.W. Skeat, some of whose editions of medieval texts are still in use). Earlier, in the 1860's, Clark and Wright had produced the Old Cambridge Shakespeare; and the founder of modern bibliography, W.W. Greg, was a Cambridge man. But until 1917, Cambridge had so few undergraduates reading English (which appeared as a minor option in the Modern and Medieval Languages Tripos from 1883) that there was no "school". As Leslie Stephen had pointed out in his *Sketches from Cambridge* (1864, pp. 89–91), the Colleges were rich and the University was poor. A Professor occupied a rather lowly position in the hierarchy, compared with Senior Tutors or First Bursars.

While London introduced English Language in 1839 and Literature twenty years later, while Oxford succumbed in 1904 and recalled Walter Raleigh from his Chair at one of the new civic universities in the North, Cambridge remained without a school of English.[2] The King Edward VII Chair of English had been founded in 1911, but the subject was eventually to be formed by a group of young veterans from the First World War, who had read History, or Classics, or in the case of Richards, Moral Science (Forbes was a historian who held that the only serious science was Heraldry). The women's Colleges were centres of English studies—long a favourite subject in girls' schools. As an undergraduate I myself was schooled by Hilda Murray, a daughter of the editor of the *Oxford English Dictionary* who, with her nine brothers and sisters, had spent her youth filling out cards for that great work at sixpence per thousand, and who greeted an early blunder in translation with "Miss Bradbrook, have you any manuscript authority for that variant?" None the less, she attended Richards' lectures on Practical Criticism which were packing the large examination hall, and filled out her "protocols" with the rest; as did Leavis and the Bennetts and other of my teachers. These occasions felt like a cross between a Welsh revivalist meeting—for Richards shews some very Welsh qualities as an orator— and the British Association's lectures in Elementary Science. The last

2. Stephen Potter, *The Muse in Chains* (Cape, 1937) gave a lively and disrespectful history of English studies, based chiefly on London and Oxford.

English school to be founded was the first school of Late Medieval and Modern Literature.

Moreover, Richards had effected a basic shift in approach which redefined the subject. What was brought into English studies was the significance of the reader's response. The King Edward VII Professor, "Q," [3] had written on *The Art of Reading*, but with Richards a new art of reading evolved. The study of literature became a collaborative social exercise; it was no longer a matter either of philology or of "history" in the old sense. At one stroke the familiar annalistic treatment was reduced in significance. There stood the monumental works of Saintsbury, there stood the *Cambridge History of English Literature, Chaucer's England, Shakespeare's England* and *Johnson's England* as before; but when Richards lectured on the Theory of Criticism (as he did until 1935), Saintsbury receded and survived only as a reference tool: our working implements were the books of Eliot and Richards.

These did not exist merely as texts however. The best of our work was done by direct contact, so that Joan Bennett's choice of a lecture course to write upon gives a true indication of where emphasis lay. In those days Cambridge was still a small and intimate place. Books were only part of the scene. Much of the best work never got into print, such as Eliot's Clark Lectures on the Metaphysical Poets (they can now be read in the Hayward Collection at King's College) or Richards' lectures on Eliot. We were not much concerned with the outside world or with publicity—we learnt by the direct method of "oral transmission."

As a group of readers who felt great literature all around us, we were constantly stimulated and so could afford to be discriminating. *The Waste Land* had opened up new possibilities in poetry (Frank Kermode records that, as late as the mid-thirties, at his school in the Isle of Man, *The Waste Land* had not been heard of). When in 1935–36 I spent a year at Oxford, I was astonished at the difference of mental climate. As an impecunious research student, I bought a copy of Eliot's *Collected Poems* and lent it to a Fellow of the college where I was staying. She returned it to me, with the following note, which I still possess:

> I am ashamed to find that I have kept this for so long, but I have very much enjoyed looking at it. Besides, it has been very useful in deciding me not to buy it!

3. Pen name of Sir Arthur Quiller-Couch.

Of course, there was opposition to Richards within Cambridge, the most notable opponent being F.L. Lucas of King's, but I don't think the opposition was as well organized as Leavis was later to imply. In 1932, when I was a fifth-year student, *The Cambridge Review*, which in Leavis's 1950 *Retrospect* [4] is singled out as an organ of opposition, published a little piece I wrote on *Coleridge's Waste Land*, comparing Eliot's poem with *The Ancient Mariner*.

Nor can I agree with Kathleen Raine that Cambridge at this time was so deeply infected by logical positivism as to impose "the denial of the imagination." [5] In my first year Yeats's volume *The Tower* came out, and Richards lectured on it immediately. This felt like the birth of a new poet; for I thought I had left behind the author of *The Wind Among the Reeds*, one of my childhood favourites, when I discovered *The Waste Land*.

The new critical school emerged at a time of greater literary excitement in prose and drama than had been known in the previous hundred years. Besides Eliot and Yeats, Lawrence and James Joyce were publishing; *Ulysses* had to be smuggled out of Paris, but Joyce's later work was evolving in little paper pamphlets; *Ash Wednesday* was appearing poem by poem in French magazines; Faulkner and Hemingway were publishing; and at the Festival Theatre on the Newmarket Road, Cambridge enjoyed one of the most advanced experimental theatres in Europe, where it was possible to see Pirandello, Elmer Rice, Eugene O'Neill, Goethe, Strindberg, Kaiser, Toller, and classical drama.

Richards helped to strengthen the ties with America; the study of Pound and Eliot brought Paris close. These connexions were felt to be more important than those with traditional schools of English in other universities. I remember the excitement of sitting under a willow tree on the Backs and reading R.P. Blackmur on Eliot in an early number of *Hound and Horn*; in 1931 Edmund Wilson's *Axel's Castle*, with its studies of Yeats, Valéry, Eliot, reached us; I still possess the copy left me by the redoubtable Hilda Murray, along with my faded little Chapbooks, and the Cambridge "little magazines" of that time, *Experiment* and *Venture*, run by Empson, Jacob Bronowski, Michael Redgrave and others. The critical bias did not prevent active production of verse, novels, sketches.

4. I.e. to *New Bearings in English Poetry* (Chatto and Windus, first published 1932).
5. Kathleen Raine, *Defending Ancient Springs*, Oxford 1967, pp. 17–18.

Something of the best cosmopolitan American literary point of view was transferred to Cambridge. We took it for granted that the context of contemporary English literature was the international context. The study of French was made part of the new Tripos, and it was possible to learn Italian also. Today's move towards comparative literature was anticipated in the English Tripos, and Richards' tastes in particular confirmed the tendency—as indeed did those of his chief opponent, F.L. Lucas, an excellent French scholar. In a sense, the situation was close to that of the present day, except that the work was felt as falling within *English* studies, which were incomplete without some comparative literature, i.e. the balance was not inter-disciplinary, but was seen from the point of view of English studies, to which the others were complementary—not ancillary. Richards' more exotic taste for the Chinese—*Mencius on the Mind* came out in 1931 after his first stay in Peking—fitted in with a school that included Forbes and that studied Pound and Joyce.

One of the early works of F.R. Leavis, *How to Teach Reading, a Primer for Ezra Pound,* appeared in 1932 from the Minority Press, a private printing press established by Gordon Fraser, an undergraduate at St. John's. The answer to Pound's *How to Read* sets out the idea of a university as Leavis then conceived it. It is based on the College "supervision," a very small private class, now universally adopted for teaching English in all English universities, at least in theory.

> Supposing, then, a university did its best to provide such an education, what would the basis be? . . .

> ### THE TRAINING OF SENSIBILITY
> Everything must start from the training of sensibility . . . the technique of analysis each teacher will, for the most part, have to develop for himself. As much theoretical apparatus as he can reasonably ask for, he will find in the works of Dr I.A. Richards, *The Principles of Literary Criticism* and *Practical Criticism*. This apparatus will not give him a technique of analysis, but with Dr Richards' account of "What is a Poem?", of rhythm, meaning, sentimentality and so on, *and* a good sensibility trained in constant analytic practice, he will be able to learn and to teach, to discuss profitably the difference between particular poems, to explain in detail and with precision why *this* is to be judged sentimental, *that* genuinely poignant; how the unrealized imagery of *this* betrays it was "faked," while the concreteness and associative subtlety of *that* comes from below and could not have been excogitated; and so on. (p. 25)

The only other book here recommended is Mr. W. Empson's *Seven Types of Ambiguity*—"those who are capable of learning from it are capable of reading it critically, and those who are not capable of learning from it were not intended by Nature for an advanced 'education in letters.'" (p. 26) Eliot's *Sacred Wood* is recommended for the stage beyond analysis of verse and prose texture.

Principles of Literary Criticism introduced the collaborative yet self-critical examination of English literature which justified it as a discipline. It appeared in a famous series issued by Routledge and Kegan Paul which included works of psychology and anthropology, and "the anthropological" or sociological approach was an essential part of Richards' work. (He was research supervisor to Q.D. Leavis, among others.) Concern with the general threat to standards which modern technological society imposed was a familiar topic at the time. Again F.R. Leavis may be cited; in the first of his pamphlets from the Minority Press, *Mass Civilization and Minority Culture* (1930), he quoted *Practical Criticism:*

> What hope is there then left to offer? The vague hope that recovery must come, somehow, in spite of all? Mr I.A. Richards, whose opinion is worth more than most people's, seems to authorize hope; he speaks of reasons for thinking this century is in a cultural trough rather than upon a crest and says "the situation is likely to get worse before it gets better." (p. 31)

and himself finally confessed, "We cannot help clinging to some such hope as that Mr Richards offers . . . that the machine will be made a tool."

More than forty years later, when Leavis has announced a book entitled *Nor Shall My Sword* (*Essays in Pluralism, Compassion and Social Hope*), the note is recognisable.

Richards is much more than a theorist. He lectured not only on Yeats but on Conrad—at that time rather an unfashionable artist—and other contemporary novelists; but he had not read English as an undergraduate, and its historic evolution did not concern him, though he could display a sense of the historic possibilities of a genre, as in his analysis of Pope's *Elegy on an Unfortunate Young Lady*. It was rather Leavis, who has recently declared that for him "practical criticism means criticism in practice," [6] who introduced a more historic method of applying the *Principles*, and devised exercises in placing poems. Some of these

6. Letter to the *Times Literary Supplement*, 3 March 1972.

derived from Eliot—a favourite comparison being that between Marvell's *Nymph Complaining for the Death of Her Faun* and Morris'
Nymph's Song to Hylas.

Richards' start at Cambridge coincided with the growing professionalism of English studies—with the foundation of such annuals as *The
Year's Work in English Studies* (1919) and *The Annual Bibliography
of English Language and Literature* (1920). In this sense Richards was
never a "professional". His technical concern was with Basic English,
in connexion with which he spent long periods of leave abroad after
1930. Although he has often returned to Cambridge and still owns the
house in which he and Dorothea Richards dispensed such lively hos-
pitality, his attachment never grew adhesive. Part, and not the least
part, of his contribution to English studies has been these wider interests, and contacts, counteracting tendencies to narrow concentration
which any academic study may incur. He acquired friends but not
disciples. He did not assume the stance of authority, although at times
his voice acquired the ring of prophecy or proclamation.

Richards' work was little understood outside Cambridge. "I don't
read to enjoy, I read to evaluate" was a remark elsewhere attributed to
a mythical female undergraduate. In 1936 Stephen Potter in *The Muse
in Chains* attacked the absurder features of traditional academic English
teaching and (despite his strong Oxford-London bias) mentioned Cambridge Aristotelianism and "a lecturer at Cambridge" who "had made a
very satisfactory ruin of the automatic use of phrases from the English
Men of Letters series—'strong vein of lyricism . . . typical of the fervid
idealism of the period' etc." (p. 245). Richards appeared to him as a
cool, dry scientist, offering something felt to be equivalent in rigour to
the bibliography with which the science-starved at London assuaged
their appetite!

Though he was too skillful a tactician to make any direct mention of
Cambridge, in *Rehabilitations* (1939) C.S. Lewis defends the annalist
ideal of English studies. Anglo-Saxon must keep its place because it is
English (p. 93): "The man who does not know it will remain all his
life a child among real English students" althought "the first thing to
do, obviously is to cut off some years from this end. . . . a hundred or
two hundred or any reasonable number of years. . . ." (pp. 90–91)
The bluff of a manly metaphor encourages the "natural" study thus
presented as distinct from "composite" courses.

> We hand over to you our tract of reality. . . . In the great
> rough countryside we throw open to you, you can choose your
> own path. Here's your gun, your spade, your fishing tackle; go
> and get yourself a dinner. Do not tell me that you would sooner
> have a nice composite menu of dishes from half the world drawn
> up for you. You are too old for that. It is time you learnt to
> wrestle with nature for yourself. (p. 93)

The reverse side of Oxford is the well-known anecdote of Robert
Graves, whose tutor rebuked him with "It seems, Mr. Graves, that you
prefer some poets to others." This has sometimes been read as irony but
the attitude is reflected in *The Business of Criticism* (Oxford, 1959),
a defence of the Oxford system written some twenty years later than
that of C.S. Lewis, by the present Merton Professor, Dame Helen
Gardner:

> To attempt to measure the amount of value, to declare or at-
> tempt to demonstrate that this poem is more valuable than that,
> or to range authors in an order of merit, does not seem to me to
> be the true business of criticism. . . . The attempt to train
> young people in this kind of discrimination seems to me a folly,
> if not a crime. (pp. 7–13)

Any hard and fast "order of merit" is something quite contrary to the
method of practical criticism; but the Cambridge approach certainly
implies that contemporary literature, as the most difficult and the most
relevant, is the most necessary of all to be taught; that the crucial test
of a knowledge of the past is to be able to apply judgment in the present, and to distinguish the first-rate from the second-rate before time has
put the labels on. As Leavis has said, "It is only in the present that the
past lives." [7]

In America, the "New Critics" met with similar academic opposition,
and established themselves only slowly in the decade following the war.
In Cambridge as late as 1955, in *Style* F.L. Lucas was trouncing "too
much English in the universities" for turning out "numbers of bright
young men and women who will trot off half a dozen pages exposing
the 'stupidity' of Tennyson or the 'insincerity' of Hardy, quite un-
cramped by their own very indifferent capacity to write English or even
to spell it." (p. 114)

English at Cambridge has remained a subject that is strongly College-
based, and there has always been room for a variety of styles in studying

---

7. *English Literature in Our Time in the University*, p. 68.

for the Tripos. In the Golden Age, only four or five colleges were really strong in the subject, and each taught in individual ways. Weekly essays and discussion were as powerful a force, though less striking, than the public lectures. King's cultivated its own epigrammatic style; Jesus and Emmanuel were strong Colleges, the latter more historically biassed; Pembroke, St Catharine's and the women's colleges were other strongholds; and after 1936, Leavis developed the most famous college school at Downing. Richards' own College, Magdalene, was a small one and offered him few pupils—but among them was William Empson, whose *Seven Types of Ambiguity* developed from his weekly undergraduate College work with Richards.

The briefest definition of Cambridge English would be: Contemporary, Comparative, College-based. We never troubled ourselves unduly about "covering the syllabus"; yet while Richards was at Cambridge, there was true balance between the centripetal force of his lectures and the more intimate college teaching. There was a general feeling that a student ought to have his wits stretched. We tended to prefer the difficult poets—Donne, or Marvell, or Eliot. "Strenuous" was a word of praise. We were not very charitable to fools. The over-earnest young woman whom C.S. Lewis depicts in *Rehabilitations* (p. 97) is myself.

The Cambridge of Wittgenstein, Richards, Empson, Leavis and Rossiter was not cosy or permissive; it was craggy and opinionated. Richards could smite vigorously in defence of a good cause; once when Empson, in a talk at the A.D.C.,[8] was being persistently heckled in a nasty way, Richards suddenly turned round with vigour and interjected at the irrelevant interrupter, "And if a sunstroke hit you on the back of the neck, you'd be dead!"

Ivor Richards cannot be met adequately through his books alone. To hear him read aloud is the best education in poetry; his voice, melancholy, slow-cadenced, sinks with an emphatic fall to clench his argument. His impish humour, his personal courtesy and his surprising union of the authoritative and the mischievous are more fully shewn in talk, lectures, or possibly—and if he has not made any, he should do so—on film.

University teaching was also, as others testify, casual, and almost improvised in the early stages, and therefore without the professional constraints that later developed. The freedom to develop as one pleased

8. The Amateur Dramatic Club—where Empson acted in Fielding's *Tom Thumb* and produced a play of his own, now lost.

conferred adult status on undergraduates without any protest being necessary.

The position has changed since those days. The finances of the University are increasingly dependent on the central government grants made through the Department of Education and Science, with all that this implies of formal appointment, limited leave of absence, specified duties. In Richards' time the one Professor, "Q", held his appointment for life. He appeared from Fowey, in Cornwall, where he was Commodore of the Yacht Club, some time about the third week of term, and departed in the fifth week. He gave popular lectures to crowds of attentive Cambridge ladies wearing marvellous hats; he was not prepared to admit the students of Girton and Newnham Colleges to his evening talks on Aristotle, and always addressed his audience as "Gentlemen," since women were not at that time given more than an associate position in the University.

"Q's" creative inertia allowed young men to take the lead, but it precluded any coherent development of the Faculty structure. I understand that he seldom came to meetings of the Faculty Board and sometimes not to meetings of Examiners. He had, after all, been appointed before the English Tripos existed.

In the 1970's there are five permanent Chairs in the English Faculty, besides personal Chairs, and the students have increased something like tenfold. The undergraduates themselves are dependent on grants from their Local Education Authorities, and the research students on grants from the Department of Education and Science. About a hundred and twenty are working for advanced degrees, whereas in Richards' time one or two a year was the norm. In these circumstances, even without any other changes, the situation that produced the English School of the Golden Age no longer exists. For some, this is a story of pure degeneration; "more means worse." In *Two Cheers for Democracy*, E.M. Forster proposed that Cambridge should be sunk without a trace before the planners got hold of her—the dons and other portable valuables being removed. But the Cambridge of the twenties and early thirties could survive in such a changed world only as a museum piece. It was the good fortune of that period that literature could provide a centre of concern; and who can say, looking at the work of Havel or Solzhenitsyn, that it cannot do so now? But in a different society with different bondings.

Looking back, it appears to me that there was a delicate balance of confidence and tentative query in the exploration of new approaches, the landing on new shores. We were innocently confident in our right to pronounce judgment; but a scientific atmosphere is one in which any thinker must be prepared to regard any position as provisional only, open to modification by new evidence. There was enough of the scientist in Richards to convey this to the rest of us. Our concentration on "the words on the page" and on the equipment which the reader could bring to bear at any given moment was itself symptomatic. We were given to words like "report" (verb and noun) and "analysis," but "insist"—that favourite Leavisism—had not made its appearance very prominently. Our strongest term of disapprobation was "odd." "At the risk of being thought impertinent" we would insert some nasty little barbs, as I did in student days in a review of Virginia Woolf, causing that eminent lady much anguish, as she records in her diary.

In a recent republication of one of his earliest works, *Science and Poetry* (1926), Richards has provided a corrective. The volume re-issued in 1970 as *Poetries and Sciences* (Routledge and Kegan Paul) originally came out in a small series including books by Emmanuel Miller and Kinnier Wilson, one by C.K. Ogden on *The Mind of a Chimpanzee* and two by Malinowski. It contains a commentary which criticizes the early version in that it failed to bring out "the connexities *within* any experience that is likely to be called "poetic" in any relevant sense. . . . the multiplicities and intricacies of its dependencies upon other experience." (p. 93) The interconnections were too lightly passed over. (p. 98) The words on the page are more than just that.

> A poem is an activity, seeking to become itself. All behaviour (or activity), as I prefer to say . . . of organisms is organic. But of course it must be *activity*. When we fall downstairs, that is not activity; going up them is.
>
> This view that poems, books, views and so on, have some degree of self-responsibility—write their own tickets and pay for their own mistakes, and so on, can go too far. (pp. 108–9)

Richards then tells a story of how Wittgenstein lamented two or three errors in *Tractatus Logico-Philosophicus*, but when it was suggested that they could be corrected by an errata slip or in a second edition, Richards

> found him staring at me as a Pillar of Society stares at a newly unmasked traitor: "How could I! It is my child! I could not murder it!" and so on.

The self-correcting process which Richards ascribes to books is certainly part of his own early work. It has been fed into minds that have re-

shaped those books from knowing them so well that they may be seldom
actually re-read. They exist as part of people, as the lectures and the
whole Cambridge of that time exists.

To conclude, as an answer to those who have felt Cambridge and
Richards were at times over-confident, I would cite the poem that ends
his latest collection, *Internal Colloquies* (1971):

Epilogue
Short poem addressed to spectators by actor at end of play
                                              —Dictionary.
"Lost, stolen, strayed."
Hearing such words,
I have been afraid.

I never, I doubt, knew
Anything about my owner;
Though, as others do,
I'ld hold
I'd some clue.

No.
My choice was between absurds
And I was proner
To consult
Some friends
Who spoke within my mind,
Unawed,
Against every cult.

I was told
I would find
These were unscreen'ds,
Might well be fiends
With their own ends
In view.

That could be true.

Either way:
Lost—at sea, overboard;
Stolen—all still to repay;
Strayed—self-betrayed?

                    December 1970

The Hammer's Ring

A splendid career, long and various, which has brought help and enlightenment wherever it has turned. Surely one might say: "Nothing is here for tears . . . no weakness, no contempt, Dispraise or blame; nothing but well and fair"; but even in Samson's case, if you remember, there was a detail which they might at least regret. Richards himself would feel impatient, I am sure, if his career were praised in this way—as if he had aimed no higher. He would feel it from the refusal of the world Departments of Education to adopt Basic English, to which he has devoted almost all his powers, with unshakeable devotion (though with readiness to improve the plan in detail), for so long a time. The same may be felt about his position in literary criticism, and even in linguistics; his views have had much recognition, with good results, but have also been widely rejected.

When I was a student at Cambridge, more people would at times come to his lectures than the hall would hold, and he would then lecture in the street outside; somebody said that this had not happened since the Middle Ages, and at any rate he was regarded as a man with a message. There were those who called him a spell-binder, implying that there must be something wrong with a lecture if it produced this effect; and I was glad of the opportunity to hear him lecture again in London shortly before writing this piece (1972)—as it has turned out, we have spent almost all our lives in different continents. I found him as spell-binding as ever, and many of the large audience seemed to be feeling the same, but as we were most of us in our sixties it didn't much matter whether we were spell-bound or not. The spell had been useful as an incitement to action in young people who were just going to choose a field of work; it held open a glimmering entry to a royal garden, or an escape route which would entirely transform common experience, or at least ordinary theoretical problems. In his moderate rueful way, Richards has gone on being fertile in proposing steps forward; but he has never lost the feeling that they are minor ones, because an immense opportunity lies unrecognised just beyond our grasp. This indeed is what is so plainly lacking from our present leaders in linguistics, and Richards demonstrated it in Chapter IV of *So Much Nearer*—where the moderation of style and manner make an exhilarating contrast to the knockdown content. One cannot see (before I read this chapter, I had been feeling guilty because I could not see) how the theories of these writers could make any difference if true, or what they could be wanted for, let alone how they could be tested. Absence of vision is not inherently scientific; and in the lecturing technique of Richards the vision itself is the spell he casts. But the dazzle of it has evidently caused delay even to himself, and a disciple would often feel that his response to it had been inadequate. One can understand a growing appetite, in Cambridge around 1930, for some casting of the idol down.

It came in a series of articles by Dr. Leavis in *Scrutiny*, largely devoted to denouncing the Benthamite Theory of Value. Till then Leavis had been adulating Richards, practically as the only known guide. It might seem odd to denounce a literary theorist for holding a philosophical belief more than a century old, and widely accepted at least in the university where he operated; but the inherent paradoxes of the doctrine allow of much chop-logic, and it was here I think that Leavis began to take his high moral tone. He was right in treating the matter as important, I cannot deny, because his own moral judgments about literature, and those of his disciples, have been wrong-headed ever since. Indeed, the whole of "Eng. Lit." as a University subject badly needs to return to the Benthamite position. Many of my colleagues, I think, reject it out of loyalty to T. S. Eliot, feeling sure that he would demand some higher criterion; and here I can offer a piece of gossip which for once might be really useful. I had gone to his office at Faber's to ask for a book to review for the *Criterion*, and he was looking at the current *Scrutiny* while talking about it to someone else; how *disgusting* the behaviour of Leavis was, what mob oratory his arguments were, couldn't something be done to stop him?—and then, with cold indignation, "Of course, I know it's going to be me next." At that time, Leavis was adulating Eliot with all the breath he had to spare from denouncing Richards. I was not an intimate friend, as the anecdote may seem to claim, but neither was I eavesdropping; he just accepted anyone who was in the office as an honorary member of the conversation. Being a disciple of Richards, I was already sure of the truth of what Eliot was saying, but I was surprised to hear him say it, and thought it did him great credit, as I still do. That is, one would expect him to think that Scientism needed putting down, but the character of the attack won all his attention.

The idea of making a calculation to secure the greatest happiness for the greatest number is perhaps inherently absurd, but it seems the only picture we can offer. Sensible people have long been accustomed to consider what would be "for the best," bearing in mind the whole situation, and have often emerged from this effort with sensible answers. To claim that God has told you to act for the general harm would surely become blasphemous if made quite specific. Short of that, the only alternatives to Bentham are arty and smarty moralising; giving unreasoned importance either to a whim of one's own or to the whim of a social clique. Leavis appeared not to be doing this because he was taking a democratic position, in defence of the underprivileged students who were then beginning to arrive at Cambridge. Oscar Wilde had a rather nasty epigram to the effect: "If a man is a gentleman he already knows enough; and, if he isn't, anything he gets to know is bad for him." Leavis adopted this, merely changing "gentleman" to "lad from a decent working-class home" or thereabouts, and when I was a student I thought this was fun as well as useful; but all too soon the decent home was being saddled with highly specialised views.

This bit of local history is not important; I was much struck in 1948 to find that Eric Bentley, who was then publishing *The Importance of Scrutiny*, regarded Leavis as a violet by a mossy stone, half hidden from the eye—he deserved praise because he had echoed without knowing it the recent developments in American criticism. They do I think have a similar fault. The main purpose of reading imaginative literature is to grasp a wide variety of experience, imagining people with codes and customs very unlike our own; and it cannot be done except in a Benthamite manner, that is, by thinking "how would such a code or custom work out?" In both countries, this whole conception seems to have been dropped; and I should think it was done, again and again, as if in solitude, by university teachers wanting to retain good relations with school teachers—who naturally want to tell the children that all decent people agree with Teacher. The influence of Eliot would be a great help.

I.A.R. in the Western Hills, China, 1931.

Two examples may help to show the wide range of the issue. *The White Devil*, if you remember, has a good old mother, Cornelia, who begins the play by protesting against the adultery of her daughter, and towards the end of the play her wicked son, who has become generally exasperated, kills her only good son in her presence. Though she goes mad almost immediately, she retains the wit to give a pathetically confused account of the quarrel, such as might almost have saved the life of her remaining son—if there had been no other witnesses, and if legal procedures had been operating at the time. Probably this has always been thought a rather crude bit of tear-jerking, and yet somehow impressive, too real to be laughed off; at least, no one has voiced any moral puzzle about it before our own confused day. But a student at Sheffield wrote down for me: "The corruption becomes total here. Cornelia has been presented as a good character, but now she tries to deceive the police in a murder case". I suspected that my pupil had adopted the ideology of her headmistress, and yet the same puzzle-headed narrowness might be found now in any academic literary magazine. And then, I had a term at Legon University, in Ghana, just before the deposition of Nkrumah. He was becoming generally suspicious, and rather a problem for our Vice-Chancellor, Conor Cruise O'Brien, but I thought one of his complaints had a considerable ring of truth. The expensively imported teachers of "Eng. Lit.," he said, were inciting the students to revive human sacrifice and other savage customs, and in every way were resisting scientific progress in Ghana. With what astonishment my colleagues would have denied this (I do not think it was reported to them); and yet how else could a vigorous-minded student in Ghana interpret their standard phraseology? Obviously Ghana, like other places, needs a Benthamite judgment of what is likely to be for the best in a rapidly changing world; and so does literature. In fact, the chapter on the Theory of Value is fundamental to the *Principles of Literary Criticism*.

I do not think he was much disturbed by the Leavis attack; when it came he was in the Far East, recommending the adoption of Basic by government schools for teaching the first few years of English. His feelings were much more deeply involved in the success of this project; after all, he had taken part in the invention of Basic, whereas Benthamism has always appeared to him merely a formulation of traditional common sense. The successive failures to get Basic adopted, over more than forty years, have continued to astonish him, and one may fairly say that he deserves credit for always keeping his temper. Often in such cases one has a lurking suspicion that an explosion might have done the trick, but here a decisive control experiment is given by the career of C. K. Ogden. There have been two major reasons for the failure. The first is that supplying the required school texts for a whole country is quite large money; not very big, but big enough to confront Ogden and Richards with methods of slander and shouting-down which they were hardly prepared for. Secondly, and as a much slower growth, there were the effects of the new English idealism, or as some would call it the retreat from empire; to use English as the international language (so their bones told them at once) opened an endless vista of whining and back-biting, creating hatred on all sides, and probably destroying the language for good and all. Clearly there has been a similar swing-back in America. Hence it was a fatal mistake for Ogden to keep on boosting the scheme as an international language; that was only a possible late incidental result of the main intention, and far more likely to grow if allowed to stay in the dark.

One needs first to realise what was already in being, and how badly it worked. Most civilised countries teach English in the schools, and nearly all the victims forget it all, except the few who go on to university and learn enough to be usable. If they were given a generally agreed word-list, without quirks of grammar, and provided with a fair amount of reading matter which was within their powers, the Government expenditure would be less likely to be a total waste. As it is, or was then, the teachers realised the hopelessness of their assignment, being themselves badly paid, educated, and equipped, and would often invent some line of evasive action. A Chinese teacher was found who took a scholarly interest in distinguishing between nouns which took the plural with S (cats) or took it with Z (dogs), and his students, year by year as their turn came, learned the contrasting lists by heart for a sheer year. Richards, being Welsh, used the S for both, or could for purposes of effect, and would insist that the Welsh are very well-thought-of in England, look you, a good example to follow. But I must not treat the subject as mild classroom fun. Two of my Chinese students, who spoke excellent English, at different times startled me by saying how much they hated their first teachers of the language, and one said that if ever confronted with the man again he would throw a bucket of night-soil in at his study window; and this was very outside their style—they would never talk so about political opponents, though they had strong political opinions. They felt that an almost unsurmountable obstacle had been piled before them at the outset of their careers. And yet the wicked teachers would have behaved normally enough if they had been given a specific task, capable of execution. In all this, please observe, there is no question of an international language.

Any reasonable word-list would have been better than none, for both teachers and students, but Basic has several merits as a first landing-stage in the learning of English. For the student who is not going further, it allows a confident movement within what he has got, because he can rely on analogy without bumping into "irregular" grammatical forms. To be sure, the eighteen fundamental verbs, called operators, are all irregular (except *seem*), as the English language requires; but after learning them you only meet nouns which can act as verbs, taking *-ing* and *-ed*, as *seem* does. Ogden insisted that they were not to be explained as verbs, to safeguard the interests of pupils with no verbs in their native languages; hence one might say "I am pricing the goods" but not "I have priced the goods" (the genders adopted by past participles in French, as they agreed with subject or object, gave a convenient marker to the dividing line). This seemed to me a quaint intrusion of theory into practice, but after all there would be no way of preventing the students from taking the further step, which is never wrong. Such quirks, I felt sure, would get cleared up once the system was operating—or might even turn out to have been justified.

So I was glad to do a little campaigning for Basic in the Far East, too little I feel now; it was nearly all a matter of writing to local papers and exposing the lies told by the opponents. Such letters were hardly ever answered; the opponents just told the same lie again later on. I translated some of the essays of J. B. S. Haldane into Basic, though I am afraid a good deal of correcting my verbal usages had to be done in the office. Still, this gave me a certain fluency in the dialect, and while refugeeing in China (1938) I once lectured for an hour in Basic, meanwhile writing everything I said on the blackboard, which gave time for a second look at the grammar. This was to a teachers' training college who were well disposed to the plan, and of course I was lecturing *about* Basic, so no aspect of the affair can have had much novelty for them, except that of a dog walking on its hind legs. They seemed mildly content. I boast of the experience because I want to support a claim often made by Richards himself. Many literary people positively fear that English would be ruined by the use of Basic as an international language, becoming a "dead jargon"; I suppose this is one of the things George Orwell feared in 1984, though he never said it outright. But the language has already shown great powers of resilience. Also, much more than French or German, maybe because it has accepted so many foreign influences, it positively likes to purge itself and act simple. If you heard Charles II talking to a Bishop, you felt not merely that he showed the man up as a fool and a pedant but that this was the right man to be King, because he spoke in such an absolutely plain-man way. If you felt so you were deluded, and I do not say that the political effects were good, only that the effects on the language were. Very few of our recent writers, in either country, seem to me to appreciate the need for this plain-man basis under an English style, readily left without losing the power to return. Practice in turning their own stuff into Basic really would be the kindest education in style you could give them, even if it made them realise how often they are talking nonsense. To pretend that it could possibly make them use the language worse than they do already sounds to me farce.

Be this as it may, the remarkable thing about the early reception of Basic abroad was the dishonesty of its opponents. The exasperating thing for us was that they kept on denouncing the whole Basic system as theoretically wrong and then, when their next year's textbooks came out, taking over whole chunks of it. The effect was of course to raise the standard of the teaching a great deal. But every change made by a firm to pretend it was not adopting Basic had to be a change for the worse, and there could be no confidence in communication between two students who had been cheated by two different firms. In the learned world, a man loses his standing if he refuses to answer a plain refutation, but not in the commercial world. We were operating on the borders between them, and I do not pretend that the situation was easy to grasp. I remember two friends of one of our major opponents, in a foreign country, describing to me how he had been summoned by one of the native experts on the subject, for a dressing down; his long succession of cheats about the matter were recited to him, patiently, and then he was permitted to go. His friends said he probably went home and drank himself silly; of course, they had no idea of ceasing to be friends. At the time I doubted what they said; I knew he had been in the wrong all along, but thought he had been able to deceive himself. Most unexpectedly, I learned better long after; this conversation happened in 1934, and I learned better in 1954. It was from an old friend describing his experiences as a pilot during the Battle of Britain; he had had a mental collapse, and was sent to a public hospital (of course there were many *ad hoc* arrangements at the time); and on return, as I remember, was put on patrol duties but no longer on raids. He had enjoyed meeting outsiders in hospital, and had positively chummed up with a dusty old teacher, returned empty from somewhere, so much so that they made a pact they would tell each other their sins. My friend probably thought this would be an excuse for boasting about his sexual triumphs, which he would earn by doing his quota of sympathetic listening; though he did also feel guilty—involuntary cowardice was very guilty. But he was quite dismayed, he said, by what the old brute told him; though he cheered up after reflection, because it showed he was really in a very innocent way of life, making war. The man's confession was about how he had destroyed Basic English; of course he was boasting in a way, but not much, because his sin had preyed fatally on his mind. "O do tell what" I kept on crying out, but no, my friend had resolutely expunged this disgusting stuff, though he had kept to his bond and listened to the end. Somehow, he felt, this procedure had turned a nasty incident into a positively health-giving one. Maybe under hypnosis he might yet give up his dead, like the sea on the Last Day; but it could hardly be of much use.

I wish I had something to tell about the negotiations of Richards with high Chinese educational committeemen, but I was never deep in his counsels, and anyhow I only reached China in 1937, on a Japanese troop-train. The Japanese conquerors had of course no interest in allowing English to be taught, and a lasting collapse of the previous broad knowledge of the language set in at once. Richards had come much nearer to success in convincing China about Basic than any other country, and had very wide contacts there; I was allowed to travel with him in 1937 from Changsha to Indochina, and was a bit startled to find him so well known and esteemed in places which seemed to me remote (all through Chinese history, I suppose, most of the really influential people have been in the provincial capitals). Actually, the disaster was an occasion that cried out for a rapid and simplified method of teaching, but there was no hope of getting the organisation for it; the east coast universities were refugeeing into the interior, and to get *that* organised was as much as the authorities could do. There were some schools already using the method, and help must be arranged for them as far as possible; but that was about all. Richards, I have no idea of denying, fought his rearguard action with all the expected pluck, grit, and panache, but he is not one to go on banging his head against a brick wall. The day came, or rather the dawn, when I walked across a few hills in the west of Hongkong to his hotel, meaning to urge him to give it a few days longer, and was distressed to find he had already left for the airport. I feel sure now that he was right.

The kiss of death was the support of Sir Winston Churchill, which began in 1943; during a grand speech in America, he recommended Basic as the way to make English the international language, and later a Government committee was set up to implement his intention. I remember Miss Lockhart, the very able secretary or manager of the Basic organisation, attempting comfort after the speech and saying that all might yet be well, so it was recognised as harmful from the start. Churchill was well able to understand that other Governments, not the British and American ones, would in the end decide the question; and if he had been serious about it he would have acted differently. It gave just what he wanted for his speech, breadth of post-war vision and co-operation between our two countries, and if it annoyed De Gaulle that was fun. So it was not surprising that foreign Governments were left in need of reassurance; what could not have been foreseen was the behaviour of the British committee. Maybe they felt that the behaviour of the Prime Minister had been unconstitutional, in not going through the proper channels; but surely a good negotiator could have cleared that point. Ogden had had reason to be exasperated, and by this time had settled into the habit of refusing to make any alterations or concessions. There must be a rapid early stage, in the file of documents, which will be interesting if made available, during which he and his committee become mortally offended with one another; after that an Ice Age was entered until his very unforeseen death from cancer in 1957. This should have been an opportunity for Richards, who has always been a much more adaptable negotiator, and indeed keen to find out the actual requirements of a given teaching problem. He devoted to it another fifteen years of intense activity, but somehow the terrible powers of nonsense had already had too long a run.

However, they may be defeated yet by some random turn of the wheel. In the poem by Richards which I take to describe this kind of process there is no actual denial that it may succeed. The princes of Abyssinia, in the poem, are trying to escape from the mountain valley which keeps them unspotted from the world; and we need hardly doubt that they often did escape from it:

Sleek slabs that lean and tilt
    And rear,
    On which to balance fear
And pride and guilt,

And learn there's no way through,
    No out,
    Whatever a stubborn doubt
May set us to

Up here with peg and sling.
    Who try
    The spider's way rely
On the hammer's ring;

Listen themselves secure,
    Until
    Will, over-reaching skill,
Its end endure.

ANGUS FLETCHER

I. A. Richards and the Art of Critical Balance

Richards' career has shown a steady concern for "critical balance," a drive to control the often conflicting forces at work in any full, lively act of reading and understanding. This emphasis on checks and balances may help to explain a recent development in his own literary life— his turn to poetry—since Richards the poet at once extends and holds in balance the dynamically opposed energies of the analytic and the visionary intelligence. His work has always been articulated through questions and question-marks, so that, for example, while he promises "space-ship" adventure in his "Goodbye Earth," the poem also proclaims a painful "comprehending," which "knows not what it knows / Nor what its knowing is—and knows thereby." Richards, questioning, forces the reader into a Platonic exercise of dramatized "internal colloquy." He follows the star of Plato's *Dialogues* and continues the tradition of late Elizabethan and seventeenth-century metaphysical verse, whose forming principle was also that of internal colloquy. Like the Metaphysicals, also, he subjects a Golden Age technique of song to the taut strain of a supervening intellectual struggle. He has come to poetry through a personal history of analytic, pragmatic response to the poetry of others. Further, he has built theories to sustain his practical criticism. How striking, then, that his poetry now should remove the methodical armor of discursive thought, to expose the more frail, human body of intuition.

To be or to become a poet, having formed major critical theory, is a dangerous game. Yet for a theorist in the Coleridgean line it is a natural shift. By turning to poetry, the philosopher modulates from the explicit to the implicit. Coleridge, perhaps first among English critics, looked for the principles of an intrinsic criticism of poetry, and one tenet of his method was a refusal to separate criticism from its object,

85

poetry. Richards has followed this tenet, both knowing and enjoying its attendant risk, whose limits he has sought to define. A speculative poetry, the *Internal Colloquies* are a natural culmination of the Coleridgean intermarriage (Richards would call it a "troth") between the poetic and the critical acts. The critical balance of poetry finally meets the poetry of critical balance.

It may seem tendentious to place Richards the critic among the artists. But such is the Coleridgean setting in which he himself has placed his work. Coleridge, who, according to the *Biographia Literaria*, early learned there is a "science" of poetry, and who sought the principles of that science in the domain of "method," further believed that a systematic understanding of poetry required a continuous contact with poetry. The truly continuous relation between the critic and the poem was so demanding of "the whole soul of man in activity" that a positivistic, purely analytic science of poetry was almost a contradiction. It is a view our recent Structuralism would void from the reading of a poem because of its inherent biographic mystery, its sense of an authorial canon, and its historical awareness of a particular author's use of particular words. The Coleridgean science of poetry is thus subject to an almost impossible semantic demand: it has to account for all the privacy as well as all the publicity that a poem displays. Guaranteeing response to this private/public mixture would seem to require the critic to be a poet, or else to act as if he were a poet—exactly the requirement a positivist would attack. The ideal Coleridgean critic suffers from identity crises in which he hovers on the edge of a poetic vocation. If not actually a poet, like the later Richards, he is forever turning into one.

If the metamorphosis of critic into poet is a Coleridgean phenomenon, it nonetheless with Richards took on a fresh, original character as a result of the systematic austerity Richards brought to his transformation of Coleridge and Bentham. Free of dogmatic belief in the religious authority of myth, though pious toward science, Richards advanced a purer semantic method than any critic of English literature before him. The systematic assault upon the "meaning of meaning," by which Ogden and Richards took the first steps toward a rhetoric of meaning which would include all necessary tropes, ended with one of the typical results of systematic clarification: semantics became a productive field, because the science of criticism acquired *instruments* of response.

The general effect of Richards' early work was a tremendous explosion of semantic energy. Everywhere poetry seemed, from his point of view, to be more "meaningful" [1] than earlier criticism could have let it be. The source of this new burden of meaning would perhaps be found by some historians in the general increase of ambiguity in our century. More particularly, however, it is to be found here in the development of new critical instruments. Whether these devices of reading, which Richards later called "speculative instruments," belong to Science or to Art is a question that may finally resist any formal answer. Their productive yield even so remains unquestionable. *The Meaning of Meaning* and *Principles of Literary Criticism* opened out wide, seemingly infinite fields of semantic exploration.

This infinity is the central Ricardian problem. Critical balance is needed precisely because there is such a richness of meaning to be held under control. "Poetry gives most pleasure when only generally and not perfectly understood"—if this scandalous Coleridgean remark is to be taken seriously, as in Richards, it must be as a call to almost infinite delicacy of response. It leads to the Coleridgean stress upon the variousness, the varieties, the multiplicities, what Empson called the "ambiguities" of poetic utterance. Richards' theoretical career can be seen as a life of interplay between the acceptance of verbal plenitude and a countering search for an instrumental austerity within that overfull semantic space. Richards first showed that poems have too many meanings, and then showed how to control or appropriately cut down on that excess of meaning. This is the art of critical balance.

Quite possibly it will be said that a sense of semantic multiplicity and an attempt to hold meanings in balance had been an implicit stress in all good criticism before Richards. There are moments when even the most dogmatic critics, hardline neoclassicists of the Renaissance or eighteenth century, allow metaphorical instability into their accounts of poetry and poems. Dr. Johnson's acceptance of "originality" is a case in point. On the other hand, criticism before Coleridge had certainly lacked a good theory of semantic range and was thus unable to deal with poetic ambiguity without falling into contradictions and awkward attitudes. By accepting the Coleridgean example,

---

1. "Meaningful," according to the *Oxford English Dictionary*, is a relatively recent arrival on the lexical scene. Whereas the *OED* gives an example from Chaucer of the word "meaning," it shows no use of "meaningful" before 1852, while its second example dates from 1879. Both uses are trivial: "meaningful gifts" and "meaningful smile." This suggests that the popular, quasi-philosophic use of the word is even more recent. "Meaningless," however, is first shown for 1797, when in a letter *to Coleridge* Charles Lamb speaks of "ill-digested, meaningless remarks."

Richards could admit a fact of pre-Coleridgean reading, the fact that in earlier periods the best criticism of poetic ambiguity had been the poetry itself. There, especially in Shakespeare, the poem had pointed to its own variety of rhetorical method. What was true of Shakespeare in the highest degree was true in lesser ways of most Elizabethan and seventeenth-century poets. Yet formal criticism never matched the implicit semantic commentary of Renaissance poetry. Formally the critics of the eighteenth century were uncomfortable in the face of this metalinguistic punning and the trail of sly rhetorical self-consciousness which so controls the abundance of metaphor in earlier poetry.

Even in Coleridge the concern with semantic range remained more often implicit than explicit (a situation Coleridge himself may have preferred). Furthermore, where the *Essay on Method*, the *Biographia*, *The Statesman's Manual* and *Aids to Reflection* did bring meaning out into the open, the revelation of semantics was largely theoretical. Grand speculator of English criticism, Coleridge pursued semantics mostly to the point of suggesting endless further work to be done. In default of the *magnum opus*, no semasiological compendium came from his pen. It was not until Ogden and Richards performed the happy fusion of Bentham and Coleridge that, with *The Meaning of Meaning*, a real start was made.

It is, however, in the works following *The Meaning of Meaning* that the implications of semantic instability and variousness come into focus. Thus Richards in his second major work, the *Principles of Literary Criticism* (1925), met the forces of chaos head-on. He set out to refine a literary theory in terms of psychology, semantics, communication and a connected "theory of value." This latter problem is a major subject in *Principles* and it haunts many later pages of Ricardian theory, largely because "the arts, if rightly approached, supply the best data available for deciding what experiences are more valuable than others." (*Principles*, 33) The final placement of problems of value is perhaps the central critical concern, nor is there, for the twentieth-century world of journalism, advertising, propaganda and pop culture, any more agonizingly important concern than this. Critics have to be valuers.

As one of its most powerful critical instruments, *Principles of Literary Criticism* developed the idea of the "stock response." Richards observed that such responses accompanied "artificial fixations of attitudes," while "against these stock responses the artist's internal and external conflicts are fought, and with them the popular writer's triumphs are made." (*Principles*, 203) The popularity of such triumphs suggests that a general narrowing in aesthetic sensitivity enlarges rather than diminishes the mere number of people who claim to have aesthetic experience. Hollywood's stock characters held the masses enthralled. (Totalitarian dictatorships took this achievement several steps further.) In retrospect the political implications of such concerns are clearer than they can have been in the twenties. What was always clear was that Richards called for a variousness in response to literature which the popular author, with his stock devices, his triggering mechanisms, could not generally work for. Gross popularity sought an art that would enslave the imagination.

Principles of Literary Criticism sought avenues of semantic variety even where it might be least expected. The powers of memory, for example, which might seem the most fixed of mental capacities, led Richards to expatiate on the sheer complexity of human symbolic process. Passages like the following are typical in their assumptions about mental and semantic complexity:

> Imagine an energy system of prodigious complexity and extreme delicacy of organization which has an indefinitely large number of stable poises. Imagine it thrown from one poise to another with great facility, each poise being the resultant of all the energies of the system. Suppose now that the *partial* return of a situation which has formerly caused it to assume a stable poise, throws it into an unstable condition from which it most easily returns to equilibrium by reassuming the former poise. Such a system would exhibit the phenomena of memory; but it would keep no records though appearing to do so. The appearances would be due merely to the extreme accuracy and sensitiveness of the system and the delicacy of its balances. (104)

The term "poise" here refers to a process of balancing by which the mind escapes the inevitable vertigo brought about when all at once too many meanings crowd into it from an uncertain symbolic situation.

Discussing the imagination, Richards observed that "impulses which commonly interfere with one another and are conflicting, independent, and mutually distractive, in him [the poet] combine into a stable poise." (*Principles*, 243) Though believing, with Coleridge, that the poet possesses a special gift of normality and command, Richards ad-

mitted that "we can only conjecture dimly what difference holds between a balance and reconciliation of impulses and a mere rivalry or
conflict. One difference is that a balance sustains one state of mind,
but a conflict two alternating states. This, however, does not take us
very far." (251) The context of this last complaint is, it should be
said, a most successful chapter on the balancing effects of irony within
the imaginative response to life's complexities. Richards had shown
how poetry of the highest order is characterized by irony's technique
of "the bringing in of the opposite, the complementary impulses."
Having shown this, however, he could still lament that current psychology could not adequately describe the relevant mental processes of
ironic contemplation. The "switchboard view of the mind," a simplified
yes-no diagram of symbolic choices, could not account for the many-
sidedness of high art. It could not account for tragedy, not to mention
the other reaches where art was polysemous. Richards insisted that
Aesthetics itself would fall into a stock response, if it failed to allow
that art, under certain conditions, most evident with high tragedy,
"can take anything into its organization, modifying it so that it finds a
place." The plenitude of meaning in a character like Falstaff had to be
seen as an aesthetic balancing-act that could occur on a very broad
range of artistic fronts.

> This balanced poise, stable through its power of inclusion, not
> through the force of its exclusions, is not peculiar to Tragedy. It
> is a general characteristic of all the most valuable experiences of
> the arts. It can be given by a carpet or a pot or by a gesture as
> unmistakably as by the Parthenon, it may come about through
> an epigram as clearly as through a Sonata. (248)

Such catholicity resulted from the method of aesthetic analysis: "We
must resist the temptation to analyse its cause into sets of opposed characters in the object. As a rule no such analysis can be made. The balance
is not in the structure of the stimulating object, it is in the response. By
remembering this we escape the danger of supposing that we have
found a formula for Beauty."

Deeply influential assumptions about the relations between subject
and object underlie such statements, and certain critics will reject the
Ricardian dismissal of "the structure of the stimulating object." On the
other hand, a concentration upon response and upon the reader as re-
sponder gave to Richards' early work much of its clarity and drive. He
was enabled to look at the way readers read, and how they get side-

tracked, and how they may succeed in closing the gap between themselves and the full range of a literary text.

The author of *Principles of Literary Criticism* knew, it would seem, better than anyone else where its case would be most vulnerable. Principles, after all, might remain merely principles—abstracted formulas, vividly enunciated with a wealth of glancing allusion, but lacking any descent from the heights of speculation. A later book, *The Philosophy of Rhetoric* (1936), quoted Hobbes: "The scope of all speculation is the performance of some action, or thing to be done." Even the most persuasively stated argument for a more fluent theory of literature needed to be backed up by a demonstration that "stock responses" (with their semantic fixations) and critical responses (with their free exploratory power) were a *fact* of common literary experience. Even with its most plausible distinctions, such as that between referential and emotive uses of language, *Principles* hewed to a line of theory. How often, indeed, have the philosopher's grand schemes turned out to be "some lovely glorious nothing." There was no special reason why Richards should possess a magic talisman of safe passage through this philosophic wasteland. At best *Principles* might have taken its place as a brilliant excursus on the consequences of taking semantic range seriously. At worst the book might have been a foray into a psychological theory of literary value whose real principles could never, or at least not yet, be established, since psychology itself was too confused to be a sound theoretical base. Critics of this and later Ricardian theory sometimes observed that he was only too willing to admit that element of almost hopeless futurity. There was in fact much of the "not yet" about the speculation on psychological models for literary response. There was at least a reasonable ground for uncertainty as to the further growth of ideas presented by *Principles of Literary Criticism*.

Readers of its Preface, nevertheless, had been forewarned: "Between the possession of ideas and their application there is a gulf. Every teacher winces when he remembers this. As an attempt to attack this difficulty, I am preparing a companion volume, *Practical Criticism*." This masterstroke of demonstration and applied theory appeared four years later, and if any had wondered before about the reality of stock responses and their associated theory, they could now sit back and relax and worry about how much too real such phenomena in fact were.

Practical Criticism is one of the great descendants of Baconian tradition. In its pragmatic curiosity about what readers actually do when they read, it manages to be vastly entertaining, informative from cover to cover. In its account of the famous "protocols" it reaches a level of high comedy seldom if ever attained by critical discourse. (I recall one of my mentors, himself a distinguished scholar and teacher, avowing to me, with undisguised pride: "*I* was one of the protocols." Prudently, I did not ask what, in the published version, his number was.) And if any had more deeply wondered about the subject-object assumptions of *Principles*, here the joyous pragmatism of Richards' "documentation" made the philosophic issues almost irrelevant.

The procedure was a major invention. Like other important inventions, it appeared on the surface to be ludicrously simple. "Extremely good and extremely bad poems were put *unsigned* before a large and able audience. The comments [the content of the protocols] they wrote at leisure give, as it were, a stereoscopic view of the poem and of possible opinion on it. This material when systematically analysed, provides, not only an interesting commentary upon the state of contemporary culture, but a new and powerful educational instrument." Thus the announcement (much like an ad) in the earlier Preface. But whereas many an ad fails to describe the actual product about to be marketed, in this case the proclamation turned out to be a fair prediction.

Once again the general effect of the method was a play between plenitude and balance. The protocols of *Practical Criticism* showed that between the extreme positions that the Cambridge students took, as they faced each unsigned text, there lay intermediate positions. The requirement of anonymity of authorship at once put readers on a basis of theoretical equality, and this in turn let loose the full flood of potential semantic response. Readers varied wildly in their reactions. While it was possible to show that certain poems led to more heavily biased responses than others (for example by eliciting undue sentiment or irrelevant moralizing), Richards the fact-finder always led *his* reader through a multiplicity of student readings. Sometimes the students were variable in the ways they did not vary; each stock response would be a particular inflexible reaction to a word or phrase or whole poem, but the overall fact of stock responses—often of a strikingly miscellaneous nature—gave to the protocols the structure of a semantic spectrum. Variability of response, including stock response, was its constant. Clearly enough, from this evidence, the poet in ideal breadth (and his corresponding ideal reader) has "the further advantage perhaps of avoiding a certain dangerous finality. Impulses which adjust themselves at so many levels may go on doing so perhaps indefinitely." (*Principles*, 213) Richards' "perhaps" applied very widely to a much larger literary area than the poems he gave his students. Even when the critic was dealing with lesser poets than Dante and Shakespeare, the example of the protocols suggested that a wide range of varying responses (within the compass of "very nice adjustments") would occur to an impartial judge.

As an experiment in reading, *Practical Criticism* set itself up to free the reader from himself, by showing him (through comparisons with other readers) where and in what modes and on what levels of sensitivity and activity he had been engaged, as he read each poem. For the reader was invited to perform the students' experiment, on the same unsigned conditions of authorship. It was an experiment whose spirit, if not letter, was to become the dominant practical influence within the large domain of the New Criticism. The educational significance of the experiment was foreseen by its author in his development of a pedagogically sturdy system of dividing meaning into a four-fold structure: sense, feeling, tone and intention. Such a structure had been implicit in *The Meaning of Meaning* and in *Principles*, and at times even approached explicit formulation. Here the semantic theorist took a further step toward questions of balance—the documented treatment of inhibiting, distracting, biasing impulses led to a new emphasis falling on tone and intention.

Practical Criticism held that intention was a type of meaning, as much a meaning as mere sense or emotive significance. Like the meanings implied by tone, those of intention were subtle and all-controlling. But unlike tone (the gestural aspect of meaning), the intention of any utterance so complex as a poem existed on a special *superordinate* level of signifying power. The gist of a poem might be "caught" through its gestures of tone, but somehow only the Intention could comprehend the detailed working of the poem's parts. Only the Intention could fully comprise the whole and the parts in a single conceptual structure.

Interest in the purposive drive of poetic utterance may have led Richards directly to his next two published works, *Coleridge on Imagination* (1935) and *The Philosophy of Rhetoric* (1936). For Coleridge the idea of intention was a problem of major, even essential importance, and to this problem Richards recurred in his discussion of the subject-object "coalescence." It is, however, in the very striking attack upon ideas about rhetoric, where Richards most clearly showed his freshened concern with the difficulties of Intention. Rhetoric has since antiquity been the art of controlled communicative intentions, the art of persuasion. Curiously, *The Philosophy of Rhetoric* might at first appear to be mistitled. It seems generally to concern itself with only one aspect of classical rhetoric, the figuration of speech. It does not seem concerned with the art of persuasion. Its subject is the "interinanimation" of words through metaphor, and especially through the subtleties of tonal manipulation. Its most celebrated novelty, the terms "tenor" and "vehicle," seems designed largely to facilitate a general theory of language rather than the special needs of rhetorical skill.

Yet perhaps in this very skewing of rhetoric implied by his title Richards indicates the core of his view of the speech act. If there is a genuine intent to persuade, on any level, be it forensic or poetical, there must be a control of metaphoric shaping. The philosophy of rhetoric is for Richards a philosophy of the omnipresent metaphoric principle. It is a philosophy of commanding style. It could be associated with the many-sided treatises on rhetoric by Kenneth Burke. But, as distinct from Burke, Richards tied rhetorical purpose to metaphor in general, yielding what appears to be a much simpler rhetorical theory than Burke's. Whatever is lost in terms of rhetorical "coverage," *The Philosophy of Rhetoric* yet makes up for this narrowness on the plane of critical interests which differ quite markedly from those of Kenneth Burke. These lectures appear to have played a specific role in Richards' own critical development, and it is to this development that they must be referred. They provided a systematic view of the link between Intention and the "meaning of meaning" as Richards had conceived these domains.

Before *The Philosophy of Rhetoric* was delivered to the audience at Bryn Mawr as the Mary Flexner Lectures in 1935, the idea of polysemous variety (as demonstrated in *Practical Criticism*) had acquired almost too much prominence and weight within Richards' whole system of literary interpretation. Theoretically a critical reading had to be a tesserated mosaic of listed, cross-referenced, lexicalized meanings. (Something of this tesseration appears in Empson, early and late.) Criticism on this plan would reach a climax when it gave for each work an entirely "overdetermined" semantic profile. In fact, a tendency toward semantic overdetermination is present throughout Richards, for whom it sometimes seems to authorize a Shelleyan view of poetry, as when, in a fairly recent lecture, he remarked that Shelley's *Defence* could well be rewritten to say: "Poems [not poets] are the unacknowledged legislation [not legislators] of the world." [2]

The desire to replace the poet by the poem is a wise precaution against the biographical forms of critical bias. But it is also the result of a view that poetry is a justified form of persuasion largely because it "legislates" in the right way, that is, it balances innumerable conflicting claims through its overdetermination of words, which in *The Philosophy of Rhetoric* is called the "interinanimation of words." Because that play among competing semantic elements is lively, there is a guarantee against the absolutism of narrower modes of interpretation. The "higher" purposiveness, in short, is a Coleridgean network (but is that the correct metaphor here?) of infinitely self-correcting pulses and counterpulses. To show how such poise could be achieved was a main aim in this transitional work.

The technical difficulties of teaching the balanced response were further explored in two subsequent treatises, *Interpretation in Teaching* (1938) and *How to Read a Page* (1942). The overdetermination of meaning for single words led naturally to the proof that even a single page of text was a vast field for active interpretation, while on a more technical level Richards here began to experiment with his system of exponential "quotation-marks," a curious method of "emphatics" which the reader can also find in the recent new edition of *Science and Poetry*, now engagingly titled *Poetries and Sciences* (1970). The emphatic marks are a device of balance on the level of phrase-by-phrase movement.

Yet quite another exploratory climb will serve to indicate how widely Richards understood the need for a critical poise. *Mencius on the Mind* (1932) had already expanded the horizon of the problem. Here the author proposed the "task of multiple definition," as it arose through interpreting the text of the ancient Chinese sage Mencius. The central idea was that "most utterances have, as well as a range of various senses, a range of gestures." (99) An emphasis on gesture recalls that intention had to be related to tone and attitude, and to a degree there was nothing especially surprising about this mention of the range of gesture. It had appeared in *Practical Criticism*, to name only one earlier study. But *Mencius on the Mind* marked off an important new context, the ex-

2. "The Future of Poetry," in *The Screens and Other Poems* (New York, 1960), p. 106.

pansion of literary studies to include cultures of such widely variant type as the Western and the Oriental. The balancing-act had now to be made comparative and intercultural, or, as anthropologists were calling it, "cross-cultural." The resulting tensions were correspondingly increased over those felt *within* any single culture such as Richards had already worked with in his readings of English and European poetry. These heightened tensions the reader of *Mencius* can experience directly, by turning to the appendix which reprints the Mencius text in Chinese characters, along with a halting, desperate, "literal" translation. Here, more graphically than is possible with even the most closely analysed English-language text, the reader is confronted with the real mysteries of context. And he is confronted with the sort of linguistic difficulties of interpretation which were almost certain to have led to the last phase of Richards' critical activity before his resolute shift into poetry.

Mencius on the Mind raised the issue of communication, which had always concerned Richards in a general sense. (*Principles* can be conceived as a machine turning on two pivotal chapters, "Communication and the Artist" and its counter-weight, "The Normality of the Artist.") Whereas Richards had been able to talk generally of the "communicative endeavour," he now had to examine a radical barrier to communication, the abyss separating Chinese and Western linguistic cultures. For not only were the ideograms of a different linguistic order from the alphabetic Western scripts, but there was also a gap to be leapt between the associated backgrounds of the remotely separated worlds of ancient China and modern Europe. Given the discrepancies, the interpreter had inevitably to look for tougher and more agile methods of reaching interpretive theory.

These Richards found in the engineer's diagram for "communication theory," and in later essays he has variously employed this diagram from cybernetics. Meaning became "information," and Intention now could be dealt with as "feedback" and "feedforward." *Speculative Instruments* (1955) freshly systematized the poet's experience that "throughout the writing of poetry, coming events cast their shadows before." The poet's willingness to try out various verbal choices found its parallel in the reader's willingness to decode and develop a message by a trial of variant responses.

> Everybody knows [a later lecture observed] how a word which is just right from one point of view may have a fatal drawback from

another; and how this trouble can be cured by finding another word or phrase, by changing some other word, maybe, in the passage, or by a more extensive reorganization, or by a radical re-start. The whole process by which possible parts accept, exclude, modify, mold one another to form a whole, which is only forefelt until it is found, operates through *feed-forward* and *feed-back* (i.e., the outcome reports as to the success or failure of tentatives in attaining ends which have been fed forward).[3]

The cybernetic notion of reading and writing which this lecture on "The Future of Poetry" developed has the advantage of linking, in another mode of balance, the interpretive theories of English- and French-speaking worlds. Richards' communication diagram now shows major stages of transmission occuring in a "two-story" schema, which attempts "to reflect the duality of a word and of a poem as a union of *signifiant* and *signifié* (in Saussure's terms), a union in which the body, while it is alive, is not to be conceived apart from that which informs it, that which it embodies, and conversely." [4] The twinning of $\frac{S}{S}$ is yet another variant of Coleridgean semantic "embodiment," as the poet and reader pursue "tentatives in attaining ends." In his most advanced meditations on information theory as it aids poetic interpretation, Richards seems to return to the Coleridge for whom poetry "is no exercise of one faculty, but of many—ideally of them all."

The control of semasiological riot has then had its curve of development from *The Meaning of Meaning* to the most recent critical essays. And at the precise moment where the curve would seem complete, with cybernetic speculations and philosophic games like the lecture "Queries," there is a fresh turn in the road. Richards begins to publish his verses. The turn to poetry seems to me a natural outcome of all the feedback and feedforward preceding its emergence. To show this in full would require an essay on Richards' verse. But a few remarks will suffice to show the sense in which poetry is his natural next step as a critic.

Perhaps the most marked characteristic of the verse of *Goodbye Earth*, *The Screens* and *Internal Colloquies* is their metrical neatness of step. They experiment prosodically in a manner that harks back directly to the Elizabethan period, when the ordering of words in complex stanzaic patterns was the highest verbal achievement possible, since it

3. *Ibid.*, p. 117.
4. *Ibid.*, p. 120.

linked the semantic freedom of metaphoric buccaneering with the elegance of courtly "measure." This neo-Elizabethan verse recalls Charles Williams' phrase, applied to the early Milton: "a ballet of ideas." The poetry, of course, is not criticism in any ordinary sense. It is, however, in direct analogy to criticism, as Richards had envisaged that mixture of science and art. Where he had previously quested for the lived forms of wordings and had whenever possible stressed the auditory life of poetry, he has now engaged himself in a private revival of Metaphysical poetry. This Metaphysical poetry belongs less to the school of Donne than to that of Jonson, the Jonson who wrote the "Cary-Morison Ode." It is thus also a continuous play upon masking and decorum, and, at its most apparently intimate moments, a play upon the idea of impersonal self-scrutiny. Richards' poetry seems intended to embody critical stance in the relatively pure state of poetic enactment. Stated differently: this verse converts judgments (sometimes of aesthetic matters, but often of philosophy and living in general) into artful performances.

One thing has always happened in the strictly discursive Richards: he is willing to scramble about, as well as climb to the summit. Communication with him is a full process, with endless admissions of the ways that theory and positive science could not match the poetic experience they were hoping to account for. "In the mountains," as Robert Lowell says, in a portrait of Richards the alpinist,

> one feels free, yes, but a mountain climber is also enslaved. Even now, taking his breather, and resting before his Byronic scenery, as if it were a landscape he had painted, he knows he should be moving on. The next lap, the middle foreground's attractively gullied and evergreen rise, is not a picture—it is a problem. Beyond and above, and really, as in the photograph, just an arm's swing away, the absolute malignly beckons. Bald, treeless peaks, lifeless as the mountains on a relief-map, spread the sail-like mirage of their deadness. Malign, too, and seepingly present, though unrepresented here, is the other busy, lower world of routine, duties, books, interviews, and chairs. In this "sporting" photograph, the narrowed eyes and cheek-shadows of the climber's face have a down-dragging gravity. The obstinate chin, the toughness, the knowledge, the muscle—Goodbye to earth at last! Nearly a lifetime it took. Richards' first book of poetry is also the first of its kind.[5]

5. "I.A. Richards as Poet," in *Encounter*, XIV (Feb. 1960), p. 77.

On this account the poetry has not abandoned the purposes of criticism. But it has shifted them to their most expressive medium, the poetic act itself. The structure-building science of balance—literally, the science of "statics"—has given way to the process of balancing. The present participle triumphs over the past. Balanced becomes balancing. In this shift of tense Richards returns to the Renaissance to relive it anew. He returns to the Jonsonian conception of an art of incisive, critical wit. His verses state and, more remarkably, enact the return.

You do not trade too long upon a lack,
And words in poems have rights, say out their say,
Exact and render strict account,
Have little mercy on what's seen its day
Or could betray: all in the troth of the pack.

Sometimes a word is wiser much than men:
"Faithful" e.g., "responsible" and "true."
And words it is, not poets, make up poems.
Our words, we say, but we are theirs too
For words made man and may unmake again.

W. K. WIMSATT

I. A. R. : What To Say About a Poem

1

About ten years ago I wrote an essay entitled "What To Say About a Poem." It was published in a typescript offset conference report, as a chap-book with the contentious commentary of some of my friends, and in a volume of my collected essays. I have no reason to think that I. A. R. ever read it, or that if he did he approved of it. It was not directly derived from him nor even written with the benefit of any recent re-study of his writings. Yet I will venture that there is probably more of Richards than of any other critic in the funded antecedents, the essential substrate, of the essay.

"What To Say About a Poem" I conceived as a teacher's concern about a poem. As I asked the question and as I tried to answer it, I had in mind the kind of things that a teacher of poetry has to say—analytic, interpretive, explicatory (celebratory perhaps, rhapsodic—at the same time, more or less sober), reliable, internally oriented to the poem itself —and in these ways distinguishable from the various kinds of things that other kinds of writers, journal essayists, reviewers, historians, biographers, might legitimately say. If now I foist my title upon Richards, I commit perhaps a degree of aggression and perhaps too casually co-opt his ideas for my own aim; yet as he is, by his own profession and in his conspicuous achievement, a critic of and for teachers of poetry, the injustice cannot be very great.

I take as a starting point one of his more recent expressions—his long TLS middle article (28 May 1970) on the analyses of grammatical structure in poems being performed nowadays by Roman Jakobson. An opening accolade greets "what may very likely prove a landmark in the long-awaited approach of descriptive linguistics to the account of poetry." Then on a second page Richards moves into a series of observations and questions that we may well think more characteristic of this shrewd, skeptical intelligence. "There are bound to be dangers. . . . There is little profit in noting that strophes I and II here present nine diphthongs /ai/ . . . if the words in which they occur don't transfix the reader." "Probably only some, not all, of the features consciously discerned and included in the *account* will be actually operative in shaping the *response*. The machinery of distinctions used in the account has developed to meet general linguistic needs and purposes. . . . It may therefore distort, may invite attention to features not essential to the poetic process."

It cannot be a large exaggeration if I say that the whole of Richards' career in poetic theory, from *The Foundations of Aesthetics*, 1922, to *So Much Nearer*, 1968, and *Poetries and Sciences*, 1970, has been an effort, canny, partly baffled yet resolute, and for his audience uniquely instructive, to describe and promote, and on occasion, with caution, to practice a certain kind of critical discourse. A discourse as nearly "positive" and reliable as such discourse can be—yet not neutral and dead; or, to reverse the emphasis, a rhapsode's explication, yet one that soberly avoids an escape into the boundless.

As a practical critic and as a promoter of practical criticism Richards has repeatedly worked to unify, to coalesce, two things (object and response) which the terms of his affective methodology have tended to separate. (I say "methodology" because I mean talk about method, rather than method itself in action.) Let me introduce here a snatch from a little-known, or at least, so far as I know, little-quoted, document, his College English Association Chap-Book, *A Certain Sort of Interest in Language*, October, 1941. It was written in an hour when the pragmatic politics of World War II were afoot in the world— widely threatening all the "values" (wherever these resided, in our hearths or in our hearts).

A certain "influential teacher" had written to Richards deploring some of the current rallying cries: "Whenever business is seriously threatened, it appears that truth, justice, freedom, religion, democracy, ethics, and everything else are all crumbling." No doubt he had expected a response of warm sympathy. Instead:

> These great words, *justice, freedom*, and the others, it seems, mean primarily . . . that someone is getting at him. Interpretation and understanding mean debunking. . . . I have to remember how I and my friends were apt to talk some ten years back. And to recall the dreams of a Heaven on Earth . . . which then

seemed to need this sort of blasphemy as their defense. . . . What simplicity in the heart and feebleness in the head made us think so? Because some scamps and villains misused them, did we have to turn against the very watchwords of all our political and moral faith, against the bearers of the truths which alone make men free?

On an earlier page he had said more succinctly: "I do not know how we separate ideas from feelings. I suspect that this division derives from a disastrous schism in the modern mind." [1]

Yet it is not as if we can detect any great divide, a pronounced change in his views on objectivity, values, and language—signaled, as some have thought, by his books of the mid-1930's, *Coleridge on Imagination* (1934) and *The Philosophy of Rhetoric* (1936). The titles "Emotive Meaning Again" and "Emotive Language Still" appear in 1948 and 1949, and I take them to be characteristic and loyal to his most persistent thinking. Perhaps the economy of the present essay is best served if I say simply that I am a partisan of Richards' practical criticism (his immense talent for reading and talking about poems), but not of his affective methodology. And in this essay I will try not to dispute with him (as I have done now and then in the past, without his ever knowing it, I guess) about the *locus* of values—whether in objects (or verbal objects) or only in our experience of objects (and "projected" speciously by us or our language onto objects). (No doubt *some* implication or reflection of these issues will occur in any account of his views on how practical criticism is, or ought to be, written.) Polysemism, ambiguity, irony or inclusiveness, the poem's verbal independence of author's plans and motives, the multiple (yet coalescing) relations of language to emotion—these are matters all more or less sagely, even triumphantly, expounded by Richards in various places. They too must be assumed if the present argument is to proceed.

The essentials of the problem are delineated vigorously (in such a way as to stress the aspect of the problematic) in the two early and basic books *Principles of Literary Criticism* (1924) and *Practical Criti-*

---

1. *Mencius on the Mind, Experiments in Multiple Definition* (London, 1932) touches on the undeveloped state of anything like the Western logical apparatus in ancient Chinese thought. (pp. 88–90) The topic merges here with Richards' characteristic concern for the question whether "feeling" does not often largely dominate when we believe we are "thinking." "Mencius Through the Looking Glass," *So Much Nearer* (New York, 1968), says more emphatically that Mencius made no division between "thought" and "feeling." (pp. 204–5)

cism (1929). Richards is ruthless (Chapter 3 of *Principles*) against two opposite kinds of critical abuse:—on the one hand, inflated terms of appreciation, our own emotive "projections," "bogus entities" (*beauty,* for instance, even *poetry*—*inspiration, rhythm*), and on the other, the tight, secure little poetic instruments (*rhyme,* for instance, or *meter*) when these, as so often, are naively promoted to poetic *ends.* What is the critic to do? Let it be understood that when he praises or damns a poem, he is talking about effects, experiences, "caused" in his own mind. Often he "goes further and affirms that the effect in his mind is due to special particular features of the object." And "this fuller kind of criticism is what we desire." Apparently not quite the same distinction is uppermost when Richards says in the next paragraph that the critic's remarks about the object, the ways and means, are all merely *technical;* they are not to be confused with *critical* remarks, which are "about the values of experiences and the reasons for regarding them as valuable."

Two kinds of remarks about poems (technical and critical) correspond to two complementary aspects of poems themselves—the communicative and the experiential, and thus (it might well seem) not to neutrality and value, but to two kinds of value, or at least to two kinds of merit. Indeed there *are* two kinds of "badness" in poetry (expounded in Chapter 25 of *Principles*), one a failure through meagerness or inefficacy of communication, the other an offense of inferior (stereotyped) values even where (or just because) communication is highly successful. Another chapter of *Principles,* however, Chapter 4, on "Communication," observes that "the very process of getting the work 'right' has itself, so far as the artist is normal, immense communicative consequences." In *Coleridge on Imagination* this recognition will exhibit a phase of almost Crocean monism. "In an examination of poetic structure the distinction [between means and ends] prevents all advance by destroying the specimens we would examine." (Chapter 9) And beginning at least as early as *How To Read a Page* (1942), Richards entertains a fully developed doctrine of the poem as autonomous linguistic artifact. Here are coils, irresolutions, and shifts of meaning which trace patterns in the puzzling dialogue of our own commonly experienced poetic speculation—but patterns which before reading Richards we may well have been aware of far less keenly.

In *Practical Criticism,* he had long since achieved a kind of maximum confrontation with the difficult implications of such dialectic for critical discourse. Two passages, on pages 11 and 302, are crucial. The earlier is the more circumstantial.

> That the one and only goal of all critical endeavours, of all interpretation, appreciation, exhortation, praise or abuse, is improvement in communication may seem an exaggeration. But in practice it is so. The whole apparatus of critical rules and principles is a means to the attainment of finer, more precise, more discriminating communication. There is, it is true, a valuation side to criticism. When we have solved, completely, the communication problem, when we have got, perfectly, the experience, *the mental condition* relevant to the poem, we have still to judge it, still to decide upon its worth. But the later question nearly always settles itself; or rather, our own inmost nature and the nature of the world in which we live decide it for us. Our prime endeavour must be to get the relevant mental condition and then see what happens.

2

What kind of critical discourse will correspond to this high ideal of understanding? What kind will cope with the paradoxical tensions of a triple fidelity to poetic objects, to "experiences" (themselves charged with emotions and hence with local values), and to the ultimate poetic evaluation? What kind of critical discourse does Richards, in the fullest and clearest moment of his vision, desire or approve? This question, perhaps unfair, no doubt insusceptible of any neat answer, is the topic of my essay.

Richards himself has written critical essays on Hopkins, on Eliot, on a cluster of Georgian poets, Hardy, De la Mare, Yeats, Lawrence, on Dostoevsky, on Forster, on Shakespeare's "The Phoenix and the Turtle" and on his *Troilus and Cressida*, on Coleridge (1950, 1959, 1960), and on Shelley. And in chapters of his books and in various detached essays there are shorter passages of similar tenor—on Denham, on Donne, on Keats, on Shakespeare, on Coleridge. But it may be said that his own orientation as a deliberate practical critic has been very largely doctrinal. That is, he characteristically adduces literary works (in a way that the title "The God of Dostoevsky" will suggest) as either statements or illustrations of literary, epistemological, or ethical doctrine. The *Living Age* essay on T. S. Eliot (1926, printed also in the same year as an appendix to the second edition of *Principles*) is mostly devoted to arguing that the coherence of *The Waste Land* is emotive rather than intellectual. The essay is methodological. A short passage on *A Cooking Egg* (in the version in *Principles*) is the main place where he says anything specific about any poem or its values. ("The reader who appreciates the emotional relevance of the title has the key to the later poems in his hand. I take Pipit to be the retired nurse of the hero of the poem, and *Views of the Oxford Colleges* to be the, still treasured, present which he sent her when he went up to the University. The middle section of the poem I read as a specimen of the rather withered pleasantry in which contemporary culture has culminated. . . . The final section gives the contrast which is pressed home by the title. Even the most mature egg was new laid once." [2]) Two essays, that which explicates *The Windhover* of Hopkins and that on *The Phoenix and the Turtle*, are analytic exceptions to the main tendency. But the poems are difficult, and the conclusions, to my mind, in one way or another, obscure.

Clearly a manageable exposition of what Richards likes in practical criticism will have to center upon some fairly compressed and close criticisms of some fairly compressed (small and rich) poetic instances. It is not necessary that these criticisms be the work of Richards himself. Perhaps it is in some ways better if they are not. We can learn something from what a critic thinks about the work of other critics—and perhaps all the more if these critics are relatively artless and unprofessional. When *Practical Criticism* appeared in 1929 and for perhaps a decade thereafter, a very startling feature was the decimally graded assemblage of student "protocols," concerning thirteen undated and anonymous short poems which Richards had set before his Cambridge classes: five clearly bad poems (1, 4, 5, 7, 9), five clearly good poems (2, 3, 6, 8, 11), three problematics (10, better; 12, more dubious; and 13, I think, the occasion for a strange pronouncement by Richards himself [3]).

From the protocols themselves and from page 3 of Richards' Introductory, it is clear that evaluative opinion was a strongly invited part of the exercise. It is a main point of the method and of the book that most of the protocols (both positive and negative critiques of good and

2. The correctness of this reading is not a relevant question here. For a later report by Richards on this poem, see "Poetic Process and Literary Analysis," in *Style in Language*, ed. Thomas A. Sebeok (New York and London, 1968), p. 21.
3. See below, note 5.

bad poems) are bad criticism—sheer ineptitudes, crashing bungles of one sort or another. Yet here and there in the crowded galleries of this modern *Dunciad*, amid all the stock responses, the sentimentalities and the inhibitions, the technical presuppositions, the doctrinal adhesions, the gauche intrusive images, the mnemonic irrelevancies, appear a certain few opinions (fewer than twenty, I should say, in the total of about 385 protocols) for which Richards deftly, almost slyly, hints a measure of approval.[4]

Certain good poems (the deceptively "sentimental" 8, Lawrence's *Piano*; the austerely mythic elegy 11, Hardy's *George Meredith*) elicited not a single criticism which met the master's approval. And so for the two middling poems, both cloudscapes, 10 and 12, by G. H. Luce [5] and Wilfrid Rowland Childe.

In more than a few bad criticisms, a conspicuously reiterated feature was the attempt to employ the raw idiom of the Richards methodology:

> I find it impossible to recreate the poet's experience (6.33); Unimportant, as the experience is capable of excitation at will by normal people (7.55) [6]; Perfect communication (7.56); Please do not think, because I consider hymns sordid, that I have an inhibition (8.2); I don't find this poem at all helpful nor does it express any feelings I have ever had or want to have (8.22); I feel myself responding to it and don't like responding (8.11); The communication is excellent (8.7); The whole poem leaves me with a sense of complete satisfaction (11.53); I feel someone is trying to play with my emotions (12.7); The impression that the author is deeply moved . . . showing in a small degree the author's attitude to life (12.7); This one seems to me a successful

---

4. 1.63, 2.7, 2.71, 3.8, 3.81, 3.82, 4.1 (?), 4.23, 4.25, 5.8, 5.81, 6.13 (?), 6.2, 6.8, 7.43 (?), 9.74, 9.75, 12.6 (?), 13.64. (The verdict on 9.74 and 9.75 appears on pp. 193–98, at a remove from the page where they are quoted. That on 4.23 and 4.25 is assisted by p. 264. See note 5.)

5. This poem elicited a good instance of Richards' own gift for posing critical problems and for delicately suggesting solutions (pp. 143–44, 198–204, 214–16). Those pages together with his analysis (pp. 193–98) of objections to the incoherence of sea-harp imagery in poem 9, Alfred Noyes' carnival on the eightieth birthday of George Meredith, add up to a keen disquisition on the general problem of mixed metaphor. Several writers (not only the approved 4.23 and 4.25, but 4.1, 4.12, 4.14, 4.31, and 4.4) registered a correct disgust for the drafty sentimentalism of poem 4, Woodbine Willy's ". . . rapture of spring in the morning." But Richards, pp. 53–60 and 264, seems especially concerned, with this group, to distinguish merely forceful expressions of distaste from critiques that have a care for reasons.

6. Cf. *Practical Criticism*, p. 266.

communication of an experience whose value is dubious (13.1);
The underlying emotion is not of sufficient value (13.31); This
form of stimulation to the mind can do it no good and may do it
harm. The poem is therefore bad (13.8).

Richards indicated no pleasure in any of these responses.

We scan the small handful of more or less approved protocols for a
plenary illustration of critical merit. If we have read *Principles* and the
Introductory to *Practical Criticism* with any care, we are prepared to
find that mere clarification of a certain level of sense, what *we* might
call seeing the plot of a poem, is not enough. Thus, with Hopkins'
Spring and Fall, to a Young Child, we are merely grateful for a "paraphrase kindly supplied by one writer."

> An elderly man, experienced in such matters, has found a girl
> grieving at the falling of leaves in autumn. . . . Even now in
> weeping at the transience of the things she enjoys in autumn, she
> is really weeping for the transience of all things. She is mourn-
> ing among other things, for the fleetingness of her own youth.
> (6.1)

What does this lack? Something very important, which is found, as it
happens, in the next protocol quoted—"an admirable power of analysis."

> . . . the accenting of the seventh line is particularly important
> —the accent falls on "will weep" and on "know why" I
> like the simple opening and closing couplet, the one answering
> the other. The first six lines begin at a low pitch and then rise
> at "Ah! as the heart grows colder," only to fall again in the sixth
> line. I like the even accentuation of the sixth line. Then there is
> great control of vowel music. . . . (6.2)

"Very detailed analyses of correspondences between sound and sense
are perhaps always open to suspicion." Still, in the chapter on Poem 2,
"Spring Quiet," by Christina Rossetti, we encounter protocol 2.7,
"persuasive as well as subtle." And 2.71 "does seem to be recording
rather than inventing."

> In its own rather tiny way, it is quite exquisite. One feels the deli-
> cate movement of the rhythm as it changes from the clear fine
> tone of the 3rd and 4th verses to the gravity and steadiness of the
> last two. The corresponding shift in vowel values might be no-
> ticed—the deepening effect given by the long "a's" and "o's."
> The adjectives are chosen with a full regard for their emo-
> tive value—in particular, "mossy stone" which at once produces

the intended atmosphere of quietness and uninterrupted peace.[7]
(2.71)

A more smashing illustration of the right way was achieved by two writers in response to one of Richards' bad poems, 5, Edna St. Vincent Millay's preposterous sonnet "What's this of death. . . ?" Several readers were troubled by a suspicion that all was not right behind a "flashy façade." "Only two, however, coupled these suspicions with detailed observation of the matter and manner of the poem and it is these observations which we seek in criticism."

> This one offers cheap reassurance in what is to most men a matter of deep and intimate concern. It opens with Browning's brisk no-nonsense-about-me directness and goes on with a cocksure movement and hearty alliteration. It contains (along with the appropriate "dust to dust") echoes of all the best people. It is full of vacuous resonances ("its essential self in its own season") and the unctuously poetic. (5.8)
> This is a studied orgasm from a "Shakespeare-R. Brooke" complex. . . . A sort of thermos vacuum, "the very thing" for a dignified picnic in this sort of Two-Seater sonnet. The "Heroic" hectoring of line 1, the hearty quasi-stoical button-holing of the unimpeachably-equipped beloved, the magisterial finger-wagging of "I tell you this"!! Via such conduits magnanimity may soon be laid on as an indispensable, if not obligatory, modern convenience. (5.81)

The closely observant celebration of poetic value which Richards prescribed, the detailed account of objects reaching out somehow to encompass also not only experiences caused by objects but the "reasons"

---

7. Poem 13, "In the Churchyard at Cambridge," which Richards had discovered among the works of Longfellow, evokes the curious instance of a vigorous negative upon its movement (13.64), "as subtly observed," says the monitor, "as it is surprisingly expressed"—"showing an altogether superior understanding of rhythm" —yet a mistake! For it depends entirely upon a misapprehension of *sense* and *tone*. A sort of Augustan urbanity and temperate social wit is mistaken for a stock exercise in provincial sanctimony. It is difficult to resist the genetic speculation that Richards prized this poem in proportion to his own success in reading certain cryptographic features, or provincial oddities, in the story of the lady buried in her family plot, with a slave at her head and another at her feet. His essay on "Gerard Hopkins" (*Dial*, LXXXI, September 1926, 196) opens with an account of the "heightened attention," the "peculiar intellectual thrill," the "awakening of other mental faculties" experienced by the reader who successfully encounters difficult poetry.

for value in such experiences, was clearly not conceived as any very severely measured description or rigorously ordered argument. There is feeling here, manifold feeling and emotion, and overall value, poetic value—directly imputed. And nearly everywhere the main descriptive technique is metaphor. (This should not surprise readers of *Coleridge on Imagination, The Philosophy of Rhetoric,* and *Interpretation in Teaching.*) There is wit. There is, I think we may say in brief, imagination.

3

Not much later than the Cambridge experiments reported in *Practical Criticism,* Richards, at work again with men and women students at Cambridge, Harvard, and Radcliffe, found that the responses to a passage from Walter Savage Landor's *Gebir* (III. 4–18) supplied a wide range of instructive aberrations. He expounded this collection of "facts of natural science," specimens of "medical" history, in *The Criterion* (April, 1933), adding some instances of critical blundering by Coleridge, Garrod, and Rupert Brooke, and then, "under shelter of these examples," venturing his own "paraphrase exposition" of the Landor passage. It is a bold and interesting departure from the reserves and indirections of *Practical Criticism.* Another difference is signaled at the outset in the explanation: "It is best . . . to eliminate, so far as possible, the question 'Is the passage good or bad poetry?' and to invite answers only to the question 'What does it mean?' " This instruction (likely enough to promote the unified ideal described in the passage I have quoted above from the Introductory of *Practical Criticism*) does much also, I conjecture, to account for the fact that now the student testimonies seem much less vivacious (either for good or ill) than the menagerie of opinions rampaging in *Practical Criticism.* On the other hand, it is no doubt the real difficulty of the Landor passage (deliberately "heightened," as Richards confesses, by his omission of lines 1–3 of *Gebir* III) which mainly accounts for the absence of any really *good* student expositions—though the shredding of their papers in short excerpts, to accommodate a convenient division of the poetry into three sections, may have done something to conceal any medium virtues that were present. The most striking feature of this essay is Richards' own virtuoso performance in manifold "paraphrase exposition"—or in "paraphrase and exposition," as he phrases it in his preliminary explanation of what he asked the students to do. The distinction between the two activities is difficult to align either with the complicated conception of means, experience, and value expounded in *Principles* or with the more severely unified poetic object of the Introductory to *Practical Criticism*. But I would not make very much of this. The essential Richards seems to me to come through very strongly in the mingled exposition of *metaphor* and *feeling* which I am soon to quote.

The fifteen lines from *Gebir* are a congenial enough Ricardian vehicle, a modern bard's richly blended reflections and feelings about his youthful infection with the poetry of Shakespeare ("I drank of Avon") and his subsequent frustrated relation to the great poetic past of magic and myth (". . . can any with outstripping voice / The parting sun's gigantic strides recall?"). *Gebir* is an Iberian-Egyptian costume epic in blank verse. The bard's personal profession in III. 1–18 corresponds in position to *Paradise Lost* III. 1–55, and in its ejaculatory opening, to IV. 1–8; in content it is a reversal of Milton's rejection of fable and romance in IX. 1–47.

> *Drank of Avon* is a "wheel within wheel" metaphor, revolving, in one set of motions, together with *panting* and, in another set of motions, together with *dangerous draught* and *feverish thirst*. The influence is thirst-arousing, perhaps salt, intoxicant, alterative. (These motions bring in a very mixed and fleeting throng of feelings.)
>
> Yet it is impossible, not allowed (feeling of injustice suffered, or of regret alone . . .) to me . . . to
>
> 1. Perform the "orphic" function of the Poet.
> 2. Write in the spirit or purpose or manner, and on the subjects, of Homer, Virgil, Dante, Shakespeare.
>
> The specific form of the metaphor here loads the statement with feelings of loss and inevitability—the vanishing of a possibility of the mind.
>
> An act in human history is over, it comes to an end like a day. . . .

This paraphrase-exposition seems pregnant with intimations of value. Yet the inquiring (the pestering) theoretical intelligence will not let us have such kinds of "profit" easily. After all, as we ought to remember if we have read *Practical Criticism* with any attention, "a judgment seemingly about a poem is primarily evidence about a reading of it." And now he adds: "There are ways of reading almost any poem so as to make it magnificent or ludicrous." *Valid* ways of reading it either magnificent or ludicrous? We might have thought in studying *Practical Criticism* that criticism was to permit us to get "perfectly, the experience, *the mental condition*, relevant to the poem,"—and thus indeed that there *was* a mental condition relevant to *the* poem. But now: the poem is magnificent (or it is ludicrous) only *if* I happen to be reading with "a mind of a certain sort," brought to this moment of experience in certain ways. This may sound appalling. We may recoil from this apparent rejection of all the "profit" we just thought we had found in the magisterial demonstration of a reading so far superior to the student naïvetés. ("Whether such a reader is likely to benefit from a university, or how he came there, are questions for another occasion.") Presumably Richards' way of reading the passage comes closer to making it magnificent than to making it ludicrous. (For purposes of the present argument, one need not feel sure that it *is* quite magnificent—a certain tumidity, a quality of straining mytho-poeticalness in the idiom—may have been left out of account.) But are we to think that the reading by the master is no nearer to being a good one than the miserable confessions of many of the students? This is not what he means. Reassurance is immediate—in the shape of this vigorous assertion:

> It may seem that . . . the difference between good and bad reading is gone; that there is no sense left for "correct" as applied to interpretations. This would be a mistake. . . . the *tests*, we should ordinarily say, for the correctness of any interpretation of a set of complex signs are its internal coherence and its coherence with all else that is relevant . . . this inner and outer coherence *is* the correctness. When an interpretation hangs together (without conflicting with anything else: history, literary tradition, etc.) we call it correct.[8]

How these dual assertions are to be managed in the logical part of our minds may be less than clear. But the second emphasis, I will take it upon myself to assert, is the operative, the athletic and militant Richards—what he is earning, by indirections, all the time. The maneuver is like the strategy spread broadly throughout *Principles*, where in some chapters we read that customs, mores, tastes, judgments do differ

8. "Correct interpretation of bad and good writing will not hang together in the same specific ways." This may send us back to the good protocols concerning both good and bad poems in *Practical Criticism* and to Chapter 25 in *Principles*, "Badness in Poetry." The problem is a nice one. See perhaps my own effort in "Explication as Criticism," *English Institute Essays* 1951, ed. Alan S. Downer (New York: Columbia University Press, 1952).

widely among men, but in other chapters that some kinds of experience and judgment are more "normal," more adequate to the human capacity than others, and hence better.

4

Having in earlier years so amply and so often demonstrated his extraordinary and sometimes bewildering faculty for seeing multiples, alternatives, ambiguities, Richards in later phases of his career, while reiterating the initial insight, seems also to have been especially concerned to assert that counter-conception of the real and important difference between correct and incorrect readings of poetry—or, more simply, the possibility (even the always imminent danger) of incorrect readings. In his volume of 1955, *Speculative Instruments*, he reached back, seven years earlier (1933) than for any other piece in the collection, to reprint "Fifteen Lines from Landor."

A few years later, or in the spring of 1958, during an "interdisciplinary conference" held at Indiana University on "verbal style and the literary process," interest in the "process" "reached its high point" at an evening public lecture, "Poetic Process and Literary Analysis," in which Richards narrated the stages of composition of a poem written by himself and now thrown upon a screen, "Harvard Yard in April / April in Harvard Yard." The main theoretical concern was the authoritative exploitation of a healthy doctrine that Richards had already asserted with emphasis as early as 1942, in *How to Read a Page:*—that a poem has a kind of internal, linguistic life of its own, independent of things its author may have intended, or thought of, or not thought of, during the process. Richards was in a commanding position to say: "This I did not think of, but consulting the dictionary now shows it is indeed in the poem; or, this choice I made in part because of certain antecedent associations, but clearly a reader does not have to know these to understand the relevance in the poem." The argument was full of witty explosions. And then, abruptly, near the end, he turned to a complementary, or postscript, doctrine—once more concerning correctness and incorrectness. If a poem has a life of its own, even a capacity for self-defense, it is the important job of critics and educators to assist that defense by correct interpretation. Reaching yet again into files of student reports (presumably recent or current) he produced a medley of incredible readings —of Eliot, of Donne, of Coleridge, of Marvell.

"Pipit sate upright. . . ." Pipit has obviously satisfied the
"I". . . . ; a state of satiation has occurred.

"Some essential control over interpretation" seemed to have been "relaxed." (At the same time, it remained "an interesting point in *linguistics* to consider why we are sure that words in such an instance do not
work like that.")

A second, somewhat more technical piece by Richards, his "work
paper" for the conference, bore the title "Variant Readings and Misreading." The obligingly obtuse student testimony was of course once
more at hand. And once more the refining theoretical conscience was
not easily appeased. "What can we allege . . . to confirm our opinion
(in which I, for one, am unshakable) that we have here a *misreading*—
and not an allowable *variant?*" [9] Later in the same year he published a
volume entitled *Goodbye Earth and Other Poems*—including "Harvard
Yard in April/April in Harvard Yard." A brief "Proem" contains echoes
of "Poetic Process and Literary Analysis" and one more swing of the
pendulum in the issue between freedom and correctness.

> When is any interpretation . . . complete? . . . Whatever ac-
> counts are offered to the reader must leave him—in a very deep
> sense—free to choose, though they may supply wherewithal for
> exercise of choice.
>   This is not—dare I note?—any general license to readers to
> differ as they please or in other ways and over other points than
> they must. For this deep freedom in reading is made possible
> only by the widest surface conformities: as to how the words in
> a poem are recognized, as to how the surface (plain sense) mean-
> ings are ascribed, as to how rhythms are followed, allusions
> caught. . . .

Does the surface determine any demarcations in the depths? The epistemology of this account of deep freedom may remind us of a much
earlier statement, in the essay "The Interactions of Words" (1942),
something perhaps even closer to a reconcilable, transcending truth.

> Understanding is not a preparation. . . . It is itself the poem
> . . . it is a constructive, hazardous, free creative process, a pro-

9. Both this paper and the evening address may be found in the proceedings of the
conference, *Style in Language*, ed. Thomas A. Sebeok (New York and London,
1960). See especially pp. 23, 245, 246, 250, 251. A note to "Variant Readings. . ."
confesses his awareness of the rise ("within my lifetime") of a school of extravagant
explicatory "squeezing." Cf. his remark on Eliot's rebuke to the "lemon-squeezer
school of criticism" ("On TSE," *Sewanee Review*, LXXIV [Winter, 1966], 28).

cess of conception through which a new being is growing in the mind.[10]

We ponder the deep principle that human understanding is *always* more than a reflex. The mind *acts*. It has this dignity, even in error.[11]

5

One other date, and the chronicle aspect of my paper is completed. In 1963 I edited for the English Institute a small collection of essays from its earlier years, under a title taken from one of my own in the *Essays* of 1951: *Explication as Criticism*. In a Foreword, looking back to the *floruit* of American explicatory criticism in the 1940's, and thinking of the free orientation within which it had operated, I invoked the five boundary forms of human awareness which Richards in *Practical Criticism* (p. 290) had seen as the conditions of "sincere" (i.e., adequate) "feeling" in the confrontation of poems:—man's fundamental loneliness, the "inexplicable oddity" of his birth and death, the "inconceivable immensity of the Universe," the vast perspective of time, the enormity of man's ignorance. These ideas seemed to me a better (a more objective, yet more flexible) frame of reference for literary criticism than the

10. In *The Language of Poetry*, ed. Allen Tate (*Princeton*, 1942), p. 76.
11. I conceive the year 1958 as a climax of Richards' speculations on the issue of incorrectness. "Variant Readings and Misreading" is republished in his collection of 1968, *So Much Nearer, Essays Toward a World English*. As the Preface indicates, "Variant Readings. . ." carries the precise issue of incorrect reading further than other essays, all of the 1960's, included in this volume. A second volume of Richards' poems, *Screens*, 1960, contained an essay, "The Future of Poetry," apparently delivered at some time as a lecture at Victoria College, Toronto; this too reappears in *So Much Nearer*; it contains an excellent assertion of the way in which *poems*, for interpreters and critics, are superior to *poets*. Another relevant essay (containing an explication of a difficult poem by Empson) is "How Does a Poem Know When It Is Fnished?" appearing in *Parts and Wholes*, ed. Daniel Lerner (New York, 1963) and also in Richards' revision of *Science and Poetry* (1926) under the new title *Poetries and Sciences* (New York, 1970). His appreciation of Shelley's *Prometheus Unbound*, in *Major British Writers*, ed. G. B. Harrison, vol. II (New York, 1959), is a complicated blend of practical criticism with some other features.

Both in "Variant Readings . . ." and in "The Future of Poetry" Richards performs for criticism the valuable service of defusing the term "encode" with which mathematical "information" engineers are currently threatening the field of literary study. The Code Napoleon as an analogue of poetic systems? Perhaps. . . with due caution. The Morse Code? One language translated into another? In the text of a poem, what is encoded into what?

fantastically pigeon-holed neo-Aristotelian categories of the then-prevalent school of mythopoeic vision. In a parallel way, I have here been celebrating the insistent, the unrelaxing or relentless, concern for *value* manifested by Richards over the many years of his career (in spite of his hypersensitivity to the difficulties), and, no less, his confidence in the integrity of poems, the difference between right and wrong readings (again in spite of his almost tortured awareness of the difficulties). The critical thinking of Richards has always cut close to the quick of poetic interest. It has been exciting. It has generated a world of ideas favorable to a general excitement with criticism. And for that reason I see it as a better kind of critical thinking than most of the now emergent vogues: —the boundless expansions of the school of "consciousness," the self-justifying apparatuses of transformational grammar, the neutralisms of historical hermeneutics, the despairs of the trope of "silence," the "aleatory" assemblage of *textes* from newspaper, dictionary, or telephone directory, the celebrations of the "death of literature," the various other attempts to play midwife to the "post-modern imagination."

Like the object of his recurrent study Coleridge, like Arnold and Eliot, Richards has always been a believer in the superior vision of the superior. He is an aristocrat of the intelligence: "Are we to think that what is thought by enough people thereby becomes what should be thought?" [12]

Those ultimate ideas framing "sincerity" which I have quoted above from *Practical Criticism* of course remind me of the large difference between sacramental religion and secular humanism. One might have thought the obstacle to any shared experience of or thinking about poetry was insurmountable. Early statements by Richards, his essays on Dostoevsky and Hopkins, might strengthen this misgiving. No doubt he would now reaffirm these. Yet there is also such a phenomenon as the assurance with which the Richards of *Practical Criticism* pronounces, on the one hand, upon a certain exercise in soft-focus nature piety ("Between the erect and solemn trees, I will go down upon my knees"— Poem 7) and, on the other, upon the clamor and the quiet of a sonnet which requires in its reader no less than an acquaintance "with the rules for attendance at the Day of Judgment" (Poem 3).[13] "It is in the nature of some performances that they leave the spectator feeling rather helpless." I have written this essay out of a happy conviction that poetry and even the criticism of poetry are places of subsumption and reconcile-

12. "Variant Readings and Misreading," in *Style in Language*, ed. Sebeok, p. 251.
13. See Richards' reflections upon this situation in *Practical Criticism*, pp. 271–73.

ment (of imagination)—where the dialogues of our opposed minds can take place without rancor, and with enlightenment.

At the Indiana conference in the spring of 1958, we sat around a big table and, after hearing papers, engaged in open debates. In a corner of the room tape recorders were busy. In a final session we heard summary papers by Roman Jakobson, George A. Miller, and René Wellek. It happened that near the end of the ensuing conversation, I got the floor and spoke briefly, urging something about the identity of "ends" and "means" in poetry. "A poem is a verbal expression which has no end except to be known." I alluded to "Harvard Yard in April." As these impromptu speeches were edited for the proceedings of the conference, only one sentence follows my little sprint. Except for a bibliography and an index, these are the closing words of the volume:

RICHARDS: Mr. Wimsatt and I are not in disagreement.

It is my hope that, with the insertion of some such word as "substantially" at some point in this sentence, he will be able to repeat it on reading this essay.

CHARLES L. STEVENSON

Richards on the Theory of Value

1

Mr. Richards' name is associated with two quite distinct theories of value. The first, emphasizing the non-symbolic, emotive function of "good" (and kindred terms), was presented in *The Meaning of Meaning*, written in collaboration with C. K. Ogden. The second, emphasizing a maximal satisfaction of appetencies, was presented in *Principles of Literary Criticism*.

I want here to summarize and discuss both theories, and to suggest that they can be united, with modifications, into a single theory.

2

The first theory, now commonly called the "emotive" theory of value, provided an important and original alternative to the views of G. E. Moore.[1] Moore had argued that such a judgment as "This is good," when "good" is used in a typically evaluative sense, is not reducible to a purely factual statement, and that the empirical methods of the sciences are insufficient to verify or falsify it. He concluded that "good" does not refer to any scientifically discernible quality but instead refers to a "non-natural" quality, whose presence or absence can be discovered only by an exercise of "intuition." Ogden and Richards suspected this view to be the relic of a long-prevalent insensitivity to the varied uses of language. They suggested that Moore's "non-natural" quality was not a quality at all, and that any alleged philosophical need of postulating its existence could be avoided by recognizing the *emotive* force of "good." The essentials of their view will be evident from this quotation:

> When we use the sentence, "This is good," we merely refer to *this*, and the addition of "is good" makes no difference whatever

1. *Principia Ethica*, by G. E. Moore (Cambridge, England, 1903).

> to our reference. When . . . we say, "This is red," the addition
> of "is red" to "this" does symbolize an extension of our reference.
> . . . But "is good" has no comparable *symbolic* function; it
> serves only as an emotive sign expressing our attitude to *this*, and
> perhaps evoking a similar attitude in other persons, or inciting
> them to actions of one kind or another.[2]

The word "attitude," as used in the quotation, presumably has a generic sense, roughly synonymous with "favor or disfavor of any sort," and thus stands in contrast to such a word as "belief"; but there is still an implied parallelism between the sense in which a sentence may "express" an attitude and the sense in which it may "express" a belief. Interpreting the view in that way, let me venture to restate it.

When a speaker says "This is red" he is normally expressing a belief, and may thereby be leading others to share it. But he is not *describing* a belief, even though he may be letting others know what belief he has; for the belief only "mediates" his description, as it were, and is not itself being described. All that the speaker is describing is the color of an indicated object. When he says "This is good," however, he is using his sentence in another way. To be sure, he is normally expressing something, and may thereby be leading others to share what he expresses. But the something is no longer a belief; it is rather an attitude. And the speaker is not describing an attitude (in the sense of "describing" here intended) even though he may be letting others know what attitude he has. Nor is he describing anything else. For the expression of an attitude does not "mediate" a description. It is simply a way of praising or recommending (etc.) something, as yet revealing nothing about the properties that may have elicited the praise or may later cause the recommendation to be accepted. Such properties (of an ordinary factual sort) may indeed exist; but if the speaker wishes to be explicit in stating what they are he must go on to use *other* sentences. His description is not "already there" in the meaning of the word "good" itself. For the usage in question, "good" has only a tendency to express or evoke attitudes, and is thus a purely emotive term.

By implication, the emotive view points to a certain kinship between "This is good" and the plural imperative, "Let us approve of this"; for note that the imperative, too, does not describe the indicated object. But of course there are differences as well. The imperative, with its overt mention of approval, is more likely to direct attention *away* from the

2. *The Meaning of Meaning*, p. 125.

indicated object, causing a self-consciousness that is stultifying; and it is less likely than the value-judgment to provoke subsequent discussion.

In calling "good" an emotive term, Ogden and Richards were not identifying it with an attitude-*designating* term. That is to say, they were distinguishing between the meanings of "This is good" and "This meets with my approval." The latter sentence, though it can sometimes do temporary service for the former, is frequently used for the purpose of describing (and now "describing" *is* the appropriate term) the speaker's attitude. It frequently expresses the speaker's *belief about* his attitude, as its attitude-designating predicate, "meets with my approval," permits—the belief, as usual, "mediating" a description. But the former sentence, with the emotive predicate "is good," expresses not the speaker's belief about his attitude but rather the attitude itself. That is one point of difference, and there is this further one: an emotive predicate, as compared with an attitude-designating predicate, is linguistically better suited to exert an influence. It has a greater power of "evoking similar attitudes in other persons," or of "inciting them to actions of one kind or another." The emotive view is not, then, open to the charge of failing to distinguish between a judgment of value and a statement that is "autobiographical."

I need scarcely add that Ogden and Richards were dealing not with *all* uses of "good," but only with *one* use that they considered typically evaluative. They were entirely free to hold, as well, that the term's emotive force is often rendered gratuitous by its context, or that the term lends itself to a variety of idioms in which its meaning is primarily descriptive—as in the context, "This is good money," where "good" can much the same meaning as "non-counterfeit."

3

In *The Meaning of Meaning* the emotive theory of value was stated with extraordinary brevity: it was outlined rather than developed. I have myself, throughout my writings on the topic, attempted to transform it into a theory that is worked out in detail; [3] but my views are too complicated, regrettably, to permit me to say very much about them here. Nor can I do more than mention the subsequent work of J. L. Austin and R. M. Hare—Austin having made a careful study of the mul-

3. See my *Ethics and Language* (New Haven, 1944) and my *Facts and Values* (New Haven, 1963).

tiple functions of language, and Hare having applied Austin-like distinctions to ethics.[4] But I must not neglect to emphasize the point that follows.

However much "good" (or "bad" or "ought," etc.) is a purely emotive term, it remains suitable for use in judgments that can be supported or attacked by *reasons*. The judgments need *not* be evaluative dogmatisms. The reasons, moreover, are of a familiar sort, even though they differ from those that are mentioned in our logic texts. They can appropriately be called "reasons for favoring or disfavoring" (as distinct from "reasons for believing or disbelieving"); and their bearing on a judgment of value can be explained in this way:

When a speaker is emotively praising an object or action, etc.—let us call it X—he will often be unwilling to continue his praise when he finds that he is mistaken or uninformed about its nature, or when he learns that it has consequences that he has not taken into account. And when his praise is intended to influence others, he will find that the others will not always concur with him without question: they will want to *know* more about X. Thus a factual inquiry into the nature and consequences of X becomes relevant both to the speaker's expression of an attitude and the hearer's inclination to share it. And it is with this sort of factual inquiry (an inquiry that can also be concerned with current customs, or with what some recognized authority says about such matters, etc.) that the reasons for a judgment of value are concerned. They attempt to reveal "the facts of the case"—facts that may tend, when brought to mind, either to strengthen a favor of X, thus supporting the initial emotive judgment, or else to weaken a favor of X, thus qualifying or attacking the initial emotive judgment.

This parallel should be noted: just as a statement expressing a belief in something often needs to be supported by reasons for believing it, so a judgment expressing favor of something often needs to be supported by reasons for favoring it. In both cases the reasons support *what is expressed*.

Thus when a man says, "It would be a good thing to appoint Smith," he may be asked "Why?"; and his reply, providing reasons for favoring Smith's appointment, will presumably be concerned with Smith's intelligence, his reliability, his efficiency, and so on. And when a man says,

4. *How to Do Things with Words*, by J. L. Austin (Cambridge, Mass., 1963, though written earlier); *The Language of Morals*, by R. M. Hare (Oxford, 1952); *Freedom and Reason*, by R. M. Hare (Oxford, 1963).

"This is a good poem," he may again be asked "Why?"; and his reply, providing reasons for favoring the poem, will presumably be concerned with these or those possibilities of interpretation, or with the likelihood that the poem will bring rewards that are permanent, rather than fleeting, and so on. (Such is the manner in which matters of taste manifestly *can* be "disputed.")

Examples of the latter sort raise a question about the need for distinguishing between aesthetic and non-aesthetic value (a distinction that Richards views with suspicion); but that is not a matter that I can here pause to discuss—save to say that it impresses me as presenting no greater problem to an emotive theory of value than it does to any other theory of value. Let me add that I must also omit any discussion of the cases in which one value-judgment is given as a reason for another, though such cases manifestly exist.

Reasons for favoring or disfavoring (of the sort to which I am limiting my discussion) can in themselves be shown true or false, or probable or improbable, by the usual empirical methods. In that respect they are like ever so many other statements. Their distinguishing feature lies rather in their relation to the emotive judgments *for* which they are given as reasons—a relation that is neither logical nor illogical but is simply psychological.

Let me spell out this psychological relation a little more fully. When a speaker is uncertain whether or not to praise X—when he partly favors it and partly disfavors it, his attitudes being in a state of conflict—then an inquiry into further properties of X (including its consequences) may disclose new objects of attitude that he definitely favors, or definitely disfavors. The attitudes to these new objects then tend to be transferred to X itself, and by strengthening one side or the other of his initial conflict they may lead him to make an emotive value-judgment with assurance. His judgment will then be "guided" by reasons—though it remains possible, of course, that there are other reasons that he has neglected to take into account. Much the same can be said of a hearer who is initially uncertain whether or not to concur with the speaker's judgment. And we have only a slightly different situation when a speaker and a hearer initially disagree about the value of X—disagree in the senses that one favors it and the other disfavors it, each wishing (in the interest of social cooperation, for instance) for a convergence of their attitudes. Reasons concerned with further properties of X may then disclose new objects of attitude that they *mutually* favor, or *mutually* disfavor; and these attitudes, when transferred to X, may resolve their disagreement.

I am speaking of what *may* happen *if* reasons are used. I am not, of course, suggesting that people always make an extensive use of reasons. And I am not suggesting that the transfer of attitudes that I mention will be automatic. Other factors may interfere with it—as in the case of the cigarette-smoker, whose strong desire to avoid the consequences of smoking may lead him to do no more than make unkept New Year's resolutions.

In general, given the psychological nature of the relation between reasons and value-judgments, we must bear in mind that the relation may be subject to individual differences. That is of particular interest with regard to *agreement* about values. Even when the transfer of attitudes is virtually automatic, it may happen that various reasons that convince A that something is good will not convince B. They will convince B only if the new objects of attitude, which are on the whole favored by A, will on the whole be favored by B as well. In some cases that may be true, but in other cases it may not be. But we must also bear in mind, for the cases in which it at first seems not to be true, that it may prove true when the reasons initially given are supplemented by further reasons. So an appeal to reasons, though it cannot guarantee a resolution of disagreements, has always a chance of resolving them, and sometimes an excellent chance.

The complexity of the reasons that bear on value-judgments, by the emotive view, can scarcely be over-estimated. Their content is no less varied than the factual considerations by which our attitudes are guided. That is why evaluative problems resist being "delegated" to those who have only a narrow, specialized knowledge. A reasoned support of a value-judgment potentially draws from the whole of our knowledge, and often requires more knowledge than we now have.

4

I must now turn to the second of Richards' theories of value—the one presented in Chapter VII of *Principles of Literary Criticism*. This is again a theory that is briefly presented, and my summary of it will have to be still more brief; but perhaps I can say enough about it to compare it with his earlier theory.

His discussion is primarily concerned with appetencies, these being desires that may or may not be accessible to introspection. In some contexts, though not in all, he seems to be identifying appetencies with "atomic" desires, or desires of maximal simplicity. Corresponding to the appetencies there are also aversions; but these, he tells us, can for practical purposes "be counted in with the appetencies." [5] Thus an aversion to X (I take it) can be considered as an appetency directed to the avoidance of X. Note that when aversions are so counted in, the term "appetency" has a close kinship with the term "attitude."

Appetencies may work together, the satisfaction of one leading to the satisfaction of others; or they may conflict, the satisfaction of one preventing the satisfaction of others. When they work together, with little conflict, they are said to have a high degree of "organization."

Now the bearing of appetencies on the theory of value, according to Richards, is so close that it can be made evident by a definition. Thus he writes:

> (A) We can now extend our definition. Anything is valuable which will satisfy an appetency without involving the frustration of some equal or more important appetency.[6]

And he then goes on to explain the sense in which one appetency is more "important" than another. The importance does not depend on strength alone: it depends as well on the difficulty of redirecting an appetency to other objects, for instance, or on the difficulty of repressing it. And any given appetency will in turn be related to a multitude of others, deriving its importance largely from them.

I trust that "valuable" is only one of the several terms that Richards wants to define in this way—that with only minor qualifications he would say the same thing of "desirable," for instance, or of "good." So to preserve terminological uniformity, in comparing this later view with his earlier one, I shall temporarily take "good" as the term defined, recasting (A) above in this form:

> (B) "X is good" has the same meaning as "X will satisfy an appetency without involving the frustration of some equal or more important appetency."

It will be evident that Richards is now saying nothing whatsoever about purely emotive uses of "good." He is no longer taking the term to be attitude-expressing, but is simply taking it to be attitude-designat-

5. *Principles of Literary Criticism*, p. 48.
6. *Idem*, p. 48.

ing. Or to put it otherwise, he is no longer taking judgments of the form X *is good* to be expressing attitudes, but is simply taking them to be expressing *beliefs about* attitudes. The beliefs will for the most part be predictive: they will be concerned with the *consequences* upon other appetencies (or attitudes) that the satisfaction of a given appetency will bring with it. So the predicate, "is good," instead of adding nothing to the reference of the judgment, will make an enormous addition to it. And that will greatly affect the status of the reasons that can be used in supporting the judgment. The reasons will no longer stand in a merely psychological, guiding relation to the judgment, but will provide ordinary *inductive evidence* for the predictions that the judgment itself has made. We have, then, in keeping with the various theories of value that are now commonly called "naturalistic," a definition that attempts to reduce value-judgments to scientific statements.

Let me add that Richards exaggerates the psychological nature of his definition; and it is for that reason that I speak of a reduction of value-judgments to "scientific statements" rather than to "psychological statements." His definition emphasizes psychology, but also has a bearing on various other sciences. Note that the question, "Will the satisfaction of an appetency whose object is X frustrate an equal or more important appetency whose object is Y?" is in part a question about the causal connection between X and Y themselves and that this connection is not always revealed by psychology alone. When a man satisfies his desire to use gasoline in starting a brush-fire, for instance, he may "frustrate" his desire to remain uninjured—that possibility being revealed less by psychology than by elementary chemistry and biology.

                    5

In attempting to *reduce* value-judgments to scientific statements, as distinct from merely *relating* the two, Richards' (second) view has its frailties. His definition, intended to effect the reduction, is incomplete. It is also misleading. So in the remainder of my paper I want to criticize the definition, and to suggest that it should give place to remarks that are recast in non-definitional form.

His definition is incomplete because it neglects to tell us *whose* appetencies are in question. Perhaps, for instance, Richards had in mind the appetencies of everyone (even including the appetencies of those still unborn). His definition as given by (A) above—and I shall now emphasize the word "valuable," as he does, rather than "good"—could then be expanded thus:

> (C) "X is valuable" has the same meaning as "X will satisfy an appentency of at least one man without frustrating equal or more important appetencies of his own or of other men."

Such a definition is democratic in its emphasis: it counts the appetencies of all men alike, much as Utilitarianism counts the happiness of all men alike.

But that is not the only way of completing the definition. Perhaps Richards was taking "valuable" to be systematically ambiguous, acknowledging that it sometimes refers to the appetencies of one group of men and sometimes to those of another group. The expanded definition might then run:

> (D) "X is valuable" has the same meaning as "X will satisfy an appetency of at least one man in group G without frustrating equal or more important appetencies of the men in that group."

Here the variable, "G," for different contexts, will have to be replaced in different ways. "Valuable" will accordingly be a relative term, with the constant replacing "G" serving as if to specify a frame of reference. If Richards was suggesting this as being related to a customary use of "valuable" he was in effect suggesting that the term can easily lead to only *seeming* disagreements; for one man, in saying that something is valuable, may be replacing "G" in one way, and another man, in denying that to is valuable, may be replacing "G" in another way. The men will then be making different assertions, and perhaps both assertions will be true.

As a further possibility, Richards may have had in mind a kind of first-person use of "valuable," each speaker using it to refer to *his own* appetencies. The expanded definition might then run:

> (E) "X is valuable," when used by Mr. M, has the same meaning as "X will satisfy one of Mr. M's appetencies without frustrating an equal or more important appetency of his."

This definition initially seems to imply that two men can *never* disagree as to whether something is valuable. When one of them affirms that X is valuable and the other affirms that it isn't, each will be relating X to his own appetencies exclusively; so their affirmations will be logically independent. That implication can be avoided (as in the emotive theory) by the claim that the disagreement is "in attitude." But such a claim would deny, contrary to what Richards was holding in the *Principles*, that evaluative discourse can be reduced to scientific discourse. Scientific discourse has a logical, inductive bearing on disagreements in *belief* (no matter whether the beliefs are about attitudes or about something else); but on disagreements in *attitude* (see Section 4 above) it has only a non-logical, psychological bearing.

In sum: Richards' "one" definition, when completed with attention to the question, "Whose appetencies?" leaves us with a choice between three definitions.

                    6

Let me now consider, more generally, the *kind* of definition that Richards was giving in the *Principles*. He was not, I trust, attempting to give a purely lexical acount of "valuable," as if revealing the common usage or usages of the term; and he could scarcely have wished to depart from common usage capriciously. So perhaps he was attempting to give the sort of definition that is often found in the sciences. Perhaps his definition can be compared to that of a physicist who defined "heat" with reference to molecular motion. The physicist is neither preserving common usage nor capriciously departing from it; he is introducing a technical sense that grows out of a non-technical sense, and one that for theoretical purposes can usefully replace or supplement it—partly because heat in the non-technical sense is nearly always heat in the technical sense as well. In the same way, presumably, Richards was attempting to provide a technical sense of "valuable" that could usefully replace or supplement its non-technical sense (or senses).

In my opinion, however, Richards was doing rather more than following this established scientific procedure; and his definition becomes misleading (quite independently of its incompleteness) on that account. To explain this I must return to a discussion of the emotive force of the value-terms.

As commonly used, "valuable" (like "good" and "desirable," etc.) virtually insists on being a term of praise. Its favorable emotive force is so strongly fixed in our linguistic habits that it can be neutralized only in very special contexts. And that must be borne in mind whenever the term is assigned, by definition, this or that "referential" or descriptive meaning. In such cases the term usually retains its favorable emotive force; and for those who accept the definition it simply acquires a descriptive meaning as well. Even when the definition seems to ignore the emotive force, it still leaves the term with a hybrid function, partly emotive and partly descriptive. In consequence, the definition tends to influence attitudes: it tends to *preempt* the term for praising whatever things or properties the definition has mentioned. I have elsewhere called such definitions "persuasive." [7]

Persuasive definitions are by no means uncommon in traditional ethics. Bentham, for instance, in defending social happiness as a standard of value, occasionally claimed that such terms as "valuable" and "good" become intelligible only when *defined* with reference to social happiness.[8] By this definitional claim he was preempting the still emotive terms (presumably without realizing that he was doing so) for exclusive use in praising the Utilitarian ideal: he was taking a step toward building the Utilitarian standard of value into our very language. In an exaggerated form, persuasive definitions are also typical of the "Newspeak" of Orwell's *Nineteen Eighty-Four*, where various favorable evaluative terms are defined to mean the same as "in accordance wth the will of Big Brother." [9] The emotive terms were again being preempted, though there with a decidedly non-Utilitarian intent.

If I were to praise Bentham's definition, or to express my horror at those of Newspeak, I would be digressing. My purpose is not to make value-judgments, but only to make them recognizable when they are expressed in a concealed way. And for that purpose the definitions of Bentham and of Big Brother are equally instructive. By wedding emotive terms to selected descriptive meanings the definitions become persuasive: they become covert value-judgments in their own right.

Now Richards' definition, as given in the *Principles*, was also persuasive, and thus covertly a value-judgment—though I suspect that he was imperfectly aware of that. For brevity, let me say that his definition of "valuable" was one that specified an *economy* in the satisfaction of appetencies. The effect of his definition, then, was to *praise* this economy, or to *advise* us to maintain it. It had that effect because it preempted the still emotively laudatory term for designating the economy, fitting it for that purpose exclusively. The specific direction of his ad-

7. *Facts and Values*, Essay III, and *Ethics and Language*, Chaps. IX, X, and XIII.
8. *Introduction to the Principles of Morals and Legislation*, by Jeremy Bentham. See particularly Chap. I, par. 10.
9. *Nineteen Eighty-Four*, by George Orwell (New York, 1949).

vice does not become evident until we complete his definition in accordance with (C), (D), or (E) of the preceding section. But it remains advice no matter how we complete it.

To some, Richards' advice will be gratuitous, but to some it will not be. Not all people look ahead to the extent that he advises. Some neglect an economy even of their own appetencies: they mirror the appetencies of those with whom they have most recently been associating; or they ignore (in the face of evidence) any beliefs that might call their habitual appetencies into question; or they satisfy only short-range appetencies, as if saying, with Edna St. Vincent Millay,[10]

My candle burns at both ends;
   It will not last the night;
But ah, my foes, and oh, my friends—
   It gives a lovely light!

But my essential point is this: in defining the value terms Richards was doing *more* than following the scientific procedure of letting a nontechnical sense give place to a technical sense. He was also, with a more-than-scientific aim, himself evaluating. He was evaluating evaluations, if I may put it so; he was encouraging us, by a definition that was persuasive, to develop a second-order appetency directed to an economy in the satisfaction of first-order appetencies. And his definition was misleading because it failed to acknowledge this more-than-scientific aim.

7

I have now discussed both of Richards' theories of value, with some additions to the earlier one and some criticisms of the later one. Let me conclude by suggesting that they need not remain as opposed theories. With certain modifications they can be reconciled, and indeed can become aspects of a broader and well-unified theory.

To understand the needed modifications we must make a distinction —a distinction between

(a) an inquiry into what value-judgments mean, and
(b) an inquiry into how people make up their minds as to whether or not something is valuable.

The distinction may at first seem elusive. The familiar remark, "To know what an assertion means, ask how you would verify it," might

10. *The Collected Lyrics of Edna St. Vincent Millay*, p. 127 (New York, 1943).

suggest the further remark, "To know what an assertion means, ask how you would make up your mind whether or not to accept it." And those who are sympathetic to the latter remark will urge that (a) and (b) yield a distinction without a difference. But the latter remark, in my opinion, is indefensible. It has no place in value-theory, where (a) and (b) stand apart as sharply as they do when applied to imperatives. Let me explain, with reference to the imperatives.

If asked about the meaning of "Please close the door," for instance, we should doubtless point out that the conventions of our language fit it for requesting that the door be closed, rather than for predicting that it will be closed. And of course we could say much more than that. But we should not, I trust, in the course of explaining what the imperative means, feel the need of discussing the detailed motivation or the degree of psychological economy that guides people in using or withholding an imperative. Perhaps Mr. A said "Please close the door" in order to avoid a draught; and perhaps Mrs. A closed it with that in mind. Perhaps both thought they were economically satisfying their wants, suspecting that the draught would give them colds; and perhaps they were actually frustrating one of their wants, since they did not take into account that the closed door would prevent them from hearing the baby cry. But such matters take us well beyond the *meaning* of the initial imperative. They are of interest not for the purpose of "unpacking" what an imperative "says," but rather for the purpose of illustrating *how people make up their minds* (with or without psychological economy) about what imperatives to use or obey.

For imperatives, then, (a) and (b) above require related but different studies; and I want to suggest that for value-judgments (a) and (b) also require related but different studies.

In dealing with (a), with its exclusive concern with meanings, Richards could safely have abided by his earlier, emotive view. In developing it he would have needed to give a more careful analysis of the conception of emotive meaning (or emotive "force"); and he would have needed to pay more attention to the terms that are less generic than "good" or "valuable"—such terms as "courageous" or "sentimental," which typically combine emotive and descriptive meaning.[11] But even in its original, schematic form the emotive view was a much-needed corrective to

11. For a discussion of terms that combine descriptive and emotive meaning, and of the circumstances under which definitions of the terms cease to be persuasive (save gratuitously), see my *Facts and Values*, pp. 221 ff.

the various forms of Platonism, Kantianism, or naturalism that had so long dominated philosophy.

Having handled (a) in emotive fashion, Richards could then have worked out his psychological views in connection with (b)—discussing how people make up their minds about evaluations. He would not, in that case, have been reducing value-theory to psychology, but he would nevertheless have been developing an aspect of value-theory on which psychology can be decidedly illuminating.

His remarks about the economy of appetencies would then belong to the same family as my own remarks (Section 3) about reasons for favoring or disfavoring. Indeed, I dealt with that topic partly in anticipation of connecting it with Richards' psychological views. I said, it will be remembered, that when a man is uncertain whether or not emotively to judge that X is good (or valuable), the reason "X leads to Y" may help to remove or diminish his uncertainty; it may transfer his favor of Y to his previously hesitant attitude to X, supporting (in his opinion) the judgment that X is valuable . . . and so on. In using reasons of that sort, or of neighboring sorts, the man will be taking steps toward letting his judgment reflect *many* of his appetencies: he will be concerned with their economy.

A study of how people make up their minds about their evaluations would not, of course, deal with the economy of appetencies exclusively. It would also deal with those departures from economy that I have previously illustrated with attention to the cigarette-smoker, or with attention to those who mirror the appetencies of others, etc. But the study could still give a central place to economy: it could ask how much people in fact preserve it, or how much they try to preserve it, or how much they could preserve it under such and such conditions. And with special reference to the arts it could ask, with reference to sublimation, whether certain works so *alter* (rather than merely satisfy) our appetencies that we can organize them with a greater economy than would otherwise be possible.

When presented in that way, Richards' discussion in the *Principles* would be free from the two criticisms that I have made of it.

It would deal with appetencies without introducing a "should." It would no longer covertly advise us, through the use of a persuasive definition, that we should economize our appetencies more than we do. It would draw conclusions about evaluations that were not themselves evaluative, thus preserving the detachment that a scientific psychology has always sought.

After developing such a study, Richards could of course *go on* to advise us, letting his advice acquire an intelligibility—and for many of us, an acceptability—from the psychological analysis that attended it. It is not my intention (as I hope my discussion has made clear) to reject his advice. I am simply pointing out that it would become less misleading if plainly labeled as such, and not presented as if it were itself a scientific conclusion.

There would be no occasion, moreover, for perplexities attending my other criticism—the one given in Section 5, where I raised the question, "With regard to *whose* appetencies is economy being mentioned?" That was an important question so long as the term "valuable" was being preempted, persuasively, for exclusive use in praising (or recommending, or advising) economy; for it is one thing to praise an economy that is preserved for a group and another thing to praise an economy that is preserved for an individual. But Richards' inquiry, so long as its psychological aspects were being developed, would not need to preempt the term. It would be a detached inquiry into the extent to which people are concerned with economy when they are making up their minds about what is valuable. Obviously, there would be *several* aspects of such an inquiry, some concerned with economy throughout society at large, some concerned with economy throughout a certain group, G, and some concerned with an economy for a given individual. A selection of one aspect to the exclusion of the others would not have to be made, since each aspect could be studied in its turn.

Suppose, for example, that Mr. M is making up his mind whether X is valuable. We might then, in psychologically explaining what he is doing, be primarily interested in discussing the extent to which he is economizing *his* appetencies—since it is *his* appetencies, guided by such reasons as *he* uses, that will eventuate in his evaluative (and emotively expressed) decision. But Mr. M's appetencies may or may not be socially directed: they may or may not, when he expresses them or acts upon them, lead to the satisfaction of the appetencies of people in group G, or of all people. So our interests may lead us to extend our inquiry, discussing the manner in which Mr. M's appetencies bear on those of others.

Until we know who Mr. M is we cannot, of course, decide about how much his appetencies are being economized, or how much they are being socially directed. We have always to reckon with individual differences. And just as the question, "Should Mr. M economize his appetencies?" is an evaluative rather than a psychological question (requiring the person who answers it to advise or recommend, etc.) so the question "Should Mr. M's appetencies be socially directed?" is an evaluative rather than a psychological question.

8

With modifications, then, Richards' two theories could be combined into a larger, unified theory—essentially an emotive theory, but deriving a greater strength from being provided with a psychological background.

The importance of the theory, if fully worked out, would lie in its freeing our evaluations from a sense of mystery. It would remind us that our value-judgments do not have a more-than-scientific subject matter, but simply have a more-than-scientific (yet scientifically intelligible) function; and it would clarify the sense in which our judgments can be supported by reasons.

As applied to literary criticism, the theory would spare us much lost motion, and much pretentiousness. It would not, however, provide us with a "science" of criticism. It would at most provide us with a criticism *guided* by science. And since the guiding effect of science depends on a psychological rather than on a logical relation between our reasons and our evaluations, the theory might prove, even in its ultimate development, to leave us with a diversity of critical opinion. It might serve partly to counteract, but beyond that merely to reveal, those differences in the nature of our appetencies that we also call differences in taste. It would not be a theory that "proves" some one standard of value. Rather, it would be one that opens the possibility of standards which, though they may still diverge, will diverge not because they are held in scientific ignorance, but only because they reflect the varied sensibilities and aspirations of human beings.

CLEANTH BROOKS

I. A. Richards and the Concept of Tension

A felt tension among its various elements is a special feature of modern poetry—and of modern literature in general. The serious writer is not ordinarily content with associating like with like, observing the requirements of a simple and obvious decorum, and furnishing his narratives with happy endings. Even his metaphors will probably be bold and sometimes disturbing. One can find this tension in modern authors as different in personality and interests as are T. S. Eliot and Allen Ginsberg.

The element of tension in literature is, of course, not new. The father of criticism discerned it in Greek tragedy and commented on it. Even that solid neo-classicist, Samuel Johnson, clearly acknowledges it—in his treatment of metaphor, at least. Tension has always been a factor in determining literary and artistic unity, regardless of the historical period. But in our own day it has emerged as an important, if sometimes problematic, aspect of literary structure, and because it upsets older ideas of decorum, it has demanded new insights into its positive functions and a fresh discussion of its proper limits.

I venture to suggest that the modern writer's need to recognize and exploit tensional elements is ultimately to be connected with the present crisis in culture; that is, with the vast imbalance between means (science) and ends (values) and the consequent breakdown of traditional systems of value. But what I want to undertake here is not a review of the emergence of our special need to harmonize the disparate and apparently conflicting; nor do I mean to attempt a history of the aesthetics of tension. My more modest purpose is to examine the role of I. A. Richards in calling attention to several important (and related) questions: the fact of disparity in poetry, the kinds of unification possible and desirable, and the positive values of a poetry that makes use of tension as its structural principle.

Richards has exerted during the last fifty years a powerful influence on our understanding of these matters—perhaps the most powerful influence of all. In the pages that follow I shall suggest some parallels between his thinking and that of other men of letters of our time, Yeats and Eliot in particular. The fact that in his stress upon a hard-won unity Richards is flanked by men who come at the same problem from quite different intellectual backgrounds makes evident that the problem is central to our culture. A concern for tensional structure does not spring from a narrow ideology or serve a special literary bias.

The concept of tension is embedded in a nexus of related concepts. Thus, as we shall see, it is impossible to talk about tension without also talking about the limits of metaphor and the possibility of (and perhaps the necessity for) incorporating the unpleasant, the ugly, and the evil into the art work. A discussion of tension must impinge on other matters also: the degree of detachment proper for the artist to adopt and its relation to the degree of his personal involvement; the whole problem of decorum and, with it, the very meaning of artistic unity.

A concern for such issues has established in our time what amounts to a new poetics. If this statement seems extravagant, the reader might look back at past theoretical criticism, particularly that written in England and America in the period from, say, 1830 to 1920. He will find that the usual formulations of poetry made during this period have little or nothing to do with a tensional element.[1] This is not to say that the modern critic cannot discern tensional structures embodied in Victorian poetry. I have elsewhere remarked that some degree of tension is basic to any poetry, but the typical Victorian critics and those critics writing in the first years of our century reveal little awareness of the tensional element.

One may well begin with Richards' *Principles of Literary Criticism* (1924). In a chapter significantly entitled "The Imagination," he describes tragedy as "perhaps the most general, all-accepting, all-ordering experience known," and its special character as a "balanced poise, stable through its power of inclusion, not through the force of its exclusions. . . ." But Richards points out that this balanced poise is not peculiar to tragedy; and it can thus become for him the norm for all the most valuable literary experience.

1. Obviously, there are exceptions to my flat generalization, notably, for example, some aspects of Coleridge, who has exerted so fruitful an influence on Richards himself.

In this description of such valuable literary experience, the terms "inclusion" and "exclusion" prove to be pivotal; for Richards observes that there are two basic ways in which the impulses of the psyche "may be organized; by exclusion and by inclusion, by synthesis and by elimination. Although every coherent state of mind," he concedes, "depends upon both, it is permissible to contrast experiences which win stability and order through narrowing of the response with those which widen it." Richards offers Tennyson's "Break, break, break," and Landor's *Rose Aylmer* as examples of poems that depend for their unity upon exclusion; Keats's *Ode to a Nightingale* and the ballad *Sir Patrick Spens* as examples of those that depend upon inclusion. Thus, in their basic groundplan, these latter poems resemble tragedy. As Richards puts it, "No one will quarrel with 'Break, break, break' . . . or with *Rose Aylmer*. . . . But they are not the greatest kind of poetry; we do not expect from them what we find in the *Ode to a Nightingale*" and poems that generally share its kind of organization.

This concept was to make its fortune in critical theory, particularly in the 1930's and 1940's, and because it has meant so much to me, I shall make bold to take it out of the special context in which Richards placed it in the *Principles* (a psychological account of the way in which impulses are aligned *within the reader's mind* as he responds to a valuable literary work) and relate it more directly to the structure of the work. Richards himself was in effect to do this in 1936 in his *Philosophy of Rhetoric*. In any case, I do not believe that the nature of his fruitful insight will be seriously distorted in the rendering that follows. In fact, I believe that something may be gained by giving to the basic distinction some of the extensions to which it was from the beginning legitimately entitled and which it has subsequently won for itself.

I would paraphrase Richards thus: there are two basic ways in which a poet may secure unity. The first is by making us see, and accept as legitimate, connections hitherto unsuspected between various elements of our experience. Thus the poet reveals patterns where we had assumed rather haphazard mixtures of experiences. The poet is good at this sort of thing. Indeed, there is reason to believe that his right to be called a poet depends upon just such ability. The poet makes meaningful (that is, unified) what we might otherwise have taken to be meaningless (unrelated, chaotic). Even the humblest poet is able to include as parts of a unified experience elements that ordinarily seem utterly disparate. But the poet—even the poet of greatest range and most compelling imagination—excludes some aspects of experience from the pattern that he is making. He must select. He can't literally put everything into his poem. There are matters of scope and depth. Besides, there probably are real incompatibles, impossible mixtures—elements that refuse to be harmonized, at least within any poem of modest dimensions. Even the most audacious poet does not dismiss all sense of what fits with what.[2] The unity of any conceivable poem is achieved by deciding what to put in and what to leave out—that is, through a reciprocal process of exclusion and inclusion.

Nevertheless, some poems depend much more on one method than the other. Because the obvious way to unify is simply to toss out the difficult item, the method of exclusion can be an easy way out for the careless or lazy or incompetent poet. A poem ruthlessly pruned so as to express only one fairly simple attitude or one specific theme may degenerate into sentimentality.

I call the reader's attention to the fact that I am here pressing an issue that Richards in the *Principles* elected to treat in a less thoroughgoing fashion. There he is concerned to make a rather delicate distinction between two kinds of poetry, one of which he regards as more valuable than the other, whereas I am using exclusion and inclusion as the opposite ends of a scale. Most actual poems fall somewhere between the extremes, but poems that lie near to either extreme undergo accordant risks, reveal characteristic virtues, and sometimes characteristic defects. Thus, too much dependence on exclusion will result in a trivial and anemic poem. Such poems do not provide the reader with new insights, i.e. new ways of putting into a pattern what we had usually taken to be unrelated and perhaps even irreconcilable elements. They do not sufficiently exhibit the power of the plastic imagination.

The muses who preside over a poetry heavily dependent on extreme exclusion are the bastard muses whose names are sentimentality, propaganda, and pornography. Under the inspiration of one or another of these, the poet tries to impose on his reader a specific short-term effect. He does so at the expense of emotional maturity, truth, and the fully human dimension. For maturity, truth, and full humanity require some comprehension of the complexities of human experience.

2. John Donne's triumphs in bringing into love poetry items so diverse as mathematical instruments and fleas do not really controvert this statement. Rather, Donne makes us aware of the special potentialities of the compass or the special associations of the flea to serve as cross-bracings and counterweights in a total structure. For Donne did not conceive of the poem as a bouquet of flowers—as the nineteenth century too often did—but as something more nearly structural, like an arched stone bridge or a hammer-beam timber roof.

By contrast, poems that achieve their basic unity through the poet's ability to include the heterogeneous and the diverse are mature and tough-minded. They wear well. They can be viewed from various angles, for their solidity does not depend upon tricky lighting and privileged perspectives.

Yet poems founded on inclusion, it must be conceded, have their characteristic failures too. If the poet tries to include too much of the heterogeneous, if he lacks the power of imagination to reconcile the disparities, if he increases tension beyond his power to control it, then the poem simply explodes into incoherence. What happens to his overambitious metaphors will illustrate: the "heterogeneous ideas yoked by violence together" have been forced by sheer will power to touch momentarily, but because merely yoked by violence and not truly reconciled, they fly apart.[3]

The unification achieved by the imagination perhaps ultimately involves a mystery—or perhaps "unification" is too bold a term.[4] But the difference between a poem that can accommodate disparate elements—however we are to describe the process by which it does it—and a poem that conveniently forgets about or deliberately refuses to acknowledge disparities is crucial. It goes to the heart of the poetic process. We shall, in the pages that follow, be referring to various insights into this process and, not least important, to some further insights by Richards himself.

How did Richards come by his seminal view? Did he make fruitful borrowings and adaptations from earlier writers? His debt to Coleridge is too well known to require comment here except that it ought to be observed that he saw something in Coleridge's celebrated fourteenth chapter of the *Biographia* that most other readers, including other Coleridge enthusiasts, had not seen.[5] He isolated, we might say, the tensional element.

3. This phenomenon was, of course, also experienced by readers brought up in the old decorum when they first encountered Donne or Eliot.

4. In his *Philosophy of Rhetoric* Richards warns us against talking about "the fusion that a metaphor effects," for in most metaphors "the disparities" between the items compared "are as much operative as the similarities."

5. William K. Wimsatt has shown, convincingly I believe, that to interpret this passage as undergirding a *general* theory of poetry, an attempt made by Richards and other modern commentators, is to extend it beyond what Coleridge probably had in mind—though Wimsatt does not deny that we can, if we like, interpret Coleridge's statement to support a general theory, one that will provide a justification for the characteristic work of a Donne or an Eliot. See Wimsatt and Cleanth Brooks, *Literary Criticism: A Short History*, New York, 1957, p. 198. I make the point here not to impugn but to assert Richards' originality. In short, he probably

Some time prior to writing the *Principles* Richards must have read George Santayana's *The Sense of Beauty* (1896). In his first book, *The Foundations of Aesthetics* (written in collaboration with C. K. Ogden and James Wood and published in 1922), there is a perfunctory reference to various definitions of Beauty proposed by Santayana, Croce, Clive Bell, *et al.*, and later in the book occurs a sentence quoted from *The Sense of Beauty*. There seem to be no further references to Santayana in Richards' work. Yet his chapter entitled "The Imagination" in the *Principles*, from which we have quoted above, clearly contains echoes of the following passage in *The Sense of Beauty:* [6]

> Now, it is the essential privilege of beauty to so *synthesize* and bring to a focus the various *impulses of the self*, so to suspend them to a single image, that a great peace falls upon that perturbed kingdom. In the experience of these momentary harmonies we have the basis of the enjoyment of beauty, and of all its mystical meanings. But there are always two methods of securing harmony: one is to unify all the given elements, and another is to reject and expunge all the elements that refuse to be unified. Unity by *inclusion* gives us the beautiful; unity by *exclusion*, opposition, and isolation gives us the sublime. Both are pleasures: but the pleasure of the one is warm, passive, and pervasive; that of the other cold, imperious, and keen. The one identifies us with the world, the other raises us above it.[7]

One notices that in this passage Santayana uses not only the terms "inclusion" and "exclusion" but also the terms "impulse" and "synthesize." Yet though I think it impossible to believe that Richards had not read this passage at some time prior to 1924, I think it entirely possible that he had forgotten where he read it, or even that he had ever read it. In any case, Richards has either deliberately or unconsciously reversed the meanings Santayana assigned to *exclusion* and *inclusion*.

The first sentence of the Santayana paragraph must have stuck in Richards' mind. The words and phrases that I italicize clearly make the

read more of a tensional element into the *Biographia* than Coleridge ever meant to put there.

6. I first called attention to the verbal parallels between these passages from Santayana and Richards in 1957 in *Literary Criticism: A Short History* (pp. 618–19), but made little of the parallels then. I now believe they have considerable significance in an examination of Richards' distinction between a poetry of exclusion and one of inclusion, though I think that such an examination tends to establish rather than deny the essential originality of Richards' concept.

7. *The Sense of Beauty*, pp. 235–36. The italics are mine.

point: bringing *the various impulses of the self* into a *synthesis*, suspending them in *a single image*, and thus composing the often troubled self so that *a great peace falls upon that perturbed kingdom*. Though Richards never uses the phrase "great peace," [8] in the later chapters of the *Principles*, his thought hovers around such a concept. Thus he explains that when "some system of impulses not ordinarily in adjustment with itself or adjusted to the world finds something which orders it or gives it fit exercise," there "follows a peculiar sense of ease, of restfulness, of free, unimpeded activity, and the feeling of acceptance, something more positive than acquiescence. . . . Such are the occasions upon which the arts seem to lift away the burden of existence, and we seem ourselves to be looking into the heart of things." This peculiar sense of balance and reconciliation within the self may even give rise to a feeling of revelation, a "revelation" that Richards, however, regards as spurious and unnecessary in order to account for the value of the experience.

To return to Santayana's account of the two methods for securing harmony among the various impulses of the self: a close inspection clarifies the real divergence between what he and Richards are saying when they refer to *exclusion* and *inclusion*. Richards is trying to distinguish between two grades of poetry; that is, between a shallow and a more profound poetry, whereas Santayana is attempting to discriminate between beauty and sublimity.

Santayana's sublimity, to be sure, is for him evidently of a deeper and more heroic order than is beauty. Whereas the pleasure of beauty is "warm, passive, and pervasive," the pleasure that results from the sublime is "cold, imperious, and keen. The one identifies us with the world; the other raises us above it." The sublime is specifically heroic:

> . . . when we come upon a great evil or an irreconcilable power, we are driven to seek our happiness by the shorter and heroic road; then we recognize the hopeless foreignness of what lies before us, and stiffen ourselves against it. We thus for the first time reach the sense of our possible separation from our world, and of our abstract stability; and with this comes the sublime.

Thus, Santayana's sublime poetry has affinities with tragedy as Richards conceives it. Just as Santayana's sublime requires us to "recog-

---

8. Some years later, in *The Philosophy of Rhetoric*, Richards did write that "a strange peace would fall upon the world," but here he is talking about what would happen if Bosanquet's Golden Rule of Scholarship were applied, and the parallel between Santayana's "great peace falls" and his own "strange peace would fall" is probably too slight to mean much.

nize the hopeless foreignness of what lies before us," so, in our experience of genuine tragedy (and of his poetry of inclusion generally),
we must, Richards tells us, rid ourselves of any notion that "somewhere,
somehow, there is Justice." In fact, tragedy, Richards declares, "is only
possible to a mind which is for the moment agnostic or Manichean."
Tragedy, in short, is what he calls "unmitigated experience."

There is a further parallel between Santayana and Richards. Just as
Richards' poetry of inclusion culminates in tragedy, so Santayana's sublime finds in tragedy its prime manifestation. Our "pity and terror,"
Santayana tells us, echoing Aristotle's passage on the catharsis effected
by tragedy, "are indeed purged; we go away knowing that, however
tangled the net may be in which we feel ourselves caught, there is
liberation beyond, and an ultimate peace." (But the liberation of which
Santayana speaks here is wrought by the soul itself when it turns away
from the world and falls back onto its own resources, and the ultimate
peace which it attains is not the Christian hope of a life of blessedness
beyond the grave. Santayana is here quite as agnostic as Richards.)

Thus, one is tempted to see Santayana's sublimity as analogous to
Richards' poetry of inclusion, until he remembers that Santayana's
beauty, which yields a "warm, passive" pleasure, is Santayana's poetry
of *inclusion,* and that Santayana's sublimity, "cold, imperious, and
keen" and tragic and heroic, like Richards' poetry of inclusion, is called
by Santayana a poetry of *exclusion.*

The two men are evidently using the terms *exclusion* and *inclusion* in
completely different senses. Richards, as we have seen, means by *exclusion* the elimination of those disparate elements that seem to threaten
the unity of the poem. Santayana, on the other hand, seems to mean by
exclusion an elimination of any delusion that we may find peace and
comfort in the world about us. In the experience of beauty we identify
beauty with the object, regarding our aesthetic pleasure "as a quality of
a thing." But our sense of the sublime is achieved by our conscious rejection of the world of things, or, as Santayana puts it in another passage, the mind is made to "recoil upon itself." The mind raises itself up
in the "glorious joy of self-assertion in the face of an uncontrollable
world," and that joy is

> so deep and entire, that it furnishes just that transcendent ele-
> ment of worth for which we were looking when we tried to un-
> derstand how the expression of pain could sometimes please. It
> can please, not in itself, but because it is balanced and annulled

by positive pleasures, especially by this final and victorious one of detachment. If the expression of evil seems necessary to the sublime, it is so only as a condition of this moral reaction.

When we compare the positions of Santayana and Richards, the fact that stands out is Richards' reinterpretation of *exclusion* and *inclusion* to fit his own purposes, a reinterpretation that emphasizes tension as an essential element in the structure of our most profound literature. Moreover, whatever the value of Santayana's distinction between the beautiful and the sublime, there can be no question about the superior "operational validity" of the distinction drawn by Richards between a poetry of exclusion and inclusion. The history of literary criticism after the publication of Richards' seminal books on the subject is sufficient proof. Santayana is a valuable and a still underrated literary critic, but his contributions have a different range of interests and his influence has worked at a different level.

There is another important figure of the latter part of the nineteenth and the first third of the twentieth century whose concern with a poetics of tension bears comparison with that of Richards: William Butler Yeats. Yet it is very unlikely that Richards—particularly the Richards of the *Principles*—was acquainted with Yeats's critical ideas. In 1924, Richards described Yeats's poetry as "a development out of the main track," and as a "minor poetry in a sense in which Mr Hardy's best work or Mr Eliot's *The Waste Land* is major poetry." In view of such opinions, there would have been little inducement to look very searchingly at Yeats's literary essays.

Richards tells us that it was not until after 1928, the year in which Yeats's *The Tower* appeared, that he came to a due appreciation of Yeats's later poetry. The later poetry Richards took very seriously indeed. I am not aware, however, that he has ever shown much interest in Yeats as a critic. Be that as it may, at his best Yeats is a very perceptive critic, and, though this may come as a surprise to many, a critic whose mature views are in some very important ways close to those of Eliot, Auden, and Richards himself.

In saying this, I have particularly in mind Yeats's celebrated remark that we make "rhetoric" out of our "quarrel with others" and that it is only out of "the quarrel with ourselves that we make poetry"; and his statement that "no mind can engender till divided into two." Both texts imply that the creation of art is a dialectical process, necessarily involving a tension between the conscious self and the buried self; between the public self that looks out on the world, and its opposite, the mask (which is the secret face of one's daimon); between the self living in the present and "that age-long memoried self, that shapes the elaborate shell of the mollusc and the child in the womb. . . ." But I am thinking also of the position he takes as early as 1907 in an essay entitled "Poetry and Tradition," where he tells us that the "nobleness of the arts is in the mingling of contraries," a phrase that locates the element of tension not only within the creative mind of the poet but in the materials out of which he makes his poem.

In this same early essay, it is interesting to see how Yeats goes about describing the essential nature of all exalted art and in particular of tragic poetry. Like Richards (and like Santayana), Yeats believes that the most profound art deals with "the great irremediable things." The poet allows his protagonist to find no way out of the tragic situation nor any religious consolation for his sorrow and loss. Yet the artist capable of coping with "the great irremediable things" endows his characters (and the reader who participates vicariously in their heroic experience) with a sense of liberation—even a sense of joy. Thus, Yeats tells us that "Shakespeare's persons"—he mentions specifically Timon of Athens and Cleopatra—"when the last darkness has gathered about them, speak out of an ecstasy that is one-half the self-surrender of sorrow, and one-half the last playing and mockery of the victorious sword before the defeated world." Clearly this experience has close affinities with Santayana's sublime, in which the self experiences the "glorious joy of self-assertion in the face of an .uncontrollable world" and "the final and victorious [pleasure] of detachment." More to our purpose here, the experience Yeats describes resembles Richards' conception of tragedy as an experience in which the mind "stands uncomforted, unintimidated, alone and self-reliant," an experience, moreover, that "strangely [has at its] heart" joy, and an experience in which the participant, in spite of his deep involvement, feels "detached" and "impersonal."

In his account of tragedy Richards goes on to record a most valuable insight, namely, that our sense of detachment as we participate in tragedy comes from the fact that as more of our own "personality is engaged the independence and individuality of other things becomes greater. We seem to see 'all round' them, to see them as they really are: we see them apart from any one particular interest which they may have for us. Of course without some interest we should not see them at all, but the less any one particular interest is indispensable, the more *detached* our attitude becomes. And to say that we are *impersonal* is merely a curious way of saying that our personality is more *completely* involved." We are reminded here of the point made by Yeats when he speaks of the artist's rising to the tragic occasion with a "touch of extravagance, of irony, of surprise, which [he brings to his work] after the desire of logic [narrative or dramatic] has been satisfied. . . ." The artist, though possessed by dramatic sympathy for his characters ("he enters upon a submissive, sorrowful contemplation"), nevertheless, as a craftsman, responds to the situation as one "caught up into the freedom of self-delight."

A like response is made by the characters, who, in suffering "the extremity of sorrow," also experience "the extremity of joy," an ecstasy in which the "perfection of personality" goes hand in hand with "the perfection of its surrender," and the character (along with the auditor or reader) is filled with a sense of "overflowing turbulent energy" but also with a sense of "marmorean stillness. . . ." A mingling of contraries indeed!

Such was Yeats's abiding faith as an artist, for thirty years later, a scant two years before his death, Yeats made these same points once more and with almost precisely the same illustrations. After quoting Lady Gregory's remark that "tragedy must be a joy to the man who dies," he appeals again to Shakespeare's tragic characters to instance this truth, and once more invokes Cleopatra. Though in her last scene she utters the poignant words "My baby at my breast," Yeats insists "all must be cold; no actress ever sobbed when she played Cleopatra, even the shallow brain of a producer has never thought of such a thing. The supernatural is present, cold winds blow across our heads, upon our faces, the thermometer falls, and because of that cold we are hated by journalists and the groundlings." [9]

One is moved to exclaim: Spoken like the poet that Yeats was, with his own characteristic touch of extravagance and his irrepressible contempt for journalists and producers infatuated with showy stage business. Nevertheless Yeats's basic point comes clear, and in its stress on a complete involvement of the self that yet transcends any merely personal concern constitutes an endorsement of Richards' thesis. [10]

I have a further reason for indicating at some length parallels between

9. "A General Introduction for My Work," *Essays and Introductions*, New York, 1961, p. 523.
10. In another passage in "Poetry and Tradition," Yeats writes that the words of Timon and Cleopatra move us "because their sorrow is not their own at tomb or asp, but for all men's fate": and in another essay he remarks, "all that is personal [in art] soon rots. . . ."

Yeats and Richards: Yeats's critical writings are a testimony to the continuing influence of the most powerful of Richards' acknowledged sources: Samuel Taylor Coleridge. I have, in later years, become more and more convinced that Yeats's intellectual debt to Coleridge was immense. A careful reading of Yeats's work reveals echoes and parallels far exceeding the number of direct references to Coleridge. (But plenty of such references occur and particularly in "Pages from a Diary in 1930." I have counted over a dozen such references in forty-odd pages.)

Yeats's critical pronouncements point to another influence related to my present purpose. Early in his career Yeats came heavily under the sway of Nietzsche and was especially influenced by *The Birth of Tragedy* (1872). In September of 1902 he wrote to Lady Gregory: "I have read [Nietzsche] so much that I have made my eyes bad again. . . . Nietzsche completes Blake and has the same roots. . . ." Yeats's much marked and annotated copy of *The Birth of Tragedy* (now in the library of Northwestern University) provides additional evidence of how thoroughly he did read him. Nietzsche's contribution to the aesthetics of tension is well known, and here I need only remind the reader that for Nietzsche, great art manifests itself "in the conquest of opposites," and that the greatest artists are those who are capable of making "harmony ring out of every discord." Nietzsche insisted that the bitter facts of life had to be faced and that the artist's genuine vitality is shown in his willingness to challenge them joyfully. There is a close parallel here with Santayana's art of the sublime in which the hero rises superior to his own misfortunes and through this action achieves "liberation" and "ultimate peace."

Richards nowhere, to my knowledge, mentions Nietzsche, and there is no particular reason why he should have done so. Long before Richards' time, Nietzsche's doctrines had become absorbed into the cultural bloodstream. He had come to be regarded as the prime opponent of the timid bourgeois, of a decadent Christianity, and of academic art; he was the recognized ally of almost any criticism that attacked what was stale, artificial, and pretentious. He had not dethroned Apollo but he had compelled him to share with the dark god, Dionysus, hegemony over the realm of art. The high art of tragedy resulted from a tension between diverse energies.

Eliot's relation to a tensional poetics is perhaps best approached through his comments on the artist's detachment and the impersonality of art. Some of his most interesting comments in this area are to be found in an early essay, "Tradition and the Individual Talent" (1917). There he told his reader that poetry is "not a turning loose of emotion, but an escape from emotion; it is not the expression of personality, but an escape from personality. But, of course, only those who have personality and emotions know what it means to want to escape from these things."

Now that in recent decades we have become aware of Eliot's terribly unhappy first marriage (into which he had entered only two years before writing "Tradition and the Individual Talent") and of the stresses and strains that, a few years later, in 1921, precipitated a nervous breakdown, we may find it easier to take seriously the personal urgency that underlies the remark that "only those who have . . . emotions know what it means to want to escape from these things." Thus Eliot's counsel to the artist to adopt a cool, classical stance did not come from phlegm and cold blood.

There is a second point to be made: though literally Eliot seems to conceive of art as escapism, his is a very peculiar kind of escapism, for it constitutes a liberation of the self through a creative act. For the suffering is not a blank waste: the artist has the satisfaction of having achieved something positive and enduring from what otherwise would be transient and merely painful. In proportion as a work of art is intelligible, it represents a reordering of the emotions and a redeeming into meaning of the painful experience. The transient passions are transformed by the action of the creative mind into something permanent. ("Mind" is the term that Eliot uses a few paragraphs further on in this essay when he observes that "the more perfect the artist, the more completely separate in him will be the man who suffers and the mind which creates; the more perfectly will the mind digest and transmute the passions which are its material." [11]) There is, in short, a sense of detach-

11. This special emphasis on the mind may also account for the rather riddling Greek epigraph that Eliot places before the fourth and last section of "Tradition and the Individual Talent." It comes from Aristotle's "De Anima" (Book I, Ch. 4) and may be translated "Whereas the intellect is doubtless a thing more divine and is impassive." But Eliot has quoted only the conclusion of Aristotle's sentence; for full sense we need to know what precedes it: "Reasoning, love, and hatred are not attributes of the thinking faculty but of its individual possessor. . . . Hence when this possessor perishes, there is neither memory nor love: for these never did belong to the thinking faculty, but to the *composite whole* [italics mine] which has perished, whereas the intellect" etc. The whole essay may be seen as a fresh exploration and special development of Horace's *Ars longa, vita brevis*, one in which

ment corresponding to that which Richards describes as a feature of his poetry of inclusion.

Moreover, the unification of disparate elements of experience which characterizes Richards' poetry of inclusion is precisely the ground plan of the poetry singled out for praise by Eliot in "Tradition and the Individual Talent." Literary works as diverse as the *Agamemnon* of Aeschylus or Shakespeare's *Othello* have a common structural feature: "a fusion of elements"; and Eliot, in offering a further illustration of the point— from Tourneur's *The Revenger's Tragedy*—describes such a fusion as "a combination of positive and negative emotions; an intensely strong attraction toward beauty and an equally intense fascination by the ugliness which is contrasted with it and which destroys it."

In "Tradition and the Individual Talent," Eliot was writing principally about the author's relationship to his work, but in "The Metaphysical Poets" and "Andrew Marvell," both published in 1921, his focus is on the structure of the poetry. Thus the matters principally discussed in these essays have to do with craftsmanship: the selection and treatment of various kinds of materials. In the work of the metaphysical poets, these tend to be quite diverse and sometimes even opposed to one another. Eliot's concern is to explore the positive effects of the tension thus generated.

Since the two essays are well known, one hardly needs to do more than remind the reader of such phrases as "a degree of heterogeneity of material compelled into unity," "sudden contrasts of associations," "contrast of ideas," "a direct sensuous apprehension of thought," and the "amalgamating [of] disparate experiences."

Holding such a view of the structure of metaphysical poetry, Eliot is forced to reexamine the nature of metaphor and its limits, the relation of wit and intellect to high seriousness, and the various kinds of ironic inflection. In general, he is forced to reconsider the nature of decorum and the larger problem of poetic unity itself.

Discussion of problems of this sort entails a further reconsideration: the place of the metaphysical poets in the general tradition of English poetry, along with a reassessment of the neoclassical poet's repudiation of the methods of the metaphysical poets and the failure of the Romantic poets to revive their methods and practices. Thus it is very much to

the permanence of art derives from unchanging principles that may be referred to the mind and not to the changing emotions experienced in the life of the artist.

Eliot's purpose to bring up here, as Richards was to do three years later in the *Principles*,[12] the distinction made by Coleridge (and Wordsworth) between fancy and the imagination. Yet he observes that, if we take into account the witty yet serious poetry of the metaphysicals, this distinction on which Wordsworth and Coleridge laid so much stress becomes so narrow as almost to disappear. To illustrate, he points out that "the elucidation of Imagination given by Coleridge" in the fourteenth chapter of the *Biographia* applies with thorough aptness to Marvell's *To His Coy Mistress*.

Was Richards, then, influenced by Eliot's account of tensional poetry? I dare say not. Richards tells us that he first met Eliot in Cambridge in 1920. Apparently their close relationship, characterized by Eliot's visits to the Richards household, did not begin until 1926. In any case, Richards has told us that "in those early days" he was not "much concerned with [Eliot's] criticism—no, only with the poetry." [13] I see no reason to question Richards' memory of these years. Such parallels between the early criticism of the two men are more easily seen by hindsight. How many were noticed in the early 1920's? In fact, up to this time, so far as I can see, they have attracted very little comment.

My reason for calling them to the reader's attention here is to make a point that has nothing to do with influences possibly exerted upon one man by the other. My concern throughout this essay has been rather to suggest that Richards, in making us aware of the importance of tension and tensional elements in poetry, was, whether or not he was aware of it, moving in a special current of ideas, and that this fact has much to do with the importance of his achievement. The times were evidently ripe for a new emphasis on these matters, and the proof that they were ripe lies in the fact that several sensitive literary minds, some of a generation earlier than Richards and others of his own, were also moving in that direction. The true originality of a thinker does not rest in his ability simply to concoct something novel, but to discover and make fruitful exploration of something that needs to be understood—some concept that the whole culture is in travail to bring forth. If this is

12. William K. Wimsatt points out that Alice D. Snyder in 1918 "was apparently the first modern writer to quote" Coleridge's famous passage on the imagination as a force revealing itself "in the balance or reconciliation of opposite or discordant qualities. . . ." See *Literary Criticism*, p. 396, n. 2.
13. See "On TSE," in *T. S. Eliot: the Man and his Work*, ed. Allen Tate, 1967, pp. 2 and 5.

true, it inevitably means that when an important discovery of this sort is made, we are very likely to find analogues—some close, some distant—elsewhere in the period.

One reason why so little notice has been taken of the similarities that exist between Richards' poetry of inclusion and related formulations by people like Santayana, Yeats, and Eliot is the fact that Richards, in his earlier books, was much occupied with stating other aspects of literature which seemed to him equally, or perhaps even more, important. I have particularly in mind the special psychological terminologies in which he described his stipulated synthesis of conflicting impulses.

Now, whatever the merit or lack of merit of such descriptions, they served in fact to disguise some of the other very important contributions that Richards was making. Without going into the various criticisms made of Richards' psychological terminology, I can say that to most of us it did not prove very helpful, for the psychological machinery was, at best, irrelevant to our interests. I mention here my own early experience in reading Richards only because it is representative of what occurred in more mature and acute minds. My experience was frankly one of tantalized bafflement. The psychological machinery not only did not help; it actually got in my way. It was worse than a distraction. On the other hand, when Richards got down to cases—in the *Principles* as well as in that great casebook on the reading of poetry, *Practical Criticism*—I found him immediately rewarding, usually very exciting, and in general a powerful educative force.

I read him hard, in part because I felt that he had to be refuted, and in the process of trying to find the refutation—it was not easy, I quickly discovered—I learned a great deal about poetry and about literary theory. In fact, it dawned on me fairly early that even those concepts of Richards which seemed to my mind most outrageous could yield—often did yield, when tilted just a little, or perhaps it was simply my willingness to alter a mite my own angle of vision—observations and insights that were true and illuminating, and that, in any case, contained matter that I needed to ponder.

A few years later I was more than commonly grateful, therefore, to find in *The Philosophy of Rhetoric* a presentation free of what had been for me largely a distraction. I found in particular that Richards' revised definition of metaphor was the most useful and illuminating that I had ever read.

In the *Principles* metaphor is said to be "the supreme agent by which disparate and hitherto unconnected things are brought together in poetry for the sake of the effects upon attitude and impulse which spring from their collocation. . . ." In such an account we seem to be dealing with the problem of literary function at several removes, and as if this description of what metaphor does were not, shall we say, sufficiently offhand—and off the point—a few sentences later metaphor is said to serve as "an excuse by which what is needed [in the poem] may be smuggled in."

There are some special senses in which this business of "smuggling in" needful elements is evidently true, but for a young man in 1929, reading the *Principles* for the first time, this notion of metaphor simply made poetry more mysterious and oblique than ever.

Curiously enough, the tensional element that is so powerfully put in the key chapters of the *Principles* is never there clearly related to metaphor, and yet metaphor is itself perhaps the most obvious example of the necessity for tension as well as being the prime imaginative instrument by which the poet reconciles and unifies matters that seem hopelessly at odds.

In pointing out that "metaphor is the omnipresent principle of language" and that thought itself is metaphoric, Richards disposed once and for all of the old notion of metaphor as mere decoration, an inessential ornament attached to the structure of thought after the fact of its creation. Instead, he insists that metaphor is of the very substance of the utterance: "it is a borrowing between and intercourse of *thoughts,* a transaction between contexts." In so defining the metaphoric process, he provided not only a proper corrective to the more one-sided traditional descriptions but also to some of his own earlier statements, or, perhaps it would be fairer and more accurate to say, an amplification and consolidation of his earlier views and one that provided a firm linguistic grounding for the concepts of tension developed in the later chapters of the *Principles.*

Take, for example, the matter of exclusion and inclusion. The didactic poet who is trying to prepare a kind of lawyer's brief for a particular code of conduct or for his outlook on life tends to leave out of his account any evidence favorable to the "other side." We feel that his presentation is thin rather than thick, calculated to elicit one kind of judgment or persuade to one course of action. Or, to take another instance of a poet too dependent on exclusion: the sentimental poet narrows the field of interest to what accords with and seems to favor a desiderated mood. He chooses metaphors and symbols possessing associations that accord with the mood that he would impose. Thus, he too "purifies" his context of disturbing and heterogeneous elements. In doing so, he tends to limit its range of interests and to oversimplify its dominant emotion.

Yeats has described such biases in one of his poems, *Ego Dominus Tuus*, denying the very title of poetry to compositions devised in this fashion. He writes:

The rhetorician would deceive his neighbours,
The sentimentalist himself. . . .

They deceive by attempting to press blinders on their reader's eyes or by covering their own eyes with rose-tinted spectacles. Richards' concept of metaphor (and poetry itself) as a "transaction" between (among) "contexts" provides a more explicit and detailed way of describing the nature of the defect. The "rhetorician" confines his poem—or novel—to a thinned-out context, allowing it no serious "transaction" with any others, shielding his readers from possible disturbing other "facts," attitudes, and concepts. The sentimentalist is simply a more naive rhetorician: his victims include himself. He takes his own medicine, whether we regard it as soothing syrup or poison. (The extreme instance of the "rhetorician" seen in these terms is the Fascist propagandist, though one can urge this point, I hope, without claiming that most rhetoricians—or writers of advertising copy—are of such political persuasion or such depraved morals.)

Such is the poetry of exclusion. The poetry of inclusion, on the other hand, is richer, more complicated, and more thoroughly detached from local issues and actions. Because of the nature of language it appears more interesting, and because of the nature of human experience, more honest. It refuses to ignore other contexts and it invites the reader to experience the poem in terms of the widest context of his experience.

In the *Principles*, Richards had offered as a test for the quality of poetry its capacity to sustain the reader's ironic contemplation. The theory of context renders the utility of the test plausible. Exposure to irony reveals the price paid in order to achieve unity. For the ironic exposure amounts in fact to relating the limited and sequestered context to other (and therefore necessarily different) contexts. It is at once disclosed that the unity of such a poem can be maintained only within its hothouse environment.

In such cases, obviously something more than formal unity is at stake. That is, the formal unity of the poem, if it is not merely specious, reflects and expresses a coherent view (account of? perspective on? vision of?) human experience. To widen the context of the poem—to challenge its ability to mesh with other contexts—tests the fidelity of its language to the language of human experience. If its coherence rests upon the poet's having conveniently forgotten about, of having deliberately ignored, other relevant areas of human experience, the act of associating the poem with such contexts exposes the spurious nature of its claims.

The English neoclassical critics described the function of metaphor as either that of heightening and ennobling the subject or of providing a clarifying illustration of what the poet means to say—or both together. In this view resides a modicum of sense, perhaps, but what that sense is and what it is not is best revealed by Richards' concept of a metaphor as a transaction between contexts. Thus, an ennoblement achieved by bringing to bear on the subject larger and more complicated fields of interest is very different from prettification—a cosmetic job; and an illustration achieved by joining to the literal description a whole new realm of interest makes the "illustration" something very different from a mechanical diagram. What the poet says through metaphor conceived in these terms constitutes indeed a new insight and involves a process of discovery. For, as Richards makes plain, the two different contexts brought together through the poet's transaction allow him to say something that can be said in no other way. To quote Richards' own words: ". . . in many of the most important uses of metaphor, the copresence of the vehicle and tenor [14] results in a meaning (to be clearly distinguished from the tenor) which is not attainable without their interaction."

The whole thrust of *The Philosophy of Rhetoric* is directed to the importance of metaphor as our prime instrument for making connections and bringing our various experiences into harmony and unity. Moreover, in the last chapter, Richards pays due—though not exclusive —attention to the factor of tension in metaphor. He writes:

> As the two things ["compared" by the poet] are more remote, the tension created is, of course, greater. That tension is the

14. So thoroughly have these two terms become part of the vocabulary of literary criticism that it may be worth reminding the reader that they were of Richards' own devising and that he used them first in *The Philosophy of Rhetoric*.

spring of the bow, the source of the energy of the shot, but we
ought not to mistake the strength of the bow for the excellence
of the shooting; or the strain for the aim. And bafflement is an
experience of which we soon tire, and rightly.

We should not indeed calculate the worth of the metaphor by the
amount of tension that it generates. Certain contemporary poets might
take note, though we should not forget on the other hand that the
complete absence of tension implies no metaphor at all—no transaction
between contexts but a mere tautology: here the difference between "My
love is like a red, red rose" and "A rose is a rose is a rose" is absolute.

The "excellence of the shooting" is indeed the main matter, but it is
also a complex matter, and is utterly different from the scientist's special
focus upon measurable identities and likenesses. As Richards puts it in
the last chapter of his *Rhetoric*: "In general, there are few metaphors in
which disparities between tenor and vehicles are not as much operative
as the similarities. Some similarity will commonly be the ostensive
ground of the shift, but the peculiar modification of the tenor which the
vehicle brings about is even more the work of their unlikeness than of
their likeness." The poet must make his pattern of likeness out of
materials which literally are unlike one another.

I have mentioned the operational validity of Richards' concept of
tension and especially of his definition of metaphor as a transaction between contexts. I think it would be useful here for me to offer a somewhat detailed illustration. Robert Frost's *Range-Finding* is not one of
his most celebrated poems and many readers would not be prepared to
concede that it has in its makeup any element of tension; but these very
lacks and deficiencies make it the better for my purposes. For the issue
is the *general* applicability of Richards' concept of tension and his definition of metaphor.

The battle rent a cobweb diamond-strung
And cut a flower beside a groundbird's nest
Before it stained a single human breast.
The stricken flower bent double and so hung.
And still the bird revisited her young.
A butterfly its fall had dispossessed,
A moment sought in air his flower of rest,
Then lightly stooped to it and fluttering clung.
On the bare upland pasture there had spread
O'ernight 'twixt mullein stalks a wheel of thread

And straining cables wet with silver dew.
A sudden passing bullet shook it dry.
The indwelling spider ran to greet the fly,
But finding nothing, sullenly withdrew.

The first shots of the battle are fairly called mere range finding. The bullets kill none of the human contestants. They effect only minor violations of nature—such as cutting the stalk of a flower half-through, or shaking the dew off a cobweb. A hasty reading of the poem may give the impression that this sonnet is simply repeating a romantic stereotype: we are shown a nature that is calm, beautiful, and peaceful, but it is about to be violated by man, with his abstract hatreds and his mechanisms of death.

If the poet had limited his context—if, discreetly removing the spider, he had presented us with such a landscape, one in which every prospect pleases and only man is vile—in that case, the poem might have tilted over into sentimentality. Sentimental poems, as we have seen, make use of highly specialized and thinned-out contexts. Because they do, when we see them from a different perspective and as part of an enlarged context, their flimsy pretentiousness is revealed.

A related simplification of context might tilt the poem over into propaganda. If here the poet had pressed the issue of man's brutality not only to nature but to his fellow man, he might have pushed the poem in the direction of an anti-war tract. At some level, to be sure, the poem does involve an indictment of war, but the poem itself is not single purposed. It does not exhaust its meaning in securing our assent to a particular proposition or our vote for a particular law.

In this general connection, one notices how delicately but firmly the poet avoids any notion that nature is being seriously disturbed by this first shot. Although the stricken flower bends double and hangs low, the mother bird is only momentarily startled, and revisits her young in the nest. The butterfly, just poised to take honey from the blossom, adjusts its flight and stoops to the flower in its altered position. Nature goes on with its immemorial processes. Even the fury of the battle will not destroy nature: the grass will eventually cover the upland pasture once more; the birds will return.

The poem moves to its climax with the appearance of the spider. In the first line its presence had been intimated by the reference to the "diamond-strung" web. But the spider had not spread the web for our aesthetic gratification. The web had been spread for strictly business reasons.

The bullet, in shaking the dewdrops from the web, has touched off a false alarm. The spider runs out to capture the fly, and finding nothing, "sullenly" withdraws. Though the adverb "sullenly" nicely puts the present mood of the spider, it does something more, for the sullen spider balances the bird and butterfly: the spider is part of nature too, and the battle on this site which the human beings are soon to begin is not only a violation of nature but also answers to something in nature. Frost has been much too subtle to insist here upon a nature "red in tooth and claw," but the sullen spider, disappointed of its prey, makes its own comment on a world in which human beings are preparing to shed the blood of their fellows.

Poetry arouses the reader's emotions and it may rouse him to act. But the emotion should be more than a self-indulgence, and if we do insist that the reader be prompted to act, then the poem that provides the best justification for an action will be not the one that is shallow and restricted in its purview, but rich and profound and related to the largest possible context.

Robert Penn Warren has pointed out that *Romeo and Juliet* is a greater love poem than Tennyson's *Now Sleeps the Crimson Petal* or Shelley's *Indian Serenade* because—to use Richards' terms here—it does include a larger context. The sordid and the realistic are not ignored: the relevant experience has a place for the bawdy jests of Mercutio who stands just outside the wall of Juliet's garden, and for Juliet's earthy and common-sense nurse, who also has her bawdy jests and who will offer her counsel of half-measures and compromise.

Because of the complexity of reality and because of the nature of language, the poet had best not try to leave Mercutio out of account, nor ought he, in the interest of a single-minded effect, reduce his peaceable natural kingdom to loving mother birds and honey-seeking butterflies. He does well to acknowledge the presence of the sullen spider with its subtle web and efficient jaws.

GEOFFREY H. HARTMAN

The Dream of Communication

> . . . why hath not the mind
> Some element to stamp her image on,
> In nature somewhat nearer to her own?
>
> WORDSWORTH

1

Aesthetics has long been linked to a study of the affective properties of art. It should really be called *psychoesthetics*, for it investigates the relation of art to the life of the mind, and particularly the affections.

Following I. A. Richards' *Principles of Literary Criticism* (1924) new interest was generated in psychoesthetics. Richards envisaged the possibility of raising our "standard of response" not only *to* art but also *through* art to experience in general. Indeed, the arts entered the picture so strongly because they were the chief instrument by which the standard of response could be raised. Or lowered—"An improvement of response is the only benefit which anyone can receive, and the degradation, the lowering of a response, is the only calamity." [1]

Eloquent and onerous words. They reflect Richards' utilitarianism and suggest that the *Principles* are implicitly a Defense of Poetry. The situation was different, of course, from that inspiring Sidney or Shelley. It was (and remains) what F. R. Leavis described five years later as "Mass Civilization and Minority Culture." [2] Richards is not frightened into aestheticism by this growing contradiction between "civilization" and "culture"; he does not restrict the name and nature of art. On the contrary, he attacks the "phantom aesthetic state"—the separation of aesthetic from ordinary patterns of experience—and he extends this way the responsibilities of both artist and critic. If art is a normal part of experience (a "criticism of life," Arnold had said), then art is capable of exerting its influence on "mass civilization"; but if art has influence, art can corrupt, and criticism must be more alive and discriminating than ever.

1. *Principles of Literary Criticism* (London and New York, 1928), p. 237.
2. Published as a pamphlet in 1930 and included in *For Continuity* (Cambridge, 1933).

The sense of art's corruptibility is unusually vivid in Richards. Indeed, it is almost Puritan. He is not concerned, of course, with its
challenge to religion or morality but rather with its substitutability for
experience. Artists can become vicars of vicariousness and erode the
capacity for direct and critical response. Art should not become, any
more than religion, a popular narcotic.

> No one can intensely and wholeheartedly enjoy and enter into
> experience whose fabric is as crude as that of the average super-
> film without a disorganization which has its effects in everyday
> life. The extent to which second-hand experience of a crass and
> inchoate type is replacing ordinary life offers a threat which has
> not yet been realized.[3]

We recognize the immediate context because it is still ours. Bad
popular art was contributing to that "stimulus flooding" and "psychic
numbing"—as modern sociologists call it—already combated by
Wordsworth in his *Lyrical Ballads*:

> . . . the human mind is capable of being excited without the
> application of gross and violent stimulants; and he must have a
> very faint perception of its beauty and dignity who does not
> know this, and who does not further know that one being is ele-
> vated above another in proportion as he possesses this capa-
> bility.[4]

The undramatic subject matter of a Wordsworth ballad was intended
to wean contemporary minds from their dependence on the novel-
making and news-mongering of urbanized society.

The situation has intensified but not changed since 1800. The jour-
nalistic economy of plenty which is ours seems more frightening than
the preceding economy of scarcity. How does one respond to sensa-
tionalism? For both Wordsworth and Richards, responsibility begins
with the ability to respond. It is easy to see, then, why Richards wrote

---

3. *Principles*, p. 231.
4. Preface (1800) to *Lyrical Ballads*. Cf. Richard Bernheimer, in his important
book *The Nature of Representation* (New York, 1961). "How disastrous the effect
can be when secondary diversions take the place of reality need hardly be emphasized, for we see all about us the loss of inner wealth, the inability to taste the savor
of things that comes from acceptance of experience in terms of manufactured
substitute capsules. Nor can it be denied that there is a specific substitutional art,
created with the weary city-dweller in mind and distinguished not only by the
predominance of certain media such as those of television and of the cinema but
also by specific artistic attitudes." (p. 204)

his most seminal book on the critic's function rather than continuing directly his work on aesthetics and semantics. If art is the instrument which might improve or re-enable our response to experience, what improves our response to art? How does art become experience, to echo John Dewey? According to Richards, the principled critic's understanding of his task should lead not only to a more competent account of how art communicates but also to a more active discrimination between the communicated responses, and so to a "premillenial" perfectibility of the whole stimulus-response relation.

2

Richards maintains, therefore, an ideal of rightness but formulates it in terms of the adequation (however complex) of stimulus and response. Among the wealth of assumptions which support his book is the classicist's belief in benevolent normativeness. His emphasis on the possibility of reconciling opposed, or stabilizing extreme, impulses (it superimposes Coleridge's definition of imagination on Wordsworth's sensibility) is only the strongest and best-known instance of this romantic classicism. The Ricardian ideal of "balanced poise, stable through its power of inclusion, not through the force of its exclusions," [5] has been as influential in our era as Winckelmann's "edle Einfalt und stille Grösse" in his.

We do not have an English Winckelmann, but we have a Dr. Johnson, and Richards' comments on the normality of art can sound like pronouncements of the great Cham, colored by the abstract vocabulary of their time:

> So much must be alike in the nature of all men, their situation in the world so much the same, and organization building upon this basis must depend upon such similar processes, that variation both wide and successful is most unlikely.[6]

This tenacious principle of uniformity supports both "pillars" of Richards' theory: his account of literary communication, and his account of literary value.

To start with the former. "The arts," says Richards, "are the supreme

5. *Principles*, p. 248. The remark comes at the end of a beautiful description of tragic catharsis.
6. *Principles*, p. 195–96. Hume's essay "Of the Standard of Taste" (1757) is also relevant.

form of the communicative activity." Moreover, though "an experience has to be formed, no doubt, before it is communicated . . . it takes the form it does largely because it may have to be communicated." In fact, "a large part of the distinctive features of the mind are due to its being an instrument for communication." If we add to this that the "priority of formal elements to content" in the arts, their most distinctive feature, is explained in terms of a communications rationale, one wonders whether the medium is not becoming the message: the phantom ideal of a perfect response to a perfect input. "What communication requires is responses which are uniform, sufficiently varied, and capable of being set off by stimuli which are physically manageable. These three requisites explain why the number of the arts are limited and why formal elements have such importance." [7]

Richards will not give up the dream of reason. Its newest version seems to be the dream of communication—of total, controllable communication. It would be foolish, of course, to try and draw a straight line from Richards to Marshall McLuhan or B. F. Skinner. For all their apparent rigor the *Principles* are, in Harry Levin's perceptive phrase, a "methodology of doubts." [8] Yet to turn to Richards' theory of value is not only to find it merging, despite disclaimers, with that of communication but also to find this merger strangely consecrated by classical ideas of order.

Richards on value sounds, at first, purely cautionary. Like certain commercials, he warns us against accepting substitutes. With imitations and inferior goods all around, he recalls the possibility of first-hand experience and the need for discrimination. But has not the spread of technical knowledge, with craft-secrets becoming available to so many, made it easier to fake the genuine "fecit"? The problem of the counterfeit troubles Richards far less than it does some of the great artists of his time, notably Borges, Gide and Mann. He always presupposes something that, if it may not be called "authority," comes through as "standard or normal criticism" based on "a class of more or less similar experiences." What kind of criterion is this?

It can be argued that Richards aims at a convergence of judgment rather than its uniformity; and that what he calls a "normal" range of

7. *Principles*, pp. 25–27 and 192–93.
8. In "Why Literary Criticism Is Not an Exact Science" (1967), now in *Grounds for Criticism* (Cambridge, Mass., 1972).

response does not involve a belief in authority. Convergence implies a coming-together of empirical acts of evaluation; and *Practical Criticism* will show more precisely what is entailed. Yet the same book also shows how much is dependent on our being exposed to a certain "class" of experiences—in this case poetry and its traditions. The notion of a "class of similar experiences" is more complex than appears, for it may involve forcible or planned exposures (as in scientific experiments) which in turn depend for evaluation on accepted notions of what is probative. If this is so, the difference between an appeal to authority and to empirically founded judgment dissolves into a difference between what, at any time, is considered scientific or probative.

Once upon a time "authority" was considered so. It is likely, then, that the categories of probative and persuasive mingle insidiously, and that all values or standards must pass also a *rhetorical test*. Yet who is to devise, evaluate or improve this test? The question not posed by Richards—yet imposing itself on the life work of F. R. Leavis—is how to determine the "class" of communicants (respondents) which would, in effect, set the standard and so become an authoritative group—if not an elite, then a clerisy.

Perhaps the reason all this is not a problem for Richards is that his account of values is deeply influenced by the managerial model of the behavioral sciences. It helps him to give a scientific updating to classicist norms. The principle of uniformity modulates into that of an ideal conformation of stimulus and response, to be achieved by a scientific type of training. As in so many thinkers of the period, a "blessed rage for order" coexists with a residual trust in nature. Science and education are still Nature methodized.

3

If there is, however, a rhetorical test which affirmations of value must pass, this should lead us beyond a renewed appreciation of literary criticism (its role in the scrutiny of the link between value and rhetoric) to a meditation on authority. Empson and Leavis, who are closest to Richards, bring this out; so does Kenneth Burke in America. Richards, instead of confronting the base-superstructure split in society (Marxist terms respected by Empson) or the potential conflict between popular and high art (Leavis) concentrates on a methodological rather than sociological dichotomy: that of poetry and science, or of the two uses (poetic and scientific) of language.[9]

What a founder omits is often what his followers find most crucial. All the more so, in the case of Richards, since the evaded meditation on authority in his theory of value tends to distort his theory of the affective structure of art. To define the poetic use of language as "pseudostatement" [10] acknowledges the special power of a discourse that does not share the referential precision of science, and so draws a *concordat* between science (or philosophy) and figurative speech; but it fails to "value" precisely enough the character of non-reference in poetic speech. While increased precision or verifiability of reference justifies, and so authorizes, scientific discourse, what can justify literary discourse?

The two paths not taken by Richards, and which are being explored today, are a theory of symbolic action, inspired in good part by Freudian psychology; and a theory of speech-acts, inspired by post-Saussurian semiology as well as by a theory of institutions that winds its way from the work on authoritarianism done at the Frankfort School of Social Research in the 1930's (Horkheimer, Adorno, Erich Fromm, Marcuse) to Gadamer's and Habermaas' reflections on the relation between interest and inter-esse, or community and interpretability.[11] A further enriching complication is Wittgenstein, and the theory of convention implicit in language rules, especially on the level of illocutionary acts.[12] Yet if there is a shared problem centering on *literary authority*, or on the philosophy of rhetoric, there is as yet little awareness of the fact. Harry Levin's "Literature as an Institution" (1946) and Richard Ohmann's recent attempts to expose the ideological content of literature by means of speech-act theory could not be more different in their intellectual debts or teaching programme. Yet both reveal, and to a degree supply, the same defect in our "Principles" of literary criticism.

That there is an evasion of the sociological issue in Richards is also suggested by the verbal style of his *Principles*. They are written in a kind of Basic Philosophical English. Everyone with a certain level of

9. *Principles*, chapters 34–35; and *Science and Poetry* (1926).

10. *Science and Poetry*, chapter 6. See also additional remarks in the reissue of the book as *Poetries and Sciences* (1970).

11. One should add, perhaps, related and important work in the area of the "sociology of knowledge," from Karl Mannheim to T. S. Kuhn.

12. See, especially, John R. Searle, *Speech Acts: An Essay in the Philosophy of Language* (Cambridge, Mass., 1969).

culture can understand the terms and follow the argument. Elements are repeated till the mind behind them becomes clear through iteration and aggregation rather than absolute logical schemes on the one hand or artistic inventiveness on the other. At no point is ordinary, common-sensical experienced threatened. We have entered a Normal School of discourse; and this would be all right if it were not accompanied by an artificial dignity that "levels" us in quite another way.

I mean that Richards' language of description, in this early work, takes what dignity it has from a highly managerial scientific model, one that is born in the laboratory or is sustained by the ideal of controlled experimentation. Propositional sentences and impersonal forms of diction are its staple, as they are in bureaucratic "organization building." The book's excessively serial structure, moreover—which promises to treat things not "now" but "later," under their proper heading—though methodologically justified [13] also greatly impedes that integration or in-teranimation of words and impulses which the actual literary theory seeks to strengthen as a whole. In short, the base is English but the superstructure is the managerial imperative of what is now called Social Science.

What I say is meant to qualify and not to diminish our debt to Richards. The dis-suasion of his style is something that reflects his criticism of contemporary criticism. He helped to rescue literary studies for our time by raising its ante, by rejecting less strenuous conceptions. Literary study was to be neither a "soothing piece of manners" (the alleged forte of Oxford dons from Raleigh to Garrod) nor ersatz politics.[14] But what was it then? After what social acts of larger design and disinterested application could it model itself?

The answer is deceptively simple, and by no means obsolete. Richards' Defense of Poetry became intertwined with a Defense of Reading, not only because of his psychological bias but also because a science of the "behavior of words" seemed to him a social act of great, even redemptive urgency. How could criticism afford to be a luxury trade, and the preserve of amateurs, when the disappearance of a homogenous intellectual tradition endangered interpretive reading as a transmitted skill? "Intellectual tradition tells us, among other things, *how literally* to read a passage. It guides us in our metaphorical, allegorical, symboli-

13. "Every object is best viewed when that which is not separate is posited in separation. . . ." Aristotle, as quoted by Richards.
14. *Coleridge on Imagination* (New York, 1935), Preface.

cal modes of interpretation. The hierarchy of these modes is elaborate and variable; and to read aright we need to shift with an at present indescribable adroitness and celerity from one mode to another." Modern heterogeneous growth—it includes the rise of other media—has "disordered" our ability to read: that which was second nature is no longer to be relied on. It is time, therefore, to begin "the reflective inquiry which may lead to a theory by which the skill may be regained— this time as a less vulnerable and more deeply grounded, because more consciously recognized, endowment." [15]

There is no need to recall how consistently Richards pursued this project for a theory, from *Practical Criticism* (1927) to *Design for Escape: World Education Through Modern Media* (1968). It is clear, at the same time, that the necessity for theory arises when a skill disintegrates or must be reintegrated on a wider, more conscious basis. The wound nurtures the bow. Richards discerns a "general drift" in Western interests that has strengthened "the aptitude of the average mind for self-dissolving introspection . . . awareness of the goings on of our own minds, merely *as goings on*, not as transitions from one well-known and linguistically recognized moral or intellectual condition to another." [16] Like Pater, in his famous essay on "Style" (1888), Beckett in his study of *Proust* (1931), and Erich Auerbach in *Mimesis* (1945), Richards values fully modernist advances in the descriptive potential of prose, though he characteristically wishes to exploit this potential for the benefit of the greatest number. The theoretical study of language (which Coleridge is said to have initiated in its modern form) should be made "capable of opening to us new powers over our minds comparable to those which systematic physical inquiries are giving us over our environment." [17] The optimistic turn in his conception of science emerges once again; the dream of communication is the dream of reason made practicable.

4

Language, says Coleridge in a high-flown allusion, is "the medium by which spirits communicate with one another." Richards seeks to envision this medium, for there is still something of the quest-hero in him.

15. *Coleridge*, pp. 193 and 195.
16. *Coleridge*, pp. 220–21.
17. *Coleridge*, p. 232.

Yet, to adapt Browning's *Childe Roland*, "What in the midst lay but language itself?"

The envisioning is aided, as well as impeded, by associationist psychology. Wordsworth had already made it the base of a new, more scientific classicism which aimed at saner relations between thoughts or feelings and their objects. He can be as scrupulously abstract (if more long-winded) than Richards:

> . . . our continued influxes of feeling are modified and directed by our thoughts, which are indeed the representatives of all our past feelings; and as by contemplating the relation of these general representatives to each other, we discover what is really important to men, so by the repetition and continuance of this act feelings connected with important subjects will be nourished, till at length, if we be originally possessed of much organic sensibility, such habits of mind will be produced that by obeying blindly and mechanically the impulses of those habits we shall describe objects and utter sentiments of such a nature and in such connection with each other, that the understanding of the being to whom we address ourselves, if he be in a healthful state of association, must necessarily be in some degree enlightened, his taste exalted, and his affections ameliorated.[18]

Yet Wordsworth's over-qualifying of the associationist thesis shows his uneasiness with the doctrine. He saw that associationism, as a model influencing self-interpretation, unbalanced the relation between psyche and environment in favor of the latter. It gave the developing mind too strong an image of its passivity, or of the complex web of relations it had to thread to be genuinely creative. Coleridge, of course, made the intellectual struggle with associationism ("Matter has no *Inward*") a major focus of his *Biographia Literaria*. He followed Leibnitz in postulating a *vis representativa*, and so anticipates (without influencing) a development also found in Schopenhauer and Nietzsche.[19] Despite its defects, however, associationist psychology emphasized several aspects of mental life which made it survive to Richards' day.

The first of these was its realistic acknowledgment that we are indeed in a basically responsive position, or strongly pressed in upon by

18. Preface (1800 and 1802) to *Lyrical Ballads*.
19. *Biographia Literaria* (1817), chapter 8. For the intellectual background of the *vis representativa* concept, and Coleridge's search for a self-active mental principle, see Thomas McFarland, "The Origin and Significance of Coleridge's Theory of Secondary Imagination," in *New Perspectives on Coleridge and Wordsworth*, ed. G. H. Hartman (New York, 1972).

our environment. Not nature alone determines us, but more inextricably a second nature: associations established early, or constructions put on experience; in short, mental habits. Mind, in these forms, surrounds us like matter; it may be, in fact, a material medium of a subtler kind. How to imagine this materiality is the challenge; and Hartley's crude explanatory schemes only kept this challenge alive.

Associationism, moreover, was *structural* (though insufficiently *dynamic*) in its undertanding of growth. The web of habit being so complex, and originating so far in the past, one cannot change the single element. The whole system must be affected: not "world" or "mind" but the stimulus-response relation, the ecology or interanimation of mind and world.

Much depends, therefore, on the quality of therapeutic intervention, another important aspect of this psychology for Richards. He displays prudent respect for old habits and a knowledge that new ones require lengthy formation. Reconstruction rather than upheaval is called for. The idea of simples (e.g. religious conversion) is discounted; indeed, recourse to simples merely continues the problem. The therapy which art—the *work* of art—suggests is de-obstruction rather than a destructive conversion-experience. The artist outwits the stock response or qualifies the immediate reflex, and so allows a new and fuller working out of experiences, a more plastic and less impulsive reaction.

Thus the main emphasis in Richards falls on the *medium of response*. Art brings the whole soul of man into activity, said Coleridge; Richards prefers to talk of this wholeness in terms of the nervous system. It is more empirical, and affords the image of an extremely sensitive "material," constituted by "stresses, preponderances, conflicts, resolutions and interanimations . . . remote relationships between different systems of impulses . . . before unapprehended and inexecutable connections." [20]

It is his vision (one can call it no less) of such a medium that invigorates Richards' quest. So responsive, so deeply interactive, and yet so powerfully if inscrutably self-unifying: what medium can this be except language itself in its ideal form? Richards tends to think of it by analogy to the nervous system, developing this way the materialist emphasis in associationism. Not the analogy is important but what it helps him to envision. Bachelard believed that the human imagination was deeply material—that always, whatever its apparent content, it was

20. *Principles*, p. 237.

also meditating air, earth, water, fire. Richards' imagination is meditating a fifth element, more visionary and more material than these: the element of language. Its workings or the "unimaginable touch" that makes it ideally responsive can be described in terms borrowed from Wordsworth:

> There is a dark
> Inscrutable workmanship that reconciles
> Discordant elements, makes them cling together
> In one society. . . .[21]

5

The early Richards was a classicist of the nervous system. Freud also sought a neurological model for mental processes. The neurotic escaped neurology, however; indeed, it seemed to many as if abnormal psychology were discontinuous with normal psychology. Richards himself remained firmly committed to the latter, for several reasons. One was the scientific stress on verifiability. "The mental processes of the poet . . . offer far too happy a hunting-ground for uncontrollable conjecture." [22] More important was the evident sanity of the work of art, its victory over disturbances that may be psychogenic but can only be guessed at. As Richards stated simply and eloquently: "One thing only perhaps is certain; what happens is the exact opposite to deadlock, for compared to the experience of great poetry every other state of mind is one of bafflement." [23] Most important, though, was his resistance to ideological impositions from any sphere, whether religion or politics or science itself.

Richards, that is, feared the violence of ideas—the violence ideas could lead to when men enforced "spiritual laws by carnal power." [24] There is something in the crude structure of most ideas that can violate minds even less finicky than that of Henry James. Psychoanalysis must

21. *The Prelude* (version of 1850), I, 341–44. The wording of this passage is very suggestive. "Cling" evokes early tactile dependency as well as, perhaps, that bee-clustering which served as a microcosmic analogy for society; while the "dark . . . workmanship" is like the "mighty working, whereby he is able to subdue all things to himself" (even the corruption of the flesh) in *The Book of Common Prayer* (Order for the Burial of the Dead).
22. *Principles*, p. 29.
23. *Principles*, p. 252.
24. Milton, *Paradise Lost*, XII.521.

have seemed full of ideas, and crudely interventionist. What Richards may not have realized is that Freud and Breuer began with the thesis that the hysteric essentially suffered from an idea.[25] The hysteric symptom was diagnosed as a "carnal" reaction to an intolerable, because intolerant, truth. Richards, in any case, preferred an "impulse" to a "compulsion" model of psychic activity. The nervous system, that brilliant ultimate, that responsive *deus in machina*, made all other explanations superfluous.[26]

This combination in him of idealism and skepticism, a strong feature of modern British thought, resisted the science of psychoanalysis as long as possible. Richards sought a critical-scientific point of view uncorrosive of art, as of all normal experience. He even subdued the troubled genius of Coleridge to his approach, as if to normalize the psychology of art. To advance beyond Richards means, therefore, to respect the findings of psychoanalysis without abandoning normal psychology or the integrity of the work of art.

Something has already been done toward such an end: insights are provided by Kenneth Burke, or similar analyses of the reader's share, by phenomenological models of the process of reading or by Jungian studies of art's affective structure (Bodkin, Werblowski, Shumaker) and the Freudian applications of Kris, Gombrich, Fletcher and Holland. Gombrich, particularly eclectic, knows that a cogent psychoesthetics would have to comprise both Freud and Richards:

> It is the ego that acquires the capacity to transmute and canalize the impulses from the id, and to unite them in these multiform crystals of miraculous complexity we call works of art. They are symbols, not symptoms, of such control. It is *our* ego which, in resonance, receives from these configurations the certainty that the resolution of conflict, the achievement of freedom without threat to our inner security, is not wholly beyond the grasp of the aspiring human mind.[27]

But this, to quote Shakespeare, "makes mouths at the invisible event." No assured general theory has yet emerged.

25. See *The Meaning of Despair*, ed. Willard Gaylin (New York, 1968), Preface.
26. E.g. *Principles*, p. 246. "The joy which is so strangely the heart of the tragic experience is not an indication that 'All's right with the world' or that 'somewhere, somehow, there is Justice'; it is an indication that all is right here and now in the nervous system."
27. From "Psychoanalysis and the History of Art," in *Freud and the Twentieth Century*, ed. B. Nelson (New York, 1957), p. 201.

6

What will be at issue in a psychoesthetics of literary representation? It should result in analyses that are neither reductionist nor crude. The discussion of the oral or anal character of the artist's impulses has continued long enough. I admire E. Kris on Messerschmidt and N. O. Brown on Swift; and I am intrigued by Norman Holland on Arnold's *Dover Beach*. But their conceptual apparatus remains strangely fixated and the interpreter's attitude resembles, inevitably, that of a methodized voyeur. The "defensive mastery" (Holland) of the artist harmonizes with that of a critic always trying to keep his cool. Representation, moreover, is considered simply as a displaced mimesis, or even mimicry: there is as yet no convincing psychogenetic theory of figurative thinking.[28]

Besides a psychogenesis of figurative (at least, of autoplastic) thinking, we would need to resolve a question raised by Kenneth Burke about the communicative (public-affective) qualities of art. He quite rightly insists on them against the Freudian analogy of art to dream, but underestimates the difficulty of elaborating a general theory of affective structures that would comprise, without falsely dichotomizing, private and public, dream and ritual, elements. "Freud's co-ordinates," writes Burke, "in stressing the poem as dream, understress the poem as a communicative structure and as a realistic gauging of human situations. Communication, rather than wish fulfillment, is the key term for literary analysis." [29]

Communication, however, is not so easily ranged on the side of the reality principle. There is, as we have suggested, a dream of communication; this dream can influence science as well as art; so that wishing returns as a visionariness shared by sister-arts. Obversely, wish fulfillment is a tricky term, for usually the only fulfillment a wish can have is to communicate itself. The wishing studied by Freud remains a craving that cannot be satisfied—a wishing unto death. It is a reality-hunger that tests reality, again and again. So in religious thought the falsified apocalyptic prediction revives; so in art reader-expectations are aroused, defeated and renewed by an indefinite series of mock closures; so in fairy

---

28. I see a movement toward it, however, in N. O. Brown's *Love's Body* (New York, 1966), in the chapter entitled "Representative" which makes strong use of Ferenczi's speculations in *Thalassa*.

29. "Freud—and the Analysis of Poetry" (1939), as in *Psychoanalysis and Literature*, ed. H. M. Ruitenbeck (New York, 1964).

tales magical wishing often returns the hero to the *status quo ante;* so dreaming cannot merge with the daylight world but must begin again each night. Wishing can lead to as much reality testing as communication; and communication is a dream that cannot find its truth.

The paradox is strengthened by the persistence of Idealism. Despite Marxism, scientific empiricism, and other critiques, it is a type of thought that has not been dislodged, either in Richards' day or in ours. And as a kind of realism—the realism of the solipsist—it will never be dislodged but will continue to nourish our skepticism vis-à-vis a true or decisive contact with "reality." [30] From the idealist's point of view all "communication" is from within a prison. The verses toward the end of *The Waste Land,*

We think of the key, each in his prison
Thinking of the key, each confirms a prison . . .

are annotated by Eliot with a reference to F. H. Bradley's *Appearance and Reality,* an important revaluation of idealist philosophy. An equally appropriate gloss, however, and less esoteric, might have been a famous passage from Anatole France's *La Vie littéraire.* It rejects "objective criticism" with the assertion that the good critic "relates the adventures of his soul among masterpieces," and continues:

> The truth is that one never gets out of oneself. That is one of our greatest miseries. . . . We cannot, like Tiresias, be men and remember having been women. We are locked into our persons as into a lasting prison. The best we can do, it seems to me, is gracefully to recognize this terrible situation and to admit that we speak of ourselves every time that we have not the strength to be silent.[31]

In this exacerbated version of Pater, idealism shows its power as a form of skeptical and realistic thought.

Nature, said Mallarmé, who never doubted its existence, is an "idée tangible pour intimer quelque réalité aux sens frustes." That is true idealism, a reality-hunger that knows it must be frustrated. In Freud

30. The significant poetical precursor here is Shelley, whose Platonism (viz. idealism) is deeply skeptical. See, for the prior tradition, "Scepticism and Platonism," in C. E. Pulos, *The Deep Truth* (Lincoln, Neb., 1954).

31. The then currency of Anatole France may be gauged by the fact that Ludwig Lewisohn's *A Modern Book of Criticism* (1919) leads off with this extract, among others, from the Preface to the *Vie littéraire.* Eliot somewhere remarks on France's influence on the intellectual life of Paris during his stay there in 1910–11.

the reality-hunger of the libido is even more radically imprisoned. Our capacity for love is basically self-love, and when it turns to others it does so only so as not to die of self. "Ultimately man must begin to love in order not to get ill." Idealism here is degraded into narcissism, yet remains so constitutive that the turn to others or "reality" always appears as if superimposed: a vulnerable conversion, a heroic and alien superstructure. Is there really a *discours de l'autre* (Lacan) or only an interrupted monologue? The analytic situation plays that drama out: it exposes the hidden wishes of the analysand, it brings to consciousness his resistances toward or projections upon others. In so doing it reveals not only the particular (repressed) thoughts that make the attempt to communicate difficult, but also the curious link between wishing and communicating.

The therapeutic alliance of patient and doctor in clinical analysis could not work if the patient were wholly passive, if he did not "wish" for dialogue or communication of some sort. More precisely, his symptoms or dreams force him to seek help or expose him to others in such a way that they seek help for him. This shows that the repressed wish not only persists in the Unconscious but continues to seek expression. Why is this? Why can't the repressed wish simply "give up"?

The early Freud views wishing as essentially libidinous, generated by a sexual energy that, *qua* energy, must discharge. The libido can be repressed but not eliminated: Freud's epigraph to *The Interpretation of Dreams* and his reference to the fallen Titans who continue to lead a subterranean and volcanic existence, indicate that the energic wish is always there, pressing against consciousness, waiting to reemerge. There is no problem about why the wish "wishes" to express itself, because, precisely, that is its nature. Freud proposes an explanatory model based on an intelligible, if mechanistic, understanding of neurological events.

Yet *The Interpretation of Dreams* is devoted chiefly to what Freud calls the "dream-work": a description of the *cunning* of dream or repressed wish. There is nothing very mechanistic about either the manifest form of dreams or the hermeneutic task of the analyst. Freud shows, for instance, that the dream often casts thoughts into a visual (rather than verbal) form to disguise their meaning or charm the mind into admitting them. He calls this the dream-work's "regard for representability." [32] Yet he does not draw from this one of two possible conclusions that would modify his mechanistic model of the libido. The wish

32. Title of section D in the chapter on "The Dream-Work."

that "wishes" to express itself shows a *vis representativa* that should be acknowledged in addition to (in place of?) the *vis libido*. Or similarly, we could posit a desire for communication which is so strong, so idealistic and hence so frustrated, that it becomes inevitably a dream-state.

Even if the primary character of the dream-wish is sexual, its passage from latency into the content of the dream can only be explained in terms of a *communication-compulsion*. The dream aspect of this compulsion, moreover, or the autoplastic character of symptom formation, would suggest an "organic" idealism that is the beginning of the cure. By substituting action upon self for action upon others, it limits the *demand* placed upon others. That demand may be described as exacting from the world a defining (accepting or accusatory) response to oneself. If this is so, the idealism of art can likewise be seen as a therapeutic modification of this demand for a defining response: for achieving self-presence despite or through the presence of others.

Describing the *vis representativa* as a communication-compulsion allows us to bring in reader or audience—the social factor. Freudian psychoesthetics fails to connect the drive for representability with the drive for presentability. This social (perhaps "phenomenological") factor of presentability, even if often noted in the case histories, does not enter the basic theory because Freud considers the sexual or criminal nature of the dream-wish sufficient to account for the latter's difficulty in presenting itself directly. Yet to talk of the dream-work's "regard" for representability subtly merges two notions: the social-ethical one of presentability ("Vorstellen") and the expressive-aesthetic one of representability ("Darstellen"). It is surely because the dream-wish cannot be admitted into our presence that explains why it must be "represented." As in legal or ritual "representation" a subject needs a "representative" because it cannot be present in its own right. It requires advocacy or seconding.

There is, then, on the one hand, an excess of (semiotic and social) demand which I have called a communication-compulsion; and, on the other, a feared defect of (semiotic and social) status which leads to oneiric or symbolic "representation." Yet whatever the reason for the defect which makes representation necessary, we cannot assume that art exists simply to compensate us for that defect. The situation, in this regard, is even more complex in art than in law or religion. The analogy between the various concepts of representation breaks down because in art "representability" is precisely the thing being questioned.

For what is sought "beyond representability" is an *unmediated presence* (which raises religious problems) or an *immediate presentability* (which goes against societal or even anthropological ideas of order).

By way of illustration, let me apply these notions briefly to Coleridge's *Ancient Mariner*. Could it be a desire for "presence" which incites the Mariner to kill the albatross? What follows this self-inaugural act certainly heightens the presence of otherness. The new distance between self and other, which the self experiences in "coming out," is part of a separation anxiety which exaggerates the other into a quasi-supernatural or spectral otherness. The spectral happenings test the victim-hero in a way which takes us beyond the obvious moral frame of the story. There is, of course, as the poem makes clear, no fully achieved presence of self or other, but rather a necessary and compulsive repetition as the self realizes its difference and deepens its sense of isolation.

O Wedding-Guest! this soul hath been
Alone on a wide wide sea:
So lonely 'twas, that God himself
Scarce seeméd there to be.

We lay ourselves under contribution until a test is found strong enough to make us feel truly present, "sufficient to have stood." "The Daemon," says Yeats, "by using his mediatorial shades, brings man again and again to the place of choice, heightening temptation that the choice may be as final as possible." Art "represents" a self which is either insufficiently "present" or feels itself as not "presentable."

Basically, then, the proposed psychoesthetics would use an unbalanced "excess" (of demand) and "defect" (of response) model, rather than an idealized stimulus and response pattern. It is not by chance that art is a formal activity whose metaphors (trial, court, judgment, initiation) converge on the idea of a place of heightened demand or intensified consciousness. Whatever the historical circumstances that color these metaphors or affect the nature of the unbalancing demand, there is always the invariant quest to get beyond "representation" to "presence." A psychoesthetics of *literary* representation, moreover, would have to associate the demand we put on ourselves or others with an anxiety for language. Words commonly help to "present" us, and should we feel that they are defective, or else that we are defective vis-à-vis them (words then becoming the "other," as is not unusual in poets who have a magnified regard for a great precursor or tradition), a complex psychological situation arises. In every case, however, art's psychic function would be seen as either limiting a demand or reenforcing a potentiality of response.

7

A final glance at these two "therapies." I have already suggested that the idealism inherent to art (as to any autoplastic shaping) is not, as the early Freud thought, the sign of a virtually limitless narcissism but rather a precarious limitation of the demand placed by the self on others. Freud, of course, respects this fact more in his later writings, which develop the concepts of introjection and super-ego. Yet the problem of the demand placed by the self on itself (via the super-ego) remains; as does the problem of the anguish involved in turning away from a mourned object toward its substitute, or the mourning self.[33] Psychoesthetic theory, as I have sketched it out, does throw a possible light on this kind of pain. It suggests that the limitation of demand we call introjection (internalization) may raise the specter of a *further* limitation: of something more properly called a *sacrifice*. This sacrifice is not the self, even if, in some way, it is the self that is being "overcome." For those who seek to overcome the self do it in the hope of a magical transformation: self-conquest is assumed to be the key step toward conquering others—that is, toward fostering a corresponding achievement in this world or the next. The sacrifice feared by one who has internalized demand is simply that of the whole principle of *mimesis*: of a magical correspondence of internal action and external effect, of a mimetic aiming at "The Real Thing." In semiotic terms, of wishing to convert symbols into signs with real, immediate reference.[34]

What of the other solution, that of strengthening adequacy of response? Both mimetic and semiotic functions of art can contribute to this, insofar as they show that the source on which the demand falls is

33. See, e.g., Freud's discussion in "Vergänglichkeit" (1916): "Warum . . . diese Ablösung der Libido von ihren Objekten ein so schmerzhafter Vorgang sein sollte, das verstehen wir nicht und können es derzeit aus keiner Annahme ableiten. Wir sehen nur, dass sich die Libido an ihre Objekte klammert und die verlorenen auch dann nicht aufgeben will wenn der Ersatz bereit liegt. Das also ist die Trauer." Freud's important essay on "Mourning and Melancholy" was published in 1917.
34. This provides, perhaps, a point of connection with Kant's important formulation, in the "Analytic of the Sublime" of *The Critique of Judgment* (section 49), that the aesthetic idea "induces much thought, yet without the possibility of any definite thought whatever, i.e., concept, being adequate to it."

resourceful, i.e. capable of being animated (animation is an important figurative device) or made as inexhaustibly responsive to demand as the Well of Life. There is an important link between representation and re-creation. Art restores the sense of powers we feared were used up, or renews images associated with them. "Imagination and taste, how impaired and restored," is the title of Books 12–13 of Wordsworth's *Prelude.* The mimetic-restorative function, moreover, may not be all that different from the semiotic, since language can be that on which the demand falls.

No complete harmony between demand and response is really possible. One reason is that though art can temper demand or strengthen the responsiveness of the (language) source, it must itself enter the cycle of demand and response. It becomes a demand as well as responding to one. Moreover, insofar as we can generalize psychoanalytically on the nature of the demand put by art on us, or to which art responds, it connects representation with reality testing. Symbols or figures point to a lack: to something used up or lost or not sufficiently "present." They do not, in short, imitate so much as test (feel out) a desired mode of being. As Freud remarks: "The first and immediate aim . . . of reality testing is not to *find* an object in real perception which corresponds to the one presented, but to *refind* such an object, to convince oneself it is still there." [35] The *one presented* points, paradoxically, to the *one absent;* the substitute or figure to the phantasm. There is a kind of harmony, a correspondence of lack with lack; but it is easy to see how this testing could incite an indefinite series of figurative substitutions. All we need suppose is, with Freud and the poets, the persistence of wishing or the endlessness of imaginative demand.

A last complication that should be mentioned, and which carries us furthest into psychoanalysis, is the *anxiety of demand* itself. I mean an anxiety generated by the very pressure of the demand we put on things, and the resultant fear that they cannot "bear" us, that what loving-patience there is must turn to resentment and even hate. This feeling is, of course, very closely allied to that of trespass—of over-stepping a limit preventatively defined in religious or moral law (the "you shall not eat" of Genesis 2:17), or not clearly defined at all, as is the case in most "existential" situations. A radical perspective could even suggest that mankind is always *hyper moron,* or its imagination always *hyperbolic.* We are doomed to disturb God's peace.

35. "Negation" (1925).

The anxiety of demand can be studied in developmental terms. As a child grows up he feels more rather than less exposed. To be in the world involves a "sowing of needs" (Traherne): we multiply, consciously or not, our bonds, though generally we call them interests rather than bonds. Part of such self-dissemination is due to anxieties that follow the feared loss of first or parental love; but it is equally due to the realization that no love-object is inexhaustible. We can't eat the breast and have it too. "The child's relationships to his first object, as primitive man's relationship to a totemic animal, is fundamentally ambivalent. The object that is eaten is 'all gone': it needs to be re-created." [36]

Thus the anxiety of demand is deeply rooted in the fear that everything that can be used can be used up; that demand creates the danger of depletion; and whether or not this danger is actual, it is always there in the form of anxiousness. The moralist is anxious about waste, the neurotic about castration or death or money; the narcissist about "Am I still beautiful and loved?" Given this basic anxiety, in whatever form, the question is obviously not whether we can scientifically determine what is in danger of being destroyed by use but rather how we can re-create what is being used—the usables including, of course, our feelings.

It is generally acknowledged that art is an effective mode of re-creation. The artist may be as prone (or more so) to depletion anxiety. He may be unsure as to where his next inspiration will come from; and he may be tempted to use all sorts of magical, compulsive tricks to summon it. Yet the new object he creates answers him in some way: it reassures him, he feels a reciprocity there, a reality he can master somehow though he cannot shake it off. In Wordsworth's utopian formula, if the mind is "insatiate," then nature should be "inexhaustible." [37]

At the end of this propaedeutic essay, I return therefore to the "psychoesthetic" ideal of perfect reciprocity, of giving and taking humanely balanced, and even of a psychic development that overcomes death, repression and discord by a "mighty working" able to subdue all things to itself. Here Richards, Freud and Wordsworth are of the

36. Arnold H. Modell, *Object Love and Reality* (New York, 1968), p. 22. Needless to say, the depletion anxiety also takes the form of fearing that one's *self* is "all gone"—that it can no longer respond feelingly or creatively to influences. Cf. Harold Bloom's psychoanalytically oriented work on the relation of poets to great precursors: *The Anxiety of Influence: A Theory of Poetry* (New York, 1973).
37. *The Prelude*, ed E. de Sélincourt and H. Darbishire (Oxford, 1959), p. 576.

same company. For invulnerability is the other side of pressure of demand. There should be something "from all internal injury exempt." [38] Such anxiety myths as Balzac's *peau de chagrin*, a skin which magically shrinks itself and its owner's life every time a wish is consummated, is balanced by that dream the rabbis had of the righteous eating Leviathan in the world to come, without fear or satiety. A "consummation" devoutly to be wished! The word is useful here, in its ambiguity: Wordsworth calls his poems a "spousal verse" to anticipate a great and blissful "consummation"—a universally shared vision of Nature as re-created rather than consumed by the demands of consciousness.[39] A consuming that does not consume but consummates: this is indeed the feast of the blessed.

38. *The Prelude*, V.65–68. Wordsworth's statement, which refers in context to "Poetry and Geometric Truth," is part of his own Dream of Communication. As regards geometry the thought is commonplace. "Except in geometry," Coleridge writes in the *Biographia*, "all symbols of necessity involve an apparent contradiction." Wordsworth is saying, by a strong metaphor, that the symbolic language of poetry heals or subsumes contradiction. Cf., for the metaphor of invulnerability, Richards' praise of Tragedy: "It can take anything into its organization, modifying it so that it finds a place. It is invulnerable . . ." (*Principles*, p. 247).
39. See the "Recluse" fragment, quoted in Wordsworth's Prospectus to *The Excursion* (1814).

HELEN VENDLER

Jakobson, Richards, and Shakespeare's Sonnet CXXIX

Th'expense of spirit in a waste of shame
Is lust in action; and till action, lust
Is perjur'd, murd'rous, bloody, full of blame,
Savage, extreme, rude, cruel, not to trust;
Enjoy'd no sooner, but despised straight;
Past reason hunted; and no sooner had,
Past reason hated as a swallow'd bait
On purpose laid to make the taker mad:
Mad in pursuit, and in possession so;
Had, having, and in quest to have, extreme;
A bliss in proof, and prov'd, a very woe;
Before, a joy propos'd; behind, a dream.
All this the world well knows; yet none knows well
To shun the heaven that leads men to this hell.[1]

In I.A. Richards' memorable Harvard courses on poetry, the exquisite commentaries heard by his students were remarkable, above all else, for the way in which they revealed aspects of famous poems which rendered those poems once again new. Paraphrase became, in Richards' lectures, the high art it rightly is. Richards never voiced formal canons of criticism, but his example was a formidable rebuke to any blurred rendering of poetic meanings. Richards' weighing of significance was

1. Edward Hubler, ed., *Shakespeare's Songs and Poems* (McGraw-Hill: New York, 1959), 139.

like the weighing of gold dust on a balance Ezra Pound's father once showed him at the Philadelphia mint, a balance able to weigh a signature. Richards always knew that hair's breadth of "internal difference/ Where the meanings are."

It is not surprising, then, that Richards should have interested himself in the recent articles of his Harvard colleague Roman Jakobson, articles which attempt to give exhaustive and careful linguistic descriptions of famous poems.[2] Richards' essay on Jakobson's recent monograph on Sonnet CXXIX[3] praised Jakobson's intent and accomplishment without agreeing entirely with Jakobson's method and conclusions. As to the method, Richards remarks:

> The machinery of distinctions used in the account has developed to meet general linguistic needs and purposes. It has only in part been devised primarily and expressly for the description of poetic structure. It may therefore distort, may invite attention to features not essential to the poetic process. . . . (590)

(Jakobson's use of binary correspondences, a method derived from information theory, is largely in question here.) Richards adds, and the italics are his, that there is *"much more"* than Jakobson's "phonogrammatic-semantic interplay" to be "in some way taken account of before a fully satisfying description of how a poem works can be given." (590) However, Richards' deepest reservations are voiced not against Jakobson's method but against his interpretation of the sonnet. Characteristically, Richards puts his objections with a dry aside: Jakobson "seems to be placing Shakespeare at a viewpoint not too far removed from that of the author of *Milton's God*" (590): Shakespeare, in Jakobson's interpretation, sees God as a cruel manipulator leading hapless passive men into a hell of lust. "The final line [of the sonnet]," says

2. The first of these articles, written in collaboration with Claude Lévi-Strauss, appeared almost a decade ago: "*Les Chats* de Charles Baudelaire," *L'Homme*, 2 (1962), 5–21. An English version, translated by Katie Furness-Lane, appears in Michael Lane's *Structuralism: A Reader* (Jonathan Cape: London, 1970), 202–21. Since that time, Jakobson has written articles on Poe's *The Raven*, a poem from the *Arcadia*, and Blake's *Infant Sorrow*. None of these is so complicated as the one on *Les Chats* or as the most recent monograph, "Shakespeare's Verbal Art in *Th'Expence of Spirit*" (Mouton: The Hague, 1970), 33 pp., to which this paper will address itself. Jakobson's method of binary correspondence remains the same from *Les Chats* onward. Page references to the monograph on Sonnet CXXIX will be incorporated in the body of this essay.

3. "Jakobson's Shakespeare: The Subliminal Structures of a Sonnet," *TLS* (28 May 1970), 589–90. Page references are in the text.

Jakobson, "seems to allude to the ultimate persona, the celestial condemner of mankind." (27) Elsewhere, Jakobson refers to "heaven's sovereign and hellish torment" (21), and notes that "the final . . . line brings the exposure of the malevolent culprit, *the heaven that leads men to this hell,* and thus discloses by what perjurer the joy was proposed and the lure laid." (18) "Many readers, many minds," Richards wryly comments, and warns against taking the sonnet as "a preachment, a hortatory discourse." (590)

One would give a great deal for a counter-essay on the sonnet by Richards. For him the sonnet exists—as it does not for Jakobson—in the matrix of all the English poems preceding it and following it, a linguistic sub-set which is its world and conditions its meanings. A counter-essay replying to Jakobson's article on *Les Chats* has been written by Michael Riffaterre,[4] and its interpretive conclusions are significantly different from those arrived at by Jakobson. The need for selection among remarked details in arriving at interpretations of poetry appears as a central point both in Riffaterre's essay and in Morton Bloomfield's recent remarks on Jakobson's monograph.[5] Bloomfield, however, reminds us as well that a poem "is only partially referential and meaningful. It is also non-referential and meaningless in the ordinary sense of the word. . . . [Jakobson's] type of analysis . . . gives us a sense of the poem's own selfness and self-reference: what it says about itself." If Jakobson's essay convinces us only in part, it nonetheless amply shows the wealth of redundancy in the formal structure and verbal patterning of a poem, at least of a certain kind of poem.

But since I agree with Richards that there is more to be taken account of in this poem than what Jakobson has seen, and since I believe that there are "phono-grammatic-semantic" aspects to the poem that Jakobson's method precludes his noticing, I should like to take careful notice here of the linguistic and grammatical and semantic and rhetorical features of the sonnet which strike me, and to ask what problems of interpretation they raise. (I omit almost entirely any attention to the phonological level, since I have not yet seen convincing evidence that as a rule sound and sense are in any degree necessarily related.) I propose

4. "Describing Poetic Structures: Two Approaches to Baudelaire's *Les Chats,*" in *Structuralism,* ed. Jacques Ehrmann (New York: Doubleday, 1970), 200–42. This book is a reprint of *Yale French Studies* 36–37 (1966).
5. "Jakobsonian Poetics and Evaluative Criticism," *The University Review* 37 (March 1971), 165–73. The quotation is from p. 172.

to remark whatever features seem useful, conspicuous, and demonstrable to others; perhaps some linguist will be able to say how my categories and Jakobson's overlap. I should also say at the beginning that I am proposing no entirely new interpretation of the sonnet: the interpretation with which I am in essential agreement is that of Richard Levin,[6] an interpretation about which Jakobson is particularly harsh:

> Finally, is it possible for a reader attentive to Shakespeare's poetry and to his "figures of grammatical construction," as Puttenham labels them, to admit R. Levin's explication of this work . . . and . . . to gloss its sequence of strophes as a successive recovery from a "bitter disgust to a recent sexual encounter," [sic] gradually "fading out in the speaker's memory," and leading him towards a more "favorable view of lust"? (31)

Jakobson's reduction of Levin's argument skews his rhetorical question; but still my answer would be yes, it is possible for a reader attentive to Shakespeare's poetry to admit Levin's interpretation, and I hope this essay will support that possibility.

I should like to point out at once that Levin's interpretation, and my own defense of it in this paper, rely on the assumption that the speaker of the poem changes his attitude constantly during the course of the fourteen lines: he is not in one static frame of mind throughout. I think it is this progressive evolution of thought which neither Jakobson nor other commentators on the sonnet recognize. They are concerned to find one attitude (usually, disgust with the sexual experience described) governing the whole poem, and whenever they express "Shakespeare's attitude" they find themselves uncomfortably appropriating lines to that attitude which to an objective mind might seem rather to contradict it. The issue is complicated by the extreme simplicity of "meaning" in the sonnet: a line like "enjoy'd no sooner but despised straight" is in no sense ambiguous, ironic, or doubtful. The difficulty of interpretation, then, is not semantic but rather inferential; not thematic, but formal. The changing attitudes of the speaker are perhaps not at first evident because a change in time (before, during, and after the act of lust) is discussed either retrospectively or in the abstract, and the speaker affects a removal from his subject. Secondly, the formal self-presentation of the sonnet as an exercise in abstract definition disguises the fluctuations existing within.

At first reading, the sonnet would seem to be proposing, after the

6. "Sonnet CXXIX as a 'Dramatic' Poem," *Shakespeare Quarterly* 16 (Spring, 1965), 175–81.

exegetical manner of a homily, a tripartite definition of lust. X is lust *in* action; Y is lust *till* action; and Z is lust *after* action. X and Y are given us so rapidly in the sonnet that we expect Z to be proffered shortly; but we are made to wait for Z, at least until line 5, and when it comes it is not what we had expected. In itself, a tripartite definition of anything is rather unsettling, since our notion of an essence contained in a definition is precisely that it does not vary with time. Shakespeare depends on that invariant quality of a definition when he writes, "Love is not Love/ Which alters when it alteration finds." A definition is, even by etymology, an ever-fixèd mark, a boundary. Definitions varying over time tend rather to be the properties of farce (e.g. a definition of love before and after marriage). We must, then, given this strange proliferation of essence, look into the sub-categories that Shakespeare uses to define each of the three phases of lust.

The first defining sub-category is, grammatically speaking, a verbal noun, more an occurrent than an existent: lust is the expense, or as we would now say, the expenditure or expending of spirit (but Shakespeare's form, "expense," has an ending more conclusive than the ongoing "-ing"). It is a process, an action, more than a thing. The semantic feature to be noticed in the first definition is the extreme indefiniteness of the nouns: expense, spirit, waste, shame. If we were asked the definition in reverse—"What is it to expend spirit in a waste of shame?"—we should scarcely answer, "Why, lust in action, of course." The terms in themselves remain largely open-ended, general, and imprecise.

But when we arrive at the next description of lust, lust till action, the terms for the most part lose their indefinite extension and become remarkably specific. Lust before action is "perjur'd, murd'rous, bloody, full of blame, savage, extreme, rude, cruel, not to trust." If we ask what the members of this series have in common, semantically, we find that in general they presuppose a victim. One perjures oneself to someone else; one murders and bloodies some prey; one is blamed by the victim; one is savage, rude, and cruel (in the normal meanings of those terms) to others; one is not to be trusted by those whose good faith one will betray in the pursuit of lust. The victims are not named, but it is the victims' point of view which is taken by this series. They are the ones—not excluding the object of the predator's lust [7]—who are injured, who

---

7. The suggestion that one victim may be the person who is the object of the hunter's lust (while not excluding as other victims those who stand in his way) was made to me by Marian Tarbox.

do the blaming, who learn that the lustful man has perjured himself, who learn not to trust him, who call him cruel and savage and murderous and bloody and extreme. The problem raised by this series of insistent adjectives is why Shakespeare here adopts the point of view of those victims who are injured, accidentally and as by-products one might almost say, by the lustful man's blind rush towards his object. To achieve his lust he will lie, murder, betray—anything. He leaves a trail of betrayed social bonds behind him. In these adjectives the corpses left by his progress are allowed, like Caesar's wounds, to be poor dumb mouths: lust is seen in its effect on others, in its *social effects*.We are not told how the lustful man *feels*; we are told, rather, how he *acts* towards his fellow men. The victims, so to speak, cause the appearance of these adjectives of relational behavior. Blame comes from others as shame comes from the self, and this difference distinguishes the point of view in the second definition from that in the first. The only adjective which is not relational is one which invokes a norm: lust till action is, says Shakespeare, extreme. The norm is not here further defined, but the very oddness and broad scope of this adjective, by comparison with others in the series, causes Shakespeare to re-employ it later on when he reaches out for the single adjective which will define all three phases of lust simultaneously. One last remark about this series: most of these adjectives are normally predicated of a person, not of an essence. The series brings to mind a similar one consisting of adjectives also normally applied to persons but in this instance as well applied to an essence: "Charity is patient, is kind. . . ."

The third set of words, which we have expected to describe lust after action, is more difficult to isolate. Already, for reasons I shall come to later, the categories of before, during, and after, so confidently displayed at the beginning of the sonnet, are beginning to blur:

Enjoy'd no sooner but despised straight;
Past reason hunted; and no sooner had,
Past reason hated.

One reason for the blurring of time-divisions is the sudden entry of the past participle.[8] One might more properly say the sudden entry of a pastness of tense, since the line might be expanded to read:

8. These "past participles" are of course used here adjectivally, but they are also immediately referred to an implied subject who does the enjoying and the despising. What masquerades as description of an impersonal essence (lust) is in fact a description of an action by a personal subject.

No sooner [has it been] enjoyed but [it is] straight despised;
Lust is despised as soon as it has been enjoyed.

Grammatically speaking, there is a priority of time here. The enjoying is more remote than the despising, and we are, we may say, stationed in the despising stage looking back on the enjoying stage. However, Shakespeare's omission of the auxiliary verb puts the two participles "enjoy'd" and "despised" on the same plane of verbal existence, and this equality is reinforced by the parallel adverbial constructions "no sooner" and "straight." The same seems true of the end of the next construction, "No sooner had,/ Past reason hated," where "had" and "hated" conceal the same priorities of time but in fact take on existential concurrence because of their apparent syntactic identity.

We are, in short, left with some words—"hated" and "despised"—to define the stage of lust after action, and those words (since we are, as I have said, "stationed" in them looking back toward earlier feelings) tell us how the author of the act feels towards his own lust after the fact. However, these phrases, with their oddly concealed tenses, also tell us something about the phase "till action" which, until now, we had only seen described in terms of its relational carnage. Now we see the phase "till action" described in terms of its own doings: the lustful man "hunts," and he hunts "past reason." This is still a judgmental summary, as the earlier adjectives were, but in its measurement of a norm—"past reason"—it focuses on the quester, not on his victims. Nevertheless, it remains a *post facto* query of the speaker's consciousness, not empathetic, but on the contrary, severe.

The effect of the conflated participles is to make all these phases of the experience, in spite of the putative division of before, during, and after, seem equally past:

Enjoy'd no sooner but *despised* straight;
Past reason *hunted*; and no sooner *had,*
Past reason *hated* as a *swallow'd* bait.

There is a magisterial distance here as experience is so definitively formulated and so neatly docketed. However, the third clause makes one important advance over the second by saying that the revulsion from lust after the fact is just as immoderate as the attraction to it before the act. Both, and not only the initial thrust, are extreme.[9] The

9. However, the self-disgust, though mitigated by this invention of a wicked bait-layer, continues in the imagery of bait, since bait is generally laid for a predator. The

hating and despising occurring in the aftermath are, by the middle of line 7, seen to be as unreasonable and exaggerated as the hunting occurring in the prelude was: as we would say today, Shakespeare is showing us that we over-react with self-disgust after, just as we over-reacted to desire before. The norm implied in the word "extreme" earlier in the poem now excludes *both* the early precipitous hunt *and* the later "waste of shame."

The lustful man has, until now, been manifest in action (whether that action has been seen in verbal adjectives like "murd'rous," in participial constructions like "hunted," or in verbal nouns like "expense"): he has expended his spirit, he has hunted down his lust and has had it and enjoyed it; on the way to his object he has perjured himself, and has been murderous and bloody and savage and cruel. He has, in short, been presented as the rapacious predator trampling over all honor and obligation, and then, afterwards, sinking into a waste of shame, loathing, despising, and hating—a condition of self-blame as extreme as his former condition of appetite. However, by the time the self-flagellation is labeled immoderate, the whole experience is brought into question, and the reliability of the presentation of the lustful man so far offered is suddenly undermined. A simile is introduced which is wholly out of keeping with the previous myth of the rapacious hunter victimizing others on the way to his desire.

In an unexpected reversal, the object of the man's lust (once he has come to hating it), is seen as "a swallow'd bait/ On purpose laid to make the taker mad." Man is still "the taker" but surely, in this simile, an innocent one. Someone else has decided to entrap him, has laid a poisoned bait; the man has seen it as wholesome food, and has taken it, and has been rendered mad by it. The "bait" is in part a visual lure, and it initiates the whole hunt or quest that we have seen earlier (and which was earlier attributed solely to the immoderate desire of the lustful man); as soon as the bait is ingested the pursuit begins. But the bait is, at the same time, the object of lust which is possessed in the act

notion of a predator hovers strongly behind the earlier objectives describing lust as "murd'rous" and "bloody." Levin (178) notes the change introduced by the second use of the phrase "past reason" and adds, "The first qualification of the speaker's revulsion [is] his admission in line five, quickly passed over, that lust is 'Enjoy'd.'" Levin also quotes J.M. Robertson's remark (from *The Problems of the Shakespeare Sonnets* [Geo. Rutledge & Sons: London, 1926], 219) that the words "Past reason hated" act "to the damage of the argument." I of course believe, with Levin, that Shakespeare intended both the qualification and the damage.

itself; you are mad after you take it, but also before you take it and while you take it: it is

> . . . a swallow'd bait
> On purpose laid to make the taker mad:
> Mad in pursuit, and in possession so.

As I understand the lines, the taker (in this analysis of the hatred now felt by the disillusioned man towards his previous lust) is innocent of all wrongdoing, since he has been made mad,[10] and mad through no fault of his own since a wicked person laid the bait on purpose to achieve just this effect. These lines show us the creation of a counter-myth on the part of the disillusioned man, who in his hatred imagines that he has been the victim, not the victimizer. For the first time in the poem all three phases of lust exist under a single rubric, have a single definition:

> . . . to make the taker *mad* [after the fact];
> *Mad* in pursuit, and in possession *so*.

The madness of all three phases yields the second panoramic rubric of definition:

Had, having, and in quest to have, *extreme*.

We have arrived, surprisingly, at an identification of all the three phases of lust. I say surprisingly because the speaker—whom we may call Shakespeare for brevity—was so utterly at pains from the beginning to separate the phases from each other, almost fussily so. We must also mention that at the beginning Shakespeare seemed excessively concerned with Phase I—lust till action—devoting to it the conspicuous spate of adjectives. Phase III—lust after action with its attendant self-loathing—has had some attention; but Phase II—lust in action—has had very little. We know that it is the expense of spirit, and that Shakespeare has used about it the words "enjoy'd," "had," and "swallow'd."

With these proportions of attention kept in mind, we can glance at the last four lines. At first, line 11 seems to be returning to the dichotomies of lines 5–7:

10. Jakobson clearly believes the person who laid the bait to be God, as his remarks on page 18 of the monograph show. Such a conception of God, though voiced by unsympathetic characters in Shakespeare ("As flies to wanton boys," etc.) is wholly out of character in the Sonnets and is I believe indefensible.

Enjoy'd no sooner, but despised straight;
Past reason hunted; and no sooner had,
Past reason hated.

A bliss in proof, and prov'd, a very woe;
Before, a joy propos'd; behind, a dream.

But where the earlier lines are judgmental, lines 11–12 are empathetic.
If lust, while it is being experienced in act, is, as these latter lines tell
us, a bliss, then we have come a long way from the previous definition
of lust in action as "a waste of shame." The definition in the first line
of the sonnet is one formulated by a mentality already in the grip of
self-loathing, while the definition formulated in line 11 is conceived by
a mentality which is able to remember (or to say objectively) what lust
felt like in action, and therefore what it then *was*. Lines 11–12 also tell
us that before, as well as during, lust is a joy (though we had been told
in lines 3–4 that "before" was a particularly repulsive phase). What we
now have, then, is competing definitions. One definition is made by
the shuddering *post facto* mind which says "Before is horrible, marked
by gross immorality," and "During is like swallowing a poisoned bait":
the second definition is formulated by a more objective mind which says
that lust is defined by what it felt like: "Before was joy in the envisag-
ing," and "During was pure bliss." In the second set of these definitions,
Shakespeare is putting himself completely within the *sequential* experience of the lustful man. It certainly seems to the man in the grip
of lust, Shakespeare tells us, that he is proposing joy, and enjoying bliss,
and naturally anyone rational would want to pursue joy and bliss. It is
only afterwards that man awakes to woe, self-loathing, or a sense of de-
ception:

So have I had thee as a dream doth flatter;
In sleep a king, but waking no such matter.

From a judgment of carnage wrought by lust (ll. 1–4) we have passed
to a rueful sympathy with its intensity of pleasure. Lust is now seen as
pure nouns: bliss, woe, joy, dream. It is no longer a verbal noun ("expense") nor an adjective of social effect ("savage," etc.) nor a past
interior experience ("enjoy'd," "despised") nor an adjective of trans-
gressed norm ("mad," "extreme"), but rather it is at last something
with nominal status. This sort of definition is rather what we might
have been expecting from the beginning—a copulative noun to define

a subject noun ("lust"). And so to reach a series of nouns at last is somewhat like the subsidence into an expected tonic at the end of a piece of music.

The appearance of these nouns at the end of the poem leads us to realize that what has been being defined up to now in the poem is not really in any objective way "lust," but rather it has been the self-definition of his lustful experience by a lustful man, and a definition springing from a particular state of mind, the unbalanced state of reaction. As I said earlier, most of the adjectives in the series occupying lines 3–4 are normally predicated of a person, not an essence, and though used here to define an ostensible essence, they arise through the manifestation of that essence in human action. The other grammatical formations, which essentially speak about lust in passive forms, imply a human agent, even if the agent remains unnamed:

lust is the expense (by someone) of spirit in a waste of shame (felt by some-
    one);
lust before action (makes someone) perjured, murderous, etc.;
lust is no sooner enjoyed (by someone) than it is despised (by that person),
    no sooner hunted and had (by someone) than it is hated (by that
    person);
lust (makes someone) mad and extreme;
lust is a bliss, a woe, a joy, a dream.

The difference in the last predication is immediately striking. For the first time we find a true copula, noun-noun, essence-essence. The predication is analytic rather than purely descriptive; something more definitive than the earlier accounts is being voiced.

With these four nouns we have returned to the distinctions between stages of lust with which the poem began, but the ethical *differentia* of the beginning have given way to the epistemological *differentia* of the end, which give no priority of reality-value to either stage, early or late, of lust. Before, it was a joy: behind, it was a dream. There is no complacency: Shakespeare does not say, "Before, it seemed a bliss, but now I know it was really a woe"; nothing of that sort is suggested. Both statements are true, and both are equally true. There is no single adequate definition of lust possible. Lust is a heaven, lust is a hell. If it were not so, if one "learned" that it was "really" a hell, then one would be more reluctant to go that way again. But it is both bliss and woe, joy and dream, heaven and hell, and therefore the heaven will keep winning converts, the hell will keep receiving sadder, but not wiser, men.

It should be very clear that Shakespeare is not stating the conventional Petrarchan paradoxes about burning and freezing at the same time. His lust is bliss at one time, woe at another, not both simultaneously. But both are true descriptions of the essence under scrutiny. It will be seen from these comments that Shakespeare's definitions (and by implication his feelings) change immensely, and progressively, through the sonnet.[11] This sonnet is one of many poems (Herbert has several such) affecting the impersonal but in fact entirely personal beneath their seeming detachment. The proper response at the end of such a poem is Herbert's at the end of "Man"—"My God, I mean myself." The speaker of this sonnet too "means himself," and though the announced aim is to define something and putatively to exhort someone else against it [12] (with a semblance of cool and clear-headed intellectual interest in describing a human phenomenon), in point of fact the sonnet begins judgmentally in a welter of feelings, the first that of shame: "I am ashamed." That broadens to a wider statement: "I am ashamed not only of what I did in the act" (which incidentally is not represented initially as an act victimizing another, since the shame is for the expenditure of self), "but also of what I did or would have been willing to do to others when I was hellbent on my desire—I was in effect a compendium of wrongdoing" (such can only be the effect of the encyclopedic calendar of adjectives of injustice). Such self-reproach will, as we already know, shortly be condemned as "past reason," but for the moment Shakespeare wallows in self-flagellation. In this mood of aftermath, the blame is at first all self-blame.

The interest next centers not on how wicked the speaker has been and how ashamed he is, but rather, as Jakobson rightly notes (19), on the mysterious metamorphosis between before and after: no sooner is lust enjoyed but it is despised, no sooner hunted and had than it is hated. "Love alters not"; but lust, it would seem, alters in a flash, in

11. Levin points out, very accurately, how this "complex reversal," as he calls it, distinguishes this sonnet from poems on similar subjects but maintaining static attitudes by Sidney and Donne (180).

12. Though Richards is I think right in warning us against a finally hortatory view of the sonnet as a moral preachment to another, my colleague Eugene Green has pointed out to me how entirely the homiletic structure of the beginning of the sonnet deludes us into taking the poem as an exhortation against lust. The poem returns as well, he points out, to its hortatory rhetoric in the ironic "wisdom" of the end. But, as he adds of the beginning, "The very tone of the preachment militates against its purpose. It puts one off; it lacks any compassion." The sestet reveals the moral falsity of the rhetoric of the octave.

the twinkling of an eye. Wonderment and perplexity, in these lines, supervene over guilt: the instantaneous curdling or souring becomes the focus of attention, and the very identity of the ego is put in question. "Am I, now despising it, the person who just enjoyed it? Am I, now hating it, the person who just hunted it?" The identity of the experience and of the ego is of course affirmed by the alliterative sequences (hunted, had, hated; purpose, pursuit, possession, proposed) noted by Jakobson (17, 24). This startling reversal in the ego may be likened to the change Troilus found in Cressida, whereupon he cried, "This is not she." The question here is, "Is this I?" The reason for the desperate invoking of the simile is a hope to save the identity of the ego before, during, and after the act, to find some way of mediating between the hunter and the hater, with the haver in between.[13] "Am I the hunter, the haver, or the hater?" The simile abandons that difficult question: "It was none of it me, I was not in charge, I was mad, and not made mad by my own fault either, it was someone else's fault, she laid the envenomed bait on purpose to make me mad, and I only came by and innocently swallowed it, and all the rest sprang from that." Harking back to an earlier excuse—"The woman tempted me, and I did eat"— this excuse contains a perfect condensed fairy tale, wicked witch, poisoned apple, innocent Snow White and all.

But we know that Shakespeare does not let matters rest in such a mythological reading of experience, in which he plays the role of a poor innocent made mad by the wicked arts of the experienced. From violent self-blame, "past reason," the poem has turned to the equally violent blame of an unspecified other (presumably the lady who was the object of his lust). It is all her fault, she is a sorceress; and his fragmented ego is now whole again since it was not really he who did those wicked things, it was a chemically induced version of himself, in a sinister Jacobean plot. Of course neither the self-blame nor the blame of the other will, in the last analysis, be allowed to stand.

Whereas the earlier adjectives the speaker used about himself ("per-

---

13. I cannot agree with Jakobson (29) in finding the simile "whimsical," since I can think of nothing less whimsical than this outbreak of hatred toward the one who laid the bait. Jakobson says that the simile, unique in the poem, is therefore out of character with the rest of the poem, and commands attention on that account. So it does, in its mythologizing, comparing experiences that are really not comparable, but though Shakespeare expects us eventually to dismiss its fiction, he does not take that fiction lightly, or expect us to see it as any less serious than the other phases of response.

jur'd" etc.) were both judgmental and accusatory, "mad" is judgmental but clinical. It is not accusatory because it is not, like the previous adjectives, voiced from the point of view of the victims. Rather, it is self-analysis: "I was mad." But "extreme" reveals another point of view. Perhaps it comes from Shakespeare's comparing his second, excusing, judgment ("I was mad") with his first pitiless one ("I was perjur'd, murd'rous . . . *extreme* . . . not to trust") and selecting from that first judgment the one neutral word. "Perhaps I was not murderous; perhaps on the other hand I was not mad; one objective thing I can note and say with certainty; I was extreme. And I was extreme before, during, and after." This objective judgment is still ethical, but it is measured not against the injuries of victims but against an implied ethical norm of temperance. The self is the norm here, the self and its appropriate scope of action, rather than the norm's being the community and its sufferings from the actions of the wicked. "Mad" (in pursuit, possession, and afterwards) unified the self under one exculpatory rubric: "extreme" (had, having, and in quest to have) unifies the self under another rubric, this one recalling the almost forgotten norm of temperance (the virtue violated by the acquisitive triple use of "to have"). It is as though, having experienced both extremes—the extreme of hating himself "past reason" and hating the lady "past reason," Shakespeare, recalling "reason," can reject both mythological arrangements of experience and think solely in terms of a violated personal norm. However, the behavior is still being measured in ethical terms, even if considerably more neutral ones.

Once this stance of descriptive neutrality has been reached, and the earlier hysteria of self-blame left behind, the sonnet can begin to be, as it had appeared to be from the beginning, a description of lust instead of an invective against it. But the description is, suddenly, no longer judgmental in the earlier sense. Lust, says Shakespeare, is a bliss early on, a woe later; a joy when proposed, a dream after the fact. This description is wholly psychological, and, for the first time in the sonnet, recovers the experienced reality of the act. The distortions of the aftermath, resulting in the initial diatribe, have been exorcised: we are not being given Sunday's view of Saturday's experience, as we were at the beginning, but rather we are being given Saturday's view as it was on Saturday, and Sunday's view as it was on Sunday, the joy and the woe, the bliss and the dream. Already, in the word "dream," as Levin remarks (179), we are passing to yet another stage—the receding of the

whole event, Saturday's bliss and Sunday's woe, into Monday's unreality. We even, by the end of the poem, pass into Tuesday's senten-
tiousness:

All this the world well knows; yet none knows well
To shun the heaven that leads men to this hell.

The summing-up, the air of aphorism, the artful use of "well" reversing
its own resolve, the paradox in the close, all show a psychological rigor-
mortis setting in: experience has passed into formula.

The course of feeling enacted in the sonnet seems common enough:
self-loathing, repentance for the self-interest and ruthlessness of desire,
a wish to explain how one could have pursued such a hateful course in
such a headlong way; a blaming of something or someone else to shift
the burden of self-blame; a realizing that to apportion blame in either
direction is only to indulge oneself in maudlin exaggeration; a recognition that we are so constituted that we cannot have foreknowledge
of endings, that sexual desire makes us pursue its object as the keenest
joy, even if afterwards it seems all woe and illusion. And, finally, that
we will do it all over again if the occasion arises, that desire is unteach-
able.

Such a recapitulation, however, does not take into account the hectic
and distracted phrases of the sonnet which, for all its formal regularity
and syntactic parallelism, so comprehensively described by Jakobson,
conveys a tone of frenzied illogic. I think the main source of the anxiety
evoked and provoked by the sonnet is the truly irrational zigzagging of
the speaker among his three phases of lust. Anyone truly in command of
himself and planning a dispassionate description would do his tripartite
division as Shakespeare "tries" to do it: X is lust in action; and till
action lust is Y . . .; but before he can neatly get to Z (lust after action) Y swells grotesquely, takes on monstrous proportions, rudely over-
balances X, and threatens never to let Z get said at all. The envisaged
proportions having been so grossly disturbed by the ballooning of Y
(and this matter of symmetry is something linguistic descriptions
should, I think, take notice of), there is a violent attempt to restore
symmetrical order:

Enjoy'd no sooner, but despised straight;
Past reason hunted; and no sooner had,
Past reason hated.

This is too elegantly said to seem quite human. And the hatred, once neatly established in its triad (hunted, had, hated) will not stay there quietly but swells into the somewhat illogically attached simile (as a bait is hated? as a bait is hunted? as a bait is had?). There is an attempt, once again, to restore analytic elegance after the explosion of "mad/ Mad" by the most rhetorically compact line of all, conflating all three stages of lust:

Had, having, and in quest to have, extreme.

But in this neutrality of elliptic dispatch, immediate feeling is lost. It is reassuring that the next line, by contrast, is suffused with remembered feeling:

A bliss in proof, and prov'd, a very woe.

(Keats, I think, was remembering this line when he came from human passion with "a heart high-sorrowful and cloy'd,/ A burning forehead and a parching tongue" to the Grecian Urn. The urn would in future days, he said, console other "woes" than his own.)

If one traces these comings and goings of Shakespeare from one phase of lust to another, the results are curious. There is clearly, in Shakespeare's mind, a wish to run over the experience again and again, to sort it out; but the mind can impose no orderly progress on its recollections. Sometimes the poet begins at the beginning and goes through to the end:

Past reason hunted; and no sooner had, past reason hated.

Sometimes he begins at the end and goes backward to the beginning:

Had, having, and in quest to have, extreme.

Sometimes the order is end, beginning, middle: the bait is laid

          . . . to make the taker mad:
Mad in pursuit, and in possession so.

Sometimes one or the other term of the three phases is left out:

[Before ?] Enjoy'd no sooner but despised straight.
Before a joy proposed; [during ?] behind, a dream.

It would be, I think, futile to attempt to schematize entirely these alogical jumpings of the mind through the hoops of lust. However, it is fair to say that the very phase which so bitterly begins the poem—lust in action—has, by the end of these nervous recapitulations, vanished entirely:

Before, a joy proposed; - - - - - - - - - - behind, a dream.

And during?

            . . . yet none knows well
To shut the heaven that leads men - - - - - - - - to this hell.

And between heaven (the prospect) and hell (the result)?

In short, what began as an ostentatiously tripartite division has ended in a simple duality: joy to dream, heaven to hell. That crucial and determining act—the deed in flesh—is overwhelmed, for poetic purposes, in favor of the mental states prefacing it and following it. The behavioral definition of lust, which must by its nature center around the sexual act, gives way to a mental evaluation, in which the non-mental act is eclipsed by its mental preface and postlude. We see in this poem an intense sketch of both these mental states—the eager anticipation and the appalled self-loathing; we also see what the eager anticipation looks like in retrospect viewed by the self-loathing mind; we also see what the self-loathing looks like when *it* is viewed in retrospect by the mind in a more equable state. It is precisely this brilliant succession of mental states viewed in the light of other mental states that gives the poem its rapid changing lights, and yet it is just this changingness that Jakobson misses in the poem, thereby missing the dramatic action which alone motivates the poem.

The development of the poem towards a simple dualism of before and after is reinforced, it seems to me, by the overriding rhythm of the lines. The prosodic norm is of course iambic pentameter, but the rhythmic norm has four stresses. This rhythmic emphasis is put into relief by various means, sometimes semantic and rhetorical ("lust in action; and till action, lust"), sometimes syntactic ("enjoy'd no sooner, but despised straight"), sometimes figurative (e.g. the chiastic constructions "Mad in pursuit, and in possession so," "A bliss in proof, and prov'd, a very woe"). In each of these cases four words are strongly stressed by emphases clearly arranged in the poem. There are some lines which do not fall into this four-stress rhythm, notably the adjectivally weighted fourth line, difficult to construe as either pentameter or tetrameter in true rhythm. The other difficult line is "Had, having, and in quest to have, extreme." The couplet, on the other hand, allows for the first time a true sustained pentameter, as rhythm and prosody finally coincide.[14] It may also be noted that it is more economical, rhythmically speaking, to describe the sonnet as trochaic. The sensible division of a line is surely

Is/ perjur'd/ murd'rous/ bloody/ full of/ blame

and not

Is per/ jur'd, murd'/ rous, blood/ y, full/ of blame.

The savagery of self-blame is considerably increased by the assaults of the essentially falling rhythm:

Th' ex/ pénse of/ spírit in a/ wáste of/ sháme
Is/ lúst in/ áction; and till/ áction,/ lúst
Is/ pérjur'd,/ múrd'rous,/ bloódy, full of/ bláme.

This is to read the sonnet as Hopkins would have read it, with falling rhythm and a free assortment of unstressed syllables, directed by the assonances and alliterations; this is I think the natural rhythmic way the voice interprets the lines, while keeping always in mind the theoretical pentameter norm over which these calculated variations are heard. These four-stress lines, present from the very beginning, help to deny from the onset the attempted tripartite division of lust, and form a dualistic counterpoint to the tripartite rhetoric:

Past reáson húnted; and no soóner hád,
Past reáson háted.

One, two, says the rhythm, as it spurts out by half-lines. One, two, three, says the rhetoric by its enumerations.

Yet riding over these antitheses in the rhythm and the logic and the rhetoric, there is the grand elementary principle of the poem which appears semantically, rhetorically, grammatically, phonologically, and thematically: we may call this the principle of concatenation. In this poem every beginning has a middle, every middle has an end, every end had a beginning, there is an after for every before, everything in proof eventually is proved. The elaborate linkages described by Jakobson [15]

14. It will be seen that I do not at all agree with Jakobson's prosodic remarks, especially his undefended and capricious placing of cesuras (reproduced on p. 9, described on p. 11), notably those in lines 3, 4, 8, 10, 11, and 14).
15. See his remarks on duplication of rhyme-words (10), the reproduction of sound-sequences and morphemes (16–17), the syntactic concatenation (21), the appearance of what Puttenham called "redouble" and "translace" (24), etc.

are the medium conveying this message. Heaven leads to hell; one unjust act begets another, as the lines in which one adjective engenders another demonstrate; "no sooner" begets "straight"; hunting yields hating; mad pursuit makes for mad possession. The elementary grammatical symbol for engendered concatenation, the sequence of tenses, reigns in the climactic line, "Had, having, and in quest to have, extreme." Such concatenations exhaust experience. There is no other tensed form of "to have" left to invoke; these have embraced all possibilities of what is past, or passing, or to come.

The distinction between "How did I act?" (especially in lines 3–4) and "How did I feel?" (especially in lines 11–12) is the fulcrum of the poem. The change from consideration of deeds to consideration of feelings enables Shakespeare finally to define lust as an essential feeling (a bliss, a woe, or a joy) or as a psychological state (a dream). The fact that Shakespeare only arrives at these noun-definitions at the end suggests that the initial desire of the poem was not to define "lust" at all, but rather to inveigh against an experience—that expense of spirit, that predatory quest. Thus the reversal of the usual definition-form: not "Lust is X" but "X is Lust." What lust causes, how others feel about its effects, what the responses of its subjects are to it—the heavily descriptive nature of the sonnet obscures its character as a definition. But by the time Shakespeare is prepared to employ nouns in his copulas, he has arrived at an epistemology of the successive feeling-states in lust which is less descriptive and more definitively analytic.

I have not mentioned here any number of minor points of difference between Jakobson's analysis of the sonnet and my own, though one would like, for the sake of clarity, that all commentators should be able to reach an agreement on relatively factual matters. What is more important, it seems to me, is to call into question Jakobson's binary method of analysis. Jakobson had hoped, it is clear, to find a useful method that could be applied to all poems, or at least to very many poems. In his method, one compares all possible combinations of parts: odd strophes against even strophes, early strophes against late stropes, outside strophes (beginning and end) against inside strophes (middle), pre-center strophes against post-center strophes, quatrains against couplet, middle two lines against the lines preceding them and following them. This method, so extraordinarily bizzare when applied to a poem, does not I think yield useful interpretations, and the linguistic features remarked by Jakobson could be described independently of his binary method. The method militates against any notion of the evolution of feeling in the poem, any progressive expansion or contradiction of thought, and, especially in this poem, the indispensable sequence of emotional logic which makes the poem a whole. The linearity of the poem is wholly lost sight of, and the many small points of suspense and climax ignored.

It seems that we are still without any "method" we can prescribe that can be applied at random to poems. Each poem will still dictate the method best suited to its own interpretation. Nevertheless, we should I think aim at the clearly demonstrable in interpretation, and Jakobson's wish to present evidence from the linguistic surface of the poem and thereby document findings is an example of candor, plainness, and truth-seeking. As I. A. Richards has even more plainly shown in his incomparable teaching and his splendid writings, there can never be any real quarrel between science and sensibility.

B. F. SKINNER

Reflections on Meaning and Structure

In their detailed analysis of the structure of Shakespeare's Sonnet 129, Jakobson and Jones [1] note that *"and very wo* instead of *a very wo* is an obvious misprint, under the assimilative influences of the antecedent *and* in the same line and in the first two lines of the same quatrain." Having written (or set in type) the word *and* three times in three lines, the poet (or typesetter) wrote (or set) it again although the meaning called for *a*. But what about the third of these four *and's*? Can we be sure that without the first two it would not have been *but*, say, or *yet*? The evidence is clearer in the fourth instance because *and* is a mistake, but there are presumably reasons why words are written when they are not mistakes.

An assimilative influence may bear on less than a whole word, and the fact that *wo* rimes with *so* is an example. Here again the evidence is better when it explains a blemish. Jakobson and Jones quote J. M. Robertson to the effect that "collapse recurs when *a very wo* fades into *a dreame* for the rime's sake" and Edward Hubler to the effect that "the anticlimactic position of *not to trust* is owing entirely to the need for a rime." But have we any reason to suppose that assimilative influences are not at work in rimes which do not show collapse or anticlimax? In Sonnet 90, for example, in the line *And other strains of wo, which now seem wo* the second *wo* may be attributed in part to the first and to an earlier occurrence in riming position in the second quatrain. In a prose version something closer to *unbearable* might have been more to the point.

The meaning of other words must also be taken into account. It is not surprising that one who has been speaking of perjury, murder, and

1. Jakobson, R., and Jones, L.G. *Shakespeare's Verbal Art in Th' Expence of Spirit.* The Hague: Mouton, 1970.

madness should say *wo*, either through word association or as the effect of a common subject matter. But meaning raises special problems. Structure has the enormous advantage of being accessible. The formal properties of Sonnet 129 are not all immediately obvious, as Jakobson and Jones have convincingly shown, but once pointed out they are there for everyone to see. But what are meanings, and where are they to be found? A dictionary does not give the meanings of words, it gives other words having the same meanings. The meaning of a poem is similarly elusive. When a person tells us what a poem means to him, he merely tells us how a meaning might be otherwise expressed. Suppose he paraphrases Sonnet 129 in some such way as this: "Sexual behavior is both rewarded and punished, and when we engage in it because of the rewards, we subject ourselves to the punishments. No one knows what to to do about it." This is not one meaning of the sonnet; it is only one other way of saying what the sonnet says.

To get closer to meaning we should have to look at the circumstances under which the sonnet was written. We cannot do that with Sonnet 129. We are limited to making a few guesses about what might have happened to Shakespeare to induce him to write as he did. It has often been pointed out that the sonnet is bitter. What could have been so bad about sex? Temporary impotence ("... *passion ending, doth the purpose lose*") is scarcely bad enough. Social, legal, or religious sanctions may have been "blouddy full of blame" and could have led Shakespeare to "dispise" himself, but they are scarcely perjured or murderous. Perhaps the best guess is the pox, but we shall probably never know. Fortunately, so far as the present point is concerned, it does not matter. Assume any plausible set of circumstances; how could they have given rise to a sonnet?

We gain nothing from supposing that the sonnet first came into existence in some preverbal form, that circumstances gave rise to an idea in Shakespeare's mind which he then put into words. If we begin in that way, we must explain how circumstances give rise to ideas, and that is much more difficult than explaining how they give rise to verbal behavior.[2] Certain events in Shakespeare's life induced him to emit two opposed and seemingly incompatible sets of responses with respect to sex. The sets are epitomized by *heaven* and *hell*. When lust is heaven it is a *bliss* and a *joy*, and it is then *hunted* and *pursued*. When lust is hell, it is uncouth (*extreame, rude*), deceptive (*perjured, not to trust*),

2. Skinner, B.F. *Verbal Behavior.* New York, 1957.

costly (a *waste*, an *expense*), demeaning (a thing of *shame*, full of *blame*), and violent (*cruel, savage, blouddy, murdrous*), and it is then *dispised* and *hated*. The two sets of responses are not really incompatible, because lust is one thing or the other depending on the time. Heaven comes first and hell follows, and this temporal aspect of the circumstances evokes several pairs of terms (*in action—till action, no sooner—straight, in pursuit—in possession, had—having*, and *before—behind*.)

These key expressions, which can be thus arranged in thematic groups, may be close to the "primordial" verbal material from which the sonnet was composed. (They were not all necessarily available when the poet began to write, since associative and assimilative influences could have generated other material as the writing proceeded.) They are far from being a sonnet, and there is much about them that any imagined set of circumstances will not easily explain. Certainly many other responses could have been evoked. Why this particular selection of synonyms? And what determined the attribution of "parts of speech"? A setting which gave rise to a *waste of shame* could easily have evoked *a shameful waste*, or *shamefully wasted*, or *a shame and a waste*. And what about the order in which the responses occur? Nine adjectives or adjectival phrases were strung together in the first quatrain: *perjurd, murdrous, blouddy, full of blame, savage, extreame, rude, cruel, not to trust*. Why that one order, when 362,879 other orders were possible? And which pair of terms was to go with which indicator of time? Why not *before injoyd, behind dispised*? Or *injoyd in proof, dispised when provd*? And what was to be done about assertion? (Very little was in fact done in Sonnet 129: only the two *is*'s in the first quatrain and the two *know*'s in the couplet assert anything. It is this lack of assertion rather than the lack of "logical organization" of which John Crowe Ransom complains that keeps 129 from being "a true sonnet.")

I have argued (using Sonnet 129 as an example; see note 2) that verbal material is worked over in this way to sharpen and improve the effect on the reader, possibly on the poet himself as his own reader. The point here is simply that at every stage the material will necessarily have form or structure. Even unworked verbal behavior has formal properties, though possibly only as by-products. At that stage it is possible that a poet's philosophy of composition could be expressed in the words of the Duchess: "Take care of the sense and the sounds will take care of themselves." But there are other sources of form or structure.

One is to be found in certain prior specifications. Shakespeare intended a sonnet, and it did not turn to an ode. But what is the role of "intention"? How does a prior specification work? One effect may be severely restrictive. Only topics of a certain size are available to the writer of a sonnet, and they must be developed with phrases of a limited length; only words or sequences of words which fit the iambic meter can be used; the rime scheme must be respected; and so on. Shakespeare did not suffer much from these restrictions. From an extraordinarily rich vocabulary suitable words were available, although some of them puzzled his contemporaries and still puzzle us today. He fudged his grammar (Jakobson and Jones point out that *not to trust* and *To shun the heaven* "seem even to transgress the grammatical standard of the Elizabethan time"). He punctuated ambiguously, so that his sentence structure was often unclear, but possibly therefore more effective. Riding and Graves [3] and Empson [4] have paid particular attention to this device. He was occasionally illogical (why *till* action, when the rest of the sonnet makes it clear that lust is perjurd, murdrous, and so on *after* action?)

We have some evidence of his success in fitting form to subject matter. He packed his lines with different quantities of meaning, and to some extent according to the position of a line in the sonnet. What might be called the density of meaning in each of the fourteen lines in the first hundred sonnets was determined in the following way. To escape from preconceptions about density, a rather mechanical method of scanning was adopted. Each line was first scanned strictly as iambic pentameter: "Bite *to* the *blood* and *burn* into the *bone*." When the accent fell on a preposition, auxiliary, possessive pronoun, article, copula, or such an ending as *-ness*, *-ing*, *-ance*, or *-ment*, it was shifted forward or backward whenever possible to an adjacent syllable not classified as above and not already included in the scanning; otherwise it was omitted. In the example the accent on *to* was shifted backward to *bite*, but the accent on *to* in *into* could not be shifted because there was no appropriate adjacent syllable and was therefore eliminated. A line of four accented syllables remained. This stage usually yielded four or five stressed syllables per line. Each line was then examined for syllables not yet included which were parts of nouns, verbs, adjectives, and adverbs, and these were added. The result was a scansion which

3. Riding, L., and Graves, R. *A Survey of Modernist Poetry.* New York, 1928.
4. Empson, William, *Seven Types of Ambiguity.* London, 1930.

took account of practically every important syllable. The method was arbitrary but yielded a plausible reading in almost every case.

The average numbers of stressed syllables in each of the fourteen lines in the hundred sonnets were then determined. The results are shown in Figure 1, which should be read as if it were the right-hand profile of a sonnet as usually printed, except that length of line is due to "density of meaning" rather than letters and spaces (the couplet not being indented). The average for the three quatrains taken together is almost exactly five syllables. The second line in each quatrain is, however, conspicuously short. Density rises toward the end of the sonnet, and both lines in the couplet are denser than any line in the quatrains. The last line is particularly so, as if Shakespeare had fallen behind in making his point and was forced to pack the line tightly. The

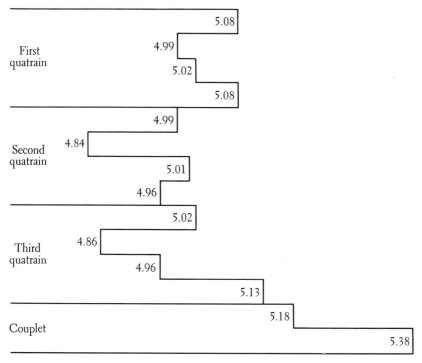

Figure 1. *Average Densities of Lines in One Hundred Shakespeare Sonnets*

The right-hand mean profile, where length of line represents density of meaning rather than number of letters and spaces. The second line in each quatrain tends to be short. Both lines of the couplet contain many meaningful syllables.

fact that the couplet often makes a point of its own and has little room in which to do so is probably relevant.

Why should a poet submit to the restrictions imposed by a prior specification of form or structure? Why write sonnets rather than maxims, aphorisms, letters, or short essays? What is gained from dancing in chains? It has been argued that early literature had the form of poetry because it was more easily remembered by those who recited it, and what is easily memorized is likely to be quoted. A philistine might say that a poet has an eye on public relations. He is concerned with putting his points across and chooses a memorable, quotable form. A philistine might also say that the structure of a poem makes what is said particularly convincing. Are we not more likely to assent to the conclusion of a syllogism if it is expressed in a meter which has been established by the premises and if it ends in a satisfying rime? Things have come out right; why ask whether they are true or false? But there are, of course, better reasons, many of which lie above and beyond prose meanings, although they are not exclusively matters of form or structure.

Formal properties which are not the result of a prior specification arise during the writing of a poem from the formal and thematic "influences" mentioned at the beginning of this paper. Word play is an example. A pun is necessarily a combination of structure and meaning, and even a vague *double entendre* may be related to structure. *In what form* can one write an opening line that means not only, as a French translation [5] has it, *L'esprit dispersé dans un abîme de honte*, but also, if Jakobson and Jones are right, ejaculation or the "spendings" of nineteenth-century pornography?

Some evidence of the mode of action of an "influence" is available. Form and meaning are both involved in alliteration and assonance. These properties are usually avoided in prose (we rewrite *pour eviter les assonances*) but are accepted in poetry. An excessive predilection for alliteration may have the effect of a prior specification and impose restrictions which are not always successfully evaded, but a moderate use is condoned and valued. It need not be "intentional." The dominant "influence" is formal rather than thematic. After emitting a response having a given sound, the poet is somewhat more likely to emit another response having that sound. The result is a structural feature which lends itself, in some degree, to objective analysis.

5. Jouve, Pierre Jean, *Mercure de France*, 1er mai, 1955.

Shakespeare's sonnets contain many alliterative lines. To what extent do they show an alliterative tendency? I have reported an attempt to answer that question.[6] The stressed syllables in the first hundred sonnets were determined in the manner described above, their initial sounds were examined, and lines containing no instances of a given sound, or one, two, three, or four instances were counted. The results were compared with the numbers of lines to be expected from chance, as calculated with a binomial expansion. The conclusions of that study were summarized as follows:

> *Lines containing four like initial consonants.*
> (Ex.: Borne on the bier with white and bristly beard.)
> Of these lines there are only eight more than would be expected from chance, and four of these are due to the repetition of the same word or words. Not more than once in twenty-five sonnets (350 lines) does Shakespeare lengthen a series of three like consonants into four, except when he repeats a word.
> *Lines containing three like initial consonants.*
> (Ex.: Save that my soul's imaginary sight.)
> Of these lines there are thirty-three too many, but twenty-nine of these are due to repetition of the same word. Only four are, therefore, "pure" alliteration. Except when he repeated a whole word, Shakespeare changed a line of two like consonants into one of three not oftener than once in twenty-five sonnets.
> *Lines containing two like initial consonants.*
> There are ninety-two excess lines of this sort, but the correction for repetition gives a *shortage* of approximately forty lines. Allowing for eight lines extended to contain three or four occurrences, we may say that once in about every three sonnets Shakespeare *discarded* a word because its initial consonant had already been used.

Jakobson and Jones note the presence of this kind of structural feature in Sonnet 129: "Each line displays a conspicuous alliteration or repetition of sound sequences and entire morphemes or words." But can we be sure that roughly the same alliteration would not have occurred if Shakespeare had drawn his words out of a hat? The result is not a statistical artifact. A similar study of Wordsworth showed, as one might expect, that he discarded many of the alliterative words which must have turned up as he wrote. In a poet like Swinburne on the other hand, alliteration is statistically conspicuous.

6. Skinner, B.F. "The Alliteration in Shakespeare's Sonnets; a Study in Literary Behavior." *Psychological Record*, 1939, 3, 186–92.

In a study of Swinburne's alliteration [7] the initial consonants in the stressed syllables of 500 lines of *Atalanta in Calydon* were examined. Instances were counted in which a sound was followed by the same sound in the next syllable, in the next syllable but one, in the next syllable but two, and so on. These observed frequencies were converted into percentages of the expected frequencies calculated from the total number of sounds. (No correction was made for the repetition of whole words.) The results are shown in Figure 2. When Swinburne uses a stressed initial sound, he shows a strong tendency to use it again in the next syllable, a slightly weaker tendency to use it in the next but one, and so on, the tendency remaining statistically significant for four syllables. The open circles show insignificant differences.

Figure 2 also shows a similar tabulation for Shakespeare. If there is any alliteration in these hundred sonnets, it is confined to successive syllables, and even there it is largely a matter of repeated whole words. (Some instances of repetition follow from Puttenham "redoubles" or "translacers," in which a word or root at the end of a line is repeated at the beginning of the next line. There are at least six of these in the first hundred sonnets.)

Writing under the control of prior specifications must be called "intentional." Only passages are allowed to stand which have the effect of fulfilling the conditions of a contract. Nevertheless, the first person who wrote three quatrains and added a couplet, all on a single theme, did not "intend" to write an English sonnet. If he found the result pleasing, however, he may have written other poems with similar structural properties, which at some point must have begun to act as a set of rules: to produce a particular kind of literary effect write three quatrains and add a couplet, all in iambic pentameter. The structural features which result from formal and thematic processes are not basically intentional (that is, they are not introduced by the writer because of their effects), but if the effects are pleasing, the writer may take steps to give these processes greater play.

Where should we place the structural properties pointed out by Jakobson and Jones? Are they "negligible accidents governed by the rule of chance," [8] are they generated by formal and thematic verbal processes, or are they the fulfillment of prior specifications? The extent

7. Skinner, B.F. "A Quantitative Estimate of Certain Types of Sound-Patterning in Poetry." *American Journal of Psychology*, 1942, 30, 64–79.
8. Jakobson, R. "Subliminal Verbal Patterning in Poetry." *Studies in General and Oriental Linguistics*, Tokyo, 1970 (Quoted by Richards in reference 9).

to which the features of Sonnet 129 are to be found in the other sonnets
is relevant. In a purely physical sense every sonnet has a center, and one
moves toward it in reading the first half and away from it in reading
the second half; the first seven lines in every sonnet are therefore
centripetal and the last centrifugal. The terminal couplet is necessarily
"asymmetrically contrasted" with the non-terminal quatrains. But other
features are quite idiosyncratic. Of how many of the sonnets can it be
said that "the odd strophes in contradistinction to the inner ones
abound in substantives and adjectives"? Or that "the outer strophes
carry a higher syntactic rank than the inner ones"? Or that "the anterior
strophes show an internal alternation of definite and indefinite articles"?
Or that "the terminal couplet opposes concrete and primary nouns to
the abstract and/or deverbative nouns of the quatrains"? Or that "each
of the six initial lines displays a grammatical parallelism of its two
hemistichs"?

Idiosyncratic or not, accidental or not, the features are there, and we

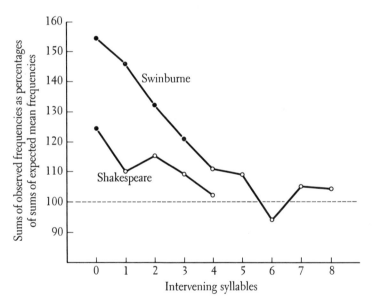

Figure 2. *The Alliterative Spans of Shakespeare and Swinburne*

The point at zero for Swinburne should be read as follows: "In 500 lines of
Atalanta in Calydon the number of successive stressed syllables beginning
with the same sound is 154 per cent of the number expected from chance."
The percentage declines but remains significant even when syllables are
separated by three intervening syllables. The figure for Shakespeare is about
124 per cent, but much of this is due to the repetition of whole words.

should perhaps turn from the conditions which may have produced them to their effect on the reader. Jakobson and Jones insist that this "amazing external and internal structuration [is] palpable to any responsive and unprejudiced reader"; but Richards certainly comes closer to the truth when he says that Sonnet 129 "is now shown to have a degree of exactly describable structural order which—could it have been pointed out to them in such precise unchallengeable detail—would certainly have thrown Shakespeare himself along with his most intent and admiring readers into deeply wondering astonishment," [9] and Jakobson has referred to "subliminal structure," as if it were out of reach of direct observation, and to "deep structure," as if it could be reached only through a penetrating analysis. Certainly the reader need not be aware of the structural features of a poem in order to enjoy it. The effect of music on a listener is due to its structure, since there is nothing else to have an effect, but few listeners—even those who are "most intent and admiring"—know anything about the structure of music and can see it only with difficulty when it is pointed out.

The visibility of structure is particularly important to the writer, who is his own first and most important reader. A writer accepts some of the verbal responses which occur to him and rejects others. He puts those he accepts into some kind of effective order, he adds grammatical tags, he asserts or denies the result, and so on. To do this he must see what he has written—the simple physical structure of his verbal behavior. Moreover, he may learn to write in given ways because what he sees pleases him. Richards has suggested "traceable linkages" between Jakobson's work and recent genetics, and I have raised the question of a different genetic linkage elsewhere.[10] The effect on the reader—particularly on the writer as reader—is important because a poem evolves under a kind of natural selection. All behavior is intimately affected by its consequences, and just as the conditions of selection are more important in the evolution of a species than the mutations, so the selective action of a pleasing effect is more important than the meaningful sources of the responses selected. Pleasing responses survive as a poem evolves.

Whether or not the structure of a poem is "subliminal" has a bearing on this issue. (The linguist's "deep structure," like Freud's "depth psychology," is a spatial metaphor which serves several functions. It is

9. Richards, I.A. "Jakobson's Shakespeare: the Subliminal Structures of a Sonnet." *Times Literary Supplement,* May 28, 1970.
10. Skinner, B.F. "On 'Having' a Poem." *Saturday Review,* July 15, 1972.

useful in referring to the visibility of behavioral processes and their effects and to the role played by visibility in the determination of behavior. It should not, of course, be used to suggest that an analysis is profound rather than superficial.) Richards has pointed to a useful distinction between two kinds of knowing. Shakespeare, to put it crudely, "knew *how*" to write Sonnet 129: but how much did he "know *about*" his behavior in doing so? He must have known about prior specifications and the extent to which what he was writing fulfilled them. A fourth quatrain might have given him useful extra space, but he did not add one. He kept to iambic pentameter. He need not have been aware of a *double entendre*, or any other kind of word play, at the time it occurred—as anyone who made a Freudian slip can testify—but he may have "seen" it after the fact and allowed it to stand if it pleased him. He need not have been aware of associative or assimilative influences or resulting features such as alliteration.

He need not have known about the greater part of the structural features pointed out by Jakobson and Jones. They could have played no part in the production of the primordial material (the "mutations"), and they are not likely to have played a part in the elaboration or selection of features as the poem evolved.[11]

11. Preparation of this paper was supported by a Career Award from the National Institutes of Mental Health (Grant K6–MH–21, 775–01).

ELSIE DUNCAN-JONES

A Reading of Marvell's *The Unfortunate Lover*

1

I have tried, however unsuccessfully, to write of Marvell's most mysterious poem in something of the way in which I.A. Richards wrote of Shakespeare's *The Phoenix and the Turtle*.[1] As in the days when I.A.R. was considering the "protocols" of us who were to be dignified by the title of his "collaborators" in *Practical Criticism*, so in this talk of 1958 the special power that I.A.R. has of making the poem itself the object of total attention is what is most striking. "You have disinterestedly stuck to the business of making my poem speak for itself, and not, as most critics do, diverged and flourished with your tendrils over my brickwork," a poet once said to a critic. This is what I.A.R. does for Shakespeare's poem and what he did for the poems read in the experiment in which we so often demonstrated our inability to write of poetry without the "impudence and vanity" which, as I.A.R. has lately said, are the occupational diseases of the critic, and one may add, the "scholar."

The unfortunate Lover

I

Alas, how pleasant are their dayes

With whom the Infant Love yet playes!

Sorted by pairs, they still are seen

By Fountains cool, and Shadows green.

But soon these Flames do lose their light,

Like Meteors of a Summers night:

1. *Daedalus*, 87, Summer 1958.

Nor can they to that Region climb,
To make impression upon Time.

II

'Twas in a Shipwrack, when the Seas
Rul'd, and the Winds did what they please,
That my poor Lover floting lay,
And, e're brought forth, was cast away:
Till at the last the master-Wave
Upon the Rock his Mother drave;
And there she split against the Stone,
In a *Cesarian Section*.

III

The Sea him lent these bitter Tears
Which at his Eyes he alwaies bears.
And from the Winds the Sighs he bore,
Which through his surging Breast do roar.
No Day he saw but that which breaks,
Through frighted Clouds in forked streaks.
While round the ratling Thunder hurl'd,
As at the Fun'ral of the World.

IV

While Nature to his Birth presents
This masque of quarrelling Elements;
A num'rous fleet of Corm'rants black,
That sail'd insulting o're the Wrack,
Receiv'd into their cruel Care,
Th' unfortunate and abject Heir:
Guardians most fit to entertain
The Orphan of the *Hurricane*.

V

They fed him up with Hopes and Air,
Which soon digested to Despair.
And as one Corm'rant fed him, still
Another on his Heart did bill.
Thus while they famish him, and feast,
He both consumed, and increast:
And languished with doubtful Breath,
Th' *Amphibium* of Life and Death.

VI

And now, when angry Heaven wou'd
Behold a spectacle of Blood,
Fortune and He are call'd to play
At sharp before it all the day:
And Tyrant Love his brest does ply
With all his wing'd Artillery.
Whilst he, betwixt the Flames and Waves,
Like *Ajax*, the mad Tempest braves.

VII

See how he nak'd and fierce does stand,
Cuffing the Thunder with one hand;
While with the other he does lock,
And grapple, with the stubborn Rock:
From which he with each Wave rebounds,
Torn into Flames, and ragg'd with Wounds.
And all he saies, a Lover drest
In his own Blood does relish best.

VIII

This is the only *Banneret*
That ever Love created yet:
Who though, by the Malignant Starrs,
Forced to live in Storms and Warrs;
Yet dying leaves a Perfume here,
And Musick within every Ear:
And he in Story only rules,
In a Field *Sable* a Lover *Gules.*

2

Are not mirth and compassion things incompatible?

DRYDEN

Literature must always represent a battle between real people and
images.   IRIS MURDOCH

"Alas," the word of pity which begins the poem, makes the whole seem
a spontaneous ejaculation. Extraordinary as the lover's history is, the
voice speaking to us about him is a natural-sounding one. "Alas," followed surprisingly by "how pleasant," is a preparation for the contrast
soon to be made between the many fortunate pairs always ("still") perceived as being still in a place of "Fountains cool and Shadows green,"
not doing or suffering, but being as yet played with; and the solitary
figure soon to be shown suffering, fighting, wrestling, in a seascape lit
only by lightning, shot at by Tyrant love: and, after he has disappeared
from the scene, said to be rewarded by Sovereign love, not with a part-
ner, not with the object of his love, who is never mentioned, but with a
title of honour, with universal posthumous compassion, and with the
sort of permanence that belongs to heraldry.

The voice speaking the poem is a natural one; but word-order is
sometimes inverted and there is something of the formalized, the conventional or fictional about even the first verse. We are not quite sure
whether the contrast between the fortunate pairs (they are never actually called lovers) in the first verse and the solitary unfortunate in the
subsequent ones is a contrast between the real and the fictional or between two kinds of fiction.

There are some suggestions that the lucky ones are creatures of the world of art or persons acting out a convention. Their feelings are "flames," the scene in which they move would be a conventional "pleasant place" if it were not so much in Marvell's idiom, anticipating *The Garden*, which too was not a place for "Passions heat": here there is not "green shade" but, slightly more formal, "shadows green." The comparison of the "flames" to "Meteors of a Summers night" gives them a sort of physical existence, however: and "Summers night" relates them to our world in which seasons come and go. These figures are at home in the world of time as the unfortunate one is not to be: they cannot

> to that Region climb
> To make impression upon Time.

"They aren't lofty enough," would be the commonplace metaphor: that they can't "climb" to that region—the empyrean, presumably, where the pure element of fire is supposed to subsist—suggests that they lack stamina—to do the impossible. Their "days" are days only and their days are "pleasant," something perhaps a little less than happy. They lack sublimity and they lack permanence.

The transient-sounding pastoral calm of these many, as yet happy, couples gives way to a scene of disaster and chaos, and a focussing on a single figure. The story of "my poor lover," the figure with whom I, the poet, am concerned,[2] whom I invent and show to you, begins with a shipwreck (the type of all human disaster) like the story of *Arcadia* and many other fictions: and like the story of every human being as represented by Lucretius in a passage much dwelt upon in Marvell's day.[3]

Here we are in a world of chaotic abandon. The seas are "ruling," but

2. It seems to me that we are prevented from thinking that it is the person loved who speaks throughout, though I do not doubt that a case could be made out for that interpretation.
3. Lucretius, *De Natura Deorum*, V. 222–5. Lucretius is demonstrating that the universe is unfriendly to man. The passage is quoted by Montaigne in the "Apology for Raymond Sebond," referred to by Burton in *The Anatomy of Melancholy*, translated as an excerpt by Dryden, etc. etc. I give Charles Cotton's translation from his version of Montaigne (1685):

Like to the wretched mariner, when tost
By raging seas, upon the desart coast
The tender babe lies naked on the earth
Of all supports of life stript by his birth.
When nature first presents him to the day
Freed from the womb where he imprisoned lay.

not in the sense of controlling anything. The word "ruling" is not
allowed a rhyming place: the seas have power, not control. The winds
are doing "what they please," which will not be pleasant. The lover is
first seen, or rather not seen, in his mother's womb, floating (in the
birth fluid and?) the sea. The witty exactness of the opposition in "ere
brought forth was cast away" is one of the features that throughout the
poem construct an element of evident artifice, worked against by the
relaxed tone of the narrative, "*Twas* in a Shipwrack," and the "low"
words in its vocabulary. "Master-wave," for instance, is not literary, but
a sailor's word, still being used by Marryat. The undisciplining rule of
the sea, its latent power, and the idle play of the winds and the floating
body are preparations for the appallingly neat accident (Lucretian
chance?) that opens the mother's womb as the master wave drives her
upon a rock that performs the Caesarian "cutting": "section" is the
usual word in Marvell's day, more precise than "operation." Marvell's
much-read Pliny says that the offspring of Caesarian births are fortunate
(*N.H.* VII. 9). Are we to remember this and mark its untruth here?
If the lover was like all mankind in that he began life as a castaway, a
shipwrecked sailor, the invention of the Caesarian birth at least marks
him out as exceptional. Lucretius had not thought of that.

The "split against the stone" is the first of the violent happenings in
the lover's story. Are there any happenings in his story not violent? The
agencies that precipitate the birth, "master-Wave" and "Stone," are
masculine-sounding. There is nothing else in the way of a father. The
mother, merely a womb, is heard of no more. So from the moment of his
birth, and to the end of his life, unless we imagine a hearer for his single
utterance, he is entirely without human companionship, or, "lover"
though he is, human relationship. Only the poet, the narrator, feels for
him, calls him "my poor lover."

The incidents of his birth were told as past. Now we are shown him,
weeping, sighing, his breast surging as he roars:

The Sea him lent these bitter Tears
Which at his Eyes he alwaies bears.
And from the Winds the Sighs he bore,
Which through his surging Breast do roar.

More exactly, the Seas and the Winds are weeping and sighing and
roaring through him: there is no feebleness nor complaint in the babe
himself. "Bears" and "bore," used of his tears and sighs, make him

seem for a moment like a figure in an emblem, and the inversion of order in "him lent" contributes to the effect of stiffness. That his tears are qualified as "bitter," though, makes him sentient. We see him and then we see what he saw when he was born, "No Day," no sunshine, no light, only lightning that frightens the clouds, not him. (He never saw the day, therefore he is a figure of fiction, might be an allowable stage in the reading of these lines.) What he hears is the thunder, "hurling," in the obsolete sense of making a hideous noise; rattling, like the drums at a seventeenth-century funeral: but this is like "the Fun'ral of the World." The unfortunate lover's birth is like the end of everything.

The comparison of the thunder to [drums] rattling at a funeral brought the scene of vigorous disorder into comparison with a sober ceremony. In verse IV the note of the ceremonious becomes still more marked, though the ceremony is not this time, a sombre one.

While Nature to his Birth presents
This masque of quarrelling Elements

—as if it were all being done on purpose, as an entertainment in his honour, as a masque might be organized at court to celebrate the birth of some seventeenth-century prince. (Masques not infrequently contained dances of "quarrelling elements" and sometimes "Nature" presented them—see Nabbes' *Microcosmos* [1637] and Benserade's *Balet Royal de la Nuit* [1654] in which the Duke of Buckingham danced as the element of fire.) Chaos is being as it were methodized.

The masque is still being performed, the storm is still raging, when a number of living creatures sail into view—the only living creatures to appear in the lover's story. They are a "fleet" and they "sail" but not to his succour. They are "cormorants black." We have left behind in the first verse the world of greenness, we are now in the world of blackness and blood.

As Marvell had sharpened and intensified the Lucretian metaphor by the additional detail of the violent birth, so here he transforms into cormorants, "marine birds" appropriate to a scene of shipwreck, the two vultures who in the ancient story of Tityus and in its derivatives prey on the breast of the victim, representing the passions that tear him. By making them a "num'rous fleet" Marvell brings the picture as it were to life: but the note of predictable symmetry comes in again with the antithesis of "cruel Care." It is appropriate in a wholly hostile universe that a child orphaned by the violence of the storm should be brought up by greedy and rapacious creatures. At this point the lover is "th' unfortunate and abject Heir." Heir to what, it has been asked? Surely to his mother's disaster and misfortune: so Shakespeare makes Richard II speak of "my sorrow's dismal heir."

Of all the verses the fifth is that in which the sense of pattern, the neat contrasts are strongest. Of all the verses this is that in which the hyperboles most seem to quiver on the verge of burlesque.

> They fed him up with Hopes and Air
> Which soon digested to Despair.

"I eat the air, promise-crammed: you cannot feed capons so," says Hamlet. Hopes and Despair, one cormorant feeding him, another pecking at him, the lover himself, in the language of the motto to an emblem; consuming and increasing: here the attempt to keep up the pretence that this is not fiction, as by "digest," giving the diet physiological consequences, and the use of the rough word "bill," seems to fail, or to be meant to fail. The supremacy in misfortune and in strength of this infant comes to a climax in the wittiest of the witty lines that have ended each verse so far: "th' *Amphibium* of Life and Death."

How he survived might puzzle a literal-minded reader like Jane Austen's Mrs. Allen. But "his life hung in the balance" would be the commonplace reduction of the monstrous-sounding "*Amphibium* of Life and Death," and life has won. In the sixth verse the "guardians" have disappeared, the figure at whose birth Nature presented a masque of quarrelling elements is no longer merely the occasion for tremendous diversions but is of age and strength to participate in another entertainment, a show, a gladiatorial spectacle for the benefit of "angry Heaven," capricious, bloody-minded, and represented by the pronoun "it."

> And now, when angry Heaven wou'd
> Behold a spectacle of Blood,[4]
> Fortune and He are call'd to play
> At sharp before it all the day.

The performances are long, the weapons unblunted, to make the performance more exciting: the antagonist, Fortune, though traditionally

---

4. Compare to Seneca's saying (*De Providentia*, V), "the gods are well pleased when they see great men contending with misfortune." Burton adds a gloss "as we are to see men fight, or a man with a beast." (*Anatomy of Melancholy*, Pt.11.Sec.III, Mem.1.Subs.1.) Burton does not show whether he is deliberately belittling the gods. There is no doubt that Marvell is.

female, is here not given a sex—a female figure would not be an appropriately formidable antagonist? While these long performances are being enacted Love—no longer Infant, but grown up like the Lover—love, now Tyrant Love, discharges all his arrows at the lover's breast. The hero has also to contend with a "mad Tempest" which he "braves," defies. Courageously? or ridiculously? But it is the Tempest that is called "mad." Heaven was belittled by the word "angry" and its wish at times for a spectacle of blood: and Love, behaving in a most unchivalrous manner, was "Tyrant." Sympathy is entirely directed to the lover, here markedly the *unfortunate* lover, for in this cruel, capricious, and unjust universe Heaven and Fortune seem to be more important enemies than love, sending its artillery ("missive weapons") presumably from a distance.

The lover at war with fortune and shot by arrows belongs to the commonplaces of mythology: what is characteristically witty, characteristic of Marvell, is the mingling of these commonplaces with the novel degradation of the Senecan sentiment: and the introduction of the comparison of the figure "betwixt the Flames and Waves" to Ajax Oileus. The comparison is introduced unemphatically and parenthetically. The story of the destruction of this Ajax is told early in the first book of the Aeneid and in the fourth book of the Odyssey. Marvell keeps close to Virgil's Latin and to Chapman's English. Ajax Oileus on his return from the siege of Troy was overtaken by a storm, defied Neptune, and was transfixed by a rock, his breast breathing out flames. The storm had been sent to punish him for ravishing Cassandra in the temple of Pallas: but he would have escaped unharmed, Homer says, if he had not impiously defied the gods. It is consonant with the degrading of Heaven and of Love in this verse that we are not invited to remember (let alone reprobate) Ajax's impiety, but only his defiance of the tempest—to which Marvell gives the epithet "mad."

In the sixth verse the activity of seeing belonged to Heaven, who would "behold" a spectacle. In the next verse *we* are to see the figure: as in antiquity the figure of Ajax was seen ("See how he . . ."). I think Marvell remembers that Pliny (N.H. XXX.9) writes of a famous painting of Ajax "all on a flaming fire with a flash of lightning." Philostratus, too, gives a picture of him, "the rocks rising out of the water, and the boiling sea about them, and on the rocks a hero glaring fiercely and with a certain proud defiance towards the sea." (*Imagines*, II. 13)

This link with the tale of Troy and the great fictions of Homer and Virgil raises the lover's status, perhaps: he is not to be thought of as

merely a creature of the world of romance [5] or emblems. But the terms
used to evoke his last appearance (perhaps he perishes like Ajax) are
vigorous rather than elevated or noble. "Cuffing," "lock," and "grapple"
might all belong to a description of a human wrestling match. What he
is disrespectfully "cuffing," however, is the Thunder that Jove traditionally "wields," and what he grapples with is the Rock that had
brought him to birth. He is naked as he was born, but fierce, con-
temptuously engaging with unyielding adversaries that are bound to
win.

The picture is not quite still: the sea still lifts him and sets him down
with "each wave": he "rebounds" from the rock, he is resilient, he does
not acknowledge defeat, but he is still in the power of the sea, the sea is
still ruling. Burning, buffeted, torn, bleeding: this is the last we see of
him: and the last we hear of the sea.

Then comes what for me is the great surprise of the poem. He speaks:

And all he saies, a lover drest
In his own Blood does relish best.

"All he saies!" We didn't expect this emblematic figure to say anything
and the poet seems to ask us to be surprised that he doesn't say more.
He had nobody to talk to. It is rather like the moment in *Upon Apple-
ton House* (1.406) when Thestylis breaks the texture of the poem by
answering the poet's thoughts "And cryes, he call'd us Israelites." The
rent in *The Unfortunate Lover* is much more striking. At the few casually introduced words the world of literary, emblematic, pictorial conventions vanishes, the shipwreck, the flames, the sighs and tears, the
birds of prey, the being a spectacle for the gods; the lover does not say
much—not as much as his extraordinary situation warranted, if he was
to say anything at all—but what he does say breaks the spell:

as when th' Inchantment ends
The Castle vanishes or rends.

He speaks and is a man like us, he speaks with conscious, with sophisticated casualness. It appears now that all that he has been, done, and
undergone is what he knew was expected of him. The lover covered
with his own blood as a garment, he says, is what is most enjoyed, gives
most delight. There is an implication too that he fully realizes the
cruelty of the convention. "Drest" together with "relish" suggests that

5. Like Amadís de Gaula, one of whose names was Oceander.

the lover is to be dressed in his own blood as a dish is "dressed" for table, to gratify a palate. For a cannibalistic lady who has never been mentioned? [6] For Tyrant love? for angry Heaven? or for us, the gentle readers of fiction and dwellers upon emblems? Is it spoken with *sprezzatura*, in an elegantly don't-care style, or with mocking acceptance, or humorous stoicism? Even if the words are to be regarded as the motto to an emblem they must have the effect of making the tissue of conventions appear as merely a tissue, a mythology of suffering enacted because it is what most gratifies somebody's, it later appears, everybody's, taste. The figure has never been shown in relation to any human being from the moment when he was ripped by an inhuman agency from a womb. The figure has been called a "Lover" but he has never been shown as loving or as being loved, in human terms. He has been created only to gratify us by the spectacle of his suffering. He exists only in relationship to the author and the reader—or so we may think till he speaks and becomes not a personage but a person; from now on it is as if the fiction of his adventures has given way to the fact of their power over those who learn of them.

The hyperboles of the poem are over. The poem is never the same after the moment of direct speech. In the last verse, which is partly a framing and contrasting one, to match the framing and contrasting first verse, the contrasts are very marked. It is not only that we pass from the figure's sufferings to its rewards, that its solitariness now becomes a distinguished uniqueness and Tyrant Love has now become (implicitly, as if in order to leave the role of the one who rules to the unfortunate lover) the grateful sovereign, who confers on his most valiant soldier the title reserved for the bravest.[7]

This is the only Banneret
That ever Love created yet.

6. Cf. *Daphnis and Chloe*, verse XVIII. Daphnis refuses the consummation of love offered by his coy mistress when he is about to depart:

Rather I away will pine
In a manly stubbornness
Than be fatted up express
For the Canibal to dine.

7. "Of Knights Bannerets. This degree of Knighthood has been used in England even since the reign of Edward I . . . bestowed on ₜthe most deserving persons. The ceremony used is very grand . . . performed by the King at the head of his Army, drawn up in battalia, after a victory, under the royal standard displayed." (*Heraldry in Miniature*, 1808, appendix)

A plain assertion, and though it is a personification who confers the honour, we are moving nearer the seventeenth-century real world: the first banneret for many years had been created by Charles I at Edgehill in 1642, as a reward for the recapturing of the royal standard. In the next lines the hero's history is summed up in a quieter, more generalized style than that in which it was previously shown to us. It might be a real person who was

> by the Malignant Starrs
> Forced to live in Storms and Warrs.

("Malignant" before "Starrs," I think, has its astrological sense, as in Shakespeare, *I Henry VI* iv.v, "malignant and ill-boding stars." Marvell never uses malignant as a political anti-Royalist term.) The question of how the unfortunate lover died is not to be asked, the participle is evasive.

> Yet dying leaves a Perfume here
> And Musick within every Ear.

"Here" is where we all are and I, the reader, must be among those subtly delighted as by perfume and. intimately conscious (*"within every Ear"*) of harmony. The language here adapts the Scriptural (Ecclus.: 49.1) praise of the remembrance of a just king. As we seem to have left the world of fiction, have we also left the world of pagan gods delighted by blood for the world that reads the Bible? I am not sure. I do think that the double sense of "dying" common in seventeenth-century poetry is excluded here by the sobriety of the tone and by the lover's being the "unfortunate" one. The progress from perfume and music to the heraldic device is called for by the development of the poem, by the need for this figure to be shown as doing what those in the first verse could not, making impression upon Time. The perfume and music that evoke the gentle aesthetic and moral delight [8] produced in us by the strenuous suffering of the lover must be evanescent: hard and

---

8. Cf. the lines in Marvell's *Poem upon the death of O.C.* in which he says that Cromwell's death will not be felt to have taken an appropriate form, since he died in his bed.

> The People, which what most they fear esteem,
> Death when more horrid so more noble deem;
> And blame the last *Act*, like *Spectators* vain,
> Unless the Prince whom they applaud be slain.

They want to be gratified by the violent death of the character they praise.

inhuman, the heraldic device in its stiffness and economy will outlast generations.

And he in Story only rules
In a Field *Sable* a Lover *Gules*.

At last it is he who rules. The simplicity of the bare assertion does not exclude ambiguity: "Story" may mean fiction, history, [9] painting. He is only supreme in these realms of the mind: and he only is supreme in them.

We know that Donne thought the end of a poem the most important part. None of Marvell's poems has a more striking, satisfying, baffling, inscrutable last line than this. All that has been suffered and done dwindles by the herald's art to seven words representing a painted device. The poem that began with the spontaneous "Alas" ends with a word from the special vocabulary of heraldry, a sinister-sounding word, what Johnson called a "barbarous word": we remember how Shakespeare in *Hamlet* used it as part of the ultra-theatrical language, language as it were at two removes from life, of the player's speech, evoking by a "dismal" heraldry the ferocity of Pyrrhus.

Now, in one sense, the figure is further from life than he ever was. A seventeenth-century hero might be rewarded by a coat of arms, [10] but this lover does not bear a coat of arms, he is a naked figure, not an armed warrior; he is *part* of a coat of arms, a semblance of man outlined—the word "lover" stands out as not heraldic—in blood against a black background. In this guise, impresa-like, he survives. The heraldic device follows as it were naturally, upon "banneret" and the artillery of Cupid: [11] it takes no account of the hero's "sea-sorrow," of the wrestling

9. Cf. Rochester, *History of Insipids*, 1677:
Fame is not founded on success:
Though victories were Caesar's glory
Lost battles made not Pompey less
But left him styled great in story.

10. One of the Royalist heroes of Edgehill was awarded an augmentation of arms immortalizing his injuries. "In a field gules, a right arm arm'd. . . . And for a Crest . . . a chevalier in a fighting posture, his left arm hanging down useless . . . his scarf red, his sword, face, arms, and horse, cruentated [bloodied]." (See *Edgehill*, 1642, by Peter Young, 1967, p. 147.) This is the mode to which Marvell's (highly simplified) device belongs.

11. Cf. *The Assault of Cupid* by Lord Vaux, published in *Tottel's Miscellany* but said by C.S. Lewis to be thoroughly medieval. Cupid bears an ensign of pierced hearts sprinkled with tears "In silver and sable to declare / The steadfast love he always meant."

with rock and tempest. A flaw in the poem? or an illustration, quite deliberate, of the exclusions of art and the inadequacy of the reward?

Hawthorne's adaptation of the last line of Marvell's poem for the last sentence of *The Scarlet Letter* shows how with a little shift of balance the representation of life by a code, a letter, a device, can seem a tragic demonstration of the tyranny of abstract ideas. Marvell's poem seems to me to unite "Mirth and compassion." It is not mere burlesque, it is not merely hyperbole undercut. Nor is it merely a protest at the tyranny of the love convention, or the injustice of the gods, or an exposure of the paradox that gentle readers demand tales of suffering.

As Helen Gardner has said, metaphysical poetry often has the flavour of the wit of conversation between friends who urge each other on to further flights. Perhaps Marvell's poem began as an attempt to outdo in some respects the poem *Dialogue: Lucasta, Alexis* in which his friend Lovelace had written that

Soldiers suspected of their courage go
Who ensigns and their breasts untorn show,
Love near his standard when his host he sets
Creates alone fresh-bleeding bannerets.

Marvell's poem may (he had his pedantic side, like most people concerned with words) have begun as an attempt to put the word "banneret," which after Edgehill must have taken on new life,[12] into a context in which "only" is important. Whether or not this was so, the poem does seem to come from an impulse to outdo, to outgo, to strain hyperbole and yet to compel belief, while all the time and, for me, most strikingly at the moment when the lover speaks, allowing what I.A. Richards calls "the bringing in of the opposite, the complementary impulses."[13] It is a poem characteristic of Marvell in this respect as in many others. The poem gets its power partly, I think, from the way in which the satirical impulse is kept subordinate. The impulse to mock at the figures created by others is balanced by the desire himself to create a figure that shall maintain some kind of hold over us in the most implausible adversities. Marvell is both smiling at and demonstrating the power of fictions of fortitude and suffering, and the paradox that, by what Sidney in his *Apology for Poetry* calls "sweet violence," portrayals of pain and suffering afford delight.

12. OED quotes a writer of the 1650's who calls Christ "God's bannerite."
13. *Principles of Literary Criticism*, 1926, p. 250.

As I write I am conscious, as an old pupil of I.A.R.'s ought to be, that there are other interpretations that can be put forward with equal or superior convincingness. More attention might be paid to the lover as lover: "My poor lover" and the snatch of direct speech might be taken differently. The poem might be interpreted as an "erotic psychomachia." "Unless we are to become most undesirably standardized, differences of opinion about poetry must continue—differences, not only between individual but between successive phases in the growth of the same personality." [14] It is difficult to imagine any reading of the poem which did not find that it gave rise to the recognition that "incompatibility and contradiction are essential parts" of it.[15]

It is also eminently a poem that awakens the "dangerous hunter's impulse" that I.A.R. has written of. There is often a surprisingly literal element in Marvell's poetry. When he says that the Escurial burns with envy at the moment that the colonnade of the Louvre is being completed, he refers to an actual fire. When he calls Lady Fairfax the "starry Vere" he is referring to the Vere coat of arms, though of course we can do very well without that information. I think that when he says "ten years before the Flood" he means 1646 Anno Mundi and hints that he is writing in 1646 Anno Domini: Ronsard had written a sonnet dating his love as beginning precisely a century earlier, 1546; etc. Precision, literalness where we are used to richly vague suggestiveness can be disconcerting. Many readers don't want to be reminded of the Vere coat of arms or the date of the Flood and here too we have a charter of liberty. "All respectable poetry invites close reading. It encourages attention to its literal sense up to the point, to be detected by the reader's discretion, at which liberty can serve the aim of the poem better than fidelity to fact." (*Practical Criticism*) It is possible that some substratum of fact remains to be detected in *The Unfortunate Lover*: if it turned out that the device at the end was the amorial bearing of Lovelace (it isn't) or of Captain John Smith, the banneret of Edgehill, *Britanniae Virtutis Imago* [16] (it isn't), the discovery would be its own reward, the sense of having recovered something Time had blurred. It would not be actually injurious to the poem, as occasionally such a fact can be for some readers in relation to some poems. Lady Caroline Lamb thought poorly of Byron's "She walks in beauty like the night"

14. *Practical Criticism*, p. 347.
15. *Practical Criticism*, p. 64.
16. The title of the pamphlet about him by Edward Walsingham, Oxford, 1644.

because she knew that it was inspired by Mrs. Robert Wilmot wearing a black evening dress with silver spangles. El Desdichado's shield I should prefer to remain mysterious. I don't much want to know that the arms of "le Prince d'Aquitaine à la tour abolie" were those of Gérard de Nerval's ancestors. Marvell's poem seems to me less vulnerable than these—I can't imagine any discovery that would injure *The Unfortunate Lover,* though I am not claiming that it is one of Marvell's greatest poems. It is "respectable poetry" at the very least and it repays "close reading": it exercises a spell.

BASIL WILLEY

I. A. Richards and Coleridge

The present volume is being prepared in 1972, which is the Bi-Centenary year of Coleridge's birth. In this there is a singular appropriateness, for Richards is not only a pre-eminent Coleridgean but is himself, in many important senses, the Coleridge of our time. Like Coleridge, he has taught us that there can be no criticism without reconsidering fundamental conceptions; that we must watch our minds as well as use them, attending especially to what we are doing when we use words like "word," "meaning," "knowledge," "truth," "belief" etc. Like Coleridge, he sees poetry as bringing the whole soul of man into activity, at the same time imposing upon it a more than usual order; and like him, he teaches that to experience poetry fully is to enjoy the bliss of "the rectified mind and the freed heart." Unlike Coleridge, he does not subordinate his critical and psychological insights to an over-riding metaphysical and religious programme; but in his impassioned defence of life-values in a world gone cold and inanimate he has more than a little of the prophetic character too.

By another fortunate coincidence (perhaps it was by design rather than chance), Richards' book *Coleridge on Imagination* came out in 1934, the centenary year of Coleridge's death. Nothing could be more satisfactory and significant than this repeated conjunction of the two luminaries, and it was for this reason (apart from their spiritual kinship) that I decided to call this essay "I.A. Richards and Coleridge."

It so happens that in 1934 I wrote a review of *Coleridge on Imagination*, of which by a near-miracle I have kept a copy. On re-reading this, I find that it says many of the things I should still want to say, and says them with a freshness which would now be hard to recapture. The review, being coeval with the book, has also perhaps a touch of "period interest," so I am going to begin by reproducing it here exactly as it stood.

Dr. Richards on Coleridge

It must be a matter for general satisfaction that Coleridge's centenary year has not passed without a contribution from Dr. Richards, whose qualifications for interpreting him to this generation are probably unique. What Coleridge said of the Imagination may be said of this book, that it is "essentially vital," as contrasted with the kind of critico-historical accounts which, however useful in their way, are relatively "fixed and dead." Dr. Richards disclaims all pretension to mere completeness of statement, and offers us instead some of the workings of a mind in growth, using Coleridge's best insights in order to investigate still more closely the "behaviour of words in poetry." This book must therefore be read, not as a "study" of Coleridge's thought, but as a development of his method—an attempt, in fact, to "reconstruct his view in the form which seems most serviceable to the critical purposes he designed it for." (p. 69)

Those readers whose interests are most purely "literary" will find plenty here to instruct and excite them, notably perhaps the fine detailed exposition of Imagination and Fancy (Ch. IV), the "paradigm" of the senses of the word *word* (Ch. V), the discussion on the uses and abuses of "theory" in literary judgments (Ch. VI), and the concluding section, critical and prophetic, on the contemporary position and the future prospects of poetry and linguistic analysis. In defence of Coleridge (and of himself) Dr. Richards urges, with convincing illustrations, that "the chief weakness of our best criticism today is the pretence that fundamental matters can be profitably discussed without prolonged and technical thinking." (p. 5) He is, of course, far too good a reader and psychologist to forget that "in no case can theory take the place of judgment." (p. 140) "The judgment that a passage is good is an act of living." But we need good theories to "protect us from worse," and, above all, Dr. Richards expects from a developed technique of literary analysis "important practical utilities"—the reconstruction of spiritual order and the conquest of a new control over our minds. Like Coleridge, he adumbrates a criticism which "would supersede all the books of metaphysics and all the books of morals too." (p. 20) An observation Dr. Richards makes on Coleridge's criticism is thus true of his own—we must be prepared, in reading him, to "reconsider our most fundamental conceptions, our conceptions of man's being—the nature of his mind and its knowledge." (p. 19) It is indeed for the reminder that "to ask about words is to ask about everything" that we are chiefly indebted to Dr. Richards in this as in his earlier books.

I think, then, in view of the very wide scope of this book (its modest size notwithstanding), that it may be permissible here to draw particular attention to Chapter VII, "The Wind Harp," and Chapter VIII, "The Boundaries of the Mythical," rather than to revive any of the discussions often evoked in literary quarters by Dr. Richards' work. For it is in these chapters that he gives us the most rigorous analysis we have yet had from him of the processes by which the Imagination, Primary and Secondary, constructs the "myths" which we call, loosely and ambiguously, "Nature"—the world of science ("Nature in Sense IV"), the world of daily routine-living or "practical" affairs ("Nature in Sense III"), and the world of "values" ("Nature in Sense II"). "Nature in Sense I" is defined as "the influences, of whatever kind, to which the mind is subject from whatever is without and independent of itself" (p. 157); while Nature in Sense II is the world "invested with characters derived from our own feelings, our hopes and fears, desires and thoughts"; "a projection of our whole response to Nature in Sense I . . . the music by which the string represents the wind" in Coleridge's Wind Harp image. I offer the brief reflections which follow less by way of "criticism" of Dr. Richards—indeed his whole method and tone preclude anything so unimaginative as crude dissent—than as an illustration of one way in which he compels us to "ask about everything." What, then, one asks, is "Nature in Sense I"—the Not-Ourselves which is symbolised by the wind in the Wind Harp image? And what is its relation to the business of living? Dr. Richards warns us that neither the inanimate cold world (Nature III) or our daily existence, nor the world which science can order and control, will suffice for our needs:

> Wisdom requires a different co-ordination of our perceptions, yielding another Nature for us to live in—a Nature in which our hopes and fears and desires, by projection, can come to terms with one another. . . . It is such a Nature that the religions in the past have attempted to provide for man. (pp. 169–70)

> Without his mythologies man is only a cruel animal without a soul—for a soul is a central part of his governing mythology— he is a congeries of possibilities without order and without aim. (p. 172)

All our "Natures" are mythologies; and all are "true" only in the sense that they are relevant to certain particular purposes and needs. Nature III is "true" because it conditions all our "practical" lives; because within the framework of its laws we live and move (or else we die). But this is not the music of the Wind Harp. To produce that music we must vibrate with our "whole souls" to the wind of the Not-Ourselves. We may live and move in Nature III, but we have our being fully only in Nature II. And we gather both from Coleridge and Dr. Richards that this wholeness of response, this union of heart with head, of deep feeling with deep thinking, is of supreme importance. Ideally our whole lives ought to be one prolonged "imaginative fact." But whence this "ought"? Why is it "better" for the mind to be performing acts of self-realizing intuition than to be a lazy looker-on, a mere passive denizen of Nature III—the world vouchsafed to the Primary Imagination? Because these acts represent a finer, fuller and subtler harmony of the impulses? Perhaps, but should we in fact cherish these imaginative moments for that reason alone? Certainly, if "states of mind" are alone real, we can have no other reason. But is it not at least reasonable to surmise that the *value* of the wind-harp music lies, not merely in itself, but in the fact of its springing from a perfect accord between the strings (the mind) and the wind (Nature I, the Not-Ourselves)?

> The saner and greater mythologies are not fancies; they are the utterance of the whole soul of man. (p. 171)

Their "truth," however, Dr. Richards teaches, is their "relevance to our purposes"—in this case our loftiest purposes—imaginative growth, "the rectified mind and the freed heart." (p. xiv) But a myth will hardly control our lives as long as it is *felt as myth*, that is, as "mere" projection. It is the utterance of the whole soul of man perhaps, but the utterance presupposes the wind and points towards it. Moreover, the conversion of "values" into "facts" does, as a matter of experience, accompany any resolute and lifelong endeavour to act "in all respects according to" the values. (p. 173) It is a pity, perhaps, that imagination should thus harden into "belief" or "faith." And there may be specially favoured mortals (I doubt if many of the poets are among them) whose shaping spirit never leaves them for long. But, for mankind in general, hours of gloom preponderate over hours of insight, and Nature III would engulf us wholly if we could not support ourselves by the belief that Nature II is both more "real" and more valuable because it is linked in some way with Nature I. How it is linked we cannot express, save by saying that Nature I, the Other-than-Ourselves, is such that when responding to it with what we take to be our "whole souls" we do

in fact project our "greatest and sanest myths." It is of the essence of
these myths that they should seem to impart "authentic tidings of invisible things." "God," the greatest and sanest of all our myths, cannot
meet the needs to which it is relevant if it is felt *merely* as projection;
and conversely, its reality is not fully felt until the life has been shaped
"in all respects according to" it. Faith, as Coleridge taught, is an act of
the Will, but the life of faith verifies the truth of its assumptions just as
daily "practical" existence verifies Nature III. The mere awareness that
we are "making" the myth true by living it (that "such as we are, such
will God himself appear to be," as John Smith said) does not render it
any the less an evidence of things not seen.

> Conscience commands us to attribute Reality and actual *Existence*
> to those Ideas, and those only, without which the conscience it-
> self would be baseless and contradictory. (*The Friend*)

There is a good deal to be said for Coleridge's view that in our search
for the Tao, for "useful hypotheses that may help us in living," a wiser
piece of advice than "Know Thyself" is "Ignore thyself and seek to
know thy God." Dr. Richards assumes that "the religions" are things
of the past. That, perhaps, is not a necessary assumption, though much
that passes for religion, now as in the past, gives colour to it. But as
Dr. Richards would probably agree, it is not by argument that such
matters are settled. It is simply the case that certain minds must hy-
postatise their values—especially "God," which comprehends them all
—in order to help themselves in living. Many others, of course, now
feel that any religious mythology is an obstacle rather than a help to
the main business of living in this age, namely the realization of a
better world-order in the social and economic spheres. For these, "living
God into a fact" may seem the formula of escape from the true task,
which is the transmutation of Nature III into Nature II on what is
known as the "material" plane. Dr. Richards is the very man to show,
by linguistic analysis, that both "believer" and dialectical materialist
may be meaning some of the same things. But both at their best are
believers; both are living their respective myths into facts. They know
that otherwise they themselves and the world would continue to be
merely "a congeries of possibilities without order and without aim." If
"All is Myth" is taken to mean "Therefore spend as much time as you
possibly can in reading poetry" it may not be the most helpful of affirmations; but if, on the other hand, it means "Therefore you are free to

live in accordance with whatsoever myth seems to you greatest and sanest," its usefulness may be immense. But all alike, in this chaotic world of ours—mystics or materialists, those who have "got religion" and those who have not—may well learn from Coleridge and Dr. Richards the value of frequent returns to poetry, to those imaginative acts which dissolve, diffuse and dissipate in order to re-create, those states in which the mind is growing, and in which its "growledge" is indistinguishable from what grows, and knowledge from what knows.

Finally, let me say of this profoundly stimulating book what Coleridge said of a certain passage of his own: "Read this over until you understand it. God bless you!"

The nature of my own debt to Richards, and that of my whole generation, is already indicated here. But its magnitude, which I have always acknowledged in principle, has been borne in upon me again irresistibly by the re-reading I have done in preparation for this essay. Richards not only founded modern literary criticism, but supplied it with a vocabulary which has become accepted currency for so long that its origin is often forgotten. Who but he coined phrases like "stock responses," "pseudo-statements," "disguised imperatives," "storehouse of recorded values," "private poem," "bogus entities," "scientific *versus* emotive language," "objectless belief," "valuable experience" and many more? It is in itself a mark of genius to be capable of putting such memorable and clinching phrases into circulation; and these are in the same class as Coleridge's own "medicated atmosphere," "suspension of disbelief," "balance or reconciliation of opposite or discordant qualities," etc. But such phrases are only effective and influential when, as with Coleridge and Richards, they are condensations of a total philosophy of the arts—or, as we may say, of a coherent world-view. And this is what both these great men achieved: they altered the whole climate of thinking about what the arts are for, how they work, and why they are important.

Here I can speak from personal experience, for I was one of the lucky few who attended Richards' first course of lectures in Cambridge nearly fifty years ago—those which went to form his epoch-making *Principles of Literary Criticism* and *Practical Criticism*. Never shall we forget the impression they made upon us then. Many of us were just back from the 1914–18 war, and we were unsatisfied with the woolly generalities and the vague mysticism of the accepted schools of criticism (Gosse,

Symons, Saintsbury and the like). The English Tripos had only just been founded, and we wanted to feel that we were not merely going to tread the hackneyed roads leading from Aristotle to Croce, but were in at the start of an exciting new enterprise and about to break new ground. This was exactly the feeling that Ivor gave us. Here was a "'subtle-souled psychologist," who, like Coleridge, was bringing scientific skills and insights to bear upon the study of literature. Here was a teacher who, before turning to literary criticism, had actually done some fundamental thinking, and grappled—as no other critic since Coleridge had done—with ultimate and basic problems: with the relations between Things, Thoughts and Words, and the Meaning of Meaning. No doubt it was at first his training in psychology which gave the new and explora- tory flavour to all he said; he taught us that critical remarks were really a branch of psychological remarks, and he showed us that "a poem" was a mental event, an experience of extreme complexity, taking place within the reader. His explanations, often illustrated by blackboard diagrams, of what goes on in the mind in response to the black marks on white paper, and delivered with matchless urbanity and wit as well as a sense of discovery, came to us like a revelation. New kinds of knowledge poured in upon us in every lecture, and Richards gave us then, as often since, the sense that a dawn was breaking in which it would be bliss to be alive: a new day in which knowledge of our own minds would give us enhanced control over ourselves and our destinies; and in which poetry, as the storehouse of recorded values, would be seen as the stronghold of the spirit of man in its struggle for the good life in the face of scientific aggression.

For this was the extraordinary thing about Richards (perhaps the heart of his mystery), that though a scientist by training and habit he was always a poet by nature and temperament; he combined "judgment ever awake and steady self-possession" *with* "enthusiasm and feeling profound or vehement." He possessed, what he himself says is indispens- able for anyone trying to explain "the high place of poetry in human affairs," "both a passionate knowledge of poetry and a capacity for dis- passionate psychological analysis." (*Science and Poetry*, 1926, p. 9; and *Poetries and Sciences*, 1970, p. 22) What he says of the poet is true of the critic as he conceives him, that no study of poets is of use to him "which is not an impassioned study." And he replaces Milton's descrip- tion of poetry as "simple, sensuous and passionate" with another trinity of terms ("passionate" being common to both): only genuine poetry, he says, will produce in a good reader "a response which is as passionate, noble and serene as the experience of the poet."

It was exciting to be told, by one who *knew* the workings of the mind, that the experience called "a poem"—or any artifact—was not different *in kind* from any other tract of experience; that it was, indeed "life" again, but better ordered and more unified. A crowded hour of glorious life, in which all our inward conflicts were resolved and all impulses freed and integrated, would feel like—would *be*—the experience called "poetry." When not experiencing good poetry and when our minds are not otherwise fixed, our thoughts usually consist of "bad private poetry." The great benefit of all this lay in the wiping-out of the old artificial distinctions between Poetry and Life, Art and Morality. To those of us who were sick of the "Art for Art's Sake" doctrines then still in vogue, and all the affectations of the "phantom aesthetic state," this teaching came as a relief and a reassurance. It did not mean, of course, that poetry was again to be valued for any didactic content or avowed moral "purpose." I did mean that the *effects* of poetry upon the conscious and unconscious mind, and thus ultimately upon action, were of the first importance; and conversely, that "good" states of mind were akin to poetry—or one might say, were themselves lived poetry.

Richards, then, taught us vastly more than we had ever known before about what actually happens when we read a poem. He also did first-rate service—to the cause of education as well as to individuals—in his subtle analyses (in *Practical Criticism* and *Interpretation in Teaching*) of the numerous wrong ways in which poetry can be read. In all this the scientist in him was uppermost. Indeed, in his earlier work he was careful to declare himself a "materialist" or neo-Benthamite. In *Principles*, he propounds a Theory of Value which is meant to be "purely psychological"—i.e. to be expressed purely in quantitative terms (in "amounts" of satisfaction) without the surreptitious introduction of "ethical" concepts or judgments. It is an interesting detective exercise to try and spot just where—if at all, as I suspect happens in this argument —ethical notions ("importance") are in fact smuggled in. Again, in *Coleridge on Imagination*, he claims to write as a "materialist," separating Coleridge's psychology from his theology, and using his metaphysics as "machinery" only, although "Coleridge himself so often took it to be much more." (p. 21)

I wonder why I could never take all this professed Benthamism and nominalism quite *au pied de la lettre?* Perhaps because it reminded me of the early Coleridge declaring himself a "compleat Necessitarian" and a believer in "the corporeality of thought—namely, that it is motion." Yet we know that soon after this Coleridge said "I love Plato—his dear *gorgeous* Nonsense!"; and both Coleridge and Richards in their later work showed how very much Plato meant to them. The minds of both men were minds in continual growth, continual movement towards self-knowledge and self-realisation; and in their forward progress they delighted to try out one system after another to see where it might lead. Just as Coleridge proved greater than his early Hartleianism and Priestleyism, so Richards has proved greater than his early Benthamism and materialism. He always gave the impression of thinking that religion was a thing of the past: useful in former times of course, and still to be spoken of with respect, but now impossible. However, he has always wanted its vital functions to be performed and perpetuated by some other agency. The chaos of human impulses must somehow be ordered and harmonised, and it was for *poetry* to supply the place formerly occupied by religion. Whether or no this is a conceivable policy for the actual conduct of human affairs (I think not), there still clings, to the image one has of Richards, the quality of religious leader, prophet or guru.

This side of him appears clearly in his frank admission (a sign of true greatness) that in the last resort "critical principles," even good ones, cannot be used as a mechanical test in literary judgments. They can protect us from worse principles, and that is something—but that is all. The critic must in the end trust his "hunch": "there comes a point in all criticism," he says, "where a sheer choice has to be made without the support of any arguments, principles, or general rules." (*Practical Criticism*, p. 302) "The lesson of all criticism is that we have nothing to rely on in making our choice but ourselves." (*Ibid.*, p. 351) "The judgment that a passage is good is an act of living." (*Coleridge on Imagination*, p. 140) Richards has always known and taught that to set up as a critic is to set up as a judge of values; and this means that the critic must believe in his own sense of values, and must say to us, in effect, "I am a better judge than you are, and you would do well to try and become as like me as possible." He will not say this harshly and arrogantly, of course; indeed, if he is Richards, he will only imply it— and do so with consummate grace and charm. Like every great critic, he just convinces us, by being himself, that he is the sort of man to whom we should defer, and whose judgments will be sound.

And so we come back, after much voyaging through strange seas of thought, to the old certainties that poetry has to do with life, that it is an appraisal of life, and that good taste is an aspect of good character. Good taste is no mere luxury or embellishment, but a first necessity—especially for those who expect the arts to become a substitute for religion: "it was never so necessary as now that we should know why the arts are important."

Richards' prophetic character was apparent to his disciples from the start, even when in his youth he was being most gaily iconoclastic. His concern for the human predicament, and his sense of things about to be, have deepened with the years. The religious affinity of his whole programme can be illustrated (in conclusion) from a remarkable passage in *Practical Criticism*—a passage which nobody but he would have dreamed of writing. He is discussing how we can be sure that our responses to a poem are genuine, deep and sincere, and he suggests a possible "ritual" for testing them:

> Sit by the fire (with eyes shut and fingers pressed firmly upon the eyeballs) and consider with as full "realisation" as possible:—
> i. Man's loneliness (the isolation of the human situation).
> ii. The facts of birth, and of death, in their inexplicable oddity.
> iii. The inconceivable immensity of the Universe.
> iv. Man's place in the perspective of time.
> v. The enormity of his ignorance,
> not as gloomy thoughts or as targets for doctrine, but as the most incomprehensible and inexhaustible objects for meditation there are. . . . (pp. 290–91)

If this is not a form of "prayer" (or of preparation for prayer), it is something very close to it, and not at all a bad technique for anyone to use when faced with an important decision—*not* only about the value of a poem.

I have dwelt upon the image of Ivor Richards as "guru," and to this I would add just one more word. For those of us who know him personally, this impression is reinforced by the wonderful poise, gentleness and serenity of his character. But the same spirit is diffused throughout his writings. Everywhere he appears as a wise and understanding guide, a "Mr. Interpreter" and "Mr. Greatheart" in one, pointing out the way and accompanying us on our hazardous pilgrimage towards The Delectable Mountains.

KATHLEEN COBURN
I.A.R. and S.T.C.

I first beheld Richards in action (and it was a beholding) one evening in Oxford in 1930 or 1931 when he came over from Cambridge to address some literary society or other. The meeting was I think in Magdalen in the Great Hall. I remember a crowded room and an atmosphere of excitement and that the subject was literary "fictions." There were a good many questions from the floor, lively objections were raised, and there was much laughter—a very active "happening." At one point Richards, the better to see and hear his questioners, leaped in mid-sentence on to one of the dining-tables that had been pushed to the side of the room, and paced up and down on it briskly, talking the while to left and right. There was a gasp of concern lest in concentration on the argument he fall off. Someone near me said cheerfully, "Oh don't worry. He's a mountaineer."

Years later I thought of this moment when I was trying to trail Coleridge in Sicily from a few sparse notebook jottings and was discovering that instead of taking the natural low road by the sea Coleridge had preferred a steep and almost trackless way over the top, for Coleridge was a climber too (one of the earliest in the English Lakes). The slant of mind is similar in the two men, with enough craggy differences to give Richards the tussle he loves with a mountain, the search for toeholds physical or intellectual. Like Coleridge he knows, in the elements as in a poem, the pleasure of the sense of difficulty overcome.

To write about Richards' contribution to Coleridge studies in our time it would be necessary, it seemed, and a good excuse, to re-read everything Richards has written. But sitting down before the daunting blank sheets of paper, I find Richards' work like education in that old definition of it, i.e. what you have left when you have forgotten everything you ever learned. The assemblage of facts and evidence, the learned references, even the specific arguments, may be more forgotten than remembered; what Richards has given to our generation is not so much detailed propositions or information about Coleridge, as a way of looking to find him for ourselves, the basic questions to ask rather than definitions or answers. As F.D. Maurice said of Coleridge himself, "He puts us into a way of seeking." Richards is above all a great educator, in the root sense of the word dear to Coleridge, an *e-ducer*; all his studies are open-ended, and this is why he finds in Coleridge so compatible and so fruitful a subject. But the world did not know this Coleridge in 1924 when Richards began to write about him in *Principles of Literary Criticism.*

Even before *Coleridge on Imagination* (1934) one could have predicted from the first two books, *The Meaning of Meaning* with C.K. Ogden (1923), and *Principles of Literary Criticism* (1924) in which Coleridge is referred to more often than any other critic, that some day Richards would write on Coleridge centrally. *Practical Criticism* (1929) took its title and some of its tactics from Coleridge; *Speculative Instruments* (1952) is another title from him. Richards tells us that these phrases come from *Biographia Literaria*, and, by not giving chapter or page, shrewdly teases us into going back to that work to search out the contexts for ourselves.

It is interesting to notice that in the first reference to Coleridge in *Principles of Literary Criticism,* a passage in which Richards is quoting from various critics their "pinnacles, the *apices* of critical theory," the Coleridge phrases he chooses are "the best words in the best order," "unity in variety," "the synthetic and magical power of the imagination," potent words and dead-centre.[1]

---

1. In discussing metre he quotes Coleridge again as dropping "his incidental remark, just beside yet extremely close to the point," quoting the sentence from Chapter XVIII of *Biographia Literaria* about metre as providing "continued excitement of surprise and . . . curiosity still gratified and still re-excited. . . ." He objects to "the surprise element," arguing that the effect of metre is rather "through the absence of surprise, through the lulling effects more than through the awakening." Richards enjoys a healthy disagreement with his heroes at times, but if one may— a *diminuendo* indulge in a similar compliment—is he right? In the first place, Coleridge provides for the lull, the pull-back, the "reciprocation," as well as the surprise, does he not? And in the second place, does not the dominance of the surprise element or the hypnotic element depend on the kind of metre in question? The horseback gallop of John Gilpin lulls one along over the whole ride, and in Yeats's *The Lake Isle of Innisfree* we could fall asleep while "noon comes dropping slow," but what of the metrical surprise of *Christabel,* for instance? Or of much of Richards' own verse, *The Ruins* for example, or *Alpine Sketches?*

Again he quotes, as an improvement on Tolstoi, "the poet described in *ideal* perfection, brings the whole soul of man into activity," adding, "As so often, Coleridge drops the invaluable hint—almost inadvertently. The wholeness of the mind in the creative moment is the essential consideration, the free participation in the evocation of the experience of all the impulses, conscious or unconscious, relevant to it, without suppressions or restrictions." Two pages onwards he tackles the most controversial sentence in *Biographia Literaria* (Chapter XIII): "The primary IMAGINATION I hold to be the living Power and prime Agent of all human perception, and as a repetition in the finite mind of the eternal act of creation in the infinite I AM." Of this he says, "The luminous hints dropped by Coleridge in the neighbourhood of this sentence would seem to have dazzled succeeding speculators. How otherwise explain why they have been overlooked?" One may well ask how much of its present familiarity this sentence owes to Richards' calling attention to it. In going on to discuss Coleridge's further descriptions of imagination in Chapter XIV, Richards made the astounding (in the 1930's) and courageous assertion that "there is enough in this description and in the many applications and elucidations scattered through the *Biographia* and the *Lectures* to justify Coleridge's claim to have put his finger more nearly than anyone else upon the essential characteristic of poetic as of all valuable experience."

In 1934 came *Coleridge on Imagination*, for one reader at least exactly the one right book at the right time. To a student already Coleridge-bent, it was a direction-finder, at once a stimulant and a reducer of the swelled head. It opened up an immense new terrain. I have elsewhere (on Richards' own pages and by his invitation, so truly Socratic is he in his love of dialogue and argument) recorded some minor difficulties with that work. But there is no doubt whatever that the forceful influence of the whole was to make us look at Coleridge afresh, and also to look again at the imagination and human communication. The world has not been the same since.

Coleridge on Imagination is one of the few works about Coleridge written in the 30's and 40's that could stand up to a re-review now, in the face of the new materials coming to light. What it did was to divert the stream of criticism into new courses, various courses. It may be said that *Principles of Literary Criticism* and *Practical Criticism* had already eminently done this. True. But *Coleridge on Imagination* delivered a special blow to the narrow moralistic rigidities of neo-humanism and to a confined historical approach to literature by taking the war even closer to the enemy ground. Babbitt in 1919 had attacked Coleridge in an essay, "Coleridge on Imagination," and the attack must have surprised those who, on the basis of some nineteenth-century views about Coleridge (Henry Nelson Coleridge's, for example), saw in Coleridge a partisan of the same establishment. Richards delivered Coleridge from reactionary claims on him and stood him before us on his own evidence.

Another impression that *Coleridge on Imagination* did much to discredit was the Coleridge of inspired fragments, the incomplete Coleridge. Not that Richards was concerned to "restore" Coleridge. It was part of the virtue of the work that it was neither a defence nor an archaeological dig. Richards began with a mind that excited him. He took the trouble to read Coleridge for himself and found there a kindred spirit useful in the ways that mattered to him: a man concerned with words and their meanings as vital to all human activity and relationships.

For words made man and may unmake again.

In his Preface Richards announced firmly his assumptions: Coleridge was a "semasiologist—aware as few have been, that to ask about the meanings of words is to ask about everything . . . that we still need to improve our understanding of language; that his unique combination of gifts enabled him to make some essential steps towards immense improvements." Undoubtedly one of the "immense improvements" that attracted Richards was Coleridge's incisiveness in distinguishing between meanings and his insistence on the proper uses of words, based on an analytical attention to roots, all this with a clear avoidance of "the one-true-meaning superstition." For Coleridge as for Richards, words are dynamic organisms that grow, change, and are related to their environment. "No passive tools," but sharp-edged, very dangerous, and vitally affecting the whole human scene. A hundred years apart, the two share a sense of human disaster, imminent unless men think and share their thoughts more clearly.

Richards said that he did not wish to catalogue historically nor to analyse Coleridge's thought as a whole, but "to extract . . . from the confusing network of his speculations and observations, those hypotheses which seem most likely to be useful in other hands," in the belief that "a further development of Coleridge's method would fundamentally change current conceptions of the relation of Poetry to Life, and with this the contemporary tone of criticism . . . it would be more experimental and less self-assertive." Perhaps Richards, in this again resembling Coleridge, was offering a prescription that could be fully effective only with a change of heart in mankind. The "delights" Coleridge offers, he says, "are most often glimpses of a new possible theoretic order—behind them hope for new power thence; behind that again a regress of visions, of the rectified mind and the freed heart. . . . He gives these best in quintessences. I take what I can and dilute it to more convenient and more controllable measure."

Yet Richards concerned himself with the whole of the mind, the "I am," in lower case, and the word, the logos, also in lower case. He had already called attention to the high-flown sentence in which Coleridge relates these to "the eternal act of creation in the infinite I AM"; he was not evading this Coleridgian analogue, only not centering his attention on it. He found in Coleridge an observer of human experience with the capacity to be disturbed, and to disturb, with far-reaching questions (not just little literary problems), a man with an inner readiness similar to his own, to strike out on an unknown track. He also found in him a great impersonality of motives and concern. Without turning Coleridge into a theorist or his ideas into abstractions, Richards, with his gift for seeing the ironical, was able to sense his principles accurately as the creatve product both of cerebration and of deep human suffering.

The key for Richards then is Coleridge's attention to words: the language of day-to-day usage, of the moral indicatives, the cultural subsumptions, and the language of poetry. But a strict regard for words is fruitful, possible even, only to the person who examines clearly and courageously his own experience of life and of literature. In demonstrating this clarity and this courage Richards did away with Coleridge the day-dreamer, also with the patronized wonder-boy, also with the half-German thief-in-the-night (or broad-daylight snatcher) who from Ferrier onwards was the victim of the cops-and-robbers approach to literary ideas. Instead Richards shows a Coleridge whose great, perhaps greatest, gift was his readiness and ability to observe truly what his own experience brought him, most notably the experiences of infinitely subtle mental and emotional states. His kind of attention to words is indicative of a mind that listens and watches and takes very little for granted. We are coming to know a Coleridge who proved things on his pulses. It is, I think, fair to say that this Coleridge is commonly the one that confronts editors of Coleridge. In attempting to annotate a text there are frequently moments of incredulity, or even of quick dismissal of a reading or a statement, and, just as frequently, corroboration comes, perhaps from some totally unexpected quarter, that he was not talking through his hat and that he rightly meant what he said. Richards taught us that we still have to catch up with Coleridge. To Richards more than to anyone else, we owe the view of Coleridge as a great experiencer, a critic not out of theory but out of experience, and a philosopher not of the remote, the over-subtle, the cob-webby, the vague generalizations, but of what he felt on the skin, heard, smelled, touched, and saw. This is not to gainsay the learning and the wide reading, but it is to understand that these had to go through the processes of a relentlessly questioning mind.

Richards bases his analyses on specific references. First of all because like Coleridge himself he talks about objects in front of him, and also because he paid Coleridge the rare honour, already mentioned, of reading Coleridge's works carefully, prose and poems, without pre-judging them. One could make a considerable list of Richards' specific revaluations, or rather his new looks at Coleridge, for as Faustus says in *To-Morrow Morning, Faustus,*

The answer to thinking's another way to think;
What you find is how to look for another thing.

For example, his was the first really critical use of *Biographia Literaria* to make us take it seriously in the context of our own time. He corrected (without chasing the usual red herrings) the view that would identify Wordsworth and Coleridge as theorists in poetics, and he dissociated Coleridge from Wordsworth's hostility to science. Coleridge's philosophy he questioned, as a system, deeming the materials inadequate, without resorting to a disparaging "fragments" theory, or undervaluing the mental prowess behind it. He called in question the lazy hackneyed notion that Coleridge, from philosophy, or frustrated love, or drugs, or some other thing, stopped being a poet about 1802; and he rescued, by quoting them as only one quotes into whose bone and flesh the poems have penetrated, the lovely almost unknown later poems. He also delivered and published a memorable lecture on them, *Coleridge's Minor Poems: A Lecture . . . in Honor of the Fortieth Anniversary of Professor Edmund L. Freeman at Montana State University on April 8th, 1960.*

These specific services to Coleridge's influence were indirect, and the greater because Richards was not concerned with reputation in any way.

To Coleridge scholars at work, his services, though considerable, have created nothing that can conceivably be called a cult. Coleridge does not attract idolaters, being rather too quizzical, even sceptical, for that. Coleridgians are as various as their subject. Yet it should be said that although Richards was never involved with the editing of Coleridge now going on—letters, notebooks, works—he helped to create the incentive for it and to point to some of the larger purposes a more complete presentation of Coleridge's mind might serve. Without him the *Collected Works* would have set sail, but his navigational aid, unknown to him, has been real. His radar is perhaps surprisingly often picked up, surely because Richards' processes and Coleridge's are in many respects akin. Both of them see poetry and the language of poetry as being at the core of the most serious human problems—the means by which, if at all, chaos must be tamed and order found. To survive we must educate our imagination to understand one another's predicaments and to communicate freely and with full awareness of the levels on which we do so. Like Coleridge, and unlike Housman, Richards sees that "*What we say*, and *how we say it* are inseparable in utterances that are entire." Both Richards and Coleridge stress the necessity of the reconciliation and co-operation of heart and head. Richards asks for exactly what Coleridge spent his life urging on his readers, a "searching and imaginative consideration of purposes and principles." Richards is with Coleridge, too, in disliking pedantry, in detesting certain kinds of power, and in distrusting the too fashionable. Neither of them as critic has dealt much in personalities—with a few notable exceptions. It is the wider horizon that beckons them (not that they ignore however, the Cambridge daffodil or the Somersetshire furze at their feet), and the deeper human plights. The arcs of their thinking are wide: for example, in *Practical Criticism* Richards links Schiller and Coleridge as two of the tough-minded critics; in "Mencius Though the Looking Glass" he sees Mencius, Plato, and Coleridge as a meeting of minds. He quotes Coleridge as giving (in his criticism of Shakespeare)

> "the only abstract rule common to" all animals, languages, and societies: that each must be judged in terms of its own organization, not that of any other. . . . Two doctrines as different as those of Mencius and Plato come remarkably close to Coleridge on this. They seem to agree on the great liberating lesson, the root of charity (as, for Plato, of Justice): for each being, its virtues and its defects are due to accordance with or departure

from itself. "A word may do what the rest of the language will let it."

So with a cell and with a citizen.

Richards gave us a new vision of the role of Coleridge. Among the critics—philosophical, literary, and social—among the poets, the language-discriminators, he saw Coleridge as one supremely useful to the world's crucial need of understanding how meanings, words, and imagination work. Here he could study the dynamics of communication with the combination of deep feeling and impersonal intellectual fervour that is the mark of minds of a certain magnitude, of that true conjunction of heart and head that he and Coleridge represent as well as advocate. Being a climber, and a responsible one, Richards not only gave his predecessor on the peaks his due, but left blazes on his trail or, one should say, set up way-marks, to indicate how one got there and to point to other possibilities worth following, if we have the will.

Guide for all comers;
Stoneman beyond
Winters and summers,
Cannot and could;
Steadfast, in bond,
Shafted secure,
With a crest of bright quartz
To sharpen the lure.

Forty years on, a recent glimpse of Richards is as characteristic as the first.

On Frying Pan Island in Georgian Bay his eye was caught by an unusual slab of granite, up-ended. It was one of two memorials, one to De La Salle, one to Champlain, and it read:

Samuel de Champlain
by Canoe
1615
As for me, I labour always to prepare a way
for those willing after me to follow it.

Richards was moved, admired it, and, one felt, had at least a split second (all one can hope for in so modest a man) of self-recognition in identification with that hardy explorer. Then, looking out over the broad sweep of waters to the horizon he said gently, "I should have liked it better without the *after me*; that was unnecessary."

JOHN PAUL RUSSO

Richards and the Classical Tradition

This essay will not concern itself solely with Richards' supposed conversion from positivism and behaviorist psychology to Plato in the early and mid-thirties, but consider his general attitude toward and specific works on classical Greece. The "conversion" has long been a question in Richards' life and it is problematic of certain preconditions in his criticism, not least of which is the matter of belief itself. Critics since Ransom have made something of a crux on the subject of Richards' detour through the second volume of the *Biographia Literaria* on his way to Greek philosophy and Homer.[1] Taking a long view, Harry Levin cites the epigram of Coleridge that every man is either a Platonist or an Aristotelian and remarks that Richards "started on the ground as an Aristotelian and moved upward into the stratosphere of eternal ideas."[2] Most recently the Italian scholar Giovanni Cianci detects "la conversione (dallo scientismo)" as early as *Science and Poetry* (1926) when T. H. Huxley's image went into eclipse before Arnold's.[3] But Richards denies such conversions. He wrote not long after finishing *Coleridge on Imagination* (1934) "I am, so far as I know, without Beliefs,"[4] and said he preferred attitudes, settings of the will, concentrations of attention, without the secondary sanction of being called Beliefs.

In recent publications Richards has begun reminiscing over the directions and "eddies" of his own career and we now know that any conversion goes back not just to his work on Coleridge, nor to his practical or

1. John Crowe Ransom, *The New Critics* (Norfolk, Conn.: New Directions, 1941), pp. 74–76.
2. Harry Levin, *Why Literary Criticism is Not an Exact Science* (Cambridge, Mass.: Harvard University Press, 1967), p. 14.
3. Giovanni Cianci, *La Scuola di Cambridge: La critica letteraria di I. A. Richards, W. Empson, F. R. Leavis* (Bari: Adriatica Editrice, 1970), p. 78.
4. "What is Belief?" *Nation*, 18 July 1934, p. 73.

psychological criticism, but all the way back, of course, to his childhood. Pope late in life remembered reading Homer in childhood "with a sort of rapture" in John Ogilby's lame verse translation, "that great edition with pictures" he told Joseph Spence. And Ruskin opens his *Praeterita* with fond recollections of reading Homer in Pope's translation. Richards begins his long autobiographical essay "Sources of Our Common Thought" with an early memory of "some large volumes of the Earl of Derby's verse translation on a reachable shelf . . . wide and spacious pages of verse as I seem to recall them." [5] Afterwards, however "desultorily" he dipped into the classics as a boy, he did pursue Latin and Greek at Clifton College, where he received a rigorous public school education on the Arnoldian model.

At Cambridge University Richards read history but changed after a term or two to Moral Sciences, and the distance between him and the classics widened. For one of the striking characteristics of Cambridge education in philosophy was and is the separation between ancient and modern philosophy. "To this day the history of philosophy begins for the student of moral science here with Descartes," writes C. D. Broad, "whilst Greek philosophy is a branch of classical studies. There is practically no overlapping either of teachers or of students." [6] Such institutional compartmentalization of humane learning can have serious consequences, as we know today from the experience of university language departments. Richards has said that McTaggart, who was his first tutor in Moral Sciences, had little influence upon him, while W. E. Johnson, his second tutor, had begun his studies in mathematics before turning to logic and psychology. A major influence, G. E. Moore, had in fact begun in classics at Cambridge, but turned early to philosophy and lectured on psychology and metaphysics. Thus Richards' studies at Cambridge were not such as to reinforce any proclivity toward classical culture or literature. When, after three years, he returned to Cambridge in 1918 to study medicine, or rather pre-medical subjects, it seemed to him as though his career were set in the direction of psychoanalysis.

There was, however, one more opportunity for an encounter with the classics at Cambridge in the years after 1918, his close friendship

5. "Sources of Our Common Thought: Homer and Plato," *The Great Ideas Today* 1971 (Chicago: Encyclopaedia Britannica, Inc., 1971), p. 281.
6. C. D. Broad, "The Local Historical Background of Contemporary Cambridge Philosophy," *British Philosophy in the Mid-Century: A Cambridge Symposium*, ed. C. A. Mace (London: George Allen and Unwin, 1957), p. 16.

and collaboration with C. K. Ogden. The polymath Ogden had received a First in the Classics Tripos, and with his many-minded attitude toward languages, classical and modern, he might have kindled Richards' interest. But Ogden was himself going in a different direction. There is little reference to classical philosophy in *The Meaning of Meaning* or their other collaborative efforts. And there is little mention of classical authors—occasional words on Aristotle, Longinus, and Horace—in *Principles of Literary Criticism, Science and Poetry,* or *Practical Criticism.*

One curious defeat at the hands of Homer, or Homer's translators, he recollects; it occurred on a journey from Moscow to China on the Trans-Siberian railroad in 1929, on his way to teach at Tsinghua University in Peking. He took along a small pocket edition of the Lang, Leaf, and Myers translation of the *Iliad.* "It bristled with *thees* and *thous, thereofs, wherebys, haths, doths,* and *eths* throughout—a 'grievous bane' indeed; but, nonetheless and despite all that, how could I have remained untouched by what—however oddly—the pages still were saying?" He relates sadly that he got nowhere and "with the failure there perked up, I recall, quite ridiculous misconceptions and suspicions of and revolts against I don't know how much of tradition." [7] Having confessed his own "humbling repulse," he goes on to say that it was his experience in teaching English literature in Peking that would lead him on much later toward designing for education basic texts of Western culture such as the *Iliad,* the *Republic,* and Plato's dialogues on the trial and death of Socrates.

What Richards discovered in teaching English to the Chinese was the incomprehensibility to his audiences of what he had to teach. This led or forced him back into considering—"as I had hardly done before —how I myself had, so I thought, come to comprehend whatever I did of what I was trying to put before them." Upon what does understanding depend? Not merely communication, but intelligent and discerning agreement, even the agreement to disagree. The serious difficulties that his Chinese students encountered were of course linguistic and cultural, springing from their lack of knowledge of Western intellectual traditions and culture. It was clear to him that before he could teach Western literature in English he had to develop programs for teaching the English language itself. And before he could develop programs in English, he had to understand Chinese and Chinese culture. Richards' first positive encounter with classical culture was, strikingly

7. "Sources of Our Common Thought: Homer and Plato," p. 281.

enough, with Chinese classical culture, especially the writings of Mencius and Confucius. We may easily dismiss the pronunciamento of Jacques Lacan that Richards' studies in Chinese are a throwback to seventeenth-century English orientalism. For Richards was one of a small group of Westerners in China (Arthur Waley, a close friend, was another) that sought genuine intellectual and imaginative understanding of Chinese poetry and philosophy—and "psychology"—long before they became fashionable. During the 1930's he labored with great effort to approach Chinese poetry and philosophy at the grammatical and semantic (and, for poetry, phonological) levels. His *Mencius on the Mind* (1932) was cautiously subtitled "Experiments in Multiple Definition." Translation, particularly between such vastly differing cultures, had to involve not singular, but multiple signs, and even at that one might easily fail. His *Basic in Teaching: East and West* (1935) was an enchiridion for Western teachers who would take Basic English into foreign cultures or into their own culture. It was also a stern warning against cultural snobbery. And his 427-page manual, *A First Book of English for Chinese Learners* (1938), climaxing one extended sojourn in mainland China, laid a seal on his claim that he was trying, and would continue in the years ahead, "(1) to do something to ease, in time, the task set the Chinese people and the Western peoples of understanding better one another's positions for living, and (2) by the same means help forward and speed up a supply of persons more competent to meet what were clearly going to be the ever more overtaxing problems of our planet." [8] A more succinct definition of the active life in the modern world is hard to come by.

Since we are now reviewing the period of Richards' career that is so often singled out as a period of conversion, we might look more closely at the influence of Coleridge. Is *Coleridge on Imagination* (1934) a long bridge-passage, a detour, a rejection of behaviorism, a stepping-stone? Let us for a moment look at the problem from the point of view of language training, that is, from the perspective of his career *after* and not (as usual) before. Language was from his earliest studies a *means* for thought. How could he develop, through training in language, a more efficient and a more moral use of the mind for children, for new learners, and for speakers? "From Criticism to Creation" (*TLS*, 27 May 1965) is the essay in which he describes the Coleridgean experience, although Coleridge, it would seem, went the other way, from Creation to Criticism. His work on Coleridge, coterminous with

8. *Ibid.*, p. 284.

his Chinese experience, marks his turn from criticism, from experimental and research studies in language deficiencies, to creation, to program designs, inventions, to translations of Homer and Plato, and in the process to the development of his own philosophy.

Coleridge's "most seminal hint" for Richards lay in the twenty-second, and not the fourteenth, chapter of the *Biographia Literaria:*

> When we consider, that the greater part of our success and comfort in life depends on distinguishing the similar from the same, that which is peculiar in each thing from that which it has in common with others, so as still to select the most probable, instead of the merely possible or positively unfit, we shall learn to value earnestly and with a practical seriousness a mean, already prepared for us by nature and society, of teaching the young mind to think well and wisely by the same unremembered process and with the same never forgotten results, as those by which it is taught to speak and converse.

Writing emerges, then, as a means of "re-examining, rearranging, reshaping" the results, conventions, and methods of man's first and most significant achievement, one that goes into the very definition of his essence, the acquisition of speech. The study of a *new* (one's second or nth) language provides an opportunity for taking up all the chances that were lost if one's first learning to write were treated as "no more than a Morse-type code, a mere transcript of speech." The transition from an oral to a written culture is a paradigm for the learning of a new language; an archetype for the transition in Western culture is that "from Homer to Plato." Moreover, such a "transition," Richards well knew, could be one of the major cultural achievements in the twentieth century—worldwide literacy. What needed to be done was to teach people, in learning to read and write, how to think. And the best method was (a) to deal with major texts that really could teach one how to think; (b) to set these texts into a simplified version of English, an international second language, designed to facilitate teaching definition, argument, etc.; and (c) to choose in the language of the particular culture texts that are in the process of transmission from oral to written statement, "for holding up and looking into the miraculous but fleeting achievements of oral utterance." [9]

---

9. In *So Much Nearer: Essays Toward a World English* (New York: Harcourt, Brace, 1968), p. 6, Richards cites Eric Havelock's discussion of this transition (*Preface to Plato* [Oxford: Blackwell, 1963]), with which he is apparently in agreement. "In the Greek case the outcome was singularly happy. But with the cultures,

D. S. *Rawson*

Dorothea and Ivor Richards, in camp on Maligne Lake, Jasper National Park, 1945. I.A.R. doing his Basic version of Plato's Republic.

In 1939 Richards attended a gathering of newcomers to Harvard University under the auspices of President Conant and met another newcomer, Werner Jaeger. Jaeger's *Paideia* was a monument to the humanistic conception of Greek classicism in its generation and is so for us today; it is a shame that its impact has fallen most often beyond classics departments. "Modern historical philology, like other simplifications (or inventions, if you like) that came to power in the eighteenth century," Richards remarks on the detritus of classical learning, "has been extremely subversive in professing to present to us 'the full facts.' It has buried Plato in the dead leaves of a wood that has vanished into trees." [10] But Richards found in the person and the work of Jaeger a model of a many-sided humanism, and expressed his in-

say, of Africa, there are grave reasons to fear that values now carried in speech will be swept away without compensating gains for any but an unhappily separated few," p. 20. Note also Bruno Snell's *The Discovery of the Mind* (Cambridge, Mass.: Harvard University Press, 1953), ch. 1.
10. "The New 'Republic,'" *Nation*, 28 March 1942, 371.

debtedness in various places, from his first preface to his translation of the *Republic* in 1942 to "Poetry as Paideia" in 1971. He had recourse to Jaeger often as he worked on his translation of the *Republic*. This version in an expanded Basic English was initially prepared for the use of men and women in the armed services during the Second World War. *Paideia* was doubtless useful to him when he taught "Humanities 1a: Homer, the Old Testament and Plato" in the fall terms of 1946–48 in the new General Education program at Harvard. (Richards had been one of the eleven members of the committee that created this program.) I have several times heard him quote Jaeger's Introduction to *Paideia*: the Greeks "considered that the only genuine forces which could form the soul were words and sounds . . . rhythm and harmony," and not the plastic arts. "For the decisive factor in all paideia is active energy." [11]

Richards' main contributions to the study of ancient Greece are his three major translations—*The Republic* (1942, 1966), *The Wrath of Achilles* (1950), and *Why So, Socrates?*, a dramatic version of Plato's *Euthyphro, Apology, Crito,* and *Phaedo* (1964)—and his unpublished philosophical inquiry on the nature of Sameness and Difference in *and* between the *Iliad*, the Book of Job, the *Republic* and other Platonic dialogues, and the *Divine Comedy*, tentatively entitled "Beyond." The translations are in expanded versions of Basic English, each designed to fit the specific needs of the text at hand. Thus for the *Iliad* Richards exceeded Basic's 850 words by almost five hundred since swords and shields were no longer Basic. Each translation is accompanied by an introduction in which he sets forth the aims of his author and his translation.

Two short, as yet unpublished plays, *Homage to Hector* (1970–71) and *The Wrath of Achilles* (1970–71), have been drawn from his version of the *Iliad*. The first was performed by students of the Harvard Dramatics Club in the Experimental Theater of the Loeb Drama Center, Harvard University, 1–3 April 1971. I have happy memories of Richards in the role of the Trojan rhapsode, dressed in a long black robe and a heavy golden necklace. I myself played the Greek rhapsode. Together we formed a choric background, providing introductory material, occasional narrative links, and voicing long Homeric similes. It was a kind of story theatre, and we offered a dialectical antiphony to the

11. Werner Jaeger, *Paideia: The Ideals of Greek Culture*, trans. Gilbert Highet (New York: Oxford University Press, 1939), I, xxvii.

real conflict there before us. A videotape of the performance was made by the Audion Corporation of Cambridge.

This casting into dramatic form of materials he had already published as narrative epic made the *Iliad* conform to a pattern of his other work on the classics, that is, a pattern of a dialectical drama. Both "drama" and "dialectic" are key words in his late criticism. When exactly these concepts arise is difficult to say, certainly early in his career, but the *Republic* translation must have focused his general disposition toward and his keenness for forensic interaction, multiple points of view, and attitude as opposed to doctrine. After he had first "fumbled" with casting the *Iliad* into two dramas, he turned his attention to dramatizing the trial and execution of Socrates. And he found that the four Platonic dialogues could be most effectively presented if he took a clue from Aristotle and provided them with a beginning, a middle, and an end. A lively drama could, moreover, be easily used in classrooms, on radio, TV, cassette, etc., especially if it were set in a simple, supple idiom. As he writes:

> One merit of such a play would come from the tension with the *Iliad* it could set up, if taken as a due sequel. I had the *Republic*, in simple form, already, as a staging of the main clashes between them. But the *Republic* called for a more dramatic presentation of Socrates; in fact, for the crucial Socratic action to balance that of Achilles. I could not, of course, explicitly and consciously look for these things in dissecting out their action. Otherwise there would be many risks of wrenchings.[12]

He must then let the dramatic action reveal the essential and unfolding idea of the work. It would be Homer's drama of ideas as cogent as those debates at the Berghof high above Davos. Only he must disengage the action from its surrounding materials.

Let us look at the transmutation of the *Euthyphro* into Act One of *Why So, Socrates?* (1964). The dialogue is seen as a prelude to the trial. The trial itself, the *Apology* (Act Two), is by nature dramatic and very little alteration is needed in translation. But the *Euthyphro* is not dramatic, it is an essay on piety, and to make it more dramatic, to make it an integral part of a whole action, Richards uses it to emphasize the "unbreakable courage" of a Socrates in confronting an insensitive and fanatical foil, a Socrates already resigned to confronting a much greater adversary, the hydra-headed beast, the Athenian popu-

12. "Sources of Our Common Thought: Homer and Plato," p. 317.

lace. We witness in the exchanges between Euthyphro and Socrates a debate between two religions, two sincerities, two pieties. "The argument is not designed to show anything beyond the fact that two such sincerities—one so complex and so self-searching, the other so simple and so unacquainted with doubts—cannot meet." The definitions of piety by which Socrates confuses Euthyphro have both a serious and a preposterous air as if Socrates were playing with the man, and at the same time buoying his spirits for the truly profound encounter to come. If we may borrow Mann's phrase, a comic counterposition thus issues from a "lord of counterpositions" himself. Thus, the scene reveals Socrates in a very characteristic mood, a mood that will yet be very much present in the tense moments in the remaining three acts. His equipoise, his wit, his immense intellectual reserves are being strikingly prepared for by an admittedly easy joust with an unequal adversary. Later there will be an " 'impetuous valour' and a moral joy of battle." [13]

From an authorial point of view, the drama can be the preeminent form for not taking sides, or allowing many sides to come into play, and this is surely a part of its appeal to Richards' mind. All the issues and "beliefs" may be debated, may be anticipated, amplified, mulled over, before by a vault of mind we touch "the truth itself." This is what Plato in Richards' interpretation means by *dialectic*, most forceful in the earlier dialogues up to the *Republic* at the outset of the founding of the Academy. Afterwards, too often, even Plato could be bedazzled "by sudden increase of light" and take *side*. Richards defines dialectic as "the continuous attempt to audit an account of the meanings used in a discussion." [14] It stands in contrast to *eristic*, wordplay or word-fighting, the art of a speaker who is arguing for victory and not for truth. Dialectic is "the art of making clear in any discussion what the participants are really saying and thinking." [15] In these later definitions of dialectic there is the impress of Richards' earlier ideas on "multiple definition," "meaning" and "symbol" in *The Meaning of*

---

13. *Ibid.*, p. 318.
14. *So Much Nearer*, p. 4. Richards uses this definition to update our understanding of our modern instruments: "Dialectic would ask us to reflect as self-correctively as we can, and with all the aids that present day computer-handled data-processing can supply, on how ideas, ambitions, pursuits, quests for being and so on, compete within as well as between minds, and on just how selection among them may be taking place," p. 4.
15. *Plato's Republic*, ed. and trans. I. A. Richards (Cambridge, Eng.: Cambridge University Press, 1966), p. 9.

BEING   REASON

The GOOD

The Intelligible

Noesis

Dialectic FORMS

Episteme

D

Hypothetical, applied thinking   UNDERSTANDING

C

Dianoia

Becoming   The Sun   Belief

The Visible

Pistis

Things

B

Representations   Picturing
Depictions
Images   Eikasia
Reflections   eikon: likeness
Shadows   eikos: likelihood

Comparison, conjecture

Meaning and *Interpretation in Teaching*. And possibly dialectic enters into his interpretation of Socrates' "divine sign": "Socrates took this feeling, this sign, this voice, whatever it was, very seriously—so seriously that when he did *not* have it (so Plato suggests) he felt that what he was going to do was right."[16] Dialectic, in fact, is seen as "the supreme study, with Philosophy as its Diplomatic Agent," with all the other arts and sciences, including poetics, subordinate.[17] A general education like Plato's leads by degrees to dialectic.

We may be permitted, knowing Richards' fondness for philosophical diagrams, to sketch Plato's Divided Line after a model in his transla-

16. *Why So, Socrates?: A Dramatic Version of Plato's Dialogues: Euthyphro, Apology, Crito, Phaedo* (Cambridge, Eng.: Cambridge University Press, 1964), p. 3.
17. "Toward a More Synoptic View," *Speculative Instruments* (Chicago: University of Chicago Press, 1955), p. 115.

tion and to quote Plato at the end of Book VI of *The Republic*. The translation is Richards':

> Take a line and cut it into two unequal parts—the short part for seeing, the long one for thought. Then cut those two parts again in the same unequal measure. Now these divisions will be representative of degrees of being clear. As the shorter part [A] of what may be *seen*, come pictures: first shadows, the images in water and in smooth, bright and polished things, glass and the like. In the longer part [B] are all the things that these copying images are of—that is, the animals about us, plants, and all the things man makes. . . .
>
> In this shorter division [C] of the line we have to do with ideas, but with these two limits. First, that here the soul is forced to use bases or starting-points; it does not go on up to what they depend on, for it is unable to escape from and get up higher than these starting-point bases; secondly, that it uses, as mere pictures or parallels, the very physical things which are themselves pictured and paralleled by the images in the sort lower down still. And in comparison with these, they are said to be very clear and are given a high position.
>
> *Glaucon.* I see. You are still talking of what comes under geometry and the sister arts.
>
> *Socrates.* And by the other, higher, division of thought [D] you will see I mean that of which reasoning itself takes hold by the power of dialectic discussion. The things reasoning takes as bases are not taken by it as unquestioned starting-points, but as hypotheses, as helps or stepping-stones, as something to give a footing, or as springboards, by which it is made able to go up to that which is no such base which needs to be taken, but. is that on which all depends. And after getting to that it takes again a grip of the first things dependent on that, and goes down again to the outcome, making no use of any of the signs of the senses but only of ideas themselves, moving on through ideas to ideas, and ending with ideas.[18]

To quote Coleridge on Plato, an aphorism from *Aids to Reflection* that Richards cites several times: "This plank from the wreck of Paradise thrown on the shores of idolatrous Greece." Hypotheses, helps or stepping-stones, something to give a footing, springboards, these are the stages from which to achieve dialectic discussion. Elsewhere Richards employs Bohr's principle of complementarity in just this fashion, most

18. *Plato's Republic*, pp. 119, 121.

recently in a memorial lecture in 1972 honoring C. A. Mace. Multiple models, definitions, and attitudes are required for the investigation of reality and of "the Good" which Richards pictures in the diagram as an inverted question mark. Multiple points of view demand representation in a complete action like the drama itself. Richards is not arguing for any simple notion of cultural or moral relativism, but for the use of Plato's "central and supreme speculative instrument with other speculative instruments in varying settings . . . in the hope of some conjoint, some mutual and collective yield." [19] The yield is a knowledge that will be virtue. It is Plato's "remedy," voiced in the *Phaedrus*, "perceiving and bringing together in one idea the scattered particulars . . . and if any other man is able to see how things can be naturally collected into one and divided into many, I walk in his footsteps as if he were a god," says Socrates. "Those who can do this I call—rightly or wrongly, God knows—*dialecticians*." (265e, 266b) [20]

There yet may be another debt to the early Plato—or should we say Socrates—in Richards' political criticism, "Psychopolitics" (1942), *Nations and Peace* (1947), and particularly his "Address to the Harvard Alumni Association," delivered on the occasion of the announcement by General Marshall of his Plan in 1947. Richards asks how man might achieve self-control when he now has on hand such an arsenal of destruction. Words are not enough; what is needed is a deed by some one nation, or group of nations, unilateral disarmament and the leaving of its (or their) defense to a world government, the U.N. I think that we have an instance here of the Socratic doctrine expressed in the *Crito*: "It is never right to return a wrong or to defend ourselves against a wrong by threat of retaliation. . . ." (48a–49b)

While the dialectical method is employed throughout the as yet unpublished "Beyond" (1974?), Richards dispenses with dialogue and brings the arguments of Homer, Job, Plato, and Dante into opposition, debate, and sometimes tentative unity on questions of justice, destiny, and "the Good." In the Prologue ("a discourse or poem," he notes, "introducing a dramatic performance") Realism, Nominalism, and modern Conceptualism are ranged against one another; there is in addition a long section concerning C. S. Pierce's Platonist linguistics. Sameness and Difference are also in opposition after the manner of Plato's form and image. One chapter is entitled, significantly, "Some

19. *So Much Nearer*, p. 90.
20. *Plato's Republic*, p. 10. Note also Irving Babbitt, *Rousseau and Romanticism* (Boston and New York: Houghton Mifflin, 1919), pp. 15–19.

Vectors on the *Iliad*." Richards describes that scene, early in the *Iliad* (I, 188–222) when Achilles is "seen in two minds, 'divided in counsel.' " Agamemnon has threatened to take away Achilles' Briseis, and Achilles begins to draw his sword in retaliation. At this moment, however, Athena descends from Olympus and appears in a vision to him alone. She tells Achilles that Hera has sent her to tell him to restrain his anger, and that greater glory and booty will come to him as a result. Achilles obeys her. In this episode Richards finds an archetype of the effect of literature, for great literature may provide such a vision of Wisdom herself. It enables us to evaluate and validate our experience and judgment and thus is essentially formative: "Poetry *as Paideia*" is the title of the essay on Jaeger. Literature offers the frame within which we may "form our critical estimates of men's conceptions and depictions (through the millennia) of the superhuman forces (outside them and within them, before them and behind them) with and against which they have somehow to pursue their ways."

"Outer testimony" is the term that Richards uses to define the experience of the past and man's written record:

> (1) the textual and circumstantial (outer) data mentioned above and especially as to how good readers have hitherto connected the items one with another.

Here Richards would include literature and "tradition," including criticism. But the other testimony is "inner"; it is the individual identity:

> (2) our own (inner) uncertainties of experience—to which, after all, how we should take (1) cannot but be subject, since what meanings we find for (1) necessarily arise from (or through) (2). In trying to order as best we can these two fields of forces (i.e. to respond most entirely and least confusedly to them) we have two loyalties to reconcile: to (A) the position we imagine our poet, ?Homer, or some substitute for him?, to be devising and managing; to (B) the position we would acknowledge to be *ours*. The probability that our view of (A) will be unduly, maybe distortingly, shaped by (B) should be a major restraint. In matters so fundamental as these the two loyalties are hardly separable. We only come by our own view of our own position through our attempts to imagine the positions of others.[21]

Inner and outer testimonies are only hypothetically antipodal, for they grow in and through each other unceasingly, "two beyond-reckoningly

21. "Beyond," ms., p. 30. By permission.

complex systems of recognitions." But their confrontation marks Richards' adherence to one of the essential tenets of classicism, the existence of truth that is beyond the individual mind. Like Arnold he affirms a *something not ourselves that makes for righteousness*. Richards emphasizes the living nature of this truth since through time it undergoes transformation in its encounter, interaction, and "interinanimation" with individual experience. Tl us, dialectically, individual experience and judgment evaluates and validates literature.

In poetry and dialectic, that is, in poetic contemplation, we have Richards' supreme study. It is the conception of thought that is virtuous.[22] Earlier he had called it "the widest and most comprehensive co-ordination of activities" (*Principles of Literary Criticism*), or, taking a page from Confucius' *Chung Yung*, "a tendency towards increased order" and "sincerity" (*Practical Criticism*). I once thought Richards' first statements of this ideal were more closely related to his teacher Moore's "enjoyment of beautiful objects" as defined in his chapter "The Ideal" in *Principia Ethica*.[23] But Richards' concept goes beyond that. It is more nearly allied to the Greek aim of disinterested philosophic contemplation without being separated from moral action. "The man who is without qualification good at deliberating," writes Aristotle in his *Nichomachean Ethics* (1141), "is the man who is capable of aiming in accordance with calculation at the best for man of things attainable by action." And this, Herschel Baker remarks, "is the most urbane kind of humanism, one that candidly names as its object an attainable good." [24] In Richards' recent *Design for Escape: World Education through Modern Media*,[25] to take just one example, we have the attainable good of, and a program toward, world literacy.

22. "The Interactions of Words," *The Language of Poetry*, ed. Allen Tate (Princeton: Princeton University Press, 1942), p. 66. Conception, taken literally and with "full metaphoric liveliness," is a philosophy of poetic language, Plato, remarks Richards, has described it in the *Phaedrus* (277): "It is true he calls them 'scientific words' there, but he was concerned with the 'dialectic art,' which I arbitrarily take here to have been the practice of a supreme sort of poetry." This, we recall, was the kind of poetry that was "to replace the poetry Plato banished from the Republic."
23. "Richards and the Search for Critical Instruments," *Twentieth-Century Literature in Retrospect*, ed. Reuben A. Brower, *Harvard English Studies* 2 (Cambridge, Mass.: Harvard University Press, 1971), pp. 150–51.
24. Herschel Baker, *The Dignity of Man: Studies in the Persistence of an Idea* (Cambridge, Mass.: Harvard University Press, 1947), p. 63; reprinted as *The Image of Man* (New York: Harper Torchbook, 1961).
25. New York: Harcourt Brace, 1968.

ERIC A. HAVELOCK

The Sophistication of Homer

For Ivor Richards, revered friend and former colleague, who in all
that he has taught and written has held a lamp for us to see by.

It is difficult for a poet who composed in one of the dead languages to
gain much success in winning the attention of our present culture. He
will enjoy that unsubstantial esteem which is due to a great and ancient name, but only the scholars are likely to spend pains upon him.
Most of us seem to have more important things to think about, like a
voyage to the moon. If he is read is his own tongue he becomes a task,
a theme at school. If he is read in translation he virtually ceases to be a
poet at all. These barriers, that interpose between the modern mind
and its classical past, are in Homer's case raised higher by special difficulties. He is the most ancient of European poets, which for practical
purposes means the oldest poet we have. Not only is he a Greek poet,
but also in some sense a pre-Greek poet. Even to the men of his own
race who came after him, and who in the classical period memorized
his poems with affection and respect, his splendor was slightly archaic.
They revered him, but did not always understand him, a fact sufficiently betrayed by their attempts to allegorize his tales, to censor his
morals, or to correct his theology. His work takes its place along with
portions of the Old Testament as not just a poem, but as a massive
milestone in the history of human culture. It is a monument hewn in a
curious shape. It is a likeness of the pattern of the human mind not as
it exists today, but as it existed in those immense pre-literate epochs
when the common man did not read or write. Man's thoughts and his
speech were different then, different even from what they became in
the age of Pericles, and far removed indeed from ours. Homer therefore addresses us, if at all, across a great gulf of literate experience and
abstract habit.

It is no use trying to leap the gulf impatiently. Modern taste has
first to be reconciled to those qualities in his style and substance which
seem alien to modern literature. There is for example the diffuseness of

the epics. The *Iliad* begins, promisingly enough, by announcing as its theme a quarrel between two chieftains with fatal consequences for the Greek host. For the space of a book the setting is then developed with the rapid economical strokes of an artist with an eye to coherent effect. But as the reader then continues the saga, he finds it well nigh impossible to hold the thread of the promised drama, so frequently is it interrupted. Books two through seven constitute an enormous pause, giving us to be sure a great deal of background material, but nothing more about the announced theme which is not resumed until books eight and nine. Homer then inserts book ten which reads like a separate episode of night operations, after which the Greeks and Trojans trade blows for six more books. There is a lot of hard fighting of which the reader grows rather weary and which has no direct bearing upon the quarrel between Achilles and Agamemnon, until, at book sixteen, Patroclus, the friend of Achilles, complicates the issue by taking his friend's place in the forefront of battle and getting himself killed. By his death he at last involves Achilles in the main action. The reader's patience, if it has lasted this far, will now be rewarded, but at the cost of feeling that the whole tale would have been more effective if boiled down to half its present length.

Diffuseness itself is not a fatal defect in a work of art. The hero of a picaresque novel may become involved in episode after episode, but he remains the hero. Yet so much of Homer is not even episodic. The materials which clog his narrative exhibit the quaintness and confusion of an ill-assorted museum. From the point of view of epic artistry, who would not gladly scrap the catalogue of Greek and Trojan contingents contained in the *Iliad*'s second book? What modern reader does not grow impatient with the endless reminiscences of other sagas, about other wars and other cities; the genealogies and histories of clans; the topographies of districts; the catalogues of properties and precious materials; itemized lists of armour and ornament; detailed descriptions of rituals and sacrifices; and a great farrago of wise saws and instances?

Then there is Homer's diction and idiom. It is tautologous and repetitious. His heroes are never allowed to just speak or act or fight or sleep. They "speak and answer and utter winged words"; they "make covenant and swear"; they "are gathered together and meet in assembly"; they "consider and take thought"; and so forth. Lines and half lines recur like entries in a ledger. His characters are always "sailing over the unharvested sea" or "the wine-dark deep," "setting in order goodly hecatombs," "putting from them the desire of meat and drink" and the like. Most of them are encumbered with a variety of ornamental titles. Achilles is always son of Peleus or noble or swift of foot. Agamemnon is always son of Atreus or wide-ruling or king of men, Hera is white-armed or golden-throned, even when her behavior is anything but regal. These are all symptomatic of a general economy of vocabulary, a rigidity of idiom, which strikes us as archaic and even primitive, and recent Homeric scholarship has tended to confirm this judgement. This is the vocabulary and style of a pre-literate poetry composed of formulaic units hoarded in the poet's memory, a vast storehouse of verbal expressions of fixed metrical shape suited for fixed positions in the hexameter line. These formulas resist change, even when the contemporary speech is changing. So linguistically they constitute a hoarded amalgam of survivals from successive dialects preserved and embalmed in the bardic diction. Homer's Greek was never spoken in daily speech by any existing Greek tribe of any given epoch. It was never a vernacular, but always archaic in relation to contemporary speech, the product of a poetic economy which sought to mitigate the strain on the oral memory by preserving the traditional at the expense of the novel.

It has become equally clear that this archaism of language is matched by a similar degree of archaism in content. Whatever Homer's own date may have been, the tales he tells, the topographies, dynasties, wars, go back to a vanished Achaean culture identified from the site of Agamemnon's palace as the "Mycenaean Age." The inhabited sites, the architecture, the armour, the art uncovered by the archeologists all have their counterparts in the Homeric tales. The inscribed records of the Hittites and Egyptians may even preserve names which roughly correspond to Homer's Achaeans and Danaans. This culture by 1100 B.C. had been swept away and a new and very different Greece, the Greece of the historical period, emerged slowly from the ashes of the old. Homer lived in this new Greece or at the edge of it. But once more, as in his language so also in his content, Homer contrives an amalgam of preserved memories. He reports the Greece not only of the Mycenaean age but of the post-Mycenaean migrations. He remembers the Achaean confederacy which warred against Anatolia. But he also recalls the Phoenicians, their voyages and their art in the period when Mycenae was becoming a memory. His material like his diction illustrates that law of oral communication whereby the collective memory slowly receives and blends successive deposits of experience and fuses them incongruously in epic structures which take on the quality of a dream, a historical fantasy belonging to no fixed time or place.

For these very good reasons, the Homeric critic, however sensitive he may grow to the presence in the poems of a reflective genius, who somehow has placed a unique stamp upon this material, falls easily into the habit of picturing Homer, whether he was author or editor, as an itinerant bard of primitive resources who recited at the command of a rude aristocracy. Were not Agamemnon, Achilles, and their like princes who commanded the uncertain allegiance of barbarous retainers? Does not Homer himself sometimes represent the minstrel as their servant, obedient to praise the exploits of princely patrons, eating at the table in the great hall, sleeping maybe on the rushes which strewed the floor? Was the Greek community which he celebrated really a community, rather than a set of scattered cantons, each dominated indeed with an edifice which passed for a palace, but united only in a confederacy of freebooting, with the loosest sort of social structure? There are no thronged city streets (except in Troy), no docks and wharves (except in Phaeacia), no parliaments, no commercial exchanges and not much in the way of domestic affluence and leisured conversation. On the plains of windy Troy, as in the island manor of Odysseus, the atmosphere of the Mycenaean age predominates. Its values can be read as those of Greek "Vikings," men of shrewd but uncultivated instincts, and we may fall into the unconscious habit of picturing their poet as a man himself of rude genius with unkempt beard, blind perchance, and led by some boy to the site of the great hearth. While the cups clink he bends to tune his lyre and waits for boisterous laughter and rude jest to subside before beginning some song of the great deeds of heroes.

From such a poet we might expect what indeed we get in Homer, tales of battles, duels, cities, voyages, genealogies of great families, tribal customs, and accumulated lore. We might expect crude dynamic power, vivid similes recalled from nature and art, portraits of princes, queens, and serving men; heroic virtues, heroically portrayed. These too we get in Homer. We can even concede the existence of an oral genius powerful enough to impose some loose dramatic unity on his lays, grouping them round a chosen theme, the anger, the prowess, the deeds, the frustration, the self-discovery and the predicted death of a single chieftain, an Achilles. This too we get in Homer. The *Iliad* is indeed, as

Aristotle divined, not just a heroic tale, but also the prototype of a Greek tragedy.

But is even this the sum of the Homeric equation? So far, the virtues of the poem are seen to be monumental, they are attained by a great act of comprehension rather than by isolation and analysis of minute situation. The vision of life is direct and in a sense uncomplicated, or at least its complexities are felt and conceived within the value system of the heroic age. But are there any traces in the *Iliad* of a rather different perspective on the human scene, one which we might identify as cultivated and even complex, not to say ironic and detached—a perspective in short in which we might discern the urbanity characteristic of a leisured culture?

Comedy on Olympus

Consider in this context the vein of the poet's comedy, a vein confined to the margins of his plot. A sampling from the first book will suffice. The outbreak of a bitter personal quarrel between two proud leaders of the Greek army, placed against the background of a military crisis brought on by plague, is told in swift drama and with mounting intensity. Already we feel danger in the air as Achilles reveals the depth and passion of his anguished mortification at the slight put upon him by the forcible deprivation of his prize. As the scene shifts to the lonely seashore, and his mermaid mother rises from the sea to comfort him, we catch in her words a premonition that the end of it all will be not triumph but tragedy. But she will do what she can for him, she will aid him in his desire to humiliate the Greeks even as he feels he has himself been humiliated. She will go to Zeus and persuade him to guarantee that if Achilles withdraws from battle, the Greek army will be defeated.

The poet has furnished himself with occasion to transfer the action to Olympus, and at this point the heroic noises begin to fade out of his story. Zeus is discovered, seated apart in solitary grandeur, and Thetis is able to engage him in purely private colloquy. At least Zeus thinks it is private. She sits down in front of him to plead, reminding him of her past services to him, and importunately demands that he arrange matters so that the Trojans prevail, and the Greeks, recognizing their mistake, will then be compelled to honor her son. Zeus, who has his own reasons for wishing to refuse, is at a loss for words, but Thetis renews the pressure and makes it more personal and petulant.

"All right," she says, in effect, "say no if you want to, and humiliate me among all the gods." Thus she converts a matter of principle concerning someone else into a personal issue concerning herself. Coping with male chauvinism, we might feel she has little choice. Having thus succeeded in making Zeus feel very uncomfortable, she wins her point. He answers with reluctant exasperation, "Oh, heavens, you will involve me in a quarrel with Hera! Think of the unpleasantness! Her tongue has such an edge to it. She will get under my skin. As it is, she is already quarrelling with me, right in front of the immortal gods, and saying that I help the Trojans in battle. Please get out of here in case she notices. I will attend to what you ask and bring it off. Look, I promise." And he affirms his promise by the imperial nod of his head which shakes all Olympus. "Whereupon," says the poet, concluding this particular scene, "the conference between the two of them broke up."

He has managed to convey the sense of a tacit conspiracy between Zeus and Thetis based on communications of long standing, even at a moment when Zeus is not at all anxious to be caught in an interview on which his wife is bound to place the worst possible construction This, alas, is exactly what happens. Though Zeus does not know it, they have been observed. As the father of gods and men enters his great hall, the children all rise with some haste and wait for the autocrat to be seated. There are no exceptions. But Hera at once offers comment upon his recent absence. A king, like any other mortal, has to divide his time between business and family life, and the business of a king is to give audience and decision in the council chamber. "Who have you been in conference with?" she asks. "You are always making secret decisions when I'm not around. You never take the trouble to tell me." With wifely skill she has converted the incident into a general grievance, which is also personal, without revealing that she already does know the truth. Do we again note Homeric perception of a role which is required by a heroic society?

Zeus, anxious to conceal his pact with Thetis, falls into the trap. "Of course, my dear," he replies rather pompously, "you should not expect to know everything that is on my mind. Some things are too difficult for a wife to grasp. On the other hand, whenever there is anything appropriate for your ears, I'll be sure to let you know. But when I have a matter to think through in private, that's not your business."

Hera now has him where she wants him. She begins submissively enough, though with a hint of sarcasm. "Most dread son of Cronos, what a thing to say! Everybody knows you have to be left alone to think—that is, when you do think. I would not dream of interrupting you. But," she continues with sudden venom, "what I'm really afraid of is that Thetis has been after you—Thetis, that silver-footed one, that daughter of the old man of the sea. Wasn't she sitting beside you early in the morning, and didn't you promise her to honour Achilles by destroying the Greeks?"

Zeus, caught off guard, has no defense left. "My good woman," he exclaims in exasperation, "you're always up to something. You won't leave me alone! But it won't do you any good," he continues, "you are making yourself detestable. If it is the way you say it is, then that is the way I want it, and so much the worse for you." So far, perhaps, he feels his rejoinder is something less than effective. Is there a half-smile on Hera's face? So then, like a thousand mortal husbands, he can take refuge in bluster. "Shut up and sit down, and do as you're told. If I lay my hand on you, do you think any of the Olympians will stop my approach?"

Hera is now a little scared—she knows her Zeus, and knows when it is politic to stop. But she does so with reluctance, and her tightened lips show it. The rest of the divine family who are sitting around (or are they still standing?) waiting for dinner to begin, are very uncomfortable at the scene. There is an awkward pause. Whereupon Hephaestus, the lame son of this happily-married pair, hurriedly intervenes to help his mother and try to smooth things over. "Come now," he pleads, "this is so unpleasant, to have you two quarrelling in front of us all. Mortals aren't worth it, and besides, we want to eat. The dinner is spoiling. Mother has to give in, and she knows it. We can't have father in another rage, and the dinner all spoiled. We all know how powerful he is, how violent he can be. Mother you've got to change your tune, and make father feel better as well. Then he'll be agreeable to everybody."

Then, not content with words, he jumps up and takes his mother a drink to talk her out of the sulks. There is a touch of pathos here lurking under the surface of the comedy, and we learn incidentally that this son is lame, and why. "I know how you feel, mother, but you've got to put up with it. You know I love you but I don't want to see you beaten before my eyes. I won't be able to help you, you know, and I shall feel awful. It is not easy to confront our Olympian. There was another time when I was aiming to help you and he took me by the foot and hurled me from the heavenly threshhold." There had, then, been thrashings before in this Olympian ménage, and the boy had tried to protect his mother, and bore the permanent marks of his father's violent temper.

However, the vein of comedy returns. "I travelled all day," he recalls ruefully, "and at set of sun I fell to earth in Lemnos, completely winded." Hera, responding to treatment, smiles and takes a drink. The crisis is over, tension is broken. Hephaestus bustles around the whole company ladling out drinks. Somehow he looks so funny. They are all relieved, and show their relief by roaring with laughter at him. It was perhaps bad taste on the part of the immortals. They were laughing at his hobble, but they were thankful enough to have something to laugh at.

Observe the essentials of this domestic comedy, this Homeric version of Life with Father. Zeus, the autocrat, a genuine power in the house and a man of affairs, authoritarian, slightly pompous, but impressively masculine. The force of his direct and uncomplicated personality finds its counterpoise in a wife who has her own grievances, and her own less direct ways of dealing with them. She has her reasons. For one thing, Zeus is susceptible, especially to mermaids. So she conducts her own guerrilla warfare against him with appropriate weapons, and on this plane of manoeuvre Zeus is no match for her. He retrieves his authority, if not his dignity, by bluster and by his ugly temper. Scenes in this household are not infrequent. One son, Hephaestus, is his mother's boy, far too sensitive to endure the sight of his father beating his mother. Once he got in the way and was hurt, and one lesson was enough. Thereafter, he plays the peacemaker. He knows mother has an edge to her tongue. Then, for heaven's sake, let her curb it. In her worst moods he can get her to smile. There is some hidden bond of sympathy between the two. As for the rest of the grown-up children, and the in-laws, they all live in the same house, a large family mansion, a patriarchal establishment, a little overcrowded. Sometimes it is very awkward with all this wrangling and bad temper going on. Their relief when things are patched up is spontaneous.

Scholars will always dispute about Homer's theology. With his Olympian apparatus he can operate at more than one level, but surely in the scene just described he is putting the apparatus to one plain purpose, which is not theological, but artistic. His tales are laid in a masculine world of fighting and voyaging. It is easy to look heroic on the battle field. In the domestic scenes staged behind the battlements of Troy, in the royal palaces, the mood of heroism is still retained, as somber destiny requires son to depart from parents and husband from wife and child, and lover from mistress. But our poet is not content till the perspective is completed, and to the human heroic tragedy there is added the human comedy. What happened to the Viking chieftains when they were off duty, and there was not more raiding to be done, and they settled down at home? The poet sets out to portray the domestic backdrop to the great deeds of heroes, and slyly labels it Olympus. Thus he blunts the edge of his satire, making it perhaps more palatable, but he also retains the artistic advantage of operating one great set of characters, the mortal ones, at a level which is consistently serious. Shakespeare, confronted with the same problem of comic relief, likewise solved it by substituting for this purpose a different social level, by moving downwards to gravediggers and porters and the like. Homer moves upwards to Zeus and Hera. Either device preserves artistic unity of mood.

I do not think that into the Olympian scene just analyzed I have put anything that is not there. Homer did not invent comic gods. Other European sagas will, on occasion, burlesque the deities of their mythologies. Perhaps it was a primitive way by which man thumbed his nose at the powers he feared. But that is not quite the spirit of these particular scenes. The characters are sharply etched, the situation delineated with realism, and with nicety, and with an unsparingly ironic eye. Homer is looking at a domestic household with complex relationships and paints these in with strokes that are sure and swift. The total effect is coherent and also comic. In short, the low comedies on Olympus, inserted here and there throughout the poem, are not just slapstick in the simpler manner of the Teutonic and Icelandic sagas. They are a little too urbane for that. They are comedies of manners. Could anything be more realistic, amusing and cynical than the scene in books 14 and 15 in which, for practical and political purposes of her own, Hera decides that it is necessary to seduce her own husband, and brings this off with a complexity of preparation and a thoroughness of execution surely worthy of the woman who has already confronted us in the first book of the epic?

Yet it must be admitted that the studied coherence of these episodes, their urbane flavour, emerges clearly only on a second or third reading.

Why is this, if not because the author, or should I say, the composer, is all the time operating in an artificial and inherited medium, an oral vehicle of formulaic language, weighted with the repetitions, the circumlocutions, the stiff brocade, so to speak, of his style, a style which he manipulates to a sophisticated purpose, but one which is alien, I suggest, to the genius of the linguistic vehicle itself. We need the colloquialisms, the quick rejoinders, the staccato conversation of domestic intercourse to convey the comedy that he in fact conveys by another medium. A comparison with Aristophanes will illustrate the point quite adequately. Here surely is a paradox of art, and one which is as complete as anything to be found in European literature.

The Heart of Helen

This kind of comic portraiture relies on an intimacy between the artist and his human material, and this intimacy can repeat itself at a second and more serious level of sympathy when the same artist turns from comedy to consider the human heart and its affections. Possibly an appreciation of this fact lay behind the Socratic proposition that the composer of comedy is also the composer of tragedy. Homer at any rate can deal with Helen and her tragic situation with a degree of sophistication which recalls his powers of comic observation. Her name and role as the stolen wife for whose sake the war is fought recur formulaically in some twenty-six contexts in the poem, none of which go further than the formula. But on three occasions and only three she intrudes into the story in her own right, in the third, the sixth and the twenty-fourth books. The contexts are so dispersed that a close comparison between them may evade the critic's attention. But in what they explicitly tell us, and still more in what they implicitly reveal, they are both congruent and cumulative in their effect and in the information that is communicated to us. They occur wholly within Helen's Trojan context. Menelaus is present only as a memory, and poignant memory at that, of what has been abandoned and lost.

The personalities who successively are brought into conjunction with her are her lover-husband (so he is prefigured in ambivalent status), her lover's father, and her lover's brother: Paris, Priam and Hector. At each conjunction, the poet has contrived that rare effect of portraying a woman herself passive yet the repository of some latent force which impinges upon the men she meets, a magnetic pull to which they respond, and in responding reveal their respective natures. In the contexts thus prepared for her she is indeed presented as a man's woman.

The third book discovers Paris leading the Trojans to battle against the Greeks, till he unexpectedly confronts Menelaus from whom he had stolen Helen. He retreats precipitately with the involuntary fear of a man who has stumbled upon a snake. This provokes his brother Hector to assail him with reproaches. The lover of Helen, he exclaims, who brought wanton disaster on his own country by stealing her away is only a lover, not a fighter. "Why cannot you confront Menelaus, and realize what a warrior is he whose lovely wife you have taken. Little use your lyre would be to you then, and those gifts of Aphrodite, your flowing hair and good looks, when you make your bed in the dust!"

Paris attempts no retort nor on the other hand is he abashed by these reproaches. He replies with equanimity that Hector's mind is ever keen, like an axe that cleaves a beam. "Cast not in my teeth the lovely gifts of golden Aphrodite. The gifts that the gods may choose to give a man cannot be discarded, any more than they can be got just because he wants them."

Already the poet has used a brief dialogue to etch two contrasted types: the responsible elder brother, obedient to the call of duty, ever mindful of what is at stake for others, with a touch of Puritanism in his character which comes out as he confronts his younger brother, the Absalom of Homer's story, no mean fighter as it turns out, but a gay irresponsible figure who gets what he wants because of his god-given charm.

Paris straightway offers to meet Menelaus in single combat, on terms that the winner shall take all and the war between Greeks and Trojans ended. At once Hector is relieved and his heart gladdened. Preparations for the duel are set in motion; the epic stage is cleared as it were, for the two men in Helen's life, the wronged husband and the successful lover. At this point, the news of the impending contest and the issues at stake is conveyed to Helen herself. The audience at the epic recital are allowed to see her for the first time. Homer's touch here is sure; there is nothing wrong with his sense of timing. Her reaction to the news is simple and profound: "It put sweet longing into her heart for the man she had before, and for her city, and for her parents." She has then not forgotten, and in her adopted city is aware of isolation.

She hastens to the Scaean gate of Troy and over the gate are sitting the

Trojan elders, and Priam with them. These are old men and frail; their days of love and fighting are spent. Yet the woman they now see provokes from them no senile imprecations, no conventional denunciation. Rather they feel a faint stirring of the blood, a warming of instincts long disused: "Now when they saw Helen coming to the tower, they spoke the winged words in whispers to each other: 'What a woman! No good blaming the Trojans and well-greaved Achaeans for suffering all these years on her account! She is incredibly like the deathless gods to look upon. Yet for all her beauty, better she take ship and go with them, rather than be left behind to our sorrow and our children's sorrow.' "

Here is the eternal tribute of man to woman released by the immortal power of sex and acknowledged with an objectivity which is characteristically Greek. Equally characteristic is the sense of danger lurking within the embodiment of beauty. The tribute is all the more forceful as it is conveyed not in the impulsive rhetoric of the young and lusty, but by the considered testimony of the old, from whom any hope of seduction has been emptied away. As Helen herself becomes the instrument of revealing others, so also it is the old men who are used to reveal Helen. The poet intends her as the living symbol of passion, and as the focus of gallant response to passion, but the method by which this quality of hers is conveyed to his audience is oblique. Let others, even the old, by their reactions, tell us what Helen was like. She also as she passes will reveal to us what they are like. This two-way system of revelation by mutual reaction is typical of Homer's technique.

From this setting, the aged Priam then emerges into sharper focus. He lifts up his voice and calls to her: "Dear child, come and sit in front of me so that you can see the husband you had before, and your kindred and friends. I do not hold anything against you. It is the gods I hold responsible for bringing dolorous war upon me." She has been the instrument of his sorrow, but he has no reproaches for her, only affection. And he realizes, with the insight of age, that she is thinking of her own people on the other side of the battlements. So she proceeds to mark the Greek host, telling him the names of those she recognizes, and the chief warriors of the Greeks pass in review before us.

The duel is the next event, and it ends summarily and unsatisfactorily, for the poet still has business to finish with Helen and Paris. His intentions in this book are not directed upon the heroic themes of battle. Paris is worsted in the contest, but his luck stays with him. He slips from under the avenging sword, and is translated by Aphrodite's help, as in a flash, to his bedchamber, unruffled, relaxed, laughing, the darling of fortune. Helen has watched the tournament, and now at her elbow an affectionate retainer of hers, an old woman from the cherished past when she lived in Sparta, plucks at her sleeve: "Come with me. I have a message from Paris. He wants you to go home. Yes, Paris is in the bedroom. He looks just beautiful. You would never think he had just been fighting another man. It is as though he was on his way to a dance, or maybe resting in one of the intervals."

She is the voice of seduction sly but tender, prototype of the affectionate nurse of Euripides and Shakespeare, and she stirs response in Helen. But the response is complex, wayward and finally bitter. Beneath the old woman's disguise she recognizes the physical splendour of the goddess of love herself: "My divine dear, why do you persist in seducing me like this? Are you going to lead me a dance from city to city—through Phrygia or Maeonia maybe? Do you have a favorite man waiting there for me, now that Menelaus has beaten Paris, and wants to hale me home in disgrace? Is that why you are here at my side with your proposition?"

This is her point of release of all the pent bitterness which her destiny self-chosen has brought upon her. Homer for once omits all connection in his verse as she bursts out: "Go and sit beside him yourself. Abandon the primrose path of the gods. Never mind returning to Olympus. Stay around him, keep agonizing over him, keep your eyes on him! Wait for him to make you into a wife—no—into a slave. Go to him I will not, nor get his bed ready. It would be too shameful. All the Trojan women will whisper about me behind my back. I have grief enough and untold in my heart." Love's only answer is a stern warning: "You are going too far. Provoke me, and I will abandon you. I have lavished my affection on you. Just as surely I can cast you off. I can arrange for you to be hated by both sides at once."

Love is her *daimon*, the second self that now controls her as she silently and secretly returns to Paris' arms. To reject her role would be to reject her sex, and the magic of her name and nature would vanish. But as she greets Paris, the mood of revulsion is still upon her: "Here you are back from battle. I wish that mighty man had beaten you—the husband I used to have. Why not challenge him again? But no! Perchance his spear may overcome you. Don't be rash and fight him again."

The formulaic not to say ceremonial style in which Homer is compelled to clothe this intimate confrontation makes it hard to be sure whether her closing sentence is inspired by sarcasm or by a revived and protective affection for her lover. At any rate, he answers her with the same equanimity with which he had earlier replied to his brother's reproaches: "I have lost today. Tomorrow I will win. But as for now, O! let us go to bed. My senses are overpowered by you. It is like when I first took you, on Lemnos, after I had snatched you away from Sparta. Only now, the tide of my desire is so much stronger!"

Thus is the tribute to immortal sex renewed, this time from the young and lusty. His fascination for her, and her magic for him, jointly prevail as she follows him to bed. But how complex and even bitter has been the revelation of her own mood and destiny!

There, at the close of the third book, Homer leaves them. Unforgettably, and at some length, he has delineated Helen's divided heart. When she reappears, it will be to fill in and confirm the portrait already presented. The next two books are filled with the noise of dolorous war, till we come to the sixth. This book, in which Hector leaves the battle to summon further aid from Troy, is memorable for the scene of parting between himself and his wife Andromache. Her tears and entreaties, his own resolute affection, and the moment when both parents dandle the little boy and play with him, denominate a domestic relationship as simple as it is profound.

But there is a brief preface to this scene. Hector, on his way to his own house, calls at his younger brother's house to summon him back to battle. The domestic interior is one of surface dignity and repose: "He found Paris in the room looking after his armour, shield, breastplate, and trying his bow. Helen was seated surrounded by her domestic staff supervising the maids in their handicrafts." It is a tranquil and civilized scene; Helen and Paris enjoy no vulgar relationship.

On this scene impinges Hector. In the third book we saw Hector with Paris and then Helen with Paris. Now here the three of them are conjoined as Hector confronts Helen. The poet has created an opportunity for a further revelation of Hector's character, a marginal revelation, irrelevant to his epic role. We see him through Helen's eyes. She, his sister-in-law, furnishes footnote to his official character, as husband, father, and protector of Troy, and in so doing further reveals herself.

He begins the dialogue with an appeal to Paris to return to battle. In effect, he seems to be saying "Let bygones be bygones between us."

Paris replies that he need not worry: "It's not that I am angry. That's not why I am staying here. I just wanted to give way to my own bitter feelings." However, Helen, he adds, has already been gently urging him to reenter the combat. "Just give me time to don my armour" he concludes, "or else let me follow you later."

Hector makes no reply. But Helen fills in the silence. "Oh my dear, she says to Hector, "my brother, vile creature that I am—horrible instrument of woe," and overcome, she bursts into passionate self-reproach. Hector has power to break her down because of his affection for her: "Would that on the day when my mother bore me at the first an evil storm wind had caught me away to a mountain, or a billow of the loud-sounding sea." Then, recovering herself, she thinks of Hector and the burden he carries, and the contrast with Paris; if only she could do something for him: "However, since these sorrows the gods saw fit to assign, O! would that then I had been mated with a better man who knew what it is to feel respect and to realize the reproach of his fellows. Paris here is so unstable. Please come in and take this chair, brother. It is you that have to bear the anxiety and responsibility, and all because of me, bitch that I am, and Paris, who began it all. Fate is too much for him and me. So Zeus decrees, that hereafter we become a song on the lips of mankind." There is no hint of coquetry, nor taint of rhetoric, in this dialogue. The poet has distanced it, by giving Helen the power to foresee her own role in his epic. In the bitter dilemma of her troubled spirit, it is to Hector she has turned for confession, if not for strength.

All he can do is to ask her not to entreat him to stop: "I realize how you feel about me, Helen, but it's no good. The Trojans miss me when I am away. Just encourage Paris. He can bestir himself to join me. I must go on to my own house, perhaps for the last time." And so he leaves her, in order to have his last meeting with his own wife and child.

Yet once again, at the very end of the long tale, in the conclusion of the twenty-fourth book, the poet adds a postscript on this relationship, and as he adds, he underlines the inferences we have drawn. Hector is dead now: his corpse has been dragged round Troy; abused and mutilated; until at length ransomed for burial and brought back to Troy. The formal lamentations, in keeping with ceremonial requirements, are performed by Andromache and Hecuba, the widow and the mother, with appropriate sentiments. The end of the epic is at hand. But now that the pride and vain glory, the conquest and killing, the fate of

Troy, the public destiny of Hector, his city, his parents, his home, are all spent and fulfilled, Helen, for whom, one would think, space could scarcely be found in such a setting, is nevertheless allowed the last word, a private footnote:

Hector of all my brethren of Troy far dearest to my heart
My mate I know is Paris of the divine form
Who brought me to Troy land—and would I had perished first.
I have now seen nineteen years go by
Since I left my own country
Yet never yet from you in all that time have I heard an evil or despiteful
    word.
Yes, and if any other man in these halls would upbraid me,
Whether brother or sister of yours, or brother's favorite wife
Or your mother—but not your father; he has always been so gentle with me,
    as if he were my own father—
Why, then you would divert him and stop him
By the loving kindness of your spirit and the loving kindness of your words.
Therefore do I now weep for you, and in weeping for you, I weep for myself,
    a castaway in my heart's grief.
For none other now remains in all wide Troy
That is to be my friend and kind to me, but they all shudder and shrink
    from me.

Readers of those reminiscences of Arnold's Rugby which Thomas Hughes incorporated in *Tom Brown's School Days* may recall how one day in Homer class the pathos of this passage was too much for one brilliant pupil, the future Dean Stanley, who broke down in tears as he construed it, to the enormous embarrassment of his shuffling school-mates. The speech is indeed charged with emotional revelation, of Helen herself and the waste spaces in her proud and passionate heart. As in the third and sixth, so also in the twenty-fourth book she speaks still as an exile, enslaved by her passion for Paris, yet utterly alone. But how vividly in her despair does she also illuminate the character of her brother-in-law! It is before him once more, before his mute corpse, that her composure breaks. And once more, with her aid, we can see that streak of romanticism, that touch of imaginative affection, which had made Hector something more than either a warrior, husband, or parent. It was the same man who, when he abode Achilles' onslaught beneath the walls of Troy in the last crisis of his career, could debate within himself whether it were worth while to offer terms to his antagonist and try and bargain for Troy's sake, to bring peace: "But it is no time now to dally with him from oak tree or from rock, like youth with maiden, as youth and maiden hold dalliance, one with the other. Better to join battle at once." Only Hector the chivalrous romantic would have allowed himself that kind of simile at such a time.

Helen, Hector, Paris and Priam emerge in joint relation only in these three widely scattered contexts. Yet the contexts are not only congruent, they supplement each other with a fine economy. On their first appearance, the poet arranges them in three separate but overlapping pairs: Hector with Paris, Priam with Helen, Helen with Paris. The sixth book follows this up by combining Hector, Paris and Helen in a trio. In the twenty-fourth, all four are finally brought together within the compass of Helen's last retrospective pronouncement. What kind of genius was it, that was capable of such subtleties, operating on the margin of his main plot?

His vehicle to be sure is still the oral saga, and though he laid it on the anvil of intellectual artistry, this artistry is muted, because it speaks with the archaic, formulaic intonation of the oral minstrel. That is why, as hero challenges hero to primitive combat and genealogy piles on genealogy and the terrific hexameter repeats its hoarded refrains, we have to attend closely, bending our ear, if we are to catch the note of urbane irony concealed in the domestic comedy on Olympus, or perceive the romantic chord which vibrates gently in Hector's gallant affection, or listen to the muffled pain of Helen's divided heart.

L. C. KNIGHTS

Literature and the Teaching of Literature

1

It is difficult to say simply and sincerely why one "teaches literature," if only because this involves trying to say what literature is "for." [1] Literature does many different things; and on the whole, criticism and teaching are most fruitful and rewarding when they engage with a particular work, or group of works, leaving the sense of why engagement with this poem—or these novels and plays—is worth while to emerge in insights that are directly related to the works in hand.

There are times, however, when one needs to stand back from what one enjoys doing and attempt some answer to the question, Why? There are special reasons in these days for attempting a periodic stock-taking. Our awareness of "the state of the world"—wars and the threat of wars, the squandering of natural resources, the struggle for mere subsistence and survival in so many countries, the steady drift towards bureaucratization in the "developed" countries—can sometimes make any particular job in hand seem very small beer, tempting us to look for some panacea, some simple saving formula. And when we turn from the universal to, so to speak, the domestic,—the job in hand of students of English literature—we can't hide from ourselves the existence, not far below the surface, of a particular kind of worry: the sense that there is just too much in English literature alone that we are expected to be knowledgeable about; the sense that the study of literature necessarily opens up towards a wide range of other in-

---

1. This paper was originally prepared for a series on "The Nature of Literature" in the English Faculty of the University of Cambridge. The series itself was in response to the prompting of the Joint (Staff/Student) Academic Committee where it was (rightly) pointed out that although there were many lectures on authors, aspects, etc., we—the staff—rarely said exactly why we thought our job worth while. It is in short the apologia of one teacher of English and is offered here as a tribute to a great teacher. I have kept the spoken form of a lecture.

tellectual interests—psychology, philosophy, social anthropology. . . Indeed I have the impression that some students—the more active-minded or more worried—want to push "English" rather strongly in the direction of other kinds of enquiry simply because these seem (at a distance) to offer more widely embracing answers to the enormous questions of which we are inescapably aware. Even if I am wrong in supposing this, the fact that the study of literature is linked in many ways with other, non-literary, interests, sharpens the question I began by asking about the nature of literature and literary studies.

Answers to that question are necessarily personal. If I were forced to make a short summary statement of the function of literature—say in answer to an enquiring scientist who could honestly see no difference between poetry and push-pin (different pleasures for different people)— I should claim that literature is a form of knowledge, an irreplaceable way of arriving at truths that are of the highest importance to us if we are to remain, or try to become, adequately human. But why "ir-replaceable?" There are two answers. One is that the truths in question are difficult to come at, not only because of "the veil of familiarity" that gets between us and the actuality of our world, but because they have to penetrate our subtle defences. As Camus said of Dostoevsky, "he teaches us only what we know, but what we refuse to recognize"; and as Melville said of Shakespeare, "All that we seek *and shun* is there." The other is that truth, in this context, is not something that we re-ceive or acquire by logical demonstration, but something that we live our way into through a complex, varying activity when we engage with formal verbal structures of a particular kind.

All this, however, is far too general. It is merely the staking of a claim for literature as a form of knowledge, and in order to validate that claim—even to make sense of it—we must start with something much simpler. What, if anything, is common to all our experience of what we intuitively recognize as significant in literature—in literature not as acquired culture, but as "meaning something" to us? It is, surely, a spurt of intellectual energy that does not dissipate itself in momentary pleasure (though it is accompanied by pleasure), but that is both sign and function of an organizing power that holds in one focus a segment of experience or potential experience (maybe fairly simple, as in a short lyric; maybe panoramic, as in a great tragedy). And the consciousness thus energized, although it starts from and will return to *this* particular work, is not simply a consciousness of this work or of that, but—even for the sake of the particular work itself—will continually make connexions with other works and with our experience as a whole.

I have, I know, raised some very large questions and left them unanswered (there is that word, "intellectual," for example, which is intended to cover far more than the usual processes of intellection), and I shall consider some of them later. For the moment all I want to insist on is the energies of art—energies that can display themselves in the smallest of ways as well as in the depth and scope of the great masterpieces. I am in a quandary here because my statement demands demonstration, and demonstration would take far too long. Fortunately I can fall back on reminding you of what you already know. Consider your experience of reading poems—poems, I mean, that immediately or after some time seem to you "worth while." You may begin with an undifferentiated feeling of pleasure (or, for that matter of bafflement); but as you get to know a particular poem in depth you are likely to find there is something that prevents the mind skating easily over the surface, that insists on it doing some work for itself. It may be a latent conflict between two words brought into conjunction, as in Wordsworth's description of London as "a sight so *touching* in its *majesty*," where you have a microcosm of the paradoxes so unobtrusively built into the poem. It may be a not easily assimilable phrase:

My thoughts are all a case of knives,
 Wounding my heart
 With scatter'd smart,
As watring pots give flowers their lives.

George Herbert's mental wounds are felt as a scattering (not a single isolated impact), like the many tiny streams from the rose of a watering-can: that is simple enough. But they don't "give life" to the poet's heart: far from it. Behind the phrase, however, lurks the so far unexpressed idea that they *ought* to, that perhaps "those powers, which work for grief" *can* "enter God's pay." To turn over in one's mind the rather complicated simile within a metaphor is to reach a new level of understanding of the movement from disintegration to integration that Herbert's *Affliction*, (iv) so powerfully expresses. The demands made on us may of course be of a different kind—to let filaments of suggestion play across from one part of the poem to another, to see if they do in fact cohere and, if so, why the whole is so much greater than the sum of its parts. I could demonstrate my point here by giving a lecture on Shakespeare's Sonnets. I will content myself with a quotation or two from Stephen Booth's recent book, *An Essay on Shakespeare's Sonnets*. Booth makes a detailed—and helpful—analysis of the different patterns of structure—formal, logical, syntactical, rhetorical, phonetic—to be found in the Sonnets. It is through these, and the complex ways in which they interact, he says, that "the mind of the reader is kept in constant motion." "The shifting of the contexts in which the reader takes the meaning of a given word is like [other] sonnet characteristics . . . in that, in making the shift from one context to another, the reader's mind is required constantly to act." Of the justly famous Sonnet 60 ("Like as the waves make towards the pebbled shore . . ."), where meanings from the world of ineluctable natural law at large, the daily and seasonal movement of heavenly bodies, and the life of man, overlap and fuse, Booth says: "He [the reader] is not conscious of all the fleeting connections his mind makes, but his mind presumably makes them all the same. The nature of the substance before him is never fixed until the last lines, and the energy expended by the reader in moving from one pattern to another transmits urgency to the poem itself." I don't want to give the impression, however, that the appeal to the reader to wake up and keep his wits about him is confined to obviously complex and "difficult" poems, like Shakespeare's Sonnets and Donne's "Songs and Sonnets." Simple-seeming poems can make similar demands. You have only to consider two short, much anthologized poems—Wordsworth's "A slumber did my spirit seal" and Frost's "The Pasture"—to see what a formidable weight of meaning "simplicity" can bear—when the reader is prepared to collaborate. As Charles Olson puts it,—"A poem is energy transferred from where the poet got it. . . , by way of the poem itself to, all the way over to, the reader. Okay. Then the poem itself must, at all points, be a high energy-construct and, at all points, an energy discharge." [2] (This, incidentally, applies *mutatis mutandis* to all the arts: Francis Bacon, for example, refers to pictorial art as "an energy system.")

The first purpose of all the devices of poetry,[3] then, is to activate the reader's mind in particular ways. This is obviously true of metaphor and

2. Charles Olson on "Projective Verse"; *The New American Poetry*, ed. Donald M. Allen (1960), p. 387.
3. If "devices" is the word, for it suggests something more deliberate and contrived than is always the case.

imagery, whose powers of suggestion we often have to explore a very long way (taking care indeed not to overstep the bounds determined by the context of the work as a whole, not to explore in modes that the context declares inappropriate). It is true of rhythm, which Theodore Roethke once called "the chief clue to the energy of the psyche." It is true of the very sound of verse (or prose), when this is what Frost called "the sound of sense," determining tone, and therefore meaning, in ways that it would be impossible to determine otherwise: that is one reason why it is so important to read poetry aloud.

What is true of the parts is true of the larger structural devices of the long poem, the play or the novel. The writer puts this episode into relation with that, he puts this character into relation with that, he keeps alive a particular series of connotations in description or imagery; and in doing so he invites the reader to think about the possible significance of those connexions, contrasts, comparisons, and so on. There's no need here to take up the well known (perhaps overworked) question of interlocking patterns of imagery in, say, Shakespeare's plays. And perhaps two simple examples will serve as a reminder of the way in which the mere placing of particular episodes or passages by the dramatist invites us to use our wits to discover what the connexion is intended to be. In *Henry V*, why—we ask ourselves—are there two sharply contrasting accounts of the battle of Crecy, one from the English and one from the French point of view? (Whereas the Archbishop of Canterbury holds up for admiration the exploits of the Black Prince,

Whiles his most mighty father on a hill
Stood smiling to behold his lion's whelp
Forage in blood of French nobility,

the French King speaks of the Prince as mangling "the work of nature," and defacing "The patterns that by God and by French fathers / Had twenty years been made.") And why is Henry's martial rhetoric in the earlier parts of the play balanced and contrasted later by the Duke of Burgundy's noble eulogy of peace? Is it merely that his country has been defeated, and he has to negotiate what terms he can? Examples of episodes that demand to be connected in our minds once we attend to what lies behind both "plot" and "character" could be endlessly multiplied.

In the novel—that large loose term—the modes of appeal to the active intelligence are as many and various as they are in poetic drama. They range from the disposition of fictive events and persons round whatever it is that most engages the author's interest (a disposition we usually call the plot, and may carelessly dismiss as "mere" narrative) to unobtrusive promptings in setting and circumstance which, when we notice them, we usually dignify with some such description as "symbolic." Here again there is an enormous range of possible effects, from the description of the female whales with their young in *Moby Dick* to the attention given to the various houses in which the destiny of Isabel Archer is worked out in *The Portrait of a Lady*. Everything in a good novel calls on us to make connexions, especially to the overriding interest or theme that dawns on us when the forward linear movement of our attention turns back on itself to ask what it is all *about*.[4] But we only do that—as in play or poem—when the writing, here and here, demands the fullness of our attention and rewards it with a quickened consciousness.

Very obviously, "close analysis" won't tell us all we need to know about, say, long prose fictions. But consider a simple example. Read carefully the opening paragraph of Chapter 74 of *Middlemarch* ("In Middlemarch a wife could not long remain ignorant that the town held a bad opinion of her husband . . ."), and ask yourself whether the analysis of what can sometimes lurk behind the big words of moral approval, "candour," "love of truth," "ardent charity," could have been undertaken without the author's power of vivid dramatic enactment in a prose where every shift of the rhythm is an invitation to see something you hadn't seen. Certainly George Eliot could not have expressed one of her major preoccupations—the sense that there is no private life that is not intimately bound up with "a wider public life"—unless she were capable of the vivacity of the passage I have referred to. Without that she must inevitably (in her own words) have lapsed "from the picture to the diagram." "Vivacity"—under that large umbrella I include the effect of *all* animating elements in an author's style, down to minutiae that may well work on us without our full conscious awareness but that it sometimes pays off to look at rather closely. A recent fairly detailed study of linguistic forms in the later work of Henry James [5] amply justifies the praise of Vernon Lee fifty years ago. "With what definiteness this man

4. Northrop Frye has some good remarks about this in "The Road of Excess," published in *Myth and Symbol*, ed. Bernice Slote (University of Nebraska Press, 1960).
5. Seymour Chatman, *The Later Style of Henry James* (Blackwell: Language and Style Series, 1972).

sees his way through the vagueness of personal motives and opinions, and with what directness and vigour he forces our thought along with him!" Our extended psychological perception is the result of "this strong, varied, co-ordinated activity forced on to our mind." This, I may add, follows an account of "the splendid variety, co-ordination, and activity of the verbal tenses" in a passage from *The Ambassadors*.[6] But of course nothing like this would be worth our while unless we had already *felt* that the writer had something important to say.

You see I am following, however clumsily, in the steps of Coleridge. Almost always, when he has occasion to touch on the primary distinguishing marks of literature, he comes back to the energy and activity of mind that it demands from, and excites in, the reader. And the imagination—we can no longer avoid the word—is not only a form of energy, it is an ordering and unifying power. This, I am afraid, must remain unsupported by anything beyond an appeal to your own experience: we are all familiar—if only through our failures—with "the great instinct of the human mind, the striving towards unity," the need to bring different parts of our experience, different parts of our personalities, into relationship. (I. A. Richards' chapter on "The Imagination" in *Principles* stays in the mind, even if he has now rejected the psychological terminology he then used.) The refreshment that we feel after reading a good poem comes partly from a kind of clarification—more, perhaps, than "a momentary stay against confusion"—in which we see, and feel, hitherto unperceived relationships. And this applies equally to the shortest lyric ("The Pasture," "A slumber did my spirit seal"), and to a great novel or a great tragedy (*The Portrait of a Lady*, *King Lear*). We are again coming close to the question of literary form, for it is through a particular form that we are enabled to see—we are, as it were, drawn into—a particular kind of order. (To quote Vernon Lee again: "FORM is not merely something we perceive; it is something which determines our mode of perception and reaction." [7]) That however is too big a question to be dealt with here. All I would say is that in talking about the ordering process which—as well as being an energizing process—any work of literature *is*, I want to avoid the suggestion of a static order, of something settled once and for all: questioning, reaching out for possible further meanings, the yielding of provisional assent and readiness

6. Vernon Lee, *The Handling of Words* (The Bodley Head Week-End Library, 1927), pp. 249–50.
7. *The Handling of Words*, p. 271.

to qualify our assent—these are all part of our "appreciation" of literature. A sense of order, coherence, comes early in our understanding of
any poem; but it is not an order we rest on: rather it is a sense of growth,
of a *direction* of consciousness that is still capable of new assimilation,
either on a fresh reading or when fresh experience (literary or non-
literary) alters the mutual interaction of the poem and the rest of our
known world.

2

The end of that last sentence contained some large assumptions which
it is time to make explicit. How *does* poetry, literature, affect that large
part of our experience which is not the reading of literature? In a review
of the recent reissue of Coleridge's *The Friend*,[8] I. A. Richards quoted
with disapproval from a twentieth-century writer: "Literature is an
individual matter and should be valued, not for its moral or intellectual
influences, but simply for what it is." As Richards went on to say, this
is merely putting up No Trespass boards. Coleridge—with his life-long
attempt to bring all sides of human life, all aspects of the mind, into
relation—was the last man to set up a special isolated province of
"aesthetic appreciation." And yet there is a sense in which the remark
could be interpreted in a proper, a Coleridgean, sense. In our dealings
with literature there are no short cuts; moralistic, political or pedagogic
simplifications have to be repelled. All the same, it is because we value
literature for what it is essentially,—and, I may add, only when we
value each work in its irreplaceable uniqueness—that we can see what
place it has in the life of the personality as a whole, what, to put it
crudely, its uses—moral, educational and even political—are.

I said earlier that literature is a form of knowledge, and I have
tried to suggest that the knowledge it brings to being in the reader is a
complex, ordering, *activity*: without that responsive activity there is no
knowledge. And surely it is obvious that if this is so, to define *how*
literature works is to indicate something of its uses, its value. It is, as
Rosalind said, not good to be a post; and although experience suggests
some caution here, it is at least possible to hope that to exercise new
modes of awareness in reading is to strengthen them for use elsewhere.
It was in discussing Wordsworth's poetry that Coleridge noted "the
advantage which language . . . presents to the instructor of impressing

8. The *Listener*, 25 September 1969.

modes of intellectual energy . . . so as to secure in due time the formation of a second nature"; and among "the beneficial after-effects of verbal
precision" he included "the preclusion of fanaticism, which masters the
feelings more especially by indistinct watch-words." Here, at one jump,
is a connexion between poetry and politics. As for the ordering or
relating that goes on when we read poetry, it is even more difficult to
define and illustrate a carry-over from habits acquired in reading to the
habits of everyday living: some of us are moderately successful readers of
poetry, but still have areas of confusion in the backyards of our emotional life! But from our acquaintance with literature we at least have
some idea of what it means to move towards completeness, some standards against which to check the unruly and the out of kilter.[9] The
idea of a carry-over of this kind needs looking at in some detail by someone
equally familiar with psychology and literature. But surely it isn't merely
fiction in the pejorative sense, when, at the end of *The Idea of Order at
Key West*, the listener to the girl's song is able to see a more meaningful
pattern in what might have been a mere jumble of lights. It is because
of the song that

> the glassy lights,
> The lights in the fishing boats at anchor there,
> As the night descended, tilting in the air,
> Mastered the night and portioned out the sea,
> Fixing emblazoned zones and fiery poles,
> Arranging, deepening, enchanting night.

I have already referred to George Herbert's *Affliction* (*iv*)—the poem
that begins, "Broken in pieces all asunder." In living through that poem
we have at least recognized the possibility of achieving some kind of
integrity, of putting chaos in its proper place by facing it with courage
and resource.

So much for the mental activity, kindled in our reading of literature,
that can (perhaps) enter into our everyday knowing. But what is it that
literature gives us direct knowledge of? In a sense the question is foolish,
and the only answer is—of all those things that authors have written
about: go and read as much as you can! But I have offered to be simple,

---

9. As Elinor Shaffer, summarizing Kant, remarks: "Our destination (by which Kant
means the spiritual end of the race, or in Christian terms, immortality) is pointed
out through art, but cannot be accomplished through it. Its reality depends on
moral action."—"Coleridge's Theory of Aesthetic Interest," *Journal of Aesthetics
and Art Criticism*, 27, Summer 1969, p. 4.

and must now take the risk of simplification—which means reminding you of a handful of platitudes that are not less true for being
obvious. Literature offers a particular kind of knowledge of the self, of
what is not self (whether nature or neighbour), and of the relations
between self and not-self; not that these are distinct and water-tight
categories.

The ways in which literature offers opportunities for self-knowledge are
of course legion. They include the invitation by the novelist or dramatist
to assess different attitudes, presented with a far higher degree of specific
realization than is possible if we use only the descriptive terms of moral
discussion.[10] Consider how many different shades of "egotism," of
aggression overt or disguised, are to be found in English fiction alone.
And in following the presented "case," always of course with an engaged
and lively sense of the particular pressures that make it what it is, and
obtaining fresh lights from the particular set of relations in which it is
presented, we not only realize "what human beings can be like," but
what we ourselves are capable of being and most want to be, or not to
be. I have of course made the whole process sound too cut and dried.
In reading literature a good deal seems to go on outside the area of
clearly focussed consciousness, in what Coleridge called the "region of
unconscious thoughts, oftentimes the more working the more indistinct
they are." [11]

As for the role of literature in relation to society; this is a topic for
a series of discussions rather than a mere paragraph. Obviously literature
"extends our sympathies," as Shelley pointed out in a notable passage
of A Defence of Poetry. It can also help in a unique way in our understanding of different social forms and relationships. I don't mean that
literature, unchecked by other sources, can often—or ever—be taken as
straight documentation in the interests of social or cultural history.
What it can do is to offer specific instances of social pressures and inter-
relationships that have a "spread" of implication outside the particular

10. See D. W. Harding, "Considered Experience: the Invitation of the Novel," English in Education, 1, 2.
11. Biographia Literaria II, 250. No one who knows Coleridge will read this as a
plea for vagueness where precision is necessary; it is simply a reminder that although knowledge demands thought, thought itself can have an antecedent phase
in feeling, which in turn is related both to the sub-conscious and to the organic
processes of the body: the poetry of self-discovery has reverberations along the
whole range. See D. W. Harding, "The Hinterland of Thought" (in Experience
into Words); and, for thought and feeling as different "phases" of a continuous
process, Susanne K. Langer, Mind: an Essay on Human Feeling (1967), Vol. I.

historical situations into which they are projected (e.g. Jane Austen's novels). And it can offer insights into social modes of which we may have no direct experience—the independence of the Lakeland "statesmen" that we sense in *The Prelude,* the strange blend of squalor, brutality, and the thrusting up of new life and kindness in unexpected places that we are vividly made aware of (even in translation) in the first volume of Gorky's Autobiography. In *Villette* Charlotte Brontë is strong when she renders the feel of psychological undernourishment, of what it means—as we say so glibly—to be lonely; and because of this she can throw light on a whole social class—that of the unmarried woman of the nineteenth century, with inadequate means of support and a cruelly limited choice of careers. The point, of course, is that the artist does not deal with "society" in the abstract, or with what can be documented, counted and assessed from the outside. With his "passion for the special case," he gives us the feel of social pressures; it is his ability to render with "the freshness, raciness and energy of immediate observation" (to borrow Johnson's phrase) that compels us to live through the presented experience: he adds a dimension to our social understanding. Not of course (and this could equally well have been said earlier) that he comes up with any "solutions." In October 1888, Chekhov wrote to a friend:

> You are right to require a conscious attitude from the artist towards his work, but you mix up two ideas: *the solution of the problem and a correct presentation of the problem.* Only the latter is obligatory for the artist. In *Anna Karenina* and *Onegin* not a single problem is solved, but they satisfy you completely just because all their problems are correctly presented. The court is obliged to submit the case fairly, but let the jury do the deciding, each according to its own judgment. . . .[12]

The social function of literature has further reaches to which I can only give a few sentences. The artist is often a radical questioner of his society. But literature and the study of literature are not only disturbing (they won't let us settle down on the assumptions of the majority, or even on those of the enlightened group to which we may happen to belong), they are also conservative and traditional. The paradox is more apparent than real. It is often by being confronted with ways of thought and feeling very different from our own (in medieval literature, for

12. *Selected Letters of Anton Chekhov,* ed. Lillian Hellman (1955), p. 57; author's emphasis retained.

example) that we gain a new perspective on the present. We all know by now that the demand for "relevance"—for what is immediately and on the short view relevant—can be misleading.[13]

The artist is a radical questioner of states of affairs for the same reason that, in writing, he hates clichés.[14] The language of the imagination and the language of the stereotype in which we do so much of our thinking are polar opposites. "Poetry is the renewal of words for ever and ever." That sentence—which comes from Robert Frost, but other poets have told us the same—points clearly enough to the connexion between "imaginative literature" and the conduct of public affairs, something which still—in spite of the computers—needs the medium of languages, as I recently tried to suggest in *Public Voices*. The case was forcibly put by Ezra Pound forty years ago (in *How to Read*), and there is no need to repeat it here. It isn't, I think, invalidated by what is rather loosely referred to as the current "retreat from the word." In 1905 Henry James, addressing the students of Bryn Mawr on "The Question of Our Speech," remarked:

> We may not be said to be able to study—and *a fortiori* do any of the things we study *for*—unless we are able to speak. All life therefore comes back to the question of our speech, the medium through which we communicate with each other; for all life comes back to the question of our relations with each other. These relations are made possible, are registered, are verily constituted, by our speech.

In public as in personal affairs we need to remember Whitehead's dictum: "Style is the ultimate morality of mind." [15]

3

In trying to define some of the things that literature does and that we value it for, I have at least partially indicated my view of how it should be "taught." Literature does many things. The teaching of literature must be correspondingly varied and flexible. If literature only works by

13. On the dangers of "relevance" as a criterion, see Stuart Hampshire's "Commitment and Imagination," in *The Morality of Scholarship*, ed. Max Black (1967), p. 51.
14. This is a crude summary of some notable passages in Edwin Muir's "The Public and the Poet," the last of his Charles Eliot Norton Lectures 1955–56, published as *The Estate of Poetry* (Cambridge, Mass.: Harvard University Press, 1962).
15. A.N. Whitehead, *The Aims of Education* (1929: Mentor Books, 1961), p. 24.

calling on a particular kind of intellectual energy in each reader, then the main business of those who offer to talk about literature is to help others, each in his own way, to direct and sharpen attention, and, I would add, to make relevant connexions. Attention is an active process, constantly reaching out and assimilating, first and foremost within this particular work, then within the work, the *œuvre*, of a writer as a whole, then within a body of work—a "kind" or a tradition—, and then within the developing life of individual minds that are likely to have many other intellectual interests besides purely literary ones; say history or psychology or the study of contemporary society.

What this means is that the teaching of literature calls for a variety of approaches. It is enough, but it is essential, that the ones we use should be directed towards the common aim of awakening the mind and suggesting to it the possibilities of self-direction and of self-discipline. Here I shall only touch briefly on two matters—the question of scholarship and the question of practical criticism—that, as a teacher, I have had to think about.

What has to be said about scholarship, if we confine our attention to the undergraduate level, is obvious enough. The student needs to acquire in an orderly and methodical way such knowledge, linguistic, historical, and so on—and it may be pretty considerable—as will enable him to make more fully his own the works that are the main objects of his attention. The only knowledge worth having is of the actively assimilative kind. The acquiring of information is *for* something, and in literary studies it is for the finer understanding and enjoyment of literature.

It is at the "higher" levels that the problems become acute. Literary scholarship—indispensable as it is, and much as we owe to the great scholars—has its dangers. I am not now referring to the kind of scholarly industry that Edmund Wilson savaged in the later years of his life; though I am concerned when I read of a centennial edition of *Moby Dick* that its 315 pages of notes and apparatus—more than half as long as the novel itself—was made a matter of congratulation: "No other American novel has ever received such liberal annotation." [16] This sort of thing is of course related to the whole system of graduate training in research which, in some parts of the world, is effectively obscuring what a future university teacher of English ought to be doing to equip himself. It is of "scholarly" training of this kind—"training in the adminis-

16. I have lost my reference to the setting of this jewel. I think it was pointed out to me by my friend, the late Stanley Edgar Hyman.

tration of a vast body . . . of facts, comments, opinions, and mere phrases"—that I. A. Richards has said:

> It may fit [a man] to continue as a specialized researcher—within areas or on "points" with no known relevance to any side of the world crisis. It quite evidently does not give him what he needs as a teacher of the humanities—reasonably rich and considered views of a person's relations to other persons. . . . It is preventing us from supplying our greatest need—teachers able to help humanity to remain humane.[17]

As long ago as 1903 William James—referring, it is true, to conditions somewhat different from our own—delivered a lecture at Harvard on what he called "The Ph.D Octopus." [18] The brute has grown since then, and has developed global ambitions. I am not for a moment belittling the work that very many graduate students in English are now doing. Nor am I saying anything so foolishly simple as, "Abolish the Ph.D." What I am saying is that among graduate students as I have known them over thirty-five years, there have been some with a coiled spring inside them, something that urged them towards a book they *wanted* to write. There have been others, equally intelligent and of equal potential, not yet ready to begin on a substantial "contribution to knowledge"— however widely we may define that phrase. The result is a groping around for "subjects" and the direction of young energies into channels which—whatever incidental benefits accrue—are not, for them, at this stage, the real right thing. To find the real right thing for those who show the necessary aptitude, and who need two or three more years after the B.A. in which to equip themselves to teach in universities, colleges of education, polytechnics etc., seems to me one of the most important tasks that Faculties in the Humanities have to face, if only because we are not only training scholars, we are (we hope) educating the educators of the future. William James said that what *made* a university was the presence of "a few men, at least, who are real geniuses," what he called "the untameables." [19] I agree about that need. But most of us are not geniuses; and in the context of what I have just said, it seems to me evident that among other necessary attributes of a university is a concern for the whole spectrum of education. An exclusive preoccupation with

17. I.A. Richards, "The Future of the Humanities in General Education," in *Speculative Instruments* (1955), p. 61.
18. Published in *Memories and Studies* (1911).
19. "Stanford's Ideal Destiny," in *Memories and Studies.*

advancing this or that particular specialism (and again I exclude the few "real geniuses," who will go their way regardless) does nothing to foster that outward-looking concern; it merely strengthens professionalism.

As for the question of Practical Criticism: active engagement with particular works without too much fumbling and irrelevance still seems to me the basis of all literary study. All the same, here too there are some dangers. Anton Ehrenzweig, in *The Hidden Order of Art*, speaks of the importance for the painter of periods of relaxed and almost unconscious "scanning"; Maritain, in *Creative Intuition in Art and Poetry*, has a chapter on the genesis of a poem in "a kind of [wordless] musical stir" in the depths of the mind; Osip Mandelstam (according to his widow Nadezhda Mandelstam, in *Hope Against Hope*) insisted that "a poem begins with a musical phrase ringing insistently in the ears"; [20] other poets have told us much the same. Readers, like artists and poets, need the capacity for relaxed and attentive *listening*. Practical Criticism, explication, *can* become an externalizing routine, inhibiting that listening, even without the aid of all those books and articles that offer to do your explication for you. The wrong kind of insistence on this necessary activity can in fact prevent what it sets out to do. It can inhibit the intuitive response to literature, which can't always easily be verbalized; it can produce unnecessary feelings of inferiority in the student who is afraid of making mistakes (mistakes are part of our growth), or who is over-anxious to produce something obviously clever and acceptable; and in—rightly—directing attention to *this* poem or *this* passage, it can have the effect of unduly narrowing the range of reading which is an essential part of an education in English. As Wordsworth said in his "Reply to Mathetes" (in Coleridge's *The Friend*), speaking of the dangers of relying too exclusively on an admired and forceful teacher:

> In spite of his [the teacher's] caution, remarks may drop insensibly from him which shall wither in the mind of his pupil a generous sympathy, destroy a sentiment of approbation or dislike, not merely innocent but salutary; and for the inexperienced disciple how many pleasures may be thus cut off . . . whilst in their stead are introduced into the ingenuous mind misgivings, a mistrust of its own evidence, disposition to affect to feel where there can be no real feeling, indecisive judgments, a superstructure of opinions that has no base to support it. . . .

20. *Op cit.*, p. 70, cf. p. 187.

The appropriate calling of Youth (Wordsworth went on) "is not to distinguish in fear of being deceived or degraded, not to analyse with scrupulous minuteness, but to accumulate in genial confidence." We may disagree with some of this, but the tenor is sound. The problem is how to combine—how to encourage the combining—of analysis in (sometimes) scrupulous minuteness with an outgoing, exploratory "accumulation in genial confidence." With which we are back to the very obvious truth that where Practical Criticism is concerned—the education of basic skills in interpretation and response—everything depends on the tact of the teacher—his awareness of and respect for his pupils as persons, with different gifts and different rates of growth, and almost all of them with something to teach *him*.

There are many other problems in the teaching of English at university level and the arrangement of university courses in English: notably the relation of literary study to other disciplines, other fields of intellectual interest and enquiry. The question is a large one, and no universally applicable solution is in sight. Perhaps all we can do for the moment is to recognize that there *is* a problem. Whitehead was right when in 1938 he said, "The increasing departmentalization of Universities during the last hundred years, however necessary for administrative purposes, tends to trivialize the mentality of the teaching profession." [21] No "subject" can be entirely isolated from other "subjects": cross-fertilization is necescessary, and something that a university exists to promote. How, when there is so much to be read in English literature alone, when English students—like their teachers—have to protect themselves from a morbid and paralysing sense of all they have *not* read, how can real cross-fertilization take place in a mere three or four years? Different universities are trying to tackle this problem in different ways. My own conviction is expressed by another remark of Whitehead's to the effect that "rightness of limitation is essential for the growth of reality," though he also said elsewhere, "We must be systematic, but we should keep our systems open." [22] An education in English has its own discipline: when a man is aware of *that*, when he knows when something is being said effectively and not merely gestured towards, then the more lively interests he has, the better for his literary studies. Insights can play across from one's reading in, say, history or psychology; but one must be careful not

21. *Modes of Thought* (1938: Capricorn Books, 1958), p. 178.
22. *Religion in the Making* (1926: Meridian Books, 1960) p. 146; *Modes of Thought*, p. 8.

to force connexions, and the fact remains that there are no short cuts to the kind of knowledge that literature offers. Formal interdisciplinary work can, and I think ought to, be encouraged at the post-graduate level, where it would inevitably have an effect on other levels. Before that (assuming that premature specialization has not got a complete stranglehold in the schools), it seems best to start from a centre—the study of literature—and to open what perspectives one can as opportunity offers.

I return briefly to the large question of what literature is *for*. I hope it won't be assumed, because the word "enjoyment" has appeared so rarely in this paper, that I regard the study of literature as a grimly solemn strengthening of the moral fibres. I take it for granted that much of what we value in literature is a celebration of the richness and variety of life. Not all literature—I would say, very little—is a simple celebration, a simple act of praise. But in all literature we value what Yeats named when he spoke of Blake's "joyous intellectual energy." We are shy of speaking of joy, but we need to use the word, even when speaking of tragedy; for it is through literature—even, and perhaps above all, through great tragedy—that the mind comes to know—to know by exercising—its own powers. Power and imaginative energy, however, are —there is no escaping it—correlatives of discipline. Only artists can speak with full authority of the discipline of their art. Those of us whose function it is to teach, to transmit, and to prompt to see, can however properly speak of the discipline of literary study. It is of course discipline for the sake of freedom—what Coleridge, in an early poem, called "a livelier impulse and a dance of thought." But freedom in this context— the ability to use creatively what has been acquired as knowledge or imaginative insight—is only possible for the mind that knows at first hand the discipline of concentration. Whitehead, in a telling phrase, speaks of "the rhythmic claims of freedom and discipline." [23] What that means each of us—teacher and pupil, teacher *with* pupil—has to discover for himself. What perhaps we may all agree on—even those of us who don't like to wave our banners too violently or too often—is that the final aim of literary study is nothing less than to set free and to foster the energies of the imagination, without which not only will our individual consciousness be less full and active than it might have been, but our collective life will be the mere "efficient" mechanism—structured over vast areas of violent unreason—that it is in danger of becoming to-day.

23. *The Aims of Education* (1929), Chap. 3.

Teacher's Debt

Fifty years ago not one teacher in a thousand would have thought it part of the elementary schoolchild's training in English to write poetry. For one who did, his pupils wrote like this—and one can say "like this" because they all wrote in the same manner, since verse-writing was a matter of manipulating spare parts from a stock of poetic phrases:

To a Celandine

In the dark and dreary nights
    When wild the winds do blow,
The little golden celandine
    Lies snug amid the snow.

This pretty little celandine
    In days so light and clear
Lives in the shade and lovely glade
    Which is so sweet and dear.

But when the days are fairer
    And milder breezes blow
The little golden celandine
    To Paradise shall go.

Half a century later verse-writing in schools is well established, and another twelve year-old writes:

My Newts

One night in thunder,
Two newts came to our back door to shelter
From the torrential rain and gusty wind;

I found them there when the rain had passed.
I caught them and kept them.
They are small and squirm when they are picked up.
Their stomachs and breasts are orange and black,
Pulsing with life.
They have four webbed feet and long shiny tails;
They are elegantly exact when they swim.

Out of the thunder night,
Came my black and orange dragons.

The two poems illustrate not only the progress that education has made, but also the changes that have taken place in the adult conception of poetry in those fifty years. Poets then were the "world-losers and world-forsakers" of O'Shaughnessy's *Ode*; poetry was Andrew Lang's synthetic sonnet, *The Odyssey*. Both poems were in the *Oxford Book of English Verse*, first published in 1900 and still a power in the 1920's. The Georgian poets were content with their mild country walks; neither Rosenberg nor Owen made any impact till the thirties. Along with the poetry of the twenties went criticism; ranging from light chat to romantic eulogy, it was, in the words of F. L. Lucas, "a charming parasite."

This was what was handed out to teachers in training, and what they in turn passed on when they entered the classroom. It was very discouraging to novice teachers seized with the Arnoldian view of the importance of poetry and its civilising function in education. The arts in the twenties seemed to attract but little of the available human talent; it was the sciences that engaged the attention of the able and established an arena within which important things happened. Thus the first two books—*Principles of Literary Criticism* (1924) and *Science and Poetry* (1926)—came as manna to hungry wanderers in the wilderness. *Principles* expounded a psychological scheme of values, in the light of which literature, especially poetry, was seen to be important. Human happiness lay in reaching a balanced adjustment of all the impulses that make up a man. Good art arose from a balanced state in the artist, and its function was to communicate that state to the spectator or reader. This neat arrangement seemed to settle so much—placing poetry in an intelligible scheme of things, and providing a "scientific" justification—in a "scientific" age—for the cultivation of literature.

Since then it has become clear that one of the achievements of *Principles* and *Science and Poetry* was their contribution to the replotting of the critical map, to the changing guidance of which can be traced the differences in the children's poems quoted above. First there was the distinction between two kinds of poetry, and the establishing as superior the one characterised by "irony"—"the bringing in of the opposite, the complementary impulses." Secondly there were the judgements on modern poets, on T.S. Eliot for example in that illuminating appendix written shortly after the publication of *The Waste Land*. Thus Richards helped to replace the Georgian poets by something more sinewy, and to form the modern taste for poetry of some complexity; so that a serious reader today cannot fail to be influenced by Richards when he approaches a poem. That is a measure of the extent to which our expectations and our understanding of poetry were altered. Especially to those seeking encouragement and direction in taking up the teaching of English the new notions of poetry were an enormous help. Further assurance was supplied by the lectures which led to *Practical Criticism*; those who attended them were impressed by the way in which poetry was taken seriously and discussed in intelligent terms that convinced many open-minded scientists.

The importance of what Richards was doing was probably not apparent to most of his audience, though he himself had been explicit: "I am preparing a companion volume, *Practical Criticism*. Extremely good and extremely bad poems were put before a large and able audience. The documents they wrote give a stereoscopic view of the poem and of possible opinion on it. This material when systematically analysed, provides, not only an interesting commentary on the state of contemporary culture, but a new and powerful educational instrument." The historic pages that record the incompetence as readers of the intelligent and cultivated people who heard the lectures are still compulsive reading. Richards then went on to ask how such inadequate readers could be expected to show themselves intelligent and imaginative in their relationship with other human beings, and how far insensitiveness, poor discrimination and a feeble capacity for poetry imply a corresponding inability to apprehend and use the values of life. The answer was that there is no gulf between poetry and life; a general insensitivity to poetry bears witness to a low level of imaginative life.

Suggestions for improving a clearly faulty education followed naturally. Richards believed that it was possible to produce more self-reliant readers; the performance of his contemporaries as speakers and readers was worse than that of comparable people only a generation before. The means to this end would be an improved technique of reading, and a fuller awareness of how our language works. Finally he offered a means of increasing this awareness by identifying the four kinds of meaning, tools of analysis which thousands of teachers have used to advantage. It was interesting to note that at an Anglo-American conference at York in 1971 one of the most effective conductors of seminars, John Dixon, started by referring to "Richards' wonderful book" (*Practical Criticism*, i.e.) as a guide to the close study of literature, and went on to supply us with unsigned poems for comment. This procedure produced examples of all the kinds of misreading that Richards had identified more than forty years earlier. The difference was that our guide and many of his hearers quickly recognised the misunderstandings and had the vocabulary to discuss them.

In addition Richards contributed to another movement in education. He surveyed the cultural scene and focused sharply on such features as commercialised entertainment. Noting that bad art was an influence "of the first importance in fixing immature and actually inapplicable attitudes to most things," he added (of the cinema) that "the extent to which secondhand experience of a crass and inchoate type is replacing ordinary life offers a threat that has not been realised." Since then a number of books with immediate implications for education have appeared, such as Mrs. Leavis' *Fiction and the Reading Public*, Raymond Williams' *Communications* and Fred Inglis' trenchant *The Englishness of English Teaching*, all of them taking directions signposted by Richards. And at school level a host of textbooks have had the common aim of encouraging pupils to criticise and analyse the working of the mass media.

The two early books, *Principles* and *Practical Criticism*, constitute their author's main contribution to education. Looking back, we see that the discussions of sincerity and the working of poetry advanced the business of criticism; the analysis of mistakes in reading is still valid and highly relevant; the "new educational instrument" was created. One result was that we, the teachers among us especially, became more self-conscious in our use of language, more scrupulous and exact in speech and writing, and (we thought) better readers of poetry. The assimilation by a generation or two of teachers of Richards' ideas, the ideas of a wide-ranging mind, was the most valuable fruit of the early work.

His influence at many universities in Britain and the Commonwealth was very great indeed—a matter of history now being forgotten. The first evidence lies in the examination papers for a degree in English at

Cambridge, England: there was a sharp change of direction after the publication of *Practical Criticism*. A comparison of 1925 with 1963 shows that a knowledge of history, social background, linguistic origins and Aristotle has ceased to be tested; scholarship and Anglo-Saxon have gone elsewhere; the examiners' main concern is with literature and the candidate's response to it. The 1925 paper on Shakespeare might have been passed by anyone who had got up information about the texts and about the period without reading a single play, but in 1963 all of the eighteen questions required the reading of at least one play. Again in 1925 you would have been helped to a degree by a knowledge of the guild system, types of medieval undergraduate, Langland's views on the labour question, or the ability to draw the ground plan of a monastery —but it would have been of no avail in 1963. It is in the additional "Passages for Comment and Appreciation" that the new course becomes even clearer; there are five quarto pages of prose and verse, including for example a question that asks, of a poem by Coleridge:

> What exactly does this poem say?
> How far is it worth saying?
> Is this the best way to say it?

From outside Britain there is the example of South Africa where, at least till a few years ago, the practical criticism approach was normal in university English courses. Moreover Ricardian methods have applications outside literature; a recent contributor to the journal *English in Education* values their assistance in making possible "a critical approach to texts of all kinds considered for their appropriateness of register and content, analysed for their meaning and tested for their efficiency in conveying that meaning to an intended destination." The teacher who has profited from *Practical Criticism* has a flexible means of reaching the heart of any reading matter, without jargon, in terms readily intelligible to his students, and without the cumbersome apparatus of any of the various types of linguistics. Of course the poor in discretion are always with us, and there have been examples of wholesale dissection of severed passages and of snap judgements on a writer based on the surface texture of a page or two.

In the schools Richards' books encouraged those who were pulling the teaching of English from under the shadow of the Greek and Roman classics and (often under the guidance of F.R. Leavis) establishing it as a more central discipline. A pre-1914 book on the teaching of English, by P. J. Hartog, wanted literary criticism in school to be "on the level of the classical teaching in our best secondary schools" and offered this prescription:

> The summarising of a passage is only the first step towards complete analysis. It is now for the teacher to indicate the general setting of the passage in the work from which it is taken, the place of that work in the life-work of the author, and its historical and moral significance; to elicit, with the help of his class, if possible, the master-idea of the piece, and to criticize the success or failure of the author in carrying out his intention; and further to criticise, if need be, the authenticity of the text.

Practical Criticism prompted a flow of textbooks that practised methods very different from that just outlined, with the common aim of concentrating on the words on the page in order to elucidate a writer's full meaning. A good example of a type which has been in evidence for more than thirty-five years and owes much to Richards and Leavis is Gilbert Phelps: *Question and Response, A Critical Anthology of English and American Poetry* (Cambridge University Press, 1969). It consists of about sixty poems, each followed by a score of questions and in the case of more difficult works by several pages of close comment "designed to provoke thought and encourage the free flow of emotional and imaginative response."

Unfortunately, as in universities, so in schools. The undiscriminating application of such textbooks has too often meant that the close examination of short passages has become an end in itself. The trend of misuse was set and strengthened by the "lords of the syllabus world" (to recall Richards' phrase of years ago), who discovered that the setting of a battery of questions on a piece of prose or verse supplied them with an easily markable test, with the result that an examination requirement has dominated teaching method. Once "comprehension" tests were set in examinations, teachers and their pupils spent their English periods years before the test in doing nothing but comprehension questions in dim little handbooks. These have proliferated, and in some schools "English" consists largely of studying fragments for analysis out of context.

The need for teachers to apply the commonsense of I.A. Richards is greater than ever. Recently Fred Inglis published a highly valuable and idiosyncratic piece of research—*The Englishness of English Teaching* (Longmans, 1969). He got teachers to say, candidly and revealingly, what they were trying to do; he gave their pupils pictures, ads, and extracts from comics and "good" books to write about—which they did with enjoyment; and he discussed their findings with them in hours of recorded interviews. He found—my paraphrasing quotations inevitably are crude—that the waste of human effort in teachers is colossal and that on children the civilising effects of literature are imperceptible; for in their response to literature and life many of the young people are cut off from contact by disabilities sadly like those identified by Richards in the 1920's. This is not surprising; the revelations of *Practical Criticism* about the inefficacy of education led to no re-thinking in ministries, universities or colleges of education.

It should be said in parenthesis that it has always been the policy of British education ministries not to interfere, so that on the one hand teachers can do much as they please within the limits set by examinations, and on the other the training provided for them is too often irrelevant and directionless. Thus when a governmental handbook for teachers salutes Professor Richards, the recommendation comes not from a fresh look at a situation and the consequent implications, but from observing what seems to be the best practice in schools. This lack of a centre lays a heavy responsibility on the two journals, *The Use of English* and *English in Education,* to give a lead, since the teaching of English in England has in recent years so much lost its way.

There is one salient pushed out by Richards from which education has benefited not at all; teachers and their advisers and publishers have missed out badly, with never a glimpse of the possibilities. Despite B.L. Whorf's sneer ("an eviscerated British English," etc.), Basic English is normal English, fully adequate for the general everyday purposes of industry, science, medicine, news and so on. Here are two examples of its value. First, in the many cases where normal attempts at communicating are under-effective: "between the manager and his labour force; the instructor and his students; in the explanation of government regulations, in directives of all sorts for the safe . . . use of machines and appliances, etc, the losses incurred are too often crippling." The second use is as a medium of paraphrase, the best remedy for unconscious misunderstanding. In Richards' words: "Basic English is . . . a sub-language into which . . . sentences of Complete English may be translated. As with all reduction or analytic translation the process is accompanied by heightened awareness of the meaning of the original." True, the translation of poetry into Basic can miss shades of feeling, but this leaves undiminished the fact that it goes a long way towards explaining the full sense; D.W. Harding has observed that Richards offers Basic "and most convincingly, as a tool in the accurate comprehension of complex writing in full English." (*The New York Review of Books*, August 5, 1969) After noting that the Basic version of a piece of inflated political journalism reveals at once that it says nothing with confused verbosity, Harding continued in words that deserve wide circulation:

> Other forms of paraphrase could achieve the same end but would not provide the same built-in safeguards against self-deception by pseudo-statement. The great disciplinary value of Basic English is that its use demands basic thinking. A wider currency of this discipline of precise statement in a simple form might do more to overcome differences between the "science" and the "arts" outlook than any spread of numeracy. The extent of confused, ambiguous utterance and slovenly half-comprehension in what passes for communication in politics, social science, and the criticism of literature and the arts can hardly be exaggerated, and it is one of Richards' services, perhaps his greatest, to have demonstrated it and at least gained some attention for the problem.

Several generations of teachers of English in England have regarded Richards as one of their special mentors. He has brought up to date the Arnold quoted in *Science and Poetry*: "The future of poetry is immense, because in poetry, where it is worthy of its high destinies, our race, as time goes on, will find an ever surer and surer stay." He has offered, as well as a rationale for the study of literature, a really effective approach to it, that could also be profitably applied to all kinds of utterance. One might hazard that Arnold himself, both the inspector of schools and the poser of the question "How to live?," would recognise the debt that teachers owe to Richards and the commonsense ways in which it could be enlarged.

Prospero

I.A. Richards is a learned poet, a formal poet, a witty poet, and a philosophical poet. One thinks mechanically of "metaphysical," but I think Richards is more advanced in metaphysics (or at least epistemology, I have trouble telling which from which) than any metaphysical poet I can think of. His erudition ranges easily from the Bible and Plato through Shakespeare and Milton to Whitehead and Wittgenstein. His own philosophy and critical theory speak for themselves where he has expounded them in prose, but they live in the poetry, to which he came last. For he is the most distinguished of beginners (a published poet only since 1958) who makes many poets acclaimed as masters seem like beginners incompetent in their craft.

Technique, though vital, is not all, but it gives me a starting point. Consider the first three stanzas of *Court of Appeal*:

Nature is better dressed than Man.
These various Birds and Fish,
Even the 'gator on his bank,
Can
Make one wish
We people weren't so rank.

And, most, the Humbled One,
Self-fluent, living Stream,
Upon his belly in the dust:
None
Of all seem
In better Taste.

His suiting modest, rich, subdued,
Choice custom drape,

In stripe and weave correct:
Shrewd
For a Shape
So bitterly abject!

Note the wonderful placing of the monosyllabic lines, and the inevitable
rightness with which their meaning always fits its place in the poem. If
there is any such thing as "mere" technique (does Swinburne prove
that there is?), there is more than that here: the synoptic eye, the con-
centrated vividness of the snake, the texture of idea. There is much delight in word-play, for words themselves are magic pieces, and this poetry is anything but non-verbal; but the very pun-sequence can express
a wry and witty pathos, as in these lines from *Retirement:*

>   In his each breath

What's past its use
     Let out must be,
          Free, since refùsed:
          Réfuse at play.

Even the cliché can be haled in and glorified (*The Screens*):

(These grids without reflect the strains within:
What feet pad round and round that empty room?
What claws scratch on against that shivering door?
What looney prisoner can now assume
No wish denied, the Universe his bin?)

or simply (*Satiation Theory*):

Pray, fingers, pray: "Let us not be all thumbs!"

Such a chameleon nature of words accords with the whole fluid
world of Richards. *Alaskan Meander*, written in elegant *terza rima*, en-
forces order on apparent wilful confusion; God or the world directs the
wiggles. "How daunting is divine Autonomy" is how we end, echoing
Milton once more. But I find this optimism unusual. Sometimes it seems
as if philosophy were nothing but a mess of cruxes, and the stuff of
Richards' philosophy and of his poetry is one and the same. Thus
Wittgenstein himself is *The Strayed Poet*. But how much is the poetry
the poet and the man? Let the poem speak for itself in *Retort* (first and
last stanzas):

A poem's not on a page
    Or in a reader's eye;
   Nor in a poet's mind
Its freedom may engage.
    For I, a poem, I
   Myself alone can find
   Myself alone could bind.

I sing, who nevertheless
    No accents have or breath.
   I neither live nor die.
But you whom I possess . . .
    You, you know life and death
   And thoroughly know; so I
   What void I fill thereby.

"Introduction" to *Birthday Thoughts* presents only a selection of aspects of self:

Its ornate and its not so
Ornate shells,
Its vestures, sociable or else.

But *The Status of the Mentionable* says that even the self, which does indeed seem to exist, cannot be so presented:

The unmentionable is with, in, of me: me.
The mentionable turns object, over against;
Not me, not me: my shell.
And we who mention, we,
Are never what is mentioned.
What pure eye
Ever yet beheld the beholder?

Nor can it be located (*Sunrise*):

Clear: we were never where we saw we were,
Nor are, nor will be, where we see we are;
Not far off from it, either; no, nor near.

Of his own poetry, Richards says: "Around every phrase—behind, on all sides, and ahead—there are other phrases: ready to compete or support, or recklessly bent on having their own way." Self and poetry alike are surrounded in a swarm of throwaways, discards, unwritten versions, unperformed acts and unthought thoughts, possibles, escaping dimensions. Yet the very constant dynamic failure to solve the insoluble is what generates the excitement of the quest and of the poetry. This poetry can turn out just and inevitable, guided by a power, "the Muse," dismissed, in *Dismission*, to attend some other poet:

Go wrench his sense and regulate his voice.
Tell him there's nothing left for verse to say
Though only you can find the way to say it.
Give him my greeting with your rates of pay
And never let him know he has no choice.

However hard the person may be to pin down, the person is there in full affecting warmth, in *Conditional* (as in *Retirement, Dismission,* and elsewhere) speaking his farewells:

Butterfly thought, sail gaily down the void,
Seeking your mate, belike—gale-borne astray,
To be destroyed, betray,
Ice-caught, the thoughts from which your life began:
Torn downy wings that will not sail again.
Fain as of old, I feign that yet I can.

In *Finhaut* the mountain-railway and the old climber go, together, over the high point of the line:

On down, past footways to
Known heights now out of reach;
To this pass come, and through:

Who, sixty-odd years ago,
Happened here first to lift
My young mere eyes to snow.

   Who writes better poetry than that?

JANET ADAM SMITH

Fare Forward, Voyagers!

I first read words of I.A. Richards in 1923, but not in *The Meaning of Meaning*, published that year: nor for many years after did I know there was any such book. The words were in the November 1923 issue of the *Alpine Journal*, in an article entitled "The North-East Arête of the Jungfrau and Other Traverses," and written in collaboration with D.E. Pilley. When their next joint article appeared in the *Alpine Journal*, in November 1931—"The North Ridge of the Dent Blanche" —the Editor appended a footnote to the effect that D.E. Pilley was Mrs. I.A. Richards. One can't begin to talk about Ivor Richards' mountaineering apart from Dorothea's: their collaboration on the hills has been as close and fruitful as in so many other aspects of their lives. What other couple has made such an art of the joint letter!

The record of their earlier climbing is to be found in Dorothea Richards' *Climbing Days*, published in 1935. I.A.R. makes his first appearance there about the end of the 1914–18 war, in North Wales, wearing a green corduroy suit and a Breton tam-o-shanter and accompanied by a faithful nondescript spaniel who could climb rocks too. He was already an old hand—he had been to the Alps as a boy, and had climbed with Cambridge friends before the war; Dorothea was in the first flush of a *grande passion* for the mountains. So begins the tale of an outstandingly enterprising partnership that has taken them all over the world; wherever they have been, they have found something to go up, from the gentle hills of the Virgin Islands to the Great Wall of China.

In the 1920's the Richardses were in the Alps nearly every summer, climbing by themselves, or with friends, or with the guide who became their dear friend, Joseph Georges le Skieur. There were classic ascents —of Matterhorn, Mont Blanc, Eiger, Weisshorn, Monte Rosa, Grépon, Géant; there were wanderings in little-frequented valleys in search of

*Ivor and Dorothea Richards, in camp with the Alpine Club of Canada,
1945. Eremite Camp; a cool morning.*

elegant climbs the crowd had passed by; there were some great expeditions—like the traverse of the North-East Arête of the Jungfrau, only
once before ascended—and two splendid new climbs. The Richardses
and Joseph Georges were the first party up the icy north ridge of the
Grivola in the Graian Alps: "The narrowing, curving, smooth unbroken
crest sweeps up unchanging; an abstract perfection of form unequalled
in the Alps." And—the high point of their Alpine days—they were the
first party up the North Ridge of the Dent Blanche, in 1928. Here
they are on the crux which had defied earlier climbers:

> Most of the passage had to be done by the oddest series of
> counterpoised pressures I have ever had to manage. All on a
> surface too steep to allow any of the usual margin of balance. An
> occasional pinch-hold was a luxury. The friction of a rubber sole
> or the palm of a hand on some small awkwardly sloping sur-
> face had to be enough. . . . The landing-place, on which I

joined I.A.R., was a nook the size of a dinner-plate, with one handhold! It needs some experience for two people to stow themselves in such a place with comfort. . . . "Ah, les amoureux!" [said the last man of the party] as he spied us clinging together to our joint and solitary hold.

This ascent confirmed their reputation in circles that had never heard of I.A.R. the writer and teacher; and *Climbing Days* gives many pictures that will be new to those who only know I.A.R. at Cambridge level. Here he is, in action on the rocks of North Wales:

I.A.R.'s speciality in those days was high steps. Being loose in the limbs he seemed to like using footholds near his chin. Analytic and scientific by disposition he would sit at the top of a pitch and give me the most extraordinarily detailed instructions as to the precise movements which would bring me up with the least stress and strain. He was in fact of the cautious-controlled type *in excelsis*, tentative in his movements and always seemed able to come back without difficulty from any position, however experimental—a sign of conscious, deliberate planning of the balance. Perhaps through being not particularly strong, he seemed to me to be more reflectively aware of how his holds were supporting him than any other leader I had ever followed.

Here, unexpectedly fierce, in the Pyrenees:

The scheduled hour of 1 o'clock had been scandalously overpast before boots were on, forgotten lanterns discovered and lit, the rope re-coiled, and the party collected at the door. At this point I.A.R., usually no aggressive disciplinarian, burst out with a diatribe on the culpable waste of precious sleep caused by early morning sluggishness. He pointed out that anyone can dress—*for a mountain*—in ten minutes and breakfast in another ten and still have ten good minutes in hand for loitering! By reflection on those figures, a whole hour could be saved either for the difficulties of the mountain or for downy rest. A meek, rebuked and surprised party then set off after a still fuming leader.

A less austere I.A.R. appears in the Bertol Hut, above Arolla, after a new route, descent in snowstorm, and trudge round a glacier in the dark:

Supper in the deserted Bertol Cabane about midnight was a festive affair. The bulkiness of I.A.R.'s sack was explained when, among other delicacies, he unpacked a bottle of champagne. He had taken it up to drink on the summit after our first ascent and had felt ashamed to mention anything so frivolous in such a desperate situation. He produced it now with the seriousness with which he might bring out a new view on the meaning of meaning.

And here, down in the bilberry pastures of Arolla, is I.A.R. on an off-day, "in a scholarly nook correcting the proofs of *Principles of Literary Criticism.*" No abrupt division between the words and the mountains!

Climbing Days ends with their exploits of 1928; what they have climbed since can be gathered from a tantalising paragraph in the introduction to a new edition of that book (1965), from articles in climbing journals, and from the letters and cards with which they keep their friends posted. In the late 1920's and the 1930's they were travelling and climbing in Sikkim, Burma, the Western Hills of Peking, the Japanese Alps, the Diamond Mountains of Korea, the Tai Shan of Shantung, Yunnan, and in the Selkirks and Bugaboo ranges of the Canadian Rockies—with now and then a return to the Alps. After the war they were back in the Alps nearly every year; for their British friends, summer was heralded by the arrival of the Richardses, I.A.R. usually with a rucksack on his back. True, it would be holding presents for friends, or books, or a script for the B.B.C. rather than sweaters, sardines and crampons; but it was a promise of high days to come, and made London or Cambridge suddenly appear as staging-posts on the Richardses' progress to the Alps. Perhaps they were less ambitious now, of expeditions that might involve eighteen hours continuous going, but they were certainly not a whit less adventurous in seeking out remote corners and unfrequented routes, and they could still, on occasion, carry on their backs enough provisions for two weeks above the snowline. In 1955 they ranged far: Adam's Peak in Ceylon, Mount Hermon in Lebanon, Ulu Dag in Turkey, Olympus and Parnassus in Greece. On winter weekends from Harvard they went snow-shoeing in the White Mountains—and it was on the way back from one of these outings, in 1958, that they were involved in a road accident that smashed Dorothea's hip. An end to climbing days? Never for them: only a difference of scale. Hut-to-hut tours in the Austrian Tyrol, with a clever use of *téléfériques* and chairlifts; traverses, but of smaller peaks than the giants of Valais or Oberland. To the Richardses, a mountain holiday has always been a complex experience, compounded of many elements: mountain people, pastures, flowers, food, wine, all go to make the experience as well as rocks and snow, peaks and glaciers. Over the years the proportions of the elements may have changed, but the total experience has not necessarily diminished.

Postcards and Christmas messages have brought news of their spirited and various doings: a night in the hay in a Tyrolean chalet; in 1966, a trip by helicopter to a hut high under the Dent Blanche, to celebrate with Swiss climbers the centenary of the first ascent, and to be toasted as the pioneers of the North Ridge, thirty-eight years before; in 1968 an ascent of Mount Hood in Oregon with the help of a snowmobile for the lower stretches. In 1970 they were off to the Cordillera Blanca of the Andes, "just donkey-boy camping mostly"; in 1971 it was camping with the Alpine Club of Canada, "then north to the Yukon, Alaska and the Arctic Ocean." A snapshot from Dawson City shows two sunburnt, check-shirted, sharp-eyed prospectors.

Prospectors is what they have always been. The note was struck early, in the first *Alpine Journal* article:

> The thrill of descent into new country outweighed the convenience of returning to a centre. To go up by a route unknown to the party, to come down over slopes never seen before into valleys where the rocks, the trees, the houses, the very flowers are different, seems to us the way to wring the best joys from mountaineering.

Later, they speak of "our scheme of travelling light and wandering." They could not always be on new ground; after the war there were returns to the Alpine centres of their best early climbs, Arolla, Saas-Fee, Zermatt. But for such climbers these are returns, not repetitions. The path, the ridge, the peak may be the same—but there will be differences, of season, weather, conditions of snow and ice, and also of mood and form and experience. However familiar the route, the climber will be a different person from what he was when last he came this way. So every expedition can be a new experience—as can every reading of a poem, however familiar. I have heard I.A.R. reading the *Ode to the West Wind* as if he were coming to it for the first time; so too it can be with the mountains he knows the best.

Twice I have seen I.A.R. angry in a gathering of climbers. Once when the lecturer, describing some difficult climb she had made, showed she knew nothing of the peaks and valleys round her own particular ascent: to her it was nothing but a physical achievement. The second time was at a television programme of some high-class rock-climbing in Wales. That this personal and subtle pleasure, to be enjoyed privately with friends, should be made a public show outraged I.A.R. For the Richardses, the mountains can never be a battleground or a stage; they are simply the place where they are completely at home, as they are in the courts of Magdalene or Harvard Yard.

Now for a little practical criticism. In 1923, the Richardses pioneered a new way up the Picion Epicoun, a minor summit in the Valais Alps; the rocks were such fun that they did not notice how time was passing. It was dusk when they reached the top: the way down lay over a tricky glacier. Here are three accounts of the descent. The first is from the *Alpine Journal:*

> A thick local mist enveloped us, inconvenient seeing the lateness of the hour (6.0), and our complete ignorance of the very confusing topography. We were lucky to get down in comfort. In fact, only ability to descend rapidly in the dark, gained through winter expeditions in Wales, enabled us to avoid a very undesirable predicament.

The second is from *Climbing Days:*

> Unfortunately the map was very sketchy and thick masses of evening mist were obscuring the view just where we most needed to see clearly. The little Upper Chardonney Glacier seemed to offer the quickest way down, but not till we were on its slopes did we discover that it was scored, under a soft coverlet of new snow, with an endless series of large crevasses. We charged as fast as the crevasses would allow down the glacier, hoping vehemently that each chasm we crossed in the misty growing darkness would be the last.
>
> Crevassed glaciers *à deux* are always anxious going. In darkness they become a nightmare. I, as the lighter and presumably the more easily fished out, went ahead. I do not know how near I came to going into some abyss. Again and again I seemed to be crawling on all-fours across frail snow-bridges, sounding with my axe in a wet, invisible, yielding, substanceless mush and almost despairing of finding solid ground. Only the knowledge that a night actually on the ice would be a very serious business drove us on from one risky passage to another. The whole thing had become unreal, like a dream, by the time the glacier smoothed out and we could creep, now in complete night, down the final ice—to find ourselves on the edge of abrupt cliffs of glacier-worn rocks. Our last candle was almost burnt out and it was obvious that we could go no further. By the final flickers of the wick we managed to find a cleft in the rocks with a chockstone. Under this roof, on a bed of sharp boulders, we settled down to watch through the night. . . . After I had felt several times that the night would never end, came suddenly the first faint light of the

dawn. Then it seemed that the vigil had passed quickly. How stiff we were as we struggled down the rocks below and stumbled across the moraine chaos! In time the sunlight came and our joints loosened. We made all speed down through the fragrant alpage, sprouting with lilac colchicum, to relieve friendly anxieties at Chamin.

The first is a dry and matter-of-fact report, by professionals for fellow-professionals, who are interested in the fact of the new rock route rather than in the misadventures of the descent (for such readers, perhaps the night out was deliberately played down). The second recreates what the experience felt like to the Richardses themselves. Finally there is I.A.R.'s poem, *Hope—to D.E.P. in hospital for a broken hip* (with a note which cites a part of the *Climbing Days* account):

. . . Recall the Epicoun:
Night, welling up so soon,
Near sank us in soft snow.
At the stiff-frozen dawn,
When Time had ceased to flow,
—The glacier ledge our unmade bed—
I hear you through your yawn:
"Leaping crevasses in the dark,
That's how to live!" you said.
No room in that to hedge:
A razor's edge of a remark.

Here the same experience produces not just a memory but a sign, a waymark to lay a course by: a real moment in time that also images a quality of their lives.

Here we are treading on literary ground as tricky as that glacier with its thinly covered crevasses. Mountains have so often been used as images of moral values, the climber's efforts as images of moral striving. It can be straightforwardly done as when Petrarch on Mont Ventoux in Provence (in a passage which forms the epigraph to I.A.R.'s *Comb and Glass*) states that:

> The life we call blessed is located on a high peak. A narrow way, they say, leads up to it. Many hills intervene, and we must proceed "from virtue to virtue" with exalted steps.

But Petrarch *had* trudged up Mont Ventoux! More often, the poet's enthusiasm for the uplift of the mountains is matched by his ignorance

Garfield White

Two prospectors in Dawson City, Yukon Territory, August, 1971.

of what actually happens on them. Think of *Excelsior*; think too of *Rugby Chapel* where Matthew Arnold compares the course of life to a journey through the mountains and his dead father to the stalwart leader of the party, now no more. The journey, the storm, the party of travellers, the inn-keeper's question—"Whom have we left in the snow?"—do not ring true to the climber; and one poet-mountaineer, Michael Roberts, had some quiet fun with *Rugby Chapel* in a paper he contributed to the *Alpine Journal*. Like *Excelsior*, he pointed out, it describes a badly organised party, setting out on a hopeless expedition, and no model for life. The trouble was that for Arnold the main subject—his father's influence—was so much more real than the mountain

journey which was the metaphor for it; but when I.A.R. (or Wordsworth, for that matter) writes about mountains in his poems, he always
starts from the concrete, particular experience; then sometimes, almost
with surprise, he will see how the moment on the mountains fits into a
larger pattern. There is no sense of making a pattern and looking out
for incidents to fit. In *Lighting Fires in Snow* there is an explicit comparison between the making of a fire and the making of a poem, but the
fire is not there to illustrate a statement about poetry; it is there in its
own right as a lived experience ("This practical poem aims to teach a
useful art") through which came the idea of how a poem starts.

Tread out a marble hollow
    Then lay the twigs athwart,
        Teepee-wise or wigwam,
So that the air can follow
    The match-flame from the start:
        As we begin a poem
    And some may win a heart.

For twig to twig will beckon
    If lightly laid above
Better than you can reckon.
        Waste no time devising.
    No, no, it is not love,
        But the drying fume arising
If the draft be free enough.

As the under cavern reddens
    Leave well alone!
Cold fuel only deadens.
        But pile across the smoke
    And give the dog a bone.
        For its life's sake, don't poke!
    The wise fire knows its own.

The wise poem knows its father
    And treats him not amiss;
        But Language is its mother
To burn where it would rather
    Choose that and by-pass this
        Only afraid of smother
    Though the thickening snow-flakes hiss.

Provided we stick as closely as he does to the facts of his days on the mountains, I think we can take I.A.R.'s climbing as a metaphor of his intellectual life. "Poking about corners for something new" was said of him on Welsh rocks, but seems as true of the corners of his mind. "An amusing and instructive adventure" was his own description of the original Cambridge experiment in Practical Criticism, and "a raid by poetry on philosophy" of his splendid poem on Wittgenstein, *The Strayed Poet*. As he delighted in crossing a ridge to come down into a new valley, so we can see him in his critical works raiding across the ridges that divide one academic discipline from another, adventuring into new country. The dedications of *Goodbye Earth* and *The Screens* are "To D.E.P. along the ridge" and "Farther along the ridge"; the poems explore language, ideas, experiences, they are "raids on the inarticulate" where "each venture is a new beginning." (Eliot's words often come to mind as one reads I.A.R.'s poems; what is the Wittgenstein one but a record of "the unbelievable wrestle with words and meanings?") In one poem, I.A.R. explores the nature and significance of his mountain days.

Resign! Resign!

Up hill, down dale . . .
So ran the tale.

We have them in our bones:
Ten thousand miles of stones,
Moraine, debris and scree;
As many, could-be twice,
Over the fissured ice,
The clinging, slippery snows
That of our feet dispose;
As many again, or more,
Beside the torrent's roar,
Within the scented gloom
Or through the sorrowing cwm.

Or by the scythe-worn dell,
And cow-placated swell
Up the redeeming grass
Lifting toward the pass.

Along the ridge itself,
The ridge that earns its pride,

Riven from either side:
Lord of the rift or shelf
Whence the awaiting cliffs
Hang out their "buts" and "ifs"
To magnetise the eye
From sweeping round the suspect sky,
That could so soon prevent
Our inexplicable intent.

Or where the driven snow
Invites our steps to show
No fluted, rearing wall,
Or plum'd crest too tall
For our impertinence.

What did we gather thence?
The bootprint in the dust,
The upward roll and thrust,
The limber footfall plunging down,
The axe-head friendly in the palm
Or snug between the sack and arm.
Clutches of delicate fears,
Qualms as the *néant* nears:
Relieved—our summit joys;
Relived—what toys!

All that—Goodbye!
And this has told you why:
Not of all that bereft,
But we, ourselves, have left . . .
Leave that behind.
And not as Fall . . .
Even resigned.

The poem, with all its Empsonian ambiguities, has no room for nostalgia: the past is "in our bones"—not lost and gone. It is like a wave of the
hand, from "farther along the ridge," to the younger selves perched
maybe on the Dent Blanche or benighted on the Epicoun: still there.

"Old men ought to be explorers" wrote T.S. Eliot—when not yet
sixty! I.A.R., passing eighty, has been one all his life.

JOHN PAUL RUSSO
A Bibliography of the Books, Articles, and Reviews of I. A. Richards

This bibliography does not include first publication of individual poems, although *editiones principes* of collected poems are entered. It does not include translations of Richards' work into foreign languages, film-strips, teaching pictures, long-playing records, taped language courses, television courses, video-cassettes, or pilot projects (even where copyrighted) of guides, texts, and workbooks in the Language Through Pictures series. Nor, save for exceptional cases where new materials are added, have I included later editions or printings of books. Since Richards often revises considerably from manuscript to printing or from printing to reprinting, "pr." (printed) and "repr." (reprinted) do not necessarily indicate a verbatim printing or reprint. If the title of the reprinted work is exactly the same as the original title, I have not entered it following "repr." but simply listed the title of the volume in which it was reprinted. The symbol "l." signifies page "leaves." Typescript and photostat copies entered are in my possession, with the exception of "Complementarities" (1972) and "Beyond" (1973), which are in Richards' possession. Several hundred books in his private library, including some of his own works, Richards has already deposited in the Old Library and the undergraduate library of Magdalene College, Cambridge. At the present time he is arranging an additional bequest.

The facts belie Richards' modest assertion that he never published widely in article form. His bibliography covers a great range of topics in an extraordinary diversity of publications. Articles have emerged from many countries, in many languages, including one "language" he helped (after its invention) to develop; they concern questions of science and poetry, in cultures classical and modern, East and West. He is himself fond of epigraphs, and few could be more apropos his bibliography than Johnson's lines:

Let observation with extensive view,
Survey mankind, from China to Peru.

I wish to thank I. A. Richards for the generous assistance he has
given me in preparing this bibliography. Christine M. Gibson was very
helpful in ascertaining the chronology of the Language Through
Pictures series and related projects. Mrs. Dorothy Pilley Richards,
William H. Youngren, Jean Slingerland, and David Walter aided in
locating some fugitive pieces. Walter Hamilton, Master of Magdalene
College, and Ronald Hyam, Fellow and Librarian, were thoughtful and
generous with their time and assistance during a stay in Cambridge
where this bibliography, as far as it could be at the time, was completed. I also wish to thank Michael Shulan for help in editing the
final copy of the manuscript.

1919

"Art and Science—I." *Athenaeum* 27 June: 534–35. ("II" by H. W. Crun-
dell, 4 July: 566.) Roger Fry hypothesized (*Athenaeum* 6 June 1919) that
the aesthetic value of a theory that disregarded facts would have equal value
for science with one that agreed with facts, since this value depends solely
on the perfection and complexity of the unity attained. R objects, arguing
that a concept of truth is decisive for science and art alike. The difference
between science and art is a difference not between fact and non-fact, or
theory and non-theory, but between the "systematic connection of propositions" and "propositions for their own sake, not as interconnected." The
term "vehicle" is introduced, while "proposition" is an early form of "tenor."

"Emotion and Art." *Athenaeum* 18 July: 630–31. Confusion over *feeling,
emotion, to feel,* and *aesthetic* in criticism could be reduced by defining
these words in ordinary contexts. The James-Lange notion that feeling
follows action is reformulated. Six ways in which emotion may be involved
in art are analyzed. "Irrelevant or mere emotions" may distort or block
meaning in art, defined as "communication of an import of a certain order."

"The Instruments of Criticism: Expression." *Athenaeum* 31 Oct.: 1131.
Contemporary critics have not explored their own aims and methods
properly. Misuse of the concept of "expression" is typical. The term is
analyzed. Croce's criticism is not rejected; but his exoteric disciples are
faulted for taking his Aesthetic without his Logic, substituting a "commonsense" logic of their own, with confusing results.

1920

"The Linguistic Conscience." [C. K. Ogden, joint author?] *Cambridge Magazine* 10: 1: 31. Repr. epigraphs and "Preface," *The Meaning of Meaning* (1923). Ten statements on language which are "mistaken." A separate science is needed for the study of the nature of signs in general and their interpretation. Historically there have been five chief methods of investigation: grammatical, metaphysical, philological, psychological, and logical. The word "symbolism" is offered to identify a new approach. Historical associations of "symbol": a sign of a Christian as distinguished from a heathen; the Symbolist Movement of the nineties; a third group of associations commences with a theory of meaning.

"Symbolism." C. K. Ogden, joint author. *Cambridge Magazine* 10: 1: 32–40. Repr. chs. 5, 2, 6, *The Meaning of Meaning* (1923). "For words, arrangements of words, images, gestures, and such representations as drawings or mimetic sounds we use the term *symbols*." The power of "the word" historically: verbal magic and medicine. Philosophers, psychologists, and logicians do not properly distinguish among sign, referent, and the process of interpretation. The theory of signs on which the doctrine of symbolism depends is formulated: the six canons of symbolism: singularity, definition, expansion, actuality, compatibility, individuality; errors in language use.

"What Is a Fact?" Adelyne More. [Pseudonym for R and C. K. Ogden.] *Cambridge Magazine* 10: 1: 41–42. Repr. Appendix E, *The Meaning of Meaning* (1923). The controversy over the existence of negative facts was initiated by Raphael Demos and expanded by Russell. The problem can be solved by the theory of signs; a fact is a "referent which belongs to the order to which its sign allocates it." Thus, the dispute lies "in the criticism of rival prose styles." R's Cambridge tutor W. E. Johnson is cited on "incompatibility."

1921

"The Sense of Beauty." C. K. Ogden, James Wood, joint authors. *Cambridge Magazine* 10: 2: 73–93. Repr. *The Foundations of Aesthetics* (1922). Sixteen theories of beauty are outlined, not to bring them into opposition, but to distinguish them from each other, and to give to each its own sphere of validity. Favored, however, is a psychological theory, Synaesthesis, "an aesthetic state in which impulses are experienced *together*. . . . Our interest is not canalised in one direction rather than another. . . . This is the explanation of that detachment so often mentioned in artistic experience." The concept of *Chung Yung* (Equilibrium and Harmony) in Confucian thought is introduced.

"The Art of Conversation." C. K. Ogden, joint author. *Cambridge Magazine* 10: 2: 94–100. Repr. chs. 1 and 6, *The Meaning of Meaning* (1923). R offers a theory of definition by which understanding, i.e. "identification of referents," may be obtained. Ten means of identifying the referent are proposed, including symbolization, similarity, and physical, psychological, and psycho-physical causation.

"Vision and Imagination: A New Basis for Physics." Adelyne More. [Pseudonym for R and C. K. Ogden.] *Cambridge Magazine* 10: 2: 101–3. Repr. ch. 4, *The Meaning of Meaning* (1923). Self-contradiction may be removed by the third canon of the theory of signs, by which a symbol is expanded to a point where the ambiguous sign-situation is discovered. Distinctions between vision and imagination follow Coleridge's distinction between primary and secondary imagination. Through the theory of signs they hope to remove "standard anti-realist paradoxes," thereby establishing a "New Basis for Physics."

"First Steps in Psychology." C. K. Ogden, joint author. *Psyche* 2:67–79. A general introduction to the nature, types, problems, and uses of the science of psychology.

"Thoughts, Words and Things." [C. K. Ogden, joint author?] *Cambridge Magazine* 11: 1: 29–31. Repr. "Summary," *The Meaning of Meaning* (1923). The main headings of the doctrine of symbolism are summarized, including sign-situations, the canons of symbolism, definition, and the meaning of beauty. When the problem of meaning is "scientifically approached, we find that no less than sixteen groups of definitions may be profitably distinguished in a field where the most rigid accuracy is desirable."

"What Happens When We Think." *Cambridge Magazine* 11: 1: 32–41. Repr. ch. 3 and Appendix B, *The Meaning of Meaning* (1923). In interpretation, when part of an external context recurs, it links up with a psychological context of causally connected groups of events, often widely separated in time, and acts as a *sign* of the rest of the external context. Whether an interpretation is "true" or "false" does not of course depend only on psychological contexts. The origins of the concept of "emotive" meaning.

"The Meaning of Meaning." C. K. Ogden, joint author. *Cambridge Magazine* 11: 1: 49–57. Repr. ch. 9, *The Meaning of Meaning* (1923). Sixteen definitions of "meaning" are analyzed. Difficulties in the control of symbols as indications of reference are considered.

"On Talking." C. K. Ogden, joint author. *Cambridge Magazine* 11: 1: 57–65. Repr. ch. 10, *The Meaning of Meaning* (1923). The context theory of interpretation is applied to the use of language. An ordering of verbal sign-situations is considered: attitude of speaker to audience, attitude of speaker to subject matter, intention, as determinants of symbolization. The antithesis is not between poetry and prose but between two functions of language. (A) In evocative (emotive) language the essential concern is the character of the attitude aroused. Sound-signs, subtle networks of association, rhythmic and metrical effects, as well as statement, imagery, and metaphor are employed for the poetic evocation of feeling and attitude. Thus metaphor elicits "new, sudden and striking collocations of references for the sake of the compound effects of contrast, conflict, harmony, interinanimation and equilibrium." (B) In symbolic (referential) language the essential concerns are the correctness of symbolization and the verification of the references. This is the language of strictly scientific prose.

1922

The Foundations of Aesthetics. C. K. Ogden, James Wood, joint authors. London: George Allen and Unwin. See "The Sense of Beauty" (1921).

1923

"The Future of Grammar." *Cambridge Magazine* 11: 2: 51–56. Repr. Appendix A, *The Meaning of Meaning* (1923). The nugatory character of several propositions made by Wittgenstein in his *Tractatus Logico-Philosophicus* on the correspondence between sign and referent. "The attempt to generalise from the exceptional cases in which symbols and referents partially correspond, to a necessity for such correspondence in all communication is invalid." A concept of belief is introduced by way of William James's formulation in *Principles of Psychology:* "a sort of feeling more allied to the emotions than to anything else." The future of grammar is bleak unless grammarians devote less effort to formalistic analysis and "mere standardisation of a score or so of convenient names," and begin to investigate the psychology of language.

The Meaning of Meaning: A Study of the Influence of Language upon Thought and of the Science of Symbolism. C. K. Ogden, joint author. London: Kegan Paul, Trench, Trubner. For origins see "An Interview with I. A. Richards" (1969) and "Beginnings and Transitions" (1973). The table of contents offers a full description. Large sections of the volume had been previously published (see above) in the *Cambridge Magazine.* Supplementary essays by B. Malinowski, "The Problem of Meaning in Primitive Languages," and F. G. Crookshank, "The Importance of a Theory of Signs and a Critique of Language in the Study of Medicine."

"Psychology and the Reading of Poetry." *Psyche* 4:6–23. Repr. ch. 16, *Principles of Literary Criticism* (1924). The qualities of a good critic: experience, sympathy, the ability to rank and subordinate experiences in value. What happens when we read a poem. Free and tied imagery are distinguished; impulses, references, emotions, attitudes are defined.

1924

"Desire and the Desirable." *Psyche* 4:213–26. Repr. chs. 6–8, *Principles of Literary Criticism* (1924). He presents a psychological theory of value based on various neurophysiological models, including that of C. S. Sherrington. The concept of impulse and attitude formation is treated at length. The ideal value "desirable" is illustrated by "those people who have achieved an ordered life, whose systems have developed clearing-houses by which the varying claims of different impulses are adjusted."

Principles of Literary Criticism. London: Kegan Paul, Trench, Trubner. "The two pillars upon which a theory of criticism must rest are an account of value and an account of communication." A psychological theory of value is articulated: the concepts of impulse, attitude, balance and equilibrium. The definition and analysis of a poem; free and tied imagery. A theory of communication. The character of the artist; "normality." Badness in poetry. Allusiveness in modern poetry. The workings of the imagination in the creation and reception of a poem. Emotive and referential language distinguished. Poetry in relation to belief. Two appendices (v. "On Value," "The Poetry of T. S. Eliot") were added in a second edition, 1926.

1925

"A Background for Contemporary Poetry." *Criterion* 3:511–28. A prolegomena to *Science and Poetry* (1926). Changes in the intellectual currents are causing a "reorganisation of our attitudes," and "neither criticism nor poetry can remain stationary." Chief consideration is given to Hardy, De La Mare, Yeats, Lawrence, and T. S. Eliot. The term "pseudo-statement" is introduced to discuss the status of literary ideas and attitudes. Thus, Eliot is praised for giving in *The Waste Land* a "perfect emotive description of a state of mind" inevitable in an alert contemporary, and for effecting a "complete severance between his poetry and *all* beliefs." Repr. chs. 5–7, *Science and Poetry* (1926).

"Science and Poetry." *Psyche* 6: 2:52–66. Repr. chs. 1–4, *Science and Poetry* (1926). One of the effects of science, especially psychology, could be an increase in our understanding and criticism of poetry. The nature and value of poetic experiences are considered from a psychological point of view. The poetic *command of life* is described as "passionate, noble and serene as the experience of the poet, the master of speech, because in the creative moment he is the master of experience itself."

"Science and Poetry." *Atlantic* 136: 481–91. Repr. chs. 1–4, *Science and Poetry* (1926). See entry immediately preceding.

1926

"Science and Poetry." *Saturday Review of Literature* 2:833–34. Repr. chs. 5–7, *Science and Poetry* (1926). The modern age is experiencing the "neutralisation of nature" and the ascendency of the scientific point of view. The distinction between scientific (symbolic, referential) statement and pseudo-statement, and between scientific truth and "truth." A pseudo-statement is "true" if it "suits and serves some attitude or links together attitudes which on other ground are desirable." The erosion of belief is inevitable, but there is consequent need for religious emotions and attitudes attached to those beliefs to survive without them: "We shall then be thrown back, as Matthew Arnold foresaw, upon poetry."

Science and Poetry. London: Kegan Paul, Trench, Trubner. 2nd ed. rev. and enlgd., 1935. Repr. *Poetries and Sciences,* with Preface and Commentary (New York: W. W. Norton, 1970). See articles "Science and Poetry" (1925, 1926). The revisions were not such as to negate any significant statement of the original.

"Sentimentality." *Forum* 76: 384–91. Repr. III.6, *Practical Criticism* (1929). Definitions of sentimentality are illustrated; only one is not pejorative. This essay is considerably revised and expanded in *Practical Criticism,* where the positive type of sentimentality is separated from the others and is used as a starting-point in the discussion of the ideal of "sincerity" (III.8).

"Gerard Hopkins." *Dial* 81:195–203. Hopkins' technical innovations are explored through analysis of *Peace, The Windhover, Spelt from Sibyl's Leaves,* and other poems. But the "belief problem" looms ominously in his poetry and his "intelligence . . . failed to remould its materials sufficiently" in attacking it.

"Count Cagliostro." Review of W. R. H. Trowbridge, *Cagliostro: The Splendour and Misery of a Master of Magic* (London: Chapman and Hall, 1910; George Allen and Unwin, 1926). *Forum* 76: 473–74. A favorable review of a biography of the famous charlatan.

"Verses and Echoes." Review of Wilfred Rowland Childe, *Ivory Palaces: Poems* (London: Kegan Paul, Trench, Trubner, 1925); Teresa Hooley, *Collected Poems* (London: Cape, 1926); C. S. Sherrington, *The Assaying of Brabantius* (London: Oxford University Press, 1925); Barrington Gates, *Poems* (London: Hogarth, 1925). *New Statesman* 17 Apr.: 16–17. Practical criticism of four volumes; only Sherrington escapes censure. *Inter alia* R discusses problems of literary influence, tradition, and the presentation of autobiographical moments or composition passing as such ("rarely successful. . . . It demands too much impersonality from the writer and asks too little from the reader").

"Mr. Eliot's Poems." Review of T. S. Eliot, *Poems 1909–1925* (London: Faber and Gwyer, 1925). *New Statesman* 20 Feb.: 584–85. Repr. "The Poetry of T. S. Eliot," *Living Age* 10 Apr.: 112–14; Appendix B, *Principles of Literary Criticism* 1926 ed. Eliot's poetry is defended against charges of being "overintellectualised." He uses allusions, for example, for their "emotional aura," for the "attitudes they incite," for "compression." " 'The Waste Land' is the equivalent in content to an epic." Obscurity and ambiguity are exploited as poetic values. Contemporary readers will find in Eliot's verse a "fuller realisation of their plight, the plight of a whole generation, than they find elsewhere."

"On Value." Appendix A, *Principles of Literary Criticism* 1926 ed. A reply to Conrad Aiken's claim that the psychological theory of value is not "sufficiently relativistic." He agrees with Aiken, adding that his (R's) definition of the best life as "that in which as much as possible of our possible personality is engaged" *is* wide of absolutism. The problem is that there are no quantitative methods of comparison, not only of experiences as they tend toward the best life, but of personalities assimilating those experiences.

Review of John B. Watson, *Behaviorism* (London: Kegan Paul, Trench, Trubner, 1925). *Criterion* 4:372–78. Watson follows modern behaviorism in excluding consciousness from its study, and in denying that it is either a definable or usable concept. R thinks contrarily that a study of consciousness may provide "valuable indications in working out a physiological theory of behavior." Watson's pages on fear- and love-transference in children mark "an extremely important contribution."

"Can Education Increase Intelligence?" "II. But We Can Be Taught To Think." *Forum* 76: 504–9. A debate with William McDougall, who takes the negative. R affirms that intelligence is the learning to exclude the irrelevant, the bringing of results of past experience to bear on new situations. Our knowledge of such processes is growing, and will help us teach ourselves to use them more efficiently.

1927

"God of Dostoevsky." *Forum* 78: 88–97. Human pain is a chief source of disbelief in God. The stages in Dostoevsky's struggle to believe are his novels. Man's attempts to "solve the universe" have been premature; they represent rationalizations of feeling. Although many of man's best traits would not have developed without religion, only those of man's "feelings" least disturbed by "beliefs" are now truly to be praised and cherished. Dostoevsky treats at length three "feelings" fostered by religion: spiritual pride, nostalgia for another world, self-humiliation.

"The Lure of High Mountaineering." *Atlantic* 139: 51–57. On the technical and intellectual attractions, as well as the dangers, of his favorite sport. See also Dorothy Pilley Richards, *Climbing Days* (London: Secker and Warburg, 1935), and the "Retrospection" to the 2nd ed., 1965.

"Changing American Mind." *Harper's* 154: 239–45. Repr. "Are We Becoming More Conscious?" *Psyche* 8: 1: 26–34. Consciousness is "an affair of integration under difficulties," and New York now epitomizes the contemporary consciousness at large, e.g. the break with tradition, and social and political problems that are the harbingers of the future.

"Nineteen Hundred and Now." *Atlantic* 140: 311–17. A growing interest in psychology, a revolt against logic, a trend toward attitude and feeling— these phenomena mark the spirit of the age. Wells and Shaw exemplify a rationalism now wearing thin, Aldous Huxley drifts through feelings too weak to support the self, Lawrence is a most extreme representative of the power of the will, but T. S. Eliot perhaps best embodies contemporary consciousness. A careful reading of Eliot will leave the reader an "impression very rarely made by anything but great poetry."

"A Passage to Forster." *Forum* 78:914–20. Forster's real audience is youth, his peculiar quality as a novelist is his hold on "fiercely critical values." The discussion concentrates on the earlier writings, including *Howards End*, "the book that still best represents the several sides of Forster's worth."

"The Teaching of English." *New Statesman* 23 July: 478. "The great work which lies before teachers of English" is the teaching of English as a foreign language. It has become "since the war . . . the world language." But we must make certain that the English that will be taught is "as favourable as possible to English poetry." Tendency to metaphor, genius for ambiguity, emotionality, are characteristic of English, making it a more fit instrument for poetry than for speculative philosophy or "general discussion." A more lively consciousness of its "peculiar traps" is what is needed to correct just these deficiencies of English as a referential language and R calls on English and American scholars for a critical study of language uses and abuses, blending logic, grammar, comparative linguistics, and psychology.

1928

"Aspects of the Novel." Review of E. M. Forster, *Aspects of the Novel* (London: Arnold, 1927). *Cambridge Review* 49: 304–5. He objects to Forster's critical devaluation of narrative line and his overly simplified con-

cept of form-content division. The interest we have in the development of
the story is a function of the novel's form.

"Time and Western Man." Review of Wyndham Lewis, *Time and Western
Man* (London: Chatto and Windus, 1927). *Cambridge Review* 49:325–26.
Modern science and philosophy render a commonsense view of the world at
best shaky and at worst untenable, according to Lewis. But an intelligence
that remains "master of itself" can always select for its particular purpose
whatever world picture seems desirable. A psychologist may be a behaviorist
and an unreservedly responsive reader of Dante "without any splitting up of
the personality into two distinct selves."

Review of Herbert Read, *English Prose Style* (London: G. Bell and Sons,
1928). *Criterion* 8: 315–24. Read's gift for detailed criticism is impaired by
a "strategic error in his choice of intellectual equipment." His distinctions
between prose and poetry, thought and word, thought and sensibility are
unclear and inadequate. On metaphor, illuminative and decorative, Read is
sounder; but he overemphasizes the visual in imagery.

1929

Practical Criticism: A Study of Literary Judgment. London: Kegan Paul,
Trench, Trubner. Thirteen poems, varying widely in quality but none
exceedingly cryptic, were given for paraphrase and analysis to Cambridge
University students and some non-academics. Half of the book consists of
their responses ("protocols") and R's analyses of their miscomprehension.
Many readers, confronted with ambiguity, irony, or obscurity, counted their
own difficulties against the author. He considers the "ten difficulties of
criticism," ·e.g. the inability to determine the plain sense, stock responses
and irrelevant associations that clog the communication channel, doctrinal
adhesions, and sentimentality. He formulates four aspects of meaning in
the analysis of a poem: sense, feeling, tone, intention. He develops concepts
of "sincerity" and "self-completion" that provide an ethical basis for criticism. The dangers of dogmatizing are pointed out: "There comes a point
in all criticism where a sheer choice has to be made without the support
of any arguments, principles, or general rules. All that arguments or principles can do is to protect us from irrelevancies, red-herrings, and disturbing misconceptions. . . . They may preserve us from bad arguments
but they cannot supply good ones."

1930

"Belief." *Symposium* 1: 423–39. Ambiguity in the use of the word "belief":
belief as an object, as a state of mind, as a relationship to what is believed.
By separating two kinds of belief, verifiable belief and imaginative assent,
one may clarify the problem of belief in poetry. "Imaginative assents are

not ordered logically"; they are based on the "compatibilities of movements of the will and the feelings and the desires."

1931

"Notes on the Practice of Interpretation." *Criterion* 10: 412–20. A reply to Montgomery Belgion's "What is Criticism?" (*Criterion* 10: 118–39). Belgion obscures the relations between science and art, between art and life. R elaborates on these relations, claiming he in no way wishes to use art to chastise life.

"Criticism of English Poetry." Review of H. W. Garrod, *Poetry and the Criticism of Life* (London: Oxford University Press, 1931), and Charles Williams, *Poetry at Present* (Oxford: Clarendon Press, 1930). *Yale Review* 21:191–93. Garrod's wit "must be enjoyed without bothersome preoccupations with the germinal value of the ideas he uses." Williams writes "the best book about modern English poets."

"Between Truth and Truth." *Symposium* 2: 226–41. A reply to J. Middleton Murry's criticism of "pseudo-statement," "truth," and "belief" in "Beauty Is Truth" (*Symposium* 1:466–501, see esp. 495–501). Murry allows that subsidiary or metaphoric statements may be "untrue" but the "total statement" of poetic utterance can be "in a very real and practical sense 'true.'" But R distinguishes, both at the subsidiary level and the level of "total statement," between truth and *truth*. "Do poetic and metaphoric statements really tell us anything about the experiences they convey to us?" Yes, they may offer facts, and they may be studied psychologically, analytically, thus revealing "true" facts as to the nature of the aroused experience. But metaphoric expression is offering a guide *to* the experience itself, "true" in the sense of "rare and desirable, important to us," meeting "deep needs in our nature," "to be accepted and integrated into the fabric of our personality."

"Chinese Personal Nomenclature: The Advantages of an Ambilateral System." *Psyche* 12: 1: 86–89. A new system of proper names is outlined, e.g. (1) "It provides perfect symmetry, and hence tends to emphasize equality between the sexes," and (10) "It would leave scope for personal whim" for the adult who would not be saddled with a name unsuited to his taste.

1932

"Human Nature: An Early Chinese Argument." *Psyche* 12: 3: 62–77. Repr. ch. 1, *Mencius on the Mind* (1932). Distinctions in interpretation available to Mencius and Kao tze are used as *"instruments of thinking even though we find no explicit formulation of them nor any grammatical* apparatus in the text for indicating them unambiguously." *Being born, nature, pleasure* in the Chinese are analyzed according to a concept of multiple definition.

Mencius on the Mind: Experiments in Multiple Definition. London: Kegan Paul, Trench, Trubner. New York: Harcourt, Brace. R elaborates on the multiple semantic possibilities involved in rendering the Chinese of Mencius into English. Translating Chinese illustrates the importance of contextual interpretation because its syntax is less highly structured than that of English. Mencius' "conception of *hsing* was in terms of activity or incipient activity—an activity which, if permitted, tended always to self-development," to the "fulfilment of the mind," which was what he meant by "goodness." His theory of the personality ranks "with the most important constructions of 'the shaping spirit of imagination.'" For origins of and problems in this volume see "Towards a Theory of Translating" (1953).

"The Chinese Renaissance." *Scrutiny* 1:102–13. The modern movement in China is essentially political, anti-traditional, "very largely a students' creation." A new literary language is now developing. What the Chinese intelligentsia read. A poem by Hsu Tze-mou. Ch. 9 of *So Much Nearer* (1968) contains later reflections on the subject.

Review of Max Eastman, *The Literary Mind: Its Place in an Age of Science* (New York and London: Charles Scribner's Sons, 1931). *Criterion* 12: 150–55. His general thesis ("very much sounder than his practice") is that "the matters which criticism has to discuss are becoming the subject of technical treatment in psychology." But Eastman describes the end of poetry airily. "If 'heightened consciousness' is all we are to ask for," answers R, "what is wrong with lumbago?" He replies to Eastman's criticism of him.

1933

Basic Rules of Reason. London: Kegan Paul, Trench, Trubner. Processes of reasoning, described in Basic English, can put thoughts into a more orderly system so that connections between them can become clarified. Reasons why Basic (in which the book is cast) is better for initial language instruction than a fuller vocabulary. Twenty-six key words such as *thought, thing, fiction, fact,* are analyzed. He shows "how their senses may be grouped," and he gives us "a machine for the better organization of our minds, which was part of the purpose of the older books on Logic" (C. K. Ogden, *The Basic Books,* Supp. to *Basic News,* Jan. 1938 [Cambridge, Eng.: The Orthological Institute, 1938], p. 15).

"Multiple Definition." *Proceedings of the Aristotelian Society* 34: 31–50. Philosophical words have the greatest multiplicity of meaning. Basic English, a controlled model of Standard English, is used as a method of analysis under this hypothesis. Philosophical words in poetry and in ordinary contexts: thought, thing, fiction, fact, knowledge, belief, sense, agreement. Repr. chs. 1–2, *Basic Rules of Reason* (1933).

"Lawrence as a Poet." Review of D. H. Lawrence, *Last Poems* (Florence: Orioli, 1932). *New Verse* 1: 15–17. "A fundamental fact about Lawrence's poetry is that its reader cannot escape the problem of belief." Two kinds of belief: "adopting the attitude as good" and "accepting the doctrine as true." Lawrence too often chose the latter. He had a "prodigious sensibility, plasticity, sincerity and courage," but "took to shutting up" his "intellectual faculties whenever they threatened his system of intuitions." The poems can be as doctrine "false" and as attitude "*merely his*, or at best sectarian." Even in his finest late verse there are prosaic passages and imperfect fusions of content and form. "What remains is the sense of passionate awareness that opened as you read."

"Preface to a Dictionary." *Psyche* 13: 10–24. The rationale for the *General Basic English Dictionary* (1940): "a dictionary technique deriving from an explicit theory of the comparison of meanings." How a sign represents meaning is analyzed by the theory of signs and symbol situations from *The Meaning of Meaning* (1923) and "The Four Kinds of Meaning" from *Practical Criticism* (1929). Logical vs. emotive metaphor.

"Meaning and Change of Meaning." Review of Gustaf Stern, *Meaning and Change of Meaning* (Göteborg: Elanders, 1931). *Psyche* 13: 185–96. Stern asks how we may treat meanings of words systematically in order to examine their history and the modes in which their changes occur. The general theory and classification of sense-changes is presented with "rare lucidity, order and design"; he has shifted the problem "to a new level of accessibility and control." There is, however, equivocation regarding the term "referent" in his method, and R resorts to sign-situations and the theory of definitions from *The Meaning of Meaning* (1923) to settle the question of belief and true and false reference.

"Fifteen Lines from Landor." *Criterion* 12: 355–70. Repr. *Speculative Instruments* (1955). Inaccurate readings of *Gebir* (III, 4–18) are analyzed and shown to prove that "a judgment seemingly about a poem is primarily evidence about a reading of it." R provides his own paraphrase.

"Our Lost Leaders." *Saturday Review of Literature* 9: 509–10. The academic machine visible in many university publications is destructive, particularly to the young students in their most susceptible years of education. A teacher of English must share a ready memory, sound learning, care in presentation, and a modicum of vivacity or impressiveness with teachers of other subjects, but in addition he must bring to his work a "fairly complete, well-balanced, and sensitive personality." He stresses the waste in "research" and the need for effective teachers.

1934

"The Sense of Musical Delight." *Psyche* 14:88–99. Repr. ch. 5, *Coleridge on Imagination* (1934). A word is not necessarily a unit of meaning. Apart from an utterance it has no meaning—or rather too many possible meanings. Through context a word may be defined as a sensory and an intellectual sign. Coleridge deduces a necessary connection between the sensory and the semantic function of meter, and between pleasure and truth in poetry.

Coleridge on Imagination. London: Kegan Paul, Trench, Trubner. Coleridge was a semiasiologist; he attempted to use Hartley's associationism and metaphysics essentially to explore and explain what a modern thinker might determine with psychological models. Topics include the coalescence of subject and object, the distinction between imagination and fancy, knowledge and "good sense" in poetry, meter, and metaphors for poetry, e.g. the wind-harp. A paperback edition was published in 1960 by Indiana University Press with an introduction by Kathleen Coburn. See "Foreword" (1962).

"What Is Belief?" *Nation* 18 July 139:71–74. Repr. *Poetries* (1973). "Prompted by arguments with Eliot," R said in conversation (see, for example, Eliot's *Selected Essays* [New York: Harcourt, Brace, 1932], pp. 229–31). Most people use "belief" to cover a heterogeneous variety of mental states, processes, and conditions, from positivism to whim. R uses "belief" to mean certain "feelings, attitudes, settings of the will, concentrations of attention," but "I am, so far as I know, without Beliefs." "The hope of skepticism is that it may uncover behind these fictions more of the actual forces by which we live."

1935

Basic in Teaching: East and West. London: Kegan Paul, Trench, Trubner. This book, not in Basic English, is designed for teachers. R relates the conditions of teaching the English language and literature, and the virtues of Basic over Chinese in teaching Western thought, in China. "Turning to parallel troubles of learners in England and America," he argues against the current system in teaching languages, and offers reasons for his opinion that "Basic may be used as a training in the right way of reading English" (C. K. Ogden, *The Basic Books*, Supp. to *Basic News*, Jan. 1938 [Cambridge, Eng.: The Orthological Institute, 1938], p. 15).

"Definiteness." *Psyche* 15:77–87. Repr. ch. 9, *Interpretation in Teaching* (1938). The definition of "definite." Do we define words or things? R takes both approaches and enumerates three senses of our defining things and eight of our defining words, including the emotive use of language.

Review of *S. T. Coleridge's Treatise on Method*, edited by Alice D. Snyder (London: Constable, 1934). *Criterion* 14: 308–11. Coleridge is "here admirably edited." Growth is the key to all Coleridge's thinking; method, the way, " 'implies both an *uniting* and a *progressive* power.' " "That knowing and what is known are no more to be separated (except for local and occasional convenience) than growing from what is grown . . . is his prime principle."

1936

The Philosophy of Rhetoric. New York: Oxford University Press. Rhetoric is defined as a "study of misunderstanding and its remedies." R focuses on varying aims of discourse; the definition of context ("a whole cluster of events that recur together—including the required conditions as well as whatever we may pick out as cause or effect"); dangers in emphasizing the visual in metaphor; mutual dependencies and "interinanimation" of words in specific contexts; the concept of *sorting* (of negating alternatives in the act of cognition); metaphor, the "omnipresent principle of language"; the relations between two halves of metaphor, tenor ("underlying idea or principal subject") and vehicle ("figure"), which together interact and bear "meaning." An intellectual model is conceived as a connecting organ, and the ability to connect is interpretation. For poetry, freedom to fill in connectives—absence of intermediate steps—is "the main source of its power."

"Empson's Poems." Review of William Empson, *Poems* (London: Chatto and Windus, 1935). *Cambridge* Review 57: 253. He praises "this superlative book of riddles" for its "wit," "deliberately complex puns," "extraordinary and inexplicable passion," and Notes that make one "laugh repeatedly in a healthy, intellectual, obscure, and satisfying fashion."

"Logical Machinery." *Psyche* 16:76–99. Repr. chs. 21–22, *Interpretation in Teaching* (1938). The uses of "concrete," "abstract," "general," "particular," are left vague in logic, and R defines them. He then classifies "properties" as: (a) "qualities," and (b) "relational properties."

1937

"Basic English in the Study of Interpretation." *Psyche* 17:35–47. Repr. ch. 11, *Interpretation in Teaching* (1938). Four duties of words: to name things, to express feelings and attitudes towards them, to represent reality through art, to indicate directions. Basic English is experimentally useful in investigating these duties since it is a rigorously controlled "model" of Standard English.

1938

Interpretation in Teaching. New York: Harcourt, Brace. In a "Retrospect" (1972) to a reprinted edition (1973?), R describes the volume as a "beginning of what should be a vast collective *clinical* study of the aberrations of average intelligence"; its aim is to "develop better judgment as to central matters upon which the health of thought depends." Passages of poetry were used for protocols in *Practical Criticism* (1929), but prose passages specifically illustrating theory and practice in Rhetoric, Grammar, and Logic (the main headings of the book) are used here. He analyzes the protocols and finds them outmoded, arbitrary, or misleading in their approach to language, while students' commentaries prove them to be "wildly and inexplicably misread." E.g. under Grammar he attacks the doctrine of good usage as the "most pernicious influence in current English teaching" for creating external standards of "what is right" or "fixing" meanings to words; he advocates instead "microscopic" analysis of the specific context through which the word is acquiring and imparting its "meaning." Under Logic he criticizes Russell's theory of descriptions. His own concept of "Freedom in Definition." The place of this volume in his career is discussed in some detail in "Beginnings and Transitions" (1973).

A First Book of English for Chinese Learners. Peking: The Orthological Institute of China. A manual, 427 pp. The preface mentions a *Teacher's Handbook* and an *Introduction* to that work which were published both with it and separately, and which I have not been able to locate.

Times of India Guide to Basic English. C. K. Ogden, joint author. Edited by Adolph Myers. Bombay: The Times of India Press. Part IV, pp. 55–88, excepting the opening section, is "from the pen of Dr. I. A. Richards" (ed. note). "Basic *versus* Word Magic," the problem of school examinations, and the use of Basic as an exercise in paraphrase, are discussed. The principles underlying Basic are found to be simple and essential; they derive from the observation that "the number of ideas we actually use in explaining or defining any meaning is a surprisingly small one." "The peculiarity of Basic is that, as an analytic instrument, it forces us to consider contexts and connections so insistently. Its 850 words are not a haphazard collection. They are those which experiment has shown are most capable, in combination with one another, of taking the place of other words in a fashion which will sensitively and accurately reflect what the other words are doing from context to context."

1939

"Basic English and Its Applications." *Royal Society of Arts Journal* 87: 735–55. Repr. *Basic English*, ed. Julia E. Johnson (New York: H. W. Wilson,

1944). An account of the origins of Basic English; its most important features and uses; the need for its adoption as an international second language.

1940

The General Basic English Dictionary. London: Evans Bros. R was one of many collaborators under the general editorship of C. K. Ogden.

"Six Sides of a Word." Typescript copy with corrections, dated 23 Mar. 1940, 9 l. A short radio play for children, delivered on WNAC, Boston. The six sides consecutively introduced are: sound, form in writing, sense, changes of form, place within a statement, and its part in the work of a statement.

"Letter from I. A. Richards to Richard Eberhart, from Magdalene College Cambridge, Dec. 15, 1938." *Furioso* 1: 3: 43. Practical criticism and revision of Eberhart's *A Meditation.*

"William Empson." *Furioso* 1: 3. Supplement: "A Special Note." In a leaflet R relates the origins of *Seven Types of Ambiguity,* and comments on the "grim wit and savage gusto" of Empson's poetry, which exhibits his "intellectual grasp of the deepest traditional themes . . . metaphysical in the root sense."

"What Is Involved in the Interpretation of Meaning?" *Reading and Pupil Development. Proceedings of the Conference on Reading Held at the University of Chicago,* Vol. II. Supplementary Educational Monographs, No. 51. Chicago: University of Chicago Press. To develop freedom in thinking one must develop basic skills in interpretation. The study of metaphor transference, such as that between perceiving and understanding, sight and knowledge, is effective in the classroom. "How to cultivate common sense" by exercises in translation into other words in the same language. Ideas in this essay are incorporated in *How To Read a Page* (1942).

"Possible Procedures in Promoting Better Interpretation of Meaning." *Reading and Pupil Development. Proceedings of the Conference on Reading Held at the University of Chicago,* Vol. II. Supplementary Educational Monographs, No. 51. Chicago: University of Chicago Press. The procedures include the study of errors in hypothetical thinking or from fixation on one single meaning. A typically "difficult" word, "must," is analyzed, by division into logical or verbal necessity, natural necessity, instrumental necessity, and imposed necessity. Which types of necessity are being presented may be ascertained by specific exercises.

1941

"Yale—Bergen Lecture (1940)." *Furioso* 1: 4: 83–90. Repr. "The Resource-fulness of Words," *Speculative Instruments* (1955). Metaphysics can no longer unify a course of study. Attention to language might, in part, supply what is lacking. We need "systematic instruction" in "the inherent and necessary opportunities for misunderstanding." This essay presents in embryo the main theme of *How to Read a Page* (1942).

"A Certain Sort of Interest in Language." *Chap Book*. 1: 1–16. An account of Basic English, stressing teacher-training. R allays fears that the teaching of Basic will replace, modify, or cripple Standard English.

"Introduction." Hugh R. Walpole, *Semantics: The Nature of Words and Their Meanings* (New York: W. W. Norton). The concept of conception, the "individual coming into being of a capacity in the individual mind." The context theory of meaning is explored. Semantics, like translation (even English to English), treats theoretically all the problems that emerge "when we compare two ways of saying the same thing."

"Basic English." *Fortune* 23: 89–91, 111–14. A popular introduction to Basic. In conclusion R asks whether Basic can deepen and sharpen interest in the essential thought of the times, e.g. differences between totalitarianism and democracy. Both ideologies are defined. "No society that is founded in consent can afford to be inefficient in its means of discussion."

1942

How To Read a Page: A Course in Effective Reading, with an Introduction to a Hundred Great Words. New York: W. W. Norton. Repr. with a new "Introduction" (Boston: Beacon Press, 1959). A response to Mortimer Adler's *How to Read a Book* (1940). Through "microscopic" analysis of key words and metaphors, determining the senses and aims of contexts, R presents a method of close efficient reading. The definitions and ambiguities of one hundred key words, all Basic, are illustrated. Under "Reason" the Richardsian concept of Dialectic derived from Plato is advanced.

"The Interactions of Words." *The Language of Poetry*, edited by Allen Tate (Princeton: Princeton University Press). Repr. "Interinanimations of Words," *Poetries* (1973). Poets, by molding and remolding words, bring *conceptions* into being. This is Plato's "dialectic art," taken "arbitrarily [as] the practice of a supreme sort of poetry—the sort which was to replace the poetry he banished from the Republic." A word is a "permanent set of possibilities of understanding." Lines 1–12 from Donne's *First Anniversary* are compared with the first stanza of Dryden's *Ode . . . to Mrs. Anne Killigrew*.

"The New 'Republic.' " *Nation* 28 March: 370–72. Repr. "Introduction," *The Republic of Plato* (1942), "Sources of our Common Thought" (1971), *Poetries* (1973). "There never was a book of such scope so well designed for *its* pupils." And to try to offer the *Republic* in English is one of the best means of studying what the Greek is trying to express. "Our purpose, which was Plato's, is saving society and our souls . . . the most inclusive of purposes."

The Republic of Plato. A Version in Simplified English. New York: W. W. Norton. See "The New 'Republic' " (1942) and *Plato's Republic* (1966). Plato's version is reduced by one-third. The language is an expanded version of Basic English.

"The Ever-New Discovery." Unpublished lecture. Photostat copy with corrections, dated 20 Oct. 1942, 11 l. Pr. *Poetries* (1973), with the subtitle "A talk to teachers (1943) [*sic*]." The discovery is how "to reconcile authority and freedom" in the classroom, thus offering a model of a well-run institution. Statements on education by Charles Hoole, Ruskin, Locke, and Plato are glossed in turn, but Aristotle on man's highest function (*Nichomachean Ethics* I,7,9) is cited as *point d'appui*. Freedom is distinguished from "doing what one wants to" after Arnold.

"Pictures in the Mind's Eye." Unpublished lecture. Typescript copy with corrections, dated 21 Oct. 1942, 3 l. R analyzes the abuse of visual metaphor in the act of understanding prose or poetry. Even Lord Kames in his *Elements of Criticism* (1762) erred as a result of "imagery obsession," for example, misinterpreting a passage from *Henry* V (IV.i. 205–7).

"Psychopolitics." *Fortune* 26: 108–9. In one of his most cogent essays in political criticism R advocates a broad internationalism, supports a U.N. where nations are but "regular embodiments or symbols of the common human effort." With regard to the individual, his ideal society fosters freedom and responsibility, but "without the traditional doctrine of human nature behind it, freedom becomes (as Plato insisted) a self-destructive aim. Freedom for what?"

1943

Basic English and Its Uses. London: Kegan Paul, Trench, Trubner. New York: W. W. Norton. The current need for an international "second" language is considered. The values and aims of Basic English in meeting this need: a "limited set of words [850] in terms of which the meaning of all words might be stated." The history of the Basic English Movement; the relation of Basic to English; the teaching of Basic by audio-visual aids. The study of Basic increases our sensitivity to and understanding of the literary language itself.

Words on Paper: First Steps in Reading. Christine M. Gibson, joint author. Cambridge, Mass.: English Language Research, Inc. A manual.

"Education for Peace." Speech delivered in Wellesley, Massachusetts, 10 May. Typescript copy with corrections, 14 l. War is a symptom, not a disease, deriving from approved and current principles of human action and social cohesion: self-interest and nationalism. Can we, after the war, redirect our will to the purpose of Education, i.e. the Socratic concepts of knowledge and virtue. We must beware of "doctrines—of thinking that it is the *doctrine,* an individual, a group, a party, or a nation" that can save us or damn us.

"The Two Rings: A Communication." *Partisan Review* 10:380–81. R comments on "The Failure of Nerve" controversy in preceding issues, and expresses the need for a creative skepticism against the ranged ideologies of the hour.

"A World Language." Speech delivered at the New York Herald Tribune Forum, 16 Nov. New York: New York Herald Tribune, 1944. Repr. "Common Language" (1943). A tract in eight pages on and in Basic English. Increase in power becomes dangerous if it is not met by like increase in understanding and control. Global travel and communications will make an international second language necessary.

"Common Language." *Vital Speeches* 10: 158–60. See above "A World Language" (1943).

"Interpretation." *Yale Review* 32:693–705. Repr. "Toward Practice in Interpretation," *Speculative Instruments* (1955). The analogy between interpreting historical events and interpreting words; Thucydides and modern historians; the concept of the universal and the particular; opposition and reconciliation. We need to heighten our power to recognize what language "is going to do to us in the next important thing it tries to say." Logic traditionally provided access to this power. Criticism, i.e. practice in interpretation, must succeed in providing it today.

"Mr. I. A. Richards Replies." *American Speech* 18: 290–96. He rebuts criticism by Chad Walsh in "The Verb System of Basic English" (*American Speech* 17: 137–43). Walsh argued that Basic made such wide use of its 850-word vocabulary that serious misunderstandings resulted, e.g. *give up* vs. *give out*, and that more difficult verb constructions are forced upon the learners in Basic than in Standard English.

"Basic English Can Be Learned Easily by All." *Rotarian* 63: 30: 56–57. He replies to Perry Reynolds, pseud. (see *Rotarian* 63: 28–30). Basic English does not impair loyalty to one's native tongue, is not unnecessarily hard for an English-speaking person to adapt to, and does not make for an irreversible transition back to Standard English. For the learner Basic English should only be considered "a clearly defined stage."

1944

"Idle Fears About Basic English." *Atlantic* June 173: 98–100. R responds to criticism by Rose Macaulay (in "Against Basic English" [*Atlantic* April 173: 58–60]), who is "too busy passing judgment on what is or is not good English." The key question remains: which is easier for the foreigner to attain competence in, Basic English or a "miscellaneous assortment of common phrases that have passed for elementary English"? Idle fears, then, are that Basic is against common usage, that it has a stinted vocabulary, that it cannot be understood by native speakers easily, that it might be taught in normal English and American classrooms.

"Education and Culture." *Partisan Review* 11:310–12. Repr. *Speculative Instruments* (1955). Taking part in a debate, R expresses several points of agreement with Eliot in his various writings on culture. The historical means for maintaining and transmitting culture are vanishing, but he objects to Eliot's disheartening prognostications. For he sees in education on a broad scale, and properly carried on, a viable medium for the pursuit of "intellectual and moral order."

1945

The Pocket Book of Basic English: A Self-Teaching Way into English. Christine M. Gibson, joint author. New York: Pocket Books. Repr. *English Self-Taught Through Pictures* (1949) and *English Through Pictures* (1952). The forerunner of the Language Through Pictures series.

General Education in a Free Society: Report of the Harvard Committee. Twelve authors, including R. Cambridge, Mass.: Harvard University Press. The nature, scope, and aims of a liberal education in a modern society. His work on the Committee led him in 1946–48 to offer Humanities 1a, *Homer, the Old Testament, and Plato,* under General Education at Harvard.

Learning the English Language. Books I–III. Christine M. Gibson, joint editor. Boston: Houghton Mifflin. Toronto: Thomas Nelson. Three workbooks and a teacher's guide were published in the same year by Houghton Mifflin; these were designed by R, Miss Gibson, and their staff. Books II–III, the accompanying workbooks, and the teacher's guide were almost completely by R and Miss Gibson.

Learning Basic English. A Practical Handbook for English-Speaking People. Christine M. Gibson, joint author. New York: W. W. Norton. The authors present an overall view of Basic English, outline a vocabulary, rules, and grammar, and provide model exercises in translation into Basic, including Coleridge's passage on the reconciling power of the imagination (*Biographia Literaria*, ch. 14).

1947

Nations and Peace. New York: Simon and Schuster. An essay in Basic English on the threat to peace (nationalism) and the way to peace (internationalism, a strong UN, a world law).

"Notes on Principles of Beginning Language Instruction." UNESCO Conference, Paris, June 19. Pr. *Design for Escape* (1968). Eighteen points of departure in sentence-in-situation instruction.

"Responsibilities in the Teaching of English." *Essays and Studies by Members of the English Association* 32: 7–20. Repr. *Speculative Instruments* (1955). The first responsibility is to reduce illiteracy. Basic English is the world's most convenient second language. The aims and methods of teaching Basic English. Greater experimentation is needed in classroom teaching. Also needed, a "recreated organon" in liberal education, a "United Studies."

"The ?Future? of the Humanities in General Education." *Journal of General Education* 1: 232–37. Repr. *Speculative Instruments* (1955). Mass education is the chief hope for man, and the problem is how to develop teachers "able to give their pupils any power to select from among the influences to which they become ever more open." In the past the study of literature produced such teachers.

"Address to the Harvard Alumni Association." 5 June. Carbon typescript copy with corrections, 5 l. Marginal note: "This was an occasion on which General Marshall, J. Robert Oppenheimer and T. S. Eliot, among others, had been receiving Honorary Degrees from Harvard and my remarks had to follow, almost immediately, the speech proposing 'the Marshall Plan.'" Title "The Nations" canceled. How might man learn to control the instruments and powers at his disposal. Not by words now, but by a deed— first by some one nation, or group of nations—laying the dangerous part of nationhood, the responsibility for self-defense, before a world government.

"Literature, Oral-Aural and Optical." A talk delivered on BBC radio, 5 Oct. Pr. "The Spoken and Written Word," *Listener* 16 Oct.: 669–70. Carbon typescript copy, "Corrected June '71," 9 l. The contrast between writing and speaking, in poetry and philosophy, is explored through Homer and Plato (esp. *Phaedrus* 274d). New inventions are restoring the opportunities once offered to the spoken word, with all the advantages of the written word behind us.

"The Voice Alone." A talk delivered on BBC radio, 12 Nov., on the twenty-fifth anniversary of the network. *Listener* 20 Nov.: 883–84. Carbon typescript copy with corrections, dated 11 Nov. 1947, 4 l.; photostat copy of the *Listener* printing with corrections, 4 l. Repr. *Poetries* (1973). The eye now dominates our reading habits to a point where we cannot comprehend the significance of the voice, defined not necessarily as a voice speaking aloud or a moving of the lips, but the inner voice, "the subtlest and most powerful instrument for exploring meaning." Alliteration is a device for conveying meaning vocally, not optically. Expression and emphasis are two broad headings for such exploration in which broadcasting might be of great value.

1948

"Emotive Meaning Again." *Philosophical Review* 57: 145–57. Repr. *Speculative Instruments* (1955). R protests the growing assumption that means to comprehension and control in language aptitude should be modeled on mathematics and the simpler sciences. A *poetic* model might serve a wider function. "Emotive" meaning does not preclude intellectual exploration or understanding. His original use of the term is defended.

"The Eye and the Ear." *The English Leaflet* 47: 65–72. The use of audio-visual aids in the classroom is invaluable, as, for example, whenever *structure* must be investigated. Structure may consist of a sentence in beginning English or a sonnet. The limited and standardized classroom voices, like stereotypical Radio Voices, are detrimental to teaching. Learning power is magnified when the eye and the ear are used together. "Words in the silence of their mere graphic form are but the footprints of thought."

"*Troilus and Cressida* and Plato." *Hudson Review* 1: 362–76. Repr. *Speculative Instruments* (1955). The central question in the play is "What is aught but as 'tis valued?" An answer from Plato; the analogy of the soul and the well-administered state. When valuations become irreconcilable (e.g. "This is, and is not Cressid," V.ii.142), "the thing splits and the thinker (or thinger) then has to remain *one* (if he can) himself."

1949

"The Places and the Figures." Review of Donald Lemen Clark, *John Milton at St. Paul's School: A Study of Ancient Rhetoric in English Renaissance Education* (New York: Columbia University Press, 1948), and Sister Miriam Joseph, C.S.C., *Shakespeare's Use of the Arts of Language* (New York: Columbia University Press, 1947). *Kenyon Review* 11:17–30. Repr. *Speculative Instruments* (1955). "The interesting question is surely NOT whether Shakespeare uses a given figure, but what *that* variation from flat writing does for him and for us just there." Rhetoric and Dialectic forgot their common aim. Plato, the source of these studies, could have redirected them, as this source could redirect our own floundering educational values.

"Emotive Language Still." *Yale Review* 39: 108–18. Six functions of language are analyzed. "An elaborate footnote on that distinction" between referential and emotive language, writes Cleanth Brooks in a prefatory remark. While the original distinctions are defended, the new formulation into six functions expands and subtilizes the theory, and proves capable of covering a wide variety of semantic situations.

1950

The Wrath of Achilles. The Iliad *of Homer, Shortened and in a New Translation.* New York: W. W. Norton. In the Introduction R argues that in the "peculiar purity" of the *Iliad* we may discover the source of many characteristics of Western culture: tragedy; the problem character in search of self-knowledge; domestic comedy; ironic skepticism toward divine control; the will in its pride; and a "poetic enjoyment of the foreknowledge of death." He discusses the language of his version and his cuts. His *Iliad* is for the advanced reader and for newcomers to English who "should find things of permanent value to read early in their progress."

French Self-Taught Through Pictures. M. H. Ilsley, Christine M. Gibson, joint authors. New York: Pocket Books. Repr. *French Through Pictures* (1953).

Spanish Self-Taught Through Pictures. Ruth Metcalf Romero, Christine M. Gibson, joint authors. New York: Pocket Books. Repr. *Spanish Through Pictures* (1953).

"Religion and the Intellectuals." *Partisan Review* 17: 138–42. Carbon typescript copy dated 29 Dec. 1949, 5 l. A concept not unlike Coleridge's clerisy is introduced, to sustain the triumph of liberalism. The decline of religion yields a spiritual vacuum ready to be filled by the State. Can we live without the civilizing cohesion provided by institutionalized belief?

"Connections between the imagination at its highest and religious feeling and ideas are not hard to see." Philosophies and religions need not tend to the unity of truth and consistency of science, for they are based on "larger and vaguer congruence among experiencings."

The Viking Portable Coleridge. Editor. New York: The Viking Press. In the lengthy introduction R takes a point of view rare in his criticism, that of biography, and assesses Coleridge the man, the poet, and the critic.

1951

"*Childermass.*" A talk delivered on BBC radio, 10 Mar. 1952. Carbon typescript copy with corrections, dated 4 Nov. 1951, 7 l. Pr. "A Talk on 'The Childermass,'" (1969). An essay on Wyndham's Lewis' eschatological narrative, "directed to the adjusting of the niceties of salvation." But nothing is certain, no speech sums up, there are no answers to the questions. Our ignorance may be a part of what Lewis' book is about. See "Jesus' Other Life" (1970).

1952

"Communication Between Men: Meaning of Language." *Cybernetics: Circular Causal and Feedback Mechanisms in Biological and Social Systems: Transactions of the Eighth Conference, March 15–16, 1951.* Edited by H. von Foerster. New York: Joseph Macy, Jr. Foundation, 1952. Repr. "Toward a More Synoptic View," *Speculative Instruments* (1955). Bohr's principle of complementarity is seen as a useful critical instrument. Relativism *vs.* the Synoptic View; feedback and feedforward. The latter term, invented by R, names the "peculiar character of tapings which arise in the service of more generic, more inclusive, tapings." A symposium discussion on R's paper follows his presentation.

"Coleridge's Tiger Cats." Review of *Inquiring Spirit, A New Presentation of Coleridge,* edited by Kathleen Coburn (New York: Pantheon Books, 1951). *New York Times Book Review* 13 Jan.: 6, 22. Carbon typescript copy with corrections, 4 l. One third of her "admirably arranged and edited" selections are new to print. The review emphasizes various sides of this "myriad-minded" man: poet, social thinker, theologian, psychologist, and mountain-climber.

1953

German Through Pictures. I. Schmidt Mackey, W. F. Mackey, Christine M. Gibson, joint authors. New York: Pocket Books.

"Toward a Theory of Translating." *Studies in Chinese Thought*, edited by Arthur F. Wright (Chicago: University of Chicago Press). Repr. "Toward a Theory of Comprehending," *Speculative Instruments* (1955). Translation provides a suitable model for comprehension in general; both are guided by any number of "partially similar situations in which partially similar utterances have occurred." The Shannon-Weaver model of communication (*The Mathematical Theory of Communication* [Urbana: University of Illinois Press, 1949], p. 5) is introduced as a critical instrument. The seven "sorts of work" an utterance may be doing: indicating, characterizing, realizing, valuing, influencing, controlling, purposing. "The translator has first to reconcile himself to conceiving his art in terms of minimal loss and then to balance and adjudicate, as best he can, the claims of the rival functions. . . . The mind-state analogy [from Plato] is at work all through, it will be perceived."

1954

Hebrew Through Pictures. David Weinstein, Christine M. Gibson, joint authors. New York: Pocket Books.

"Percy Bysshe Shelley." *Major British Writers, II*, edited by G. B. Harrison. New York: Harcourt, Brace. A biographical and critical introduction. R's most extended treatment of *Prometheus Unbound* is given here, and he concurs with Yeats's epithet for this poetic drama, "a sacred book."

"Notes Toward an Agreement Between Literary Criticism and Some of the Sciences." *Confluence* 3: 41–53. Repr. *Speculative Instruments* (1955). While science and criticism can have no "clear, precise, or consistent" view of each other, there are grounds for some agreement and ways to ease conflict. The sciences, including linguistics, deal with what is done, or can be done; the humanities deal with what should be done. A discussion of free will *vs.* determinism.

1955

Speculative Instruments. Chicago: University of Chicago Press. R's first volume of collected essays and addresses, 1933–54. Notes toward an agreement between literary criticism and some of the sciences—Toward a theory of comprehending—Emotive meaning again—The future of the humanities in general education—Education and culture—The resourcefulness of words —Toward practice in interpretation—Responsibilities in the teaching of English—The idea of a university—Toward a more synoptic view—General education in the humanities—Queries—Language and value—Poetry as an instrument of research—The places and the figures—Dependence of thought on its milieu—fifteen lines from Landor—*Troilus and Cressida* and Plato.

Italian Through Pictures, Book I. Italo Evangelista, Christine M. Gibson, joint authors. New York: Pocket Books.

Hebrew Reader. David Weinstein, Christine M. Gibson, joint authors. New York: Pocket Books. An adaptation of *Words on Paper* (1943), featuring slow letter-intake (initially five of thirty-two symbols), simple sentences selected from *Hebrew Through Pictures* (1954), a narrow range of syntax patterns (mostly assertions and questions), and a basic vocabulary of less than two hundred widely used words.

1956

A Leak in the Universe. Playbook. New York: New Directions. A play in prose and verse, with a prologue and five scenes. First performed in the home of Mr. and Mrs. William James in Cambridge, Mass., on 25 Feb. 1954, by the Poet's Theatre of Cambridge.

1957

First Steps in Reading English: A First Book for Readers To Be. Christine M. Gibson, joint author. New York: Pocket Books. Control of letter as well as word intake, picture clues to simple sentences, and freedom from distracting materials characterize this manual.

A First Workbook of French. M. H. Ilsley, Christine M. Gibson, joint authors. New York: Pocket Books.

First Steps in Reading Hebrew. David Weinstein, Christine M. Gibson, joint authors. New York: Pocket Books. Mimeographed workbooks and a teacher's guide were printed separately.

"Mechanical Aids in Language Teaching." Christine M. Gibson, joint author. *English Language Teaching* 12: 3–9. Ogden's concept of linguistic "work"—how much a given supply of words can do—is a useful guide in designing programs with machines. Film should display, "through essential animation, relations between semantic and syntactic elements" within a sentence.

"Recollections of C. K. Ogden." *Encounter* Sept.: 10–12. The origins of the *Cambridge Magazine* and its varying perspective; his collaboration with Ogden on *The Meaning of Meaning,* beginning in 1918; their use of pseudonyms; the development of Basic English and related projects; and a portrait of the polymath leader of the worldwide movement in Basic.

"Design and Control in Language Teaching." *Harvard Alumni Bulletin* 59: 673–74. He relates his long and close collaborative efforts with Miss

Christine M. Gibson in designing language programs, the Language Through Pictures series, films, and video-tapes. "Film is the answer to illiteracy."

1958

Goodbye Earth and Other Poems. New York: Harcourt, Brace. London: Routledge and Kegan Paul. Repr. *Internal Colloquies* (1971). His first collected poems, nearly all of which date from 1950.

English Through Pictures, Book II. Christine M. Gibson, joint author. New York: Pocket Books. This volume takes a reader up to one thousand words, doubling the vocabulary from the first volume (1945). Furthermore it is a kind of primary general education, with information in history, geography, biology, literature, mathematics, astronomy, and politics. It builds into a form of Everyman's English (1000 words).

"Reversals in Poetry." Script used in a series of TV broadcasts over WGBH-TV, Boston. Carbon typescript copy with corrections, 19 l. (One section entitled "Line-breaks," 4 l.) Pr. *Poetries* (1973). The effect of irony, particularly in ballad literature. "White was the sheet," Sir Walter Scott's "Proud Maisie" and "The Deluge," Thomas Hood's "Faithless Nelly Gray," are read and criticized. Four pages are concerned with accommodating longish lines to the restrictions of television, giving rise to reflections on the visual aspects of printed verse and on cooperations between ear and eye in reading.

"The Exstasie." Script used in a series of TV broadcasts over WGBH-TV, Boston. Carbon typescript copy with corrections, 16 l., and photostat copy, 7 l., both with corrections. Pr. *Master Poems of the English Language*, edited by Oscar Williams (New York: The Trident Press, 1966); repr. *Poetries* (1973). A line-by-line reading of the Donne poem, with reflections on the controversies that the poem has stirred.

"The Garden." Script used in a series of TV broadcasts over WGBH-TV, Boston. Photostat copy with corrections, 20 l. Pr. *Poetries* (1973). Close analysis of the structure and detail of the Marvell poem that "describes an ecstasy."

"The Sense of Poetry: Shakespeare's 'The Phoenix and the Turtle.'" Script used in a series of TV broadcasts over WGBH-TV, Boston. Pr. *Daedalus* 87: 3: 86–94; repr. *Poetries* (1973). A close analysis of a text which concerns the experience of ecstasy. The poem directs itself steadily toward "poetry," the end of the poetic endeavor itself. For the endeavor is "the mystery of being" which is "forever dying into cinders and arising to flame and die anew; and always, perhaps, demanding a sacrifice of constancy for the sake of that to which it is loyal and true."

"A Valediction: Forbidding Mourning." Script used in a series of TV broadcasts over WGBH-TV, Boston? Photostat copy with corrections, 4 l. Pr. *Master Poems of the English Language*, edited by Oscar Williams (New York: The Trident Press, 1966). A close analysis of the Donne poem. On stanza nine: "There has been discussion as to whether the image here is of the completion of a circle or of the closing of the compass when its task is done. Each seems equally relevant." Plato's *Timaeus* is cited on the circle as the emblem of perfection and the soul's proper course; and Eliot's "In my beginning is my end" is quoted to explicate the two final lines of the poem.

1959

A First Workbook of English. Christine M. Gibson, joint author. New York: Pocket Books.

"The Mystical Element in Shelley's Poetry—I." *The Aryan Path* 30: 250–56. Three passages in *Prometheus Unbound* may be justifiably described as mystical: the colloquy between Asia and Demogorgon (II.iv.1–30), the transfiguration of Asia (II.v.6–47), and Prometheus' account of the Role of Poetry and the Arts (III.iii.6–63). Shelley's "provocative agnosticism" rejects the creative deity of Christianity, but recognizes nonetheless a Power co-eternal with the universe. Paul Tillich's "unconditioned transcendent," a "language without symbols," elucidates the negativism of Demogorgon's "the deep truth is imageless." Asia as Love.

"The Mystical Element in Shelley's Poetry—II." *The Aryan Path* 30: 290–95. Photostat copy with corrections, 6 l. As "hierophants of an *unapprehended* inspiration" poets use words which may express "*what they understand not.*" Analysis of Prometheus' prophecy of the "mystery of the service of the imagination to man." Shelley's mysticism is true to the Plotinian tradition, is an apprehension of "the influence which is moved not but moves," is marked by its "involvedness" and introversion, both in its psychology and its syntax. The confluence of Eastern and Western symbolism in Shelley's cave and Temple metaphors is described.

"Poetry as an Instrument of Research." A talk delivered on BBC radio, 14 Sept., not to be confused with ch. 14 of *Speculative Instruments* (1955) which bears the same title. *Listener* 17 Sept.: 443–44. Photostat copy of the *Listener* printing with typescript and handwritten interleaves, with corrections, 8 l. Repr. *Poetries* (1973). Expansion in human possibility now lies in logic, methodology, linguistics, and education. Such instruments have much to teach us about poetry, which remains the chief instrument. The poetic use of language can release a poet into "larger freedoms." "Instead of having to express himself, say, he finds himself serving a possibility of language."

"Coleridge: The Vulnerable Poet." *Yale Review* 48: 491–504. Photostat copy of the *Yale Review* printing, with corrections, 8 l. Repr. *Poetries* (1973). In new editions of Coleridge's notebooks and letters one may observe evidence of the mutual harm, as well as good, Coleridge and Wordsworth did to each other. "Coleridge lacked that great protection: vanity."

1960

The Screens and Other Poems. New York: Harcourt, Brace. London: Routledge and Kegan Paul. Repr. *Internal Colloquies* (1971). "What connections, if any, hold between a critic's theories about poetry and his practice when he professes as a poet?" R's view is that no such connections should be discernible. "Screens" is a metaphor for "filters bringing out interesting speculative possibilities" and for a sheet (or sheets) upon which an image (or multiple images) may be cast, thus relating to the principle of "complementarity."

"The Future of Poetry." *The Screens and Other Poems* (1960). Repr. *So Much Nearer* (1968). Poetry will depend (a) upon understanding of the reserves and potentials of language and (b) upon the training of an audience of readers. Attention should be focused not on poets, but on poetry. The Shannon-Weaver communications model is used to clarify the process by which a poem is communicated from poet to reader (though neither should consider himself the ultimate source or end of a process of language). But the model is not fully adequate, for signals are mathematical entities, while poetry exemplifies the unity of message and signal, content and form, spirit and letter, and thus, potentially, our most humanizing instrument. He discredits the view that language "packages" a poetic experience.

Learning the English Language, Book IV. Christine M. Gibson, joint author. Toronto: Thomas Nelson. Boston: Houghton Mifflin. The workbook to this volume was published by Educational Series in 1970. As in the case of the three workbooks published previously, it was designed by R, Miss Gibson, and their staff.

A First Workbook of Spanish. Ruth Metcalf Romero, Christine M. Gibson, joint authors. New York: Pocket Books.

"More Meanings for Meaning." Review of *On Translation*, edited by Reuben Brower (Cambridge, Mass.: Harvard University Press, 1959). *Contemporary Psychology* 5:20–21. R praises the volume for its many-sided approach and the high level of generality given to translation, "the replacement of any sign by some equivalent sign." "Communication theory is now shaping the language, at least, of the forward-looking."

"Coleridge's Minor Poems: A Lecture . . . Delivered in Honor of the Fortieth Anniversary of Professor Edmund L. Freeman at Montana State University on April 8, 1960." [Missoula, Montana, 1960] Typescript copy with corrections, entitled "Coleridge's Other Poems," 27 l. Repr. *Coleridge's Minor Poems* (Cambridge, Mass.: Harvard Graduate School of Education [?]); *Poetries* (1973). A slide-lecture. Themes and symbols in Coleridge's *Dejection: An Ode, The Aeolian Harp, Self-Knowledge, Phantom,* and other poems are analyzed closely and related to one another, concluding with *Epitaph* and *Sunset.*

"Poetic Process and Literary Analysis." *Style in Language*, edited by Thomas A. Sebeok (Cambridge, Mass.: the MIT Press). The author in his "Poetic Process, in his actual work on the poem, is an imaginary construct . . . based on our understanding of the poem." A reader employs this imaginary construct in his paralleling Literary Analysis to further his interpretation, forgetting that "the author" is a theoretical invention. R offers himself, as poet and critic, in a type situation where he analyzes the creation of his own poem *Harvard Yard in April/April in Harvard Yard.*

"Variant Readings and Misreading." *Style in Language*, edited by Thomas A. Sebeok (Cambridge, Mass.: the MIT Press). Repr. *So Much Nearer* (1968). As the title suggests, the range of accepted readings and miscomprehensions is explored in various ways, e.g. by analysis of a line in Shakespeare's Sonnet 66, "As to behold desert a beggar born." The context holds the meaning of a word in quasi-control. These "restrictive-permissive, controlling-enabling inter-relations, which tie the utterances possible within a language into a system, give us our means of distinguishing between variant readings and misreading."

1961

Russian Through Pictures, Book I. Evelyn Jasiulko Harden, Christine M. Gibson, joint authors. New York: Pocket Books.

Arabic Through Pictures. Graham Leonard, Christine M. Gibson, joint authors. Cambridge, Mass.; Language Research.

Translation of Meng Tzu, "Ox Mountain Parable." *Commonweal* 12 May 74: 174. Introduction by Thomas Merton.

"Language and World Crisis." Christine M. Gibson, joint author. *Harvard Graduate School Association Bulletin* 6: 2–7. Methods of language instruction are developing fast through new media. These media are proving the only ways to teach language on a mass scale.

"Technology to the Rescue: Elementary Language Teaching by Film and Tape." Christine M. Gibson, joint author. *Harvard Alumni Bulletin* 63:548–50. Methods by which languages can be taught by film and tape, suitably combined, are illustrated. The authors describe their experience in the Arlington Project, language training in elementary schools, by means of a "teaching van," a movable laboratory.

1962

Tommorow Morning, Faustus! An Infernal Comedy. New York: Harcourt, Brace. London: Routledge and Kegan Paul. Repr. *Internal Colloquies* (1971). R took the role of Faustus in the first production at the Loeb Drama Center, Harvard University, 12–13 May 1961.

A Second Workbook of Spanish. Ruth Metcalf Romero, Christine M. Gibson, joint authors. New York: Pocket Books.

"What Future Educational Needs of Society Will the Teaching Profession Be Called Upon to Meet?" Speech delivered at the University of Alberta, Calgary, 17 Mar. Pr. "The Technological Crisis," *So Much Nearer* (1968). Technological advances are accelerating at such a rate that education must meet these emergencies with advances of its own—in programming, audio-visual aids such as film and television, and teacher-training.

"Foreword." *Coleridge on Imagination* (1934). 3rd edition. London: Routledge and Kegan Paul.

1963

A First Workbook of Russian. Evelyn Jasiulko Harden, Christine M. Gibson, joint authors. New York: Pocket Books.

A Workbook of Italian. Italo Evangelista, Christine M. Gibson, joint authors. New York: Pocket Books.

"How Does a Poem Know When It Is Finished?" *Parts and Wholes: The Hayden Colloqium on Scientific Method and Concept,* edited by Daniel Lerner (New York: The Free Press of Glencoe; London: Macmillan New York [*sic*]). Repr. *Poetries and Sciences* (1970). Quotations from Coleridge and Shelley on the organic nature of poetry form guiding principles. ". . . the minimal problem a poem can set itself is the mere finding or creation" of some situation which will "permit its growth." Poems are "living, feeling, knowing *beings* in their own right"; the so-called metaphor treating poetry as organic is "not a metaphor, but a literal description." The seven functions of language (see "Toward a Theory of Translating" [1953]) are illustrated. Shortcomings of the comparative, historical, linguistic, and biographical approaches to poetic wholeness. Analysis of William Empson's *Legal Fiction.* Two versions of R's *By the Pool* are printed in parallel, with remarks suggesting why one pattern of stanzas should be regarded as a final form replacing an imperfect draft.

1964

Why So, Socrates? A Dramatic Version of Plato's Dialogues: Euthyphro, Apology, Crito, Phaedo. Cambridge, Eng.: Cambridge University Press. A translation into a simplified, but elegant, English. An Introduction provides historical and biographical background material. R ponders the meaning of Socrates' "divine sign," that is, "his way of asking himself what he was doing"; his voice; his mission as Apollo's servant, i.e. to teach the value and acquisition of self-knowledge and self-control; and his ethical principle: "It is never right to return a wrong or to defend ourselves against a wrong by threat of retaliation."

1965

Opening Address, 32nd International Congress of P.E.N., Oslo, 21 June 1964. Pr. *Arena* 24: 4–14, 20–22; repr. ch. 2, *Design for Escape* (1968). R contrasts types of utterance, in Amos, Socrates, and the Book of Job, and considers other kinds of contrast: between cultures, between scientific experimentation and moral choice, between points of view. He quotes Shakespeare's metaphor on the eye of the spiritual faculty, man's "glassy essence" (*Measure for Measure* II.ii.120), the profound "activity through which we see whatever we ever see, our very self."

Development of Experimental Audio-Visual Devices and Materials for Beginning Readers. Cooperative Research Project No. 5 0642. Christine M. Gibson, joint author. Cambridge, Mass.: Harvard University. The research for this government report was supported by the Cooperative Research Program of the Office of Education, U.S. Department of Health, Education, and Welfare. Problems of reading impairment and failure are investigated. New principles of instructional design through audio-visual aid are needed to guide primary reading programs. The objective is to develop a wide range of experimental materials which can "set up for the learner a gradation of intelligent explorations of writing and print as notations for speech." A description of programmed teaching sequences and devices, analysis, and report on results of programs of Language Research, Inc., form the bulk of the project.

A Second Workbook of French. Christine M. Gibson, joint author. New York: Pocket Books.

A Second Workbook of English. Christine M. Gibson, joint author. New York: Pocket Books.

"From Criticism to Creation." *Times Literary Supplement* 27 May: 438–39. Repr. "Prologue: From Criticism to Creation," *So Much Nearer* (1968). The title calls attention to what R believes is the direction of his career. Early investigative and experimental studies pointed to a need for designing and inventing more effective instruments for instruction. "I let Coleridge lead me." He discusses major features of his designs in language training: proper sequencing, the concept of opposition, association by contiguity and by similarity, and complementarity. Reflections on the Chomsky-Skinner language controversy. Creation also includes his poetry and translations. His poem *Verbal Behavior*, a flyting with B. F. Skinner, is cited in n. 18 of the reprinted version (v. Skinner's "On Having a Poem," *Saturday Review*, 15 July 1972: 32–35).

"What is Saying?" [1964–65?] Photostat copy with corrections and ms. additions, 17 l. Pr. *Poetries* (1973). "Knocking about for some time," he replied when I inquired about the date. A *terminus a quo* is 1964 since he cites a long passage from *Why So, Socrates?* But the photostat reproduction is "primitive," and therefore it is unlikely that the essay dates much latter than 1965. Semantics presents us with a paradox: we must use the process, language, to analyze that very process. To gain perspective, he casts his essay, after Plato, in dialogue form, between Author and Reader; only it is an "internal dialogue," one mind questioning and answering itself, a form of dialectic. The topics include: saying what one means, tone, argument, the seven functions of language (see "Toward a Theory of Translating," [1953]) and how they operate together, and imagining.

1966

Russian Through Pictures, Book II. Evelyn Jasiulko Harden, Christine M. Gibson, joint authors. New York: Pocket Books.

Plato's Republic. Cambridge, Eng.: Cambridge University Press. "After various revisions, through decades," this is his latest edition. See *The Republic of Plato* (1942). A new "Introduction" stresses reasons why the *Republic* remains invaluable: the concepts of Being and Becoming, the Divided Line, and "dialectic."

"On TSE: Notes for a Talk at the Institute of Contemporary Arts, London, June 29, 1965." *Sewanee Review* 74: 21–30. Repr. *T. S. Eliot: The Man and His Work*, edited by Allen Tate (New York: Delacorte Press). A personal memoir and encomium.

"Comment" on "The Construction of *Seven Types of Ambiguity*," by James Jensen. *Modern Language Quarterly* 27: 255. Jensen asserts (*Modern Language Quarterly* 27: 243–55, 258–59) that Empson's book was not sired by R alone, but that Robert Graves and Laura Riding in their *Survey of Modernist Poetry* (1927) played a large role. In a three-sentence comment R describes Jensen's piece as "fiction . . . not *bad* fiction." Comments by Graves, Empson, and Jensen follow.

"Growing Pains." Review of R. H. Robins, *General Linguistics: An Introductory Survey* (Bloomington: University of Indiana Press, 1965), and M. A. K. Halliday, Angus McIntosh, and Peter Strevens, *The Linguistic Sciences and Language Teaching* (London: Longmans, 1964). *New York Review of Books* 14 Apr.: 20–24. Repr. ch. 4, "Some Glances at Current Linguistics," *So Much Nearer* (1968). A survey of contemporary linguistics, particularly in America, where R believes that grammarians, in trying to seek the status of a new science, are making the same mistakes as their forerunners. "It was *not* the badness of the grammar descriptions which caused the failure [in teaching] . . . learning how to *describe* a language is not at all the same thing as learning how to *use* it with power and discernment."

" 'A Valediction: Forbidding Mourning' by John Donne." *Master Poems of the English Language*, edited by Oscar Williams (New York: The Trident Press). See "A Valediction . . ." (1958).

" 'The Extasie' by John Donne." *Master Poems of the English Language*, edited by Oscar Williams (New York: The Trident Press). See "The Exstasie . . ."(*sic*) (1958).

1967

"A Sacred Mountain." Review of Heinz Skrobucha, *Sinai*, tr. G. Hunt (New York: Oxford University Press, 1966). *Yale Review* 57: 115–17. "A rich repository, studded and stuffed with precious things . . . beautifully presented."

"The Creative Aim in Instruction." "Foreword," *The Computer in American Education*, edited by Don D. Bushnell and Dwight W. Allen (New York: John Wiley, 1967). Repr. ch. 3, "Computer-Conveyed Instruction," *So Much Nearer* (1968). The computer will extend the resources of the central nervous system, be our "Caliban-Ariel attendant, advisor, executant." Thoughts on the psychology of teaching. Objections to the use of computers in education are analyzed and dismissed. The physical sciences and mathematics should be no more obvious disciplines for computer instruction than reading. A design for such a program is outlined.

"Introduction." C. K. Ogden, *Opposition: A Linguistic and Psychological Analysis* (Bloomington: University of Indiana Press). In a reissue of Ogden's book (orig. pub. 1932), R explains that the theory of Opposition sprang from their joint work on the germ of Basic English, sending them back to this essential principle by which language operates. He stresses the importance of Ogden's classic in a time when binary opposition is becoming a key concept in many scientific methodologies.

"Why Generative Grammar Does Not Help: I." *English Language Teaching* 22: 3–9. Repr. ch. 4, "Some Glances at Current Linguistics," *So Much Nearer* (1968). There are two questions here: help toward what end? and where generative grammar fails to further our efforts toward that end. On the first, he claims that the end is "world communciation": to meet linguistic needs by modernized and methodized techniques, and, in learning a language, to learn to think. "The *minutiae* of theories of linguistic theory seem to be incommensurate with global mutual murder." On the second, he asserts that in his analysis of surface structure N. Chomsky gives a central position to grammar. Grammar has traditionally been the most formalized of language studies, with phonology second, and semantics, the most important, unfortunately a far-back third. In addition, from a psychological standpoint, the distinction between surface and deep structure is less between two types of abstraction than between both abstractions and the apprehending *subject* dealing with a situation. "Linguistic theory is, as Jakobson has many times reminded us, a matter of much more than language; it is a reflection of all that is relevant to how any use of language does, or does not work."

"Learning and Looking." A lecture given at the Carpenter Center for the Visual Arts, Harvard University, 30 November. Pr. *Design for Escape* (1968). The use of slide images in the learning process. A new urgency, due to (1) the coming into world circulation and communication of peoples who have not in the past participated in world affairs, (2) the availability of computer-controlled, satellite-distributed TV, and (3) the alarming disparity between the rich and the poor nations. Edwin Reischauer's two world "maps" are used to illustrate this disparity (they depict nations' relative population and GNP by geographical distortion). Learning and looking are then related through Opposition, Comparison, Perceptual Exercises, and Points of View.

1968

"Why Generative Grammar Does Not Help: II." *English Language Teaching* 22: 101–6. Repr. ch. 4, "Some Glances at Current Linguistics," *So*

Much Nearer (1968). Any one point of view regarding language must of necessity suffer distortion. E.g. (1) Rival linguistic ideologies, Chomsky's Cartesian linguistics and Skinner's positivist behaviorism, require corroboration. How are competent corroborators to be selected? (2) Individuals vary greatly with regard to expression: the fluent speaker is an abstract unreality of modern theorizing. (3) Likewise, dictionary definitions: words require contexts.

So Much Nearer: Essays Toward a World English. New York: Harcourt, Brace and World. R's second collected essays (1934–68), on language, technology, education, and literature. The title is from Frost's *Desert Places.* Prologue: from criticism to creation—The technological crisis—Computer-conveyed instruction—Some glances at current linguistics—Meanings anew—The future of poetry—Variant readings and misreading—Mencius through the looking-glass—Sources of conflict—Toward a world English.

Design for Escape: World Education Through Modern Media. New York: Harcourt, Brace and World. "To fit together" with *So Much Nearer,* this enchiridion collects essays from 1943 to 1968. Design for instruction concerns the use of film, tape, records, picture, text, TV—modern media extant or to be computer-handled—for the purpose of education on a mass scale, particularly in language, and in some form of English. Contents: The design—Grounds for responsibility—Basic English: the forerunner—Learning and looking—Notes on principles of beginning language instruction—The Chelsea closed circuit television project—Delmar project report—From "A Controlled Evaluation of Semantically Sequenced Program of Instruction in English as a Foreign Language" (by Morris E. Eson).

"The Secret of 'Feedforward.' " *Saturday Review* 3 Feb.: 14–17. In the series "What I Have Learned," R contemplates guiding lights in his own career. Of high importance has been the heuristic "feedforward" in the process of thinking and artistic creation. It is the "before the event" relation to feedback, a "selective reflection of what has been relevant in similar activity in our past." Hence the wisdom of doubt, instead of doctrine, in the thinking process. "Feedforward" may be as highly articulate as a scientific hypothesis, or "hardly cognized or embodied at all, even in the vaguest schematic image . . . no more than a readiness to be surprised or disturbed."

Review of Jeanne S. Chall, *Learning To Read: The Great Debate* (New York: McGraw-Hill, 1967). *Harvard Educational Review* 38: 357–64. Repr. "Instructional Engineering" (1971). Do children learn better with a beginning method that stresses meaning or with one that stresses learning the code? Chall favors an increase in code-emphasis. R examines presuppositions in the use of *code, meaning, learning the code, stress,* and *emphasis.*

R favors a combination of sound-letter relations with a progressively full use of script in the study of meanings. Meanings, depictions, letter-intake, and sequencing are considered. "We should remember always . . . that children are learning to read not *just to read*, not even *just to enjoy stories*, not *just to be able to spell and pronounce correctly*, and not *just to get jobs* —but to develop further their distinctive quality as human beings: resourceful, self-corrigible, discernment."

1969

"An Angel's Talk." Review of Samuel Taylor Coleridge, *The Friend*, edited by Barbara E. Rooke. *The Collected Works*. Vols. I–II (Princeton: Princeton University Press, 1969). *Listener* 25 Sept.: 423–24. Repr. *Poetries* (1973). "The peculiar appropriateness of its title." Coleridge is talking about "the things that matter most—not the less alluringly for so frequently skating along the brink of the incomprehensible." The distinction between Reason and Understanding is analyzed. Coleridge and Shakespeare.

"Tipi e campioni." *Strumenti Critici* 9: 187–93. To be repr. in English trans., "Prologue," "Beyond" (1973). Starting points for discussion are C. S. Pierce's distinction between type and token and Nelson Goodman's nominalism and language theory.

"A Talk on 'The Childermass.' " *Agenda* 7: 3: 16–21. See "*Childermass*" (1952).

"An Interview with I. A. Richards." Conducted by B. A. Boucher and J. P. Russo, 12·Dec. 1968. *Harvard Crimson* 11 Mar.: 3, 5 (excerpts). *Harvard Advocate* 103: 3–8. Typescript copies with corrections, 22 l. and 29 l. He discusses his early years at Cambridge University, his readings in moral sciences, C. K. Ogden and *The Meaning of Meaning*, the English radical tradition, Coleridge, G. E. Moore, Bertrand Russell, the origins of the distinction between emotive and referential language, Ogden and Basic English, Jerome Bruner's *Toward a Theory of Instruction*, travels and teaching in China, the importance of reading aloud, English graduate studies, and world literacy: "I think we have a better way of teaching English, but while you're teaching beginning English, you might as well teach everything else. That is to say, a world position, what's needed for living, a philosophy of religion, how to find things out and the whole works—mental and moral seed for the planet."

"A Philosophy of Education." *Wellesley Alumnae Magazine* 53: 3, 21, 41. A note on scientist and educator John Pilley. Pilley left off being a research scientist in chemistry for "that far rarer thing, an originative influence in Education." He diagnosed the prevailing disease in liberal education, "preferment of peripheral exploit to central penetration," cloaked by the labels of scholarship, research, or specialization, and he anticipated the famous debate on the split between science and the humanities. An expert classroom teacher, choosing not to affirm as much as to ask the revealing question, Pilley also wrote a succinct and forceful prose. "Studies in Education at Wellesley" (*Education*, Nov. 1942) and "Science and Liberal Education" (*The Journal of Education*, June 1955) are particularly recommended.

[A talk delivered before the Brookline Reading Institute, Brookline, Mass.] Handwritten notes and carbon typescript, dated 1 Mar. 1969, 11 l. An introduction to the Richards theory and practice of language training. He analyzes the channels and controls that operate in the process of beginning reading: how one hears interplaying with how one would say it; how one sees marks on paper interplaying with how one would make them; what one thinks they mean interplaying with "what he can do about it." Distinctions between meanings and codings are introduced by the concept of the seven functions of language ("Toward a Theory of Translating," 1953); the concept of sentence-in-situation; an arrangement of elements in the code which facilitates learning, e.g. fewness, easy differentiability, connection, and opposition.

1970

Poetries and Sciences. A Reissue of Science and Poetry (1926, 1935) with Commentary. New York: W. W. Norton. An old "Introduction," "from 1940 or 1941," is set within a new Preface. There are explanatory notes, a "Reorientation" in which he clarifies ideas that may have been wrongly taken in the original, and the essay "How Does a Poem . . ." (1963).

Review of Samuel Taylor Coleridge, *The Friend*, edited by Barbara E. Rooke. *The Collected Works.* Vols. I–II (Princeton: Princeton University Press, 1969); J. R. deJ. Jackson, *Method and Imagination in Coleridge's Criticism* (London: Routledge and Kegan Paul, 1969). *University of Toronto Quarterly* 40:102–3. Coleridge never stopped talking about himself: "In his uncommon humility he thought that his true self (if he could only find it) was about all he had to repay creation with." *The Friend* is an installment of this repayment, a work dedicated to finding "true PRINCIPLES." His key topics, Reason, Understanding, Imagination, Fancy, Sense, etc. help us to comprehend our "endeavours in living." Jackson's work is praised as a "devoted, careful guidebook."

A Fourth Workbook of English. Christine M. Gibson, joint author. New York: Pocket Books. This supplies a workbook both to *Learning the English Language, Book IV,* and *English Through Pictures, Book II,* bringing the vocabulary up to one thousand words.

"Draft for a Yale Lecture." A speech, entitled "Relevance and Remoteness as Illustrated by the Book of Job," delivered at Yale University, 26 Feb. Carbon typescript copy with corrections, 14 l. The "dynamic oppositions" between a folk tale and a poem together make up the Book of Job. "There are two Jobs, two Gods, two dramas of their dealings with one another— extremely different one from the other." He formulates the central question of Job: "What—for a human being—is a fair deal? And why do we think he is entitled to it?" Themes and ideas in this lecture are subsumed in the Job chapter of "Beyond" (1973).

"Jakobson's Shakespeare: The Subliminal Structures of a Sonnet." Review of Roman Jakobson, *Shakespeare's Verbal Art in "Th'expence of Spirit"* (The Hague: Mouton, 1969). *Times Literary Supplement* 28 May: 589–90. Offprint with corrections, 2 l. Repr. "Linguistics into Poetics," *Poetries* (1973). "May very likely prove a landmark in the long-awaited approach of descriptive linguistics to the account of poetry." But R differentiates between powers of knowing *about* and *how*, between the processes (including language) by which values are articulated and the initial (or final) choice of those values. It is an error to treat these issues totally apart, as much an error to confuse them. Under consideration are Jakobson's analysis of sound-character, grammar and syntactic form, utterance aim, the binary oppositions of rime patterns, and the repetitions of its rime words.

"Jesus' Other Life." Review of George Moore, *The Brook Kerith: A Syrian Story* (1916) (New York: Liveright, 1969). *New York Review of Books* 3 Dec.: 47–49. Carbon typescript copy with corrections, 4 l. The novel is "about the religious quest" without "doctrinal or historical discussions." Its narrative concerns piety, not religion, advancing through "differing minds whose idiosyncrasies are in the utmost degree realized, displayed, allowed for," and with astonishing technique in plot-handling. See "God of Dostoevsky" (1927) for further comment.

"On Reading." *Michigan Quarterly* 9: 3–6, 24–25. Repr. "Instructional Engineering" (1971). Remarks on reading at a conference at Queens College, New York, 29 Mar. 1969. Subtlety of discrimination, "vital to levels of communication and mutual comprehension, is dependent for maintenance and development far more upon *writtens* than upon *spokens*." Speech cannot be easily compared with another way of saying the same thing unless they are written down. Man's increased power over his *meants* has been the most decisive factor in creating civilization.

"The Future of Reading." Speech delivered before the American Academy of Arts and Sciences, Brookline, Mass., 13 May. Report of the speech, in the third person, by W. M. Whitehill, *Bulletin of the American Academy of Arts and Sciences* 24: 2: 2–12. The speech itself is reprinted with considerable emendation in *The Written Word* (Rowley, Mass.: Newbury

House, 1971). A memoir and an apologia: "why and how . . . I adjusted from *Theory of Literary Criticism* to *Design of Instruction in Reading*." What should form the basis of reading in a free society and how it might be taught.

1971

"Homage to Hector" [1970–71]. An unpublished play in prose taken from R's version of the *Iliad* (*The Wrath of Achilles* [1950]). Three photostat copies with corrections, 31 l., 31 l., 30 l. Originally titled "To Honor Hector." First performed by the Harvard Dramatic Club, Experimental Theater, Loeb Drama Center, 1–3 Apr. 1971. R took the role of the Trojan rhapsode.

"The Wrath of Achilles" [1970–71]. An unpublished play in prose taken from R's version of the *Iliad* (*The Wrath of Achilles* [1950]). Two photostat copies, 25 l. and 25 l. With "Homage to Hector" (see entry immediately preceding), it forms one of two dramatic points of view on the action at Troy.

Job's Comforting. Internal Colloquies (1971). Typescript copy with corrections, 18 l. A play, written in the winter of 1970–71, is taken from the Book of Job, "abridged and re-arranged, and with one single sentence added."

Internal Colloquies. Poems and Plays. New York: Harcourt Brace Jovanovich. The volume contains "Further Poems (1960–70)," *Goodbye Earth and Other Poems* (1958), *The Screens and Other Poems* (1960), *Tomorrow Morning, Faustus!* (1962), and *Job's Comforting* (1970–71).

"Sources of Our Common Thought: Homer and Plato." *The Great Ideas Today* 1971 (Chicago: Encyclopedia Britannica, Inc.). Photostat copy with corrections, 91 l. Repr. "Sources of our Common Aim," *Poetries* (1973). "I've changed the title to 'Sources of our Common Aim' which seems now to me much better." R relates the development of his own readings in Homer and Plato, from an early defeat to his later translations of the *Republic, the Iliad*, and the dialogues concerning the trial and death of Socrates. His own experience was instructive in designing texts and plays out of his translations, because earlier translations failed to make such great "sources of our common thought" relevant to our age and situation. He concludes with thoughts on the inspiration of Socrates, "belonging, I too, to Apollo" (*Phaedo* 85).

"Poetry as Paideia." Photostat copy with corrections, 3 l. Pr. *Poetries* (1973). R values Werner Jaeger's discussion of the Greek concept of education (*Paideia: The Ideals of Greek Culture*, I, xxvi.) with regard to the priority of language in the development of the individual and of man.

What place today should poetry have in the shaping of character by ideals? In the "diminishment of the book it is poetry which suffers most."

"Instructional Engineering." *The Written Word.* Rowley, Mass.: Newbury House. An essay based on materials drawn from the review of Jeanne S. Chall's *Learning to Read* (1968) and "On Reading" (1970).

"Semantics." Unpublished essay. Photostat copy with corrections, 15 l. A dictionary or encyclopedia article on the nature and scope of semantics from its first formulation by Bréal in 1883. R discusses the sorts of work sentences can do, the diverse meanings they may carry simultaneously, the encoding and decoding of messages, and the breakdown in transaction between communicators and how such breakdown can be remedied. "Probably semantics should, as yet at least, make no claims to regulate or supervise other studies. It might well be defined as the science of miscomprehensions. Its service to other endeavors is to make what it discovers more available." In the future the computer may well provide "our best means" for ascertaining and controlling meaning through comparisons.

"Foreword." *Poetries: Their Media and Ends* (1973). Photostat copy with corrections dated 11 Oct. 1971, 8 l. See *Poetries* (1973). A defense of R's use of specialized quotation marks introduced in *How To Read a Page* (1942) as a "compact meta-semantic means of indicating" something about the way a word or phrase is used. The theme of the book, emerging from essays over thirty years, is the aid that media have to offer one another to improve their separate and mutual efficacies when the "illiteracy that is spreading is a more *general* disability." Thus far, modern media have on the contrary counted toward the decline of literacy.

1972

Spanish Through Pictures, Book II, and A Second Workbook of Spanish [1962]. Ruth Metcalf Romero, Christine M. Gibson, joint authors. New York: Pocket Books. This volume was published together with the text and workbook of Book One in a two-volume edition.

"Functions of and Factors in Language." *Journal of Literary Semantics* 1: 25–40. Photostat copy with corrections, 20 l. Repr. *Poetries* (1973). Roman Jakobson's formulation summarizing what language does (the six factors and six functions in "Linguistics and Poetics," *Style in Language*, ed. Thomas A. Sebeok [Cambridge, Mass.: MIT Press, 1960], pp. 350–77) is related systematically to the means through which language does it. Citing Pierce's doctrine on the translation of signs, R "translates" Jakobson's key passages into an exploratory paraphrase in Everyman's English, with gloss and commentary, and with particular attention to "context" and "message."

"Complementarities. A Lecture in Honor of C. A. Mace, Birkbeck College, June 28, 1972." Typescript copy, 27 l. To be published by Birkbeck College, University of London, 1973? A memoir of life at Cambridge University, 1912–15, 1918–19, when C. A. Mace, Marjorie Mace, and R studied under G. E. Moore. Bohr's principle of complementarity is presented in its fullest treatment as a critical model of "multiple models." The key idea of mutual exclusiveness in atomic physics is transferred to more complex investigations among intelligential procedures along lines of a theory of non-contradiction. New thoughts on the relation between tenor and vehicle. A reading of poems illustrating the concept of Dialectic and Points of View.

"Retrospect" to *Interpretation in Teaching* (1938, 1973). Photostat copy with corrections, 5 l. ". . . Of all my writings, the most worthwhile." He calls attention to the clinical nature of the book, "an extensive piece of natural history, collecting, arranging, displaying . . . the aim being just to develop better judgment as to central matters upon which the health of thought depends." He notes currently a shrinking from attempts to correct judgment in criticism, a preoccupation with belletristic questions rather than with "what is *necessary*," among other symptoms of "the corruption that has been spreading so widely since the Greater Wars." *I in T* was in fact the "grand hinge" on which he moved from literary into educative pursuits, and many later writings stem from positions adopted here.

1973[–74]

"Literature for the Unlettered." *Uses of Literature*, edited by Monroe Engel. *Harvard English Studies* 4 (Cambridge, Mass.: Harvard University Press). The new media—TV, tape, cassette—have not supported our cultural inheritance as variously, imaginatively, and venturesomely as they could, "specifically, as means of helping literature to have more impact upon those deprived or, unprepared for, access to it." The qualities of good oral reading; why neither poets on their own poems, nor actors in performance are necessarily the best interpreters. The development of the reading voice is a chief means for analyzing meanings. Likewise, comparison of phrasings—"different ways of saying what may profess to be the same thing"—is a sound semantic exercise. In *Biographia Literaria* XIV (1817) Coleridge alters stanzas from Davies' *Nosce Teipsum* (1599), aiding both our interpretation of Davies on the soul and Coleridge on the imagination. R cites Coleridge's definition of the workings of the imagination in the same chapter and renders it into Everyman's English. Controlled paraphrase into simplified English will extend our spiritual inheritance to newcomers to the language or to beginning readers.

Poetries: Their Media and Ends. The Hague: Mouton. A fourth collected essays (1934–73). In a draft of the "Foreword" (1971), he writes: "The terms of the title are in the plural, because *Poetry* is to *poems* as *life* is to *living beings.* We can make endless progress in studying organisms. Meditation on what Life is has not been—for many—of much help." *Media* is plural to call attention to the multiple uses and purposes of words: as types and as tokens; as speech dispositions and acts; as auditory patterns and images; and as script. *Ends* is plural: "It may be that poetries, along with all else, have some ultimate goal. But the way to useful speculation as to that seems to require the finest discrimination we can attain to of subordinate ends serving, each in its place, as means." Contents: Factors and functions of linguistics—Powers and limits of signs—Linguistics into poetics—"The Phoenix and the Turtle"—Poetic reversals—Interinanimations of words— "The Ecstasy"—"The Garden"—Coleridge's other poems—The vulnerable poet and *The Friend*—Poetry as paideia—Literature for the unlettered— Sources of our common aim—Poetry as an instrument of research—What is saying?—What is belief?—The ever-new discovery. [There may be additional titles or some deletions.]

"Beginnings and Transitions." An interview with Reuben Brower, 19 Mar. 1971. *I. A. Richards: Essays in His Honor*, edited by Reuben Brower, Helen Vendler, and John Hollander (New York: Oxford University Press). Carbon typescript copy with corrections, 28 l. R discusses early reading, Kipling and Swinburne, early classroom experiences, Cambridge University, C. K. Ogden, the classroom of G. E. Moore and Wittgenstein, mountaineering, Ruskin's *Modern Painters*, the origins of *The Meaning of Meaning*, James Wood and *The Foundations of Aesthetics*, the makings of *Principles of Literary Criticism, Interpretation in Teaching*, and other works, his transition from literary criticism into educational and literacy problems, T. S. Eliot's friendship, coming to Harvard University in 1939, his interest in and translation of Plato's dialogues, his work in the Chinese of Mencius, Coleridge, *How To Read a Page* and the Chicago experiment in great books, the *English Through Pictures* series, modern media, concluding with a reading of his most recent poem, *Acquiescence*.

"Beyond." Unpublished ms. Typescript copy with corrections, 166 l. Begun "several years ago." Philosophical and religious questions in the *Iliad*, the Book of Job, Plato's *Republic*, the *Divine Comedy*, and three cantos by R after Dante, *Whose Endless Jar* (Dec.–Jan. 1972) are brought into opposition, debate, and partial reconciliation with one another. The questions concern moral freedom, divine and human justice, fate, and man's future. Two major "shaping positions" are "the interdiction figured by the forbidden fruit and the Socratic belief that Knowledge—could we attain it—would be Virtue." R sees in the ultimate consequences of "Eve's trespass" the inevitably recurrent problem that Socrates posed to Phaedrus: "I am not yet able, as the Delphic inscription has it, to know myself; so it seems to be absurd, when I do not as yet know that, to inquire into extraneous matters." The method of the volume is dialectic (in Plato's definition), seeking *sameness* through *difference*, by a proper knowledge of both, in major works of the European experience.

Addenda

Review of Ralph B. Crum, *Scientific Thought in Poetry* (New York: Columbia University Press, 1931). *Modern Language Notes* 48 (1933), 64–65.

Review of Bernard C. Heyl, *New Bearings in Esthetics and Art Criticism: A Study in Semantics and Evaluation* (New Haven: Yale University Press, 1943). *Modern Language Notes* 60 (1945), 349–50. Carbon typescript with corrections, 2 l.

" 'A Cooking Egg': Final Scramble." *Essays in Criticism* 4 (1954), 103–5.

Contributors

Joan Bennett is a Life Fellow of Girton College and formerly a Lecturer in English, Cambridge University.

M. C. Bradbrook is Professor of English and Mistress of Girton College, Cambridge University.

Cleanth Brooks is Gray Professor of Rhetoric, Yale University.

Reuben A. Brower is Henry B. and Anne M. Cabot Professor of English Literature, Harvard University.

Kathleen Coburn is Professor of English, Victoria College, University of Toronto.

Elsie Duncan-Jones was until recently Senior Lecturer, University of Birmingham.

Richard Eberhart is Class of '25 Professor of English, Emeritus, and Poet in Residence, Dartmouth College.

William Empson is Professor of English Emeritus, Sheffield University.

Angus Fletcher is Professor of English, State University of New York, Buffalo.

Geoffrey Hartman is Professor of English and Comparative Literature, Yale University.

Eric A. Havelock, formerly Chairman of the Harvard Classics Department, is Sterling Professor of Classics Emeritus, Yale University.

John Hollander is Professor of English, Hunter College and the Doctoral Program, City University of New York.

L. C. Knights was until recently King Edward VII Professor of English Literature and a Fellow of Queens' College, Cambridge University.

Richmond Lattimore is Professor of Greek Emeritus, Bryn Mawr College.

Robert Lowell is Lecturer in English, Harvard University.

John Paul Russo is Assistant Professor of English, University of Chicago.

B. F. Skinner is Edgar Pierce Professor of Psychology, Harvard University.

Janet Adam Smith is former literary editor of *New Statesman* and former President of the Ladies' Alpine Club.

Charles L. Stevenson is Professor of Philosophy, University of Michigan.

Denys Thompson is Headmaster Emeritus, Yeovil School.

Helen Vendler is Professor of English, Boston University.

Robert Penn Warren is Professor of English, Yale University.

Basil Willey is King Edward VII Professor Emeritus of English Literature and President Emeritus of Pembroke College, Cambridge University.

W. K. Wimsatt is Frederick Clifford Ford Professor of English, Yale University.